FUN CITY

FUN CITY

JOHN LINDSAY, JOE NAMATH,
AND HOW SPORTS SAVED
NEW YORK IN THE 1960s

SEAN DEVENEY

Sports Publishing books may be purchased in bulk at special discounts for sales promotion, corporate gifts, fund-raising, or educational purposes. Special editions can also be created to specifications. For details, contact the Special Sales Department, Sports Publishing, 307 West 36th Street, 11th Floor, New York, NY 10018 or sportspubbooks@ skyhorsepublishing.com.

Sports Publishing® is a registered trademark of Skyhorse Publishing, Inc.®, a Delaware corporation.

Visit our website at www.sportspubbooks.com.

10 9 8 7 6 5 4 3 2 1

Library of Congress Cataloging-in-Publication Data is available on file.

Cover design by Owen Corrigan
Cover photo credits: Associated Press

ISBN: 978-1-61321-815-0
Ebook ISBN: 978-1-61321-859-4

Printed in the United States of America

Contents

Preface   *vii*

Chapter 1   "I believe the Jets have found their star"   1

Chapter 2   Enter John Vliet Lindsay   16

Chapter 3   Decline and Fall   28

Chapter 4   "What's the matter, rookie?"   40

Chapter 5   Ten Million Lunatics   52

Chapter 6   Meet the Mets   67

Chapter 7   The Fun City Has a Fun Mayor   80

Chapter 8   White and Black and Redneck   97

Chapter 9   "I think we're going to have a riot"   113

Chapter 10   No Quarrel with Them Vietcong   132

Chapter 11   Backlash   147

Chapter 12   "Nothing but garbage and rats"   163

Chapter 13 Of Riot, Revolt, and Hair   178

Chapter 14 "What kind of people are we?"   193

Chapter 15 Confrontation   207

Chapter 16 "I'll guarantee you"   223

Chapter 17 Light, Meaningless, Dippy and Lovely Few Days 236

Chapter 18 Eating Crow   251

Chapter 19 "A year ago I would have felt
            it was pretty hopeless"   264

Chapter 20 The Saints of Lost Causes   277

Chapter 21 "It is best not to plan on promises and dreams" 291

Source Notes   304

Index   343

Preface

THE SCOTTISH POET, THOMAS CAMPBELL, once wrote, "Coming events cast their shadows before." For New York in the late 1960s, those shadows dated back to 1957. Consider some of the events that unfolded that year, some of which were clearly momentous at the time, some whose impact would not fully be felt until the end of the next decade:

- On January 1, thirty-five-year-old lawyer John Lindsay left his post as an assistant to Attorney General Herbert Brownell. During his tenure with Brownell, the two had become close, and Brownell would be Lindsay's mentor for years. Though he was moving back into the private sector with his old law firm, Lindsay—who helped Brownell draft the legislation that would become the 1957 Civil Rights Act—had gained a taste for public service and was eyeing the congressional seat in his home district, Manhattan's 17th.
- On January 3, Harry Wismer, a broadcaster and 20 percent stockholder in the Washington Redskins, charged the team with racial bias while speaking at an event for black journalists. George Preston Marshall, the team's owner and president, was blatantly racist, and the Redskins had no black players on the roster. The race issue would be one reason Wismer would split with the Redskins and, two years later, buy into a new football

venture known as the American Football League. Wismer's team, the Titans, would play in New York's Polo Grounds.

- On one evening in April, a man named Hinton X. Johnson (also sometimes referred to as Johnson X. Hinton) witnessed a police officer beating a black citizen in Harlem. When Johnson intervened, he, too was beaten. Johnson was a member of the Black Muslims, led by a preacher named Malcolm X. After word of Johnson's beating spread, hundreds of members of the mosque began demonstrating in front of the Harlem police precinct. Fearing violence, the authorities arranged a meeting with Malcolm X. Assurances were given that Hinton X. Johnson would be given care in a hospital and those responsible for his injuries would be punished. Satisfied, Malcom X stunned police when he, according to one account, "strode to the head of the angry, impatient mob, and then flicked his hands." Moments later, as if by magic, the crowd dispersed and the street was empty. "No man should have that much power," one officer said.

- On May 28, the eight owners of National League clubs met in Chicago and voted unanimously to grant permission for the two N.L. teams located in New York—the Giants and Dodgers—to seek new homes. Ebbets Field in Brooklyn and the Polo Grounds in upper Manhattan were growing increasingly decrepit, and efforts to have new stadiums built had been long stymied. By the end of the 1957 season, the Dodgers had agreed to move to Los Angeles, and the Giants would head to San Francisco.

- On October 22, in Saigon, Vietnam—still a distant and unknown corner of the globe to most Americans—three bombs detonated by Communist terrorists injured thirteen American soldiers who were part of a team that had been training South Vietnam's anti-Communist army. The injuries marked the first casualties the United States suffered in Vietnam.

- On December 30, the *New York Times* reported on the state of New York's economy. All told, 1957 had been a bad year—

50,000 jobs had been lost in New York, while consumer prices continued to rise, by 2.7 percent. The report noted that the city's factory employment was hard hit, especially the garment industry, which accounted for 38,000 lost jobs—about 12 percent of its total, in just one year. The report also stated that unemployment was expected to rise, and that the average age of an unemployment insurance claimant had gone from forty-seven to thirty-eight in one year. Good-paying, low-skilled jobs in New York City disappeared at an alarming rate in 1957.

These events were all seeds that would sprout separately but become intertwined in New York City during coming years of dramatic change. New York in the 1960s would be a fast-evolving and nearly ungovernable city. There would be, concurrently, an overhaul in the sports culture, which had long bound together the heterogeneous citizenry that made up the city. Wismer's AFL Titans would nearly fold, until new owners stabilized the team and turned them into the Jets. The Dodgers and Giants were gone, but an endearingly hapless group of losers, the Mets, replaced them. A couple new sports teams were not going to bring back disappearing manufacturing jobs, end overseas wars or ease racial frustrations. But there could be a time—couldn't there?—at which the exploits of those teams would help.

. . . .

The Jets introduced rookie quarterback Joe Namath, the western Pennsylvania slinger who'd picked up a treacly Southern drawl playing for Bear Bryant at Alabama, to New York in January 1965, giving him an astronomical $400,000. Just four months behind him, Lindsay, the handsome, young liberal Republican hailed in some corners as the next John F. Kennedy, entered his name into the race for mayor of New York, an almost unheard-of act of audacity for a member of the GOP in a city where Democrats had a 3-to-1 advantage. On the day the shaggy-maned Namath was introduced, the Giants retired thirty-eight-year-old Y.A. Tittle, who was known as the "Bald Eagle" for his long-bare scalp. And the man Lindsay was seeking to replace was fifty-five-year-old Mayor Robert Wagner, whose three terms in office had left him looking every bit his age. The symbolism was obvious, as was the new-guard optimism that Namath and Lindsay each brought to his field. Lindsay's campaign slogan, taken from a New York columnist, was, "He is fresh and everyone else is tired." As it was for Lindsay, so it was for Namath. He was fresh, and everyone else—the New York Giants, the NFL, Mickey Mantle's Yankees—was tired.

The five years that followed Lindsay's arrival in the city from Washington DC and Namath's arrival from Tuscaloosa were unlike any other period in the county's history. Racial politics dominated, and as the civil rights movement evolved into the black power and separatist movement, the Vietnam War reached its peak and sparked a level of public protest and dissent not seen in the United States before or since. Frustrated minority city dwellers led violent eruptions in ghettoes across the country, pushing the issue of the fate of American cities to the fore. The violence was not only carried out in mass settings—this was a time during which Dr. Martin Luther King Jr. and Senator Robert F. Kennedy were murdered, within two months of each other. While the political and demographic order was giving way, the underpinnings of the nation's culture and social norms were shifting, too. Sexual promiscuity and drug experimentation were becoming more acceptable, and anti-authority symbols gained popularity. Men even had the audacity to grow bushy sideburns.

In New York's political milieu, Lindsay was a symbol: the White Urban Crusader.

In New York's social milieu, Namath was a symbol: the Hedonist's Quarterback.

. . . .

Ultimately, the validity of Lindsay and Namath as symbols would rest on job performance, and each would have his own troubling disappointments, low points, and vocal opponents. Namath would be doused with hot coffee, engage in a verbal war with sportswriters, engage in an actual fistfight with a sports editor, have his cheekbone broken by an antagonistic opponent, and find his bitterest critics in his own locker room. Lindsay would alienate just about every prominent Republican in the country, was called an "ungrateful son of a bitch" by fellow Republican and fierce enemy Governor Nelson Rockefeller, was labeled a "pipsqueak" by a prominent labor leader, was hated by rank-and-file police officers and firemen, had to escape an unruly mob at a Jewish center in Flatbush, contended with major municipal labor strikes in each of his first three years in office, and saw himself burned in effigy from his City Hall office. But both Lindsay and Namath would have incredible highs. Lindsay's willingness and ability to stride into ghetto communities, even in the severest of crises, earned him the kind of respect from minorities few white politicians ever could claim. There was a moment, however brief, when it looked like Lindsay *could* solve the urban crisis, when national magazines hailed him as a potential political savior. Namath, too, for all the physical and verbal abuse he endured early in his career (and later, too) had that one magical season, that one year in which he took the Jets to the Super Bowl, shattered myths, and wrote his name forever into American sports lore.

Lindsay and Namath were just the headliners of the era. New York City was a battlefield for Lindsay's fight to save cities, but it also began to regain its lost status as a cultural leader with a rebirth of theater and filmmaking in the city, became an epicenter for anti-war protest, saw a massive building boom that reshaped the architecture of the city's financial districts and followed through on a commitment to green spaces that led to the creation of vest-pocket parks and the closing of Central Park to automobile traffic. During late-1960s ascendancy of Lindsay and Namath in New York, the Knicks would win their first NBA championship in twenty-four years, Muhammad Ali would defend his title at the old Madison Square Garden, the new Madison Square Garden would open and host a track meet that featured the forerunner of what would become the 1968 Olympic black power salute. And there were the Mets, who doused Lindsay with champagne in the locker room during their incredible run to the 1969 World Series championship and helped him win reelection a month later.

During his first month in office, Lindsay oversaw a crippling transit strike that shutdown the subways in the city for nearly two weeks. He tried to maintain a positive outlook, saying he still thought New York was a "fun city." Columnist Dick Schaap lampooned his cheery attitude, writing, "He certainly has a wonderful sense of humor. A little while later, Lindsay cheerfully walked four miles from his hotel room to City Hall, a gesture which proved that the fun city had a fun Mayor." Over the course of his time in office, Lindsay would reclaim the "Fun City" moniker, using it to describe the kind of place where he'd like to be mayor. Others, though, would continue to use it as Schaap had— loaded with irony—so that even the words Fun City were endowed with layers of meaning and symbolism, capable of carrying opposite meanings depending on context.

It remains the best way to think about the positives and negatives of New York in those years. It was a Fun City.

CHAPTER 1

"I believe the Jets have found their star"

IT HAD BEEN AN EXHAUSTING, bizarre five weeks. On Thanksgiving, Joe Namath had helped Alabama defeat rival Auburn, 21–14, to cap an undefeated season and win the 1964 national championship. The time in between had been a haze of rumors, meetings, negotiations, handshakes, new faces. And cities. Lots of cities: Tuscaloosa, Birmingham, Atlanta, Los Angeles, San Diego, Miami, New York, Nassau (yes, the one in the Bahamas), and back to Miami. Even with all those miles logged, all Namath could think about now was the one foot he had *not* traveled. Namath, despite a heroic performance, sat on the Alabama bench in the rainy Miami night and reprimanded himself over that one foot. The 1965 Orange Bowl had been historic, the first collegiate bowl game played at night in prime time, beamed out on NBC to 25 million households, the first time an outdoor sporting event was shown on television at night in color, with instant replay (also for the first time), in front of a sellout crowd of 72,647 that included dignitaries from parade marshal and television star Jackie Gleason to former Vice President Richard Nixon to the Rev. Dr. Billy Graham to the pride of Greece, the recently crowned Miss Universe, Corinna Tsopei.

That Namath was on the field at all was a surprise. Back on October 10, Namath had suffered a badly wrenched knee in a win over North Carolina State, and the injury had limited him to spot duty for the bulk of the 1964 season. He still managed to make appearances in all ten Alabama games, on a limited basis—in one, on the road against Georgia Tech in early November, Namath cemented his legend by coming off the bench, leading two touchdown drives in just under ninety seconds just before halftime, and leaving the game having set up a 24–7 Alabama win. After a month of rest, there was hope that Namath would be nearly healthy before the Orange Bowl against No. 5 Texas, but he re-injured the knee during practice in the run-up to the game, and Namath was supposed to be out altogether. In Miami and across the nation, the question of whether Namath would play dominated sports pages and beyond. Alabama Governor George Wallace, on hand in South Florida that week, was asked on the day before the game whether Namath would play. "I run a lot of things in Alabama," Wallace said, "but one thing I don't run is the football team. Bear Bryant runs that department."

Namath himself didn't know that he might see action until he was standing on the field next to coach Bear Bryant, awaiting the national anthem, and overheard Alabama trainer Jim Goostree give Bryant the OK to play Namath if he was needed, as in the Georgia Tech game. Once the Orange Bowl got underway, it didn't take Bryant long to figure out the Tide did need Namath, even at less than 100 percent health. Texas established a 14–0 lead early in the second quarter, leaving Alabama reeling and forcing Bryant to call for Namath at quarterback in relief of Steve Sloan. Namath's knee was singing with pain, but still, he was dynamic. Namath set an Orange Bowl record by completing 18 of his 37 passes (on a windy night, his receivers dropped several of his throws), hitting for two touchdowns and, with time running out in the fourth quarter, dramatically driving the Crimson Tide to the 1-yard line facing a 21–17 deficit. But that's when Namath, who had the freedom to call his own plays, faltered. He called for fullback Steve Bowman, the team's touchdown leader and a usually reliable force at the goal line, three times, but Bowman could not break through the Texas line.

On fourth down, with the game in the balance, Namath knew the play he needed to call: the run-pass option, a play that called for him to roll out and use his agility to find a hole if he elected to run or flick a toss if he saw a receiver open. It was that play that had made Namath famous in his time with the Tide, because it emphasized his three advantages—his speed, his arm, and his ability to make quick decisions—but the pain in his knee made him reconsider the option play. Maybe a timeout, a moment to consult with Bryant? No. The heck with it. It was Namath's talent that boosted the Tide to this game, let Namath's talent decide it. He called his own number, a quarterback sneak. "When the officials pulled the bodies away," sportswriter Jimmy Burns noted, "Namath was short by the width of the shoulders of Tom Nobis, the Longhorn guard who stopped the plunge."

Texas had held. Alabama suffered its only loss of the season. Namath had been certain he had crossed the goal line, so sure that he saw one referee begin to raise his arms to signal a score that he shouted, "Touchdown!" He would insist that he had scored that touchdown as long as he lived, but he knew it should not have been that close, anyway. Namath would, even in defeat, win the game's MVP award, but he was so stunned by the failed sneak, one writer described him in the locker room as, "looking like a child who had just been spanked for something bad," and Namath would later say he just plain forgot to pick up the Orange Bowl MVP trophy altogether. Bryant consoled Namath, who, despite an individualist streak that had created a handful of headaches for the iconic coach, would go down as one of Bryant's favorite players. Bryant told the media, "I sent in all the plays when we were on the one-yard line," taking the blame for Namath's failed play-calling even though it was not true. Namath could not stop thinking, "I shoulda, shoulda, shoulda . . ." But as he sat on the Alabama bench, muddy and surrounded by fans from both teams, a bespectacled gentleman sidled up to Namath, pulled a sheaf of papers from one jacket pocket and a pen from another. The two spoke briefly. Namath took the pen and scribbled his name on the papers.

. . . .

The man behind the spectacles was fifty-four-year-old Sonny Werblin, president of the television arm of Music Corporation of America, who would retire from the showbiz game later in 1965 as what *Variety* called broadcasting's, "greatest promoter and salesman." For Namath's purposes, though, Werblin was one of the five owners, and the frontman, for the New York Jets of the American Football League. By the time of the Orange Bowl, Werblin had much invested in Namath, having spent more than a month traversing the country to engage in contract deliberations with Namath and his representative, lawyer Mike Bite of Alabama, trying to persuade Namath to come to New York and play for the Jets. Despite his knee injury, Jets scouts had been raving about Namath. More important, coach Weeb Ewbank had watched Namath throughout the 1963 season and, lured by the arm strength and quick release he saw, was determined to find a way to bring Namath to his team. In November 1963, a full year before Namath would be available in the draft, Ewbank had been talking with a small group of writers about quarterback prospects, and he was not particularly enthused about anyone on hand, especially not incumbent Jet quarterback Dick Wood. "The guy I'm thinking about is a junior at Alabama," Ewbank confessed. "I'm going to give Dick Wood one more year as our quarterback, and then I'm going after that Namath kid from Alabama." The Jets followed through, selecting Namath with the first pick in the AFL's 1965 draft. That was the easy part. Selling him on signing an AFL contract was far more difficult.

The AFL was, in the terms of the time, "at war" with the National Football League, still just an upstart group of teams founded by (mostly) well-funded owners who had been shut out of the small group that made up the NFL buyers' club. The league had begun in 1960, and was still a second-rate operation compared with the long-established NFL, whose history stretched back even before 1922, when it became the

National Football League for the first time. Of all AFL teams, the Jets (at first known as the Titans) were a particularly moribund lot in the early 1960s, led by overmatched owner Harry Wismer, who constantly dealt with the dual threat of his own bankruptcy and direct competition with the New York Giants, one of the most consistently successful franchises in the NFL. Two years earlier, Werblin was part of a group that purchased the AFL's Titans from Wismer, which were deeply in debt, often unable to meet payroll and had averaged just 5,166 fans per game in 1962. But the arrival of Werblin (with co-owners oilman Leon Hess, horse trainer Townsend Martin, stockbroker Donald Lillis, and women's clothing magnate Phil Iselin) gave the Jets stability and legitimacy. The move out of the battered old Polo Grounds and into the newly built Shea Stadium (Werblin changed the team name to "Jets" to create a link to their popular Shea co-tenants, the Mets) in Queens bolstered attendance. NBC's agreement with the AFL on a five-year, $36 million television package signed that year gave the fledgling league something more tangible than legitimacy with which to fight the NFL: money.

Werblin aimed to spend that money. By 1964, the Jets' attendance had blossomed to almost 43,000 per game, but they were still dwarfed in attention and adulation by the Giants. If there was something that the AFL in general—and the Jets specifically—were missing, it was the kind of star players who attracted fan and media attention, who drew in casual viewers on Sundays, and made a ticket to a home game a sort of entrée into a social event. This was Werblin's terrain. He had represented Hollywood types ranging from Ronald Reagan to Elizabeth Taylor to Johnny Carson, and had gotten shows for Ed Sullivan and Jackie Gleason on television. He'd also been employed by the *New York Times* in his early twenties (quitting journalism, it was said, when he learned how little the paper's managing editor actually was paid), and had an understanding of how to manipulate press coverage. Most sports owners operated under the simple labor-management model, which dictated that depressing player salaries was in the team's best interest, helping the bottom line, but in Hollywood, Werblin learned that you throw out standard labor rules when it came to mass entertainment.

There, you made big money when you paid your talent big money, because that big money attracted attention, and attention translated into profits. "Louis B. Mayer built the mighty Metro-Goldwyn-Mayer studio with the star system," Werblin explained. "It's a lesson that has stuck with me. Maybe it can be done with the Jets, too. At least I'm going to give it a try."

Werblin, having been assured of Namath's ability by Ewbank, quickly came to believe that Namath was that star—not only could Namath play, but he was different than the dull, crew-cutted boys Werblin typically encountered coming out of college. Namath was handsome, wore his hair long and the rebelliousness that sometimes irked Bryant and others in Tuscaloosa could be a selling point to the public as a pro in New York. The problem was that Namath had also been drafted by the St. Louis Cardinals, with the twelfth pick in the NFL draft. In 1964, the warring AFL and NFL held their drafts simultaneously for the first time, on November 28, and in the days after the draft, the leagues raced to beat each other in signing those draftees, sometimes resorting to underhanded methods like pre-signing players while they were still eligible for college and "babysitting" draftees to block access from the opposing league. Approaching star collegians, the AFL was always at a disadvantage because of its reputation as a lesser league with unstable franchises. That forced it to make far more lavish offers than its NFL competitors just to get the attention of players. The new television money would help make those offers even more lavish, and with a stake in the outcome of the bidding wars, NBC sent letters to all top college players, "informing them that NBC would soon begin televising some, and maybe all, AFL games in living color." The network needed the AFL to have star players as much as the AFL did.

Still, among Namath's draft class, the experience of Kansas star running back Gale Sayers was typical. He was chosen with the fourth pick by the Bears of the NFL and with the fifth pick by the Chiefs in the AFL. The Bears made Sayers an offer of $25,000 per year for four years. Chiefs owner Lamar Hunt came back with an offer of $27,500 per year—10 percent better than Chicago's deal. But Sayers had thought

Hunt would come up with a bigger offer than that. "I thought, 'New league, no, I can't do that,'" Sayers said. "You didn't know it was going to be a good league, so I decided to go with the Bears."

When it came to Namath, the Cardinals' approach was in line with how the NFL typically did business—the league acted as though the AFL was second class and as though the NFL was entitled to whichever players it wanted. From the beginning, St. Louis' Bidwill family, which owned and ran the Cardinals, made missteps with Namath. He had told them from the beginning he'd rather play in the better league. But Namath, unschooled on the process of contract negotiations, trusted his gut as much as his brain. Shortly after the draft, the Bidwill brothers (Stormy and Billy, who had inherited the team founded by their father after their mother died in 1962) showed up in the lobby of Namath's dorm, unannounced. Namath had to go down and sign them into the visitor's log, as though they were high-school friends who stopped by to pal around. "I was totally embarrassed and all," Namath later wrote. "It was just me and these two guys in my room, right?"

The Cardinals men were direct, asking Namath what it would take to sign him. Namath thought back to a conversation he'd had with Bear Bryant on Thanksgiving. Bryant had asked what Namath would ask for from the teams that drafted him, and when Namath suggested he would ask for $100,000, Bryant told him no, he should start at $200,000. He wouldn't necessarily get it, Bryant said, but it was a better starting point for a negotiation. He also told Namath not to sign anything without first checking with the other league. Namath, heeding Bryant's advice, told the Cardinals' reps he wanted $200,000. Namath has since told the story of his dorm room negotiation with a variety of flourishes, all of which illustrate the level of shock registered by the Cardinals at his request. In one, Namath said, "I told them $200,000, and they both leaned back, 'Oh my goodness!' fell down on the bed, guy was standing there, leaned back against the wall screaming like they were in agony." In another: "They didn't say anything but they seemed a little shook up. They didn't quite believe me." And Namath relishes recounting that he then mentioned one added demand: a new car. A convertible Lincoln

Continental. Putting on a mock-fancy voice, Namath described their incredulous reaction: "Oh, suuuure. A Lincoln Continental convertible! Yeah, boy wants a LIN-coln Con-ti-NEN-tal!"

Either way, Namath knew he was onto something when the Cardinals quickly came back, agreeing to his terms (Con-ti-NEN-tal included) and eager to have him sign. *No, no*, Namath insisted he would not yet sign. Alabama's regular season was over, but he would not sign until after the Orange Bowl, because he didn't want to jeopardize his eligibility. Also, he'd not spoken to the Jets, who had a couple of important advantages when it came to Namath. First they had Chuck Knox, the team's line coach, who had been a high school football coach in Ellwood, Pennsylvania, just ten miles north of Namath's home in Beaver Falls. Namath first caught Knox's eye when he was just fourteen years old and not even playing football—Knox was coaching basketball at the time, and was impressed by Namath's innate ability. "I could see then," Knox later remembered, "that Joe Namath was going to be a really good athlete." When Namath was a senior in high school trying to pick a college, Knox had taken a job at Kentucky, and developed a friendship with Namath as he tried to get him to play for the Wildcats. Now with the Jets, Knox was able to give more than just another scouting report. Namath would always have a soft spot for fellow Western Pennsylvanians, and before the draft, Knox had a friendly conversation with Namath about the perks of playing in New York, trying to divine where Namath would like to go. He reported back to Ewbank that Namath wanted to come to the Jets, wanted to play in New York, and would be willing to consider forgoing the NFL to do so.

Besides Knox, the Jets' other advantage was Werblin. When it came to Namath, he would leave the typical football approach to the Cardinals. Werblin would take the Hollywood approach, because where the Bidwills were recruiting a quarterback, Werblin was courting a star.

. . . .

Werblin did not show up unannounced at Namath's dorm room. Instead, Knox arranged a meeting in early December at a Birmingham hotel. It was just an informal discussion, Werblin hoping to establish a rapport. Werblin did not even bring up money. Neither did Namath—he was too scared. Instead, Namath and Bite agreed to go to California that Sunday for the Jets' game in San Diego, where they would be guests of the team. When Namath and Bite arrived in Los Angeles, Werblin gave them first-class treatment, booking them at the Beverly Hills Hotel. Namath had been familiar with nice accommodations from his travels with the Crimson Tide, but this was different. Every detail was elegant. "I marveled at the wallpaper," Namath remembered. "It was like walking through a jungle with all the leaves, flowers, and colors."

If the goal was to sell Namath on the Jets, the game in San Diego did not go well. The Chargers played on a decrepit field—Balboa Stadium, built in 1914—that held 34,000 fans, and though San Diego had the opportunity to clinch the AFL's West Division with a win, only 25,753 fans showed up. They witnessed a Chargers blowout, drubbing the Jets, 38–9, as Ewbank cycled through hapless quarterbacks (Dick Wood, Mike Taliaferro, and Pete Liske) who combined to go 13-for-36 passing, for 95 yards and three interceptions. "I thought the Jets stunk," Namath later said. "I really did." But at dinner that night, the negotiations with Werblin began in earnest. He told Namath and Bite he did not want to get into a bidding war. Where the Cardinals had given Namath histrionics and fainting attacks when he made his request for $200,000, Werblin calmly made the first move: $300,000. Namath wasn't scared anymore. He was stunned. He and Bite had to be excused in order to catch their combined breath and confer. Namath wanted a little more—he had hoped to have his family taken care of, too. Bite thought there was room to make additions. "Just like blowing up a balloon," he kept saying. "You got to go as far as you can without popping it."

After their meeting with Werblin, Namath and Bite went back to the Cardinals. There was a sense that St. Louis would, indeed, raise its offer, but negotiations with the Cardinals had become somewhat disjointed. Whomever Bite called in St. Louis, he could never get a straight answer. He was always told by Cardinals representatives that they had to consult and get back to him. Werblin figured out what was happening—the Giants were pulling the strings for the Cardinals, at first in an effort to keep Namath out of New York, and then perhaps to have him traded from St. Louis to play for the Giants. In one of their final meetings, Namath later said, the Cardinals dropped the front and flat-out asked him if he would play for the Giants. Had that been the approach the NFL had taken from the beginning, Namath might have been more inclined to join the Giants in New York, but he was disenchanted with what he saw as the underhanded approach the NFL had taken. Besides, he liked Werblin, and the idea of bucking the established order and playing for the fast-and-loose AFL had grown on him. On December 30, a spokesman for the Cardinals announced that the team was withdrawing from the bidding for Namath, saying that their offer had gone as high as $400,000 for three years or $500,000 for five years. "We have abandoned hopes of getting Namath—we know he wants to play in New York," the spokesman said. Werblin had good reason to be confident in the weeks before the Orange Bowl, but it wasn't until Namath skipped out on Miami and visited Werblin with his family in Nassau over the holidays that the deal was all but consummated. Namath also reportedly went to New York for tax advice on his impending windfall. Perhaps Namath could not sign until after Alabama's game against Texas, but Werblin made sure everything was in place beforehand, including having the Lincoln Continental convertible (price: $7,000; color: Jet green) shipped to South Florida ahead of time. There were rumors that the Jets would pay Namath the $400,000 the Cardinals had offered, which seemed incomprehensible to the sports reporters gathered in Miami for the Orange Bowl. But the rumors were only close. With perks, Namath's deal was actually worth $427,000.

Werblin was not all that concerned about the one foot that Namath failed to gain to end the loss to Texas. He'd gotten just what he had hoped for out of Namath's Orange Bowl appearance—star-making performance witnessed by about one-eighth of the nation's population. A friend told Werblin, "You just got the benefit of the greatest pilot film in TV history." During the game, Ewbank felt justified in his faith in Namath, telling anyone who would listen in the pressbox: "Fabulous, fabulous, fabulous. He could take a pro team right now." Werblin was more effusive. He was sitting with friend Joe Hirsch, the horse-racing writer and future roommate of Namath, during the game. "When Sonny saw how great Joe was," Hirsch said, "he was standing on a chair and screaming, 'My God, I'm not paying this guy enough.'"

....

The day after the Orange Bowl, at Werblin's request, Namath pulled up at the Bal Harbour Inn on Miami Beach in the brand-new green Lincoln. Perhaps Werblin wanted to make sure the Bidwills would see Joe in the car they'd made such a fuss about—they were staying in a hotel just a few doors down. There was to be a press conference announcing Namath's deal with the Jets, and Werblin's strategy was clear: keep the media guessing as to the deal's actual value, while hinting that that it was as big (or bigger) than expected. Mystery was more titillating than reality, and if that mystery could be punctuated by a high-class new car, all the better. The word had already been circulating that Namath was getting $400,000, and that was perfect. Werblin understood that Namath's salary immediately would become part of his lore. He was not just the Jets' new quarterback from Alabama. He was the *$400,000 quarterback*.

"I believe the Jets have found their star in Joe Namath," Werblin said. "In all my theatrical experience I've met few Hollywood stars with the indefinable quality of being able to walk into a room and electrify everyone there by the magnetism of their presence—Clark Gable, Gregory Peck, Joan Crawford, and Marilyn Monroe. It's the same quality that Jack Dempsey and Babe Ruth had. My feeling is that Namath has much of the demeanor and attitude of Joe DiMaggio." Gable? Peck? Ruth? DiMaggio? Namath was twenty-one years old, stooped at the shoulders and, when he spoke, affected a syrupy Southern drawl that spilled awkwardly from his mining-town mouth. Here he was, being presented as a pro for the first time, at the bright pastel Bal Harbour Inn, the kind of place that utterly lacked DiMaggio's pomaded dignity, and Werblin already had him on a pedestal. The event proceeded, one writer noted, "with no more pomp than Cleopatra might expect for her Saturday night bath. . . . Joe wore a new jacket and tie but had a hole in the sole of his right shoe." Repeatedly, the question was posed to Namath and Werblin: Is it really $400,000? Interviewed on television, all Werblin would offer was, with an intentional lack of specificity, "To my knowledge, it's the largest amount ever given to an athlete for professional services. Let me say, we're very happy to do it."

If publicity was Werblin's goal, he got it, and not just in New York (though there was plenty of Namath coverage in the local papers). In the days after the Miami press conference, Namath was a national story. On the West Coast, *Los Angeles Times* columnist Sid Ziff led off his January 5 offering (under the headline, "Namath Hot Copy") with, "Everybody is talking about Joe Namath, the Jets' $400,000 bonus baby," and went on to discuss Namath's prospects with star Rams lineman Merlin Olsen. The *Associated Press* contacted legendary Red Grange—who was the first true football star and had a $100,000 contract in his playing career—for his thoughts on Namath ("I think it's wonderful," the Galloping Ghost said). The Senior Bowl in Mobile, Alabama, was a sellout for the first time in the game's sixteen-year history, drawing 40,605, and it was unquestionably Namath who was driving the attention.

The *Boston Globe* sent a reporter (legend-to-be Gloria Negri) to Beaver Falls, Pennsylvania, for two days' worth of stories about Namath's background. Under the headline, "Beaver Falls Waits for Joey and His Car," Negri wrote that Beaver Falls was a steel mill and manufacturing town, with a population of 17,000 constituting 4,135 families—744 of those earning under $3,000 annually (the federal poverty line), 434 earning more than $10,000 annually, and the great mass in the middle. One resident said, "Though we're not in Appalachia, we might be considered on the fringe of it." Namath had grown up the youngest of four brothers, with an adopted sister, in the Lower End of Beaver Falls, an especially hardscrabble area. His father, John—a Hungarian native—and his mother, Rose, were divorced, and it was Rose who primarily raised Joey, the baby of the family with a penchant for mischief.

Namath had gained a reputation as a troublemaker even before going to Alabama, but back home, locals insisted that was exaggerated. "I'm not trying to say Joe had wings and flew around like an angel," Bill Ross, the athletic director at Beaver Falls High at the time, said, "but everything he did that other kids would do was blown out of proportion." Negri also spoke with Namath's usually publicity-shy father, John Namath, a "rugged man," who earned a living in a steel tubing mill. "I'm not a rich man and I'm not a poor man," John Namath said. "Just an ordinary working man." Venerable sportswriter Will McDonough interviewed Larry Bruno, Namath's high school coach, who said, "There are stories that Joe was a real bad kid—a Peck's Bad Boy—but he wasn't. Sure, he hung around the pool room, smoked, had long hair and sported dark glasses. But in Beaver Falls, there are two shows and a pool room. What else are you going to do?" Rags-to-riches, wrong-side-of-the-tracks . . . for Werblin it was all pure gold.

But Namath was ready for the big city, wanted to be associated with New York. On January 22, Werblin brought Namath to Manhattan for a grand unveiling in front of the local media. It was impeccable timing. That afternoon, at Mamma Leone's on 48th St., the Giants were giving a press luncheon for the great Y.A. Tittle, who was officially retiring at age thirty-eight after seventeen seasons. Two years earlier, Tittle had, amazingly, set an NFL record for passing touchdowns with 36, but the following season had been unkind, and Tittle said he'd rather step away than continue as a "mediocre" player. At the gathering, Tittle—known as the "Bald Eagle" for his long-bare pate—joked that he knew it was time to retire when Giants rookie quarterback Gary Wood not only took his starting job, "but started to ask permission to date my daughter." Turning serious, Tittle said, "This is a moment I have dreaded."

Just a few blocks away, in an upstairs function room at Toots Shor's—the smoky, dim old-boys' club that long attracted New York celebrities and journalists—the Jets were hosting a media cocktail party for much the same gang that had just witnessed Tittle being put out to pasture. The contrast was not subtle: the Giants were Tittle, the Jets were Namath. It wasn't necessarily Namath's kind of place, but Toots

Shor's still had a certain amount of cachet. "Toots Shor was the kind of guy who thought dumping a scotch in your lap was high comedy and lukewarm roumaki (liver with bacon wrapped around it) was five-star cuisine," Namath later said. "And his joint was old-school. This was the home of the New York Giants' Frank Gifford, the New York Yankees' Joe DiMaggio, TV's Jackie Gleason and even the Catholic Church's Cardinal Spellman. And in 1965, the New York Jets were no school, a joke. We got no respect from these people."

While Namath was in the midst of meeting various New York media types, he was approached by a smiling Greek man who, he would say, "sort of looks like Ernest Borgnine." The face belonged to Dr. Jim Nicholas, the Jets' team orthopedist. Moments before, Weeb Ewbank had pulled Dr. Nicholas aside with a special instruction—check out that gimpy right knee of Namath's, pronto. It was no secret that Namath was going to need knee surgery, and that it was going to have to happen at some point that winter. Ewbank wanted Nicholas to see what he was up against. But where was Nicholas supposed to perform this exam?

"I don't care," Ewbank whispered to the doctor. "The men's room."

Nicholas told Namath he needed to examine his knee, immediately. Namath, slightly taken aback, followed Nicholas into the men's room at Toots Shor's, where he reluctantly dropped his pants. "We're standing there where anybody could see us in the men's room foyer, and I'm standing there with my pants down to my ankles now," Namath recalled. "He's down on his knees, examining my knee. A guy came in and gave us a look and made a U-turn. I don't know what the hell he was thinking, but he split." After ten minutes, Nicholas and Namath emerged. Nicholas didn't tell Namath, but his knee had been damaged enough that, as Nicholas later told it, "I thought that even with an operation he might not ever be able to play."

He approached Ewbank with his diagnosis: "You had better get yourself another quarterback."

Meanwhile, Namath—pants now pulled up into place—was back among the press horde. The questions about his contract kept coming.

So much had been made of the $400,000 Namath windfall, the gathered media members were fixated on advancing the story and seemed to feel almost entitled to details. Namath simply shrugged. One writer characterized the encounter: "It wasn't very friendly. For the next two hours, the major interest in Namath was trying to find out the extent to which the reported $400,000 he actually signed for." A writer from the *New York Times* chimed in, wondering, with all the pressure and attention and the knee injury, what would happen to that $400,000 if he didn't make it?

The question made sense. After all it was New York. This city could chew up Namath quickly, and he would not be the first. But Namath furrowed his brow. To him, the premise of the question was incomprehensible. It was 1965 and he was taking over in New York now, and it was better that the establishment in town get used to that idea.

Didn't make it?

"Take everything into account," Namath said, "my injury, all the publicity, all those things you've mentioned, and just throw them away." He paused. "Because I am going to make it."

CHAPTER 2

Enter John Vliet Lindsay

IN JANUARY 1965, WHILE JOE Namath was being given his Toots Shor's baptism, the *New York Herald-Tribune* was preparing to run a major series of stories that its editorial team had been working on for months. Namath might have been, as Werblin suggested, a new DiMaggio, but it was clear that the New York of 1965 was not DiMaggio's New York, and the *Herald-Tribune* planned to illuminate that. The city, for much of the 1960s and even before, was deteriorating. This was part of a trend. Nationwide, tugged by technology, economic shifts, and fast-changing demographics, urban life was in serious peril, and as the monarch of all US cities, New York's problems were most publicized and most acute. *Time* magazine would call the city in 1965, "a cruel parody of its legend. Compared with the sparkling, sophisticated city hymned by Cole Porter and Scott Fitzgerald, the world-admired paradigm of urbanity and elegance, New York seemed a shiftless slattern, mired in problems that had been allowed to proliferate for decades." Reacting to the city's deterioration, on January 25, the *Herald-Tribune* began running a special report called, *City in Crisis*, which was part scathing indictment of New York City's institutions, part incitement to action. The lead of the story opened: "New York is the world's financial and cultural center, the nation's tastemaker and home of the power elite, but to many of its eight million citizens, it is no longer the greatest place in which to live."

The issues were many, and they were profound—the *Herald-Tribune* outlined twenty-two areas of concern that would be explored in the series, under headlines ranging from "Youth, Traffic and Press" to "Poverty, Welfare and Police." In the section, "Politicians," the paper first quoted entrenched three-term Democratic Mayor Robert Wagner, who defended his part in the city's political decline by placing blame on a lack of participation by local Republicans, whose ranks were thin. "OK, so they don't agree with the way I run the city," Wagner said. "But what do they offer in my place? . . . I'm willing to listen to anybody." Immediately thereafter, forty-three-year-old Congressman John V. Lindsay, born and raised in New York City, educated at Yale and now, the city's most prominent Republican as the representative from the 17th district in Manhattan, rebuffed Wagner. "I think that under Mayor Wagner New York has lost its will power, its great energy and its great leadership," Lindsay said. "You hear a lot of people say that the city is too big to be governed by one man. I don't agree with that at all. It's just a cliché. But to run this city properly and get it going again, the Mayor has to be very tough. He's got to ask for the moon and he's got to convince the people to make sacrifices. It will take a man who loves the city and a man who loves its people. If we don't get going again soon, New York will become a second-class city."

The *Herald-Tribune*'s Wagner-Lindsay juxtaposition was no accident. Sure, the paper was civic-minded and the "City in Crisis" series was an important, illuminating and prize-winning piece of work. For a newspaper that was on the brink of dissolution—as many papers across the country were—the series was an attempt to prop up its standing and boost readership. But there was more to it than crusading journalism. If the series was a call to action aimed at New York's citizenry, it was also a call to action for Lindsay to, as Wagner put it, offer something in the current administration's place.

About a year earlier, Lindsay attended a private luncheon hosted by Jock Whitney, the publisher of the *Herald-Tribune*, and Walter Thayer, the paper's president, along with members of the editorial board. Whitney and Thayer had an active hand in progressive Republican politics, and Lindsay was a worthwhile project. The question was raised: how could Lindsay, heading toward a fourth term as a Congressman, attain a higher national profile that could be a springboard to a run for president? Already, he had established himself as an up-and-comer, a resolute voice for the increasingly muzzled liberal wing of the Republican Party. He was enormously popular in his home district, known as the Silk Stocking District (because it included swanky addresses on Park Avenue and Fifth Avenue). Lindsay had won his first election there back in 1958, by a narrow margin of 7,800 votes. In the 1960 election, he extended that to 26,000 votes. In 1964, despite a nationwide Republican collapse under the leadership of especially conservative nominee Barry Goldwater, Lindsay's personal popularity was perspicuous, as he took 71.5 percent of his district's vote despite incumbent Democrat Lyndon Johnson getting 70 percent of the votes for president.

It helped that Lindsay was a looker, 6-foot-4 and blue-eyed, somehow always tanned and sporting a healthy carpet of hair. When his name came up in the press at the time, there were usually three footnotes attached: The first was his looks, the second was his aspiration for higher office, and the third was a combination of the two wrapped up in the inevitable comparison to John F. Kennedy. In December 1964, political columnist James Reston managed to include all three in one paragraph: "Lindsay is a young, tall, handsome Yale character—sort of an incipient Republican Kennedy—who opposed Goldwater in the election and survived the Democratic avalanche in New York. The lady journalists in Washington were so impressed with his looks that they invited him to address a splashy luncheon, where his wit, candor, and sophistication fluttered one of the most influential Washington audiences."

But for the editors at the *Herald-Tribune*, it was something that Reston wrote later in his column that provided the substance of conversation: "The tragedy of the Republican Party in Washington today is that it smothers and devours its young." Lindsay was young and ambitious, but he was also ripe for devouring. During his tenure in Washington, he had made few friends among national Republicans because of his willingness to buck the conservative dogma in favor of his own liberal leanings. He cast one of only two votes against a bill that would have granted the postmaster general the right to impound obscene mail, and he cast the lone Republican vote against a bill that would allow the federal government to seize mail from Communist countries. Lindsay, when asked how he could cast votes against monitoring Communism and pornography, said that obscene mail and Communist literature were two of the major industries of his constituents, and without them, "the 17th district would be a depressed area." His shaky credentials as a Republican left Lindsay open to being smothered by his party. His repudiation of Goldwater was one thing, but after his renegade votes, Lindsay watched his hopes for a spot on the House Foreign Affairs Committee vanish. Minority Whip Leslie Arends reportedly told him, "Boy, I never saw a man talk himself off the Foreign Affairs Committee so fast in my life." During the 1965 congressional session, he would vote with House Republicans only 6 percent of the time. Cinching his lack of friends in Washington, Lindsay found that the Kennedy comparison worked two ways. "He was not wildly popular among his colleagues in the Congress," Reston later observed, "who regarded him, as they regarded John Kennedy, as a little too good-looking, a little too Ivy Leaguish, and a little too curt and abrasive."

Lindsay could not find a natural path for his ambition. At the Whitney-Thayer luncheon, the prospect of the Senate was raised. "We have two of those," Lindsay said, referring to liberal Republicans Kenneth Keating (who would be replaced later in 1964 by Democrat Robert F. Kennedy) and Jacob Javits, who had handily defeated Wagner for the seat in 1956 and was re-elected in 1962. Governor? "We've got one," Lindsay said. Though Governor Nelson Rockefeller had already twice tried and failed to get the Republican presidential nomination, he was not up for reelection until 1966 and the feeling was that he would hold his chair in Albany for the foreseeable future, though he had not yet made an official announcement about his intentions.

Then Lindsay piped up: "You left out something—the Mayor of New York."

If the response to this suggestion was underwhelming, it was not difficult to figure out why. While the job had national significance and profile, it also was a dead end. Only two of the 102 men who had filled the New York mayor's office over the previous 300 years had moved on to a higher political office than the congressional seat Lindsay was proposing to leave. The first was DeWitt Clinton (who actually was a US Senator before stepping down to the mayoralty in 1803, lost a presidential race to James Madison in 1812, then became New York's governor in 1817), and the second, John T. Hoffman, had been elected governor in 1869. It was one thing to orate on the floor in Congress or to run the business of the state from on high in Albany, but the quotidian demands of the city called for a level of minute decision making and horse trading that was unseemly for a would-be president of the United States. You don't leapfrog from fixing potholes in Astoria and brokering deals with sanitation workers to dealing with the Russians, your finger on the button. Political analyst Nick Thimmesch called the job a, "political prison," and noted, "New York mayors of this century left office beaten, shamed, or dying men."

Lindsay pitched the idea differently. America's cities, as he saw it, had been neglected too long, and increasingly were becoming a fulcrum in politics. About 75 percent of the country's population lived in cities, and that number was projected to grow—a study by the Institute of Urban Life in October 1964 said that "within a relatively few years, 90 per cent of Americans will be living in metropolitan areas." Additionally, a Supreme Court ruling was forcing change in election districting, putting more of an emphasis on cities over rural areas. Wouldn't it be vital, if the Republican Party really wanted to resurrect itself, to win back some measure of urban support? New York was a good example, with registered Democrats outnumbering Republicans by a margin of 2.4 million to 700,000. No Republican had been mayor since 1946, when

Fiorello LaGuardia headed a fusion government. Lindsay wanted to be Mr. New York. Lindsay was making some sense, and, "gradually the idea emerged that a mayor of New York who qualified legitimately as, 'Mr. City,' and who did not alienate the fast-growing suburbs around the center cities might go all the way to the White House."

When the *Herald-Tribune* came out with the "City in Crisis" series, Thayer and Whitney were providing an undercurrent of support for a potential Lindsay-for-mayor campaign. (The *Herald-Tribune*'s Dick Schaap, later to help Joe Namath with his autobiography, recruited Barry Gottehrer, later to be a controversial aide to Lindsay, to be the lead editor for the package.) The stories didn't necessarily lay the blame for the city's deterioration at Mayor Wagner's feet or attack him personally, but Wagner came off as disconnected, blind to the ruins around him. Wagner was a savvy politician and understood his job as a zero-sum game, where abrupt moves to please one constituency would anger others. Wagner had a very deliberate style that emphasized the status quo and allowed change only at a slow pace. "I like the Mayor, everybody likes the Mayor," the story quoted one prominent educator as saying. "He's always available and he's always pleasant. But when you leave his office or Gracie Mansion, it suddenly dawns on you that he hasn't really said a damn thing. . . . We need a Mayor who doesn't care about his image and his political popularity. We need a Mayor who cares about the city and has the ability to cope with its problems."

Lindsay would later say that the "City in Crisis" series helped inspire him politically. "The weight of the articles was overwhelming," Lindsay said. "It was a gloomy tale of crisis everywhere in the city—and provided a raison d'etre for me to run." Wagner, who was only fifty-five but looked much older because of the grind of the job and some personal hardship (he lost his wife to cancer in 1964), had indicated he would run for a fourth term that fall. He was less impressed with the "City in Crisis" series than Lindsay. A *Herald-Tribune* reporter called his office seeking comment on the series from Wagner. A spokesman for Wagner, who knew Jock Whitney's political leanings, responded, "The Mayor says to tell Jock to shove it up his ass."

....

The *Herald-Tribune* helped pave the way for a Lindsay mayoral bid, but there was still a matter of the party elders devouring their young. Lindsay was the budding GOP star, but he was still a second-tier guy in the political establishment. Within the state, he was behind Governor Rockefeller and Senator Javits at the New York political trough, and that meant he would not be in position to run a credible campaign against Wagner unless he had their backing. In the winter of 1964–65, he didn't.

Javits was considering a run at the mayoralty himself. Though he was comfortable in his Senate seat, he was sixty and the idea of closing out his career in politics as New York's first Jewish mayor appealed to him. But he knew he would need Rockefeller's help to round up Republican resources, and he would need plenty of time to set up a citywide political organization. He wanted Rockefeller to make a decision on the mayor's race by January 1, so that he could begin to formulate a campaign against Wagner. Rockefeller, though, stonewalled Javits. He was not eager to see an anti-Wagner race get rolling early, mostly for his own purposes—as part of the anti-Goldwater wave, the New York State Assembly had turned Democratic for the first time in thirty years, and Rockefeller knew he would need the help of Wagner (with whom he had a cordial and even productive working relationship based on mutual political survival) to get Democrats on board with necessary legislation. Rockefeller also was not so sure he wanted to see Wagner gone. If he were ousted, statewide control of the Democrats in New York would likely go to newly elected Senator Robert F. Kennedy, who would be a much bigger threat to Rockefeller. Wagner was trying to run New York City, and had to engage in niceties and wink-and-nod agreements with Rockefeller. Kennedy didn't.

As the Javits-Rockefeller mayoral feud simmered, Lindsay was feeling out his own prospects, which hinged on Javits pulling out. Richard

Aurelio, then an aide to Javits, said, "There was one night when he went into a meeting and told me to get some rest, because when I got up in the morning, we may be running for Mayor of New York. He was very serious about it. Gave me a sleepless night." At the end of January 1965, Lindsay was, according to the *Times*, "quietly circulating" a list of requirements any Republican mayoral candidate would need fulfilled before making a run: a decision from Rockefeller by March 1; a campaign fund worth at least $1.5 million; and the ability to select his own running mates, allowing for a LaGuardia-style fusion ticket. Rockefeller was not about to budge, though. He would not give in to the deadlines imposed by Javits or Lindsay. In Washington on February 25, a meeting that included Rockefeller, Javits, and Lindsay devolved into a shouting match that lasted more than an hour. At the end of February, Javits—without ever having entered the race—took his name out of consideration. On March 1, Lindsay followed suit, resigned to sticking with his congressional seat. "Mr. Lindsay is still stymied," R.W. Apple wrote in the *Times*. "A fine future is predicted for him by everyone, but no one can say just how he will get from here to there."

While in between here and there, Lindsay maintained his public celebrity—he preferred to be known as something more than just a palm-greased politician, but as an educated, well-rounded man with a sense of humor. He could come across as a moralizing, patrician New York blueblood, but his background was actually much more humble. Lindsay had been brought up an Episcopalian on the West Side of New York, and his schooling—St. Paul's in New Hampshire for school, Yale for college and law school—was that of a typical country-club conservative. But that wasn't Lindsay, personally or philosophically. His father, George, was a successful investment broker when he retired, but he was the son of an immigrant factory worker from the Isle of Wight. George Lindsay had never finished high school and had risen through the ranks on Wall Street only after starting as a runner at age fifteen. This was no patriarch of a political dynasty. In fact, he would have preferred his son stay out of politics altogether. "The candidate's father was no Joe Kennedy and the candidate's family is hardly Rooseveltian," wrote political reporter Alvin Davis, "and despite what you'll be hearing in the days to come, the candidate is no Jack Kennedy or FDR, either. For one thing, he's a New Yorker, and his accents are West Side. . . . He doesn't have Kennedy money and he doesn't have a Roosevelt barony, but he has their sense of people-politics." When he died in 1961, George Lindsay left his five children (John had a twin brother, David, as well as brothers, George and Rod, and a sister, Eleanor) portions of his estate, valued at about $700,000 each. Lindsay was certainly comfortable, but his father left the family with no pretensions of upper-class status. "My father never forgot that he had been very poor as a child and as a young man," Lindsay said. "And he never let us forget it."

Lindsay thus tried to maintain a common-man political touch while debating his potential mayoral run. In February, Lindsay appeared as a special guest at a Fashion Group luncheon on the topic of men's toiletries, alongside such fellow panelists as pianist/comedian Victor Borge, entertainer Sammy Davis Jr., and future tennis Hall of Famer Bill Talbert. Lindsay flushed and grinned when one speaker called him, "the future president of the United States of America," and then, "got a long round of applause for merely being there." He also worked on one of his favorite side gigs, reviewing books for newspapers and magazines (he gave the book, *Spanish Harlem,* a positive endorsement for the *New York Times* that spring). On March 28, he made an appearance on TV's *What's My Line?* hosted by John Charles Daly. Lindsay was able to guess that Mrs. Mary Proctor of Bossier City, Louisiana, was a tax technician, but when movie star Robert Mitchum appeared as the celebrity guest in the blindfold portion of the program, Lindsay was stumped.

It was around late March, though, that Lindsay began having second thoughts about his decision not to run for mayor. It was depressing him, he would later report. He lost sleep. He lost weight. Sure, unseating Wagner was a near impossible task, but Lindsay was being told that, even if he ran and lost, it would not doom his career. If he had good ideas, spoke passionately about urban issues and at least made a credible showing, he would bolster his credentials as Mr. City in the eyes of New Yorkers and the nation. Besides, Lindsay's top political aide—Robert

Price, a thirty-two-year-old lawyer and political wiz—wanted Lindsay to give it a try. Price is credited with getting Lindsay back into the race, especially after Rockefeller (to the surprise of no one) announced in early May that he would run for governor again in 1966, formally closing off that avenue of advancement to Lindsay. On May 12, the *Times* ran a front-page story, leaked by Price to a reporter friend, saying that Lindsay was again considering challenging Wagner despite the fact that Lindsay had not yet made the decision himself. Price was quoted in the story: "He is deeply troubled about the condition of the city and believes it is his responsibility to offer the people a viable alternative to what they now have at City Hall. . . . I know, too, that he believes the Republican party has to show its interest in the problems of the cities, because its future depends on its success in the cities."

Price had persuaded Rockefeller to give Lindsay his support, morally and financially. In addition to the front-page story in the *Times*, the paper followed up with an editorial that stopped short of endorsing a potential Lindsay candidacy, but said, "for the first time in years, the minority party is presenting a candidate who offers a real choice to the voter, who will fight a real contest and who has a real chance to win." There had been polls leaking out, too, going back to December, showing Lindsay at least tied with the mayor in a head-to-head race, if not leading by several points. And the matchup of the lithe, energetic Lindsay against the perpetually ragged Wagner was almost too tempting to pass up. "It is now Lindsay who is the hero-knight of the good guys," wrote national columnist William S. White. "It is now Wagner to whom befalls the painful part of the line-faced character actor, the spear carrier for the bad guys." For Lindsay, there was no resisting the momentum Price's machinations had started. He skipped a theater date with his wife, Mary—they had been married for sixteen years, with four children, and this qualified as a marital misstep on Lindsay's part—to spend a night conferring with Price. When he was done, he met Mary for a post-performance drink at Sardi's in Times Square. That's when he told her he would run for mayor. She would be behind him, on one condition: that he put off making the announcement until the following day. She had already planned a birthday party for their son, John Jr., who was turning five.

On May 13, the announcement came. Lindsay, a Manhattanite through and through, made a tour of all five boroughs, ticking off—nervously at times—the points he hoped to get across in his declaration of candidacy. He was new at this, and his first day of campaigning outside the Silk Stocking District was uneven at best. He was met with wild enthusiasm in the Bronx, for example, and when he closed his day by speaking at what would become his headquarters in the Roosevelt Hotel in Manhattan, he got a ten-minute ovation from the crowd. In Brooklyn, though, the *Village Voice* reported, "In the dreary Stardust Room of the St. George (Hotel), a few old ladies, perhaps permanent tenants of the hotel, sat and waited. . . . A few, very few, Brooklyn Republican politicians filtered in." When the grand tour was through, Lindsay was back at campaign headquarters, talking on the air with popular WMCA radio host Barry Gray. He gave a rationale for the risks of running for mayor as a Republican in such a heavily Democratic city. "One of the great things about living is being willing to stake all," he said. "If you are not a little bit of a gambler then you are a fuddy-duddy." Lindsay had a reputation as a Boy Scout politician ("Prince Valiant" and "Captain Marvel" were among his nicknames), and probably did not help that reputation by suggesting that he was no "fuddy-duddy."

In the *New York World-Telegram*, writer Murray Kempton agreed that Lindsay's opening message seemed disjointed. Traveling to Staten Island, for example, Lindsay did not alter his speech, saying, "In our city our streets are dirty and unsafe. The air we breathe increasingly and dangerously is polluted. Crime, brutality, and narcotics are rampant." Kempton pointed out that, "the effect was odd," because Staten Island is, "at least transiently rural." The air wasn't so bad there, and the narcotics problem was minimal. In his initial tour of the boroughs, Lindsay was only just getting a grasp on how big and varied New York City really is. A city in crisis, certainly, but the crises affecting Manhattan were not necessarily the same as those affecting the Bronx or Brooklyn or Staten Island or Queens.

But Kempton saw a glimmer of what Lindsay could be on that first day, despite the occasional awkwardness. "He will walk more easily when he knows the terrain better," Kempton wrote. "Before long what he sees will instruct him to cease talking about this magnificent city as a ruin and begin to describe it in those real terms upon which his essential appeal rests, as a community whose failure is in not having achieved its proper greatness. At the moment, he is a little unformed."

Still, Kempton could see what was going on. It was 1965 and Lindsay was prepared to take over in New York, and it was better that the establishment get used to that idea. Murray wrote the line that would quickly define not only Lindsay and his candidacy, but the rest of the political order, in New York and beyond—Wagner, Javits, and Rockefeller, certainly, but also Barry Goldwater and Lyndon Johnson and every other establishment member of either party.

"He is fresh," Kempton wrote, "and everyone else is tired."

CHAPTER 3

Decline and Fall

Y.A. TITTLE WOKE UP ON the morning of December 12, 1964, in his bed on the eighth floor of the Roosevelt Hotel in Manhattan, and his first thought was of Vince Costello. The Cleveland linebacker was known for, "dogging," meaning he would shadow the movements of the opposing quarterback, prepared to get in the way of a pass or to step in and make a tackle himself. As Tittle lay in bed, mentally preparing to face the Browns—who needed a win to seal the Eastern Division championship of the NFL at Yankee Stadium that afternoon—he could not escape the image of Costello. This was the 209th time that Tittle awoke on the day of one of his own professional football games. It would be the last. Tittle had not made a formal announcement, but at age thirty-eight and having suffered a rib injury in Week 2 that sapped his effectiveness, he knew he would be retiring. "This game Saturday is important to me for a lot of reasons," he said. "A lot of reasons. I want to have a good day Saturday so much."

He didn't. Playing in a steady rain that muddied the field, the Giants led, briefly, by a 7–3 count, but after that, the Cleveland onslaught arrived. The Browns scored 42 straight points. Tittle, in his final play of the game, was chased by Cleveland tackle Dick Modzelewski and, under pressure, unleashed a pass to avoid the sack. Modzelewski still hit Tittle, slamming him into the mud. As he was going down, Tittle saw the ball, then saw the image which had jolted him from his slumber that morning: Vince Costello, dogging him. The pass floated into Costello's arms for an interception. It was the final pass Tittle would throw in the NFL. He was replaced in the game by rookie Gary Wood.

Trailing Cleveland, 52–14, in the closing moments, the Giants registered a meaningless touchdown, before a wave of fans spilled onto the field at Yankee Stadium, laying assault to the grounds. It was the worst season in Giants history, a record of 2–10–2. For the past month, Giants loyalists—who registered the twentieth consecutive home sell-out at Yankee Stadium that afternoon—had grown incredulous over what had happened to their team, and developed a derisive anthem aimed at coach Allie Sherman. "Good-bye, Al-lie!" they sang. "We hate to see you go!" As the clock expired, Sherman was again serenaded, only this time, fans stood in the end zone, ripping out the goalposts as they did. With no goalposts, the Giants couldn't kick the extra point. The referees, one report noted, "merely said, 'The hell with it.'" The game ended, 52–20.

The following day, from his home, Sherman told a reporter that he'd been able to find some calm in the wake of the loss—his son, Randy, had just turned eleven. "We invited some of the kids in to see some sound films," Sherman said. "There was a Lewis and Martin picture and some cartoons."

When it was suggested that Sherman should have shown Giants games, he retorted, "Those were the cartoons."

If the Mara brothers, powerful owners of the Giants, were concerned about Namath going to the Jets in the winter of 1964–65, it was with good reason. Their Giants were, for the first time in their history, terrible. Tittle's age and ineffectiveness was a storyline for the season, but it was hardly the only reason for the disintegration of the team. Particularly galling was the play of the Giants defense, so long the spine that held up the team during its run of five playoff appearances in six years. They'd finished first in the NFL in team defense three times in that span, but in 1964, they were dead last in the league, allowing 28.5 points. The blame fell to Sherman, a good-natured and intelligent Brooklyner who was, perhaps, doomed to a bleak denouement from the outset of his head-coaching career. In 1959 Sherman had the bad luck to take over the chair of Giants offensive coordinator from none other than Vince Lombardi, who left the Giants for Green Bay and went on to be arguably the greatest coach in football history. The Giants' defensive coordinator at the time? Tom Landry, who would head to Dallas and become a legend himself with the Cowboys, in 1960. (Jim Lee Howell, the Giants' head coach when Landry and Lombardi were genius coordinators, supposedly once described his job by saying, "I just blow up the footballs and keep order.") The departures of Landry and Lombardi left Sherman to take over when Howell retired in 1960, but only after the Maras failed to persuade Lombardi to leave Green Bay and come back to the Giants. Sherman led the Giants to the playoffs three straight years, but they lost each time. It seemed Sherman's lot to take blame for what went wrong without receiving credit for what went right.

The hostility of the local boosters had been building. Sherman was the target of that resentment. The Giants' old reliables had aged, and it had been Sherman's lot to either trade away popular but faded stars, or accept a steady decline into old age that would ultimately leave the Giants at the bottom of the NFL. Amazingly, Sherman managed to do both simultaneously. He had already traded away lineman Rosey Grier in 1963, and in 1964, he did the unthinkable, dealing two franchise stalwarts: Modzelewski, an understated and mild-mannered eleven-year veteran who was sent to the Browns in March, and linebacker Sam Huff. After having sent Tittle into a muddy faceplant in the Browns win, Modzelewski was polite, almost apologetic. "I hate seeing it come against my ex-teammates," he said.

Huff, though, was neither understated nor mild-mannered. While starring for the Giants in 1959, he had become the face of the rising NFL, appearing on the cover of *Time* magazine, with an accompanying story that lauded the masculinity of Huff's gridiron exploits: "The crash of Huff's tackle can stir the Giant bench to bellowing glee, set the rabid fans in Yankee Stadium to rumbling out their own rapid-fire cheer like the chugging of a steam engine: 'Huff-Huff-Huff-Huff-Huff.' When Sam is on the field, the toughest fans in the U.S.'s toughest sport see what they came to see." The following year, CBS ran a half-hour special hosted by Walter Cronkite called, "The Violent World of Sam Huff." In it, the crew-cutted Huff told the audience, "Anytime you play football, on the field there is no place for nice guys. You have to be tough, you have to go all out. I always feel real good whenever I hit someone, you just hear that old leather thud in there. You feel as though you accomplished something, you made a beautiful tackle. . . . It's either, the expression is, kill or be killed."

Huff felt the Giants had betrayed him. After the trade of Modzelewski, Huff had gone to the Maras to seek assurances that he, too, would not be traded. He got those assurances but was shocked to learn that Sherman still sent him to Washington the following month. Huff would never forgive Sherman. When the Redskins played the Giants in 1966, Washington had a 69–41 lead and was prepared to let the clock run down to end the game. But Huff, as he later told it, called a time out and urged Redskins coach Otto Graham to "show no mercy." Washington kicked a field goal and completed their humiliation of the Giants by putting 72 points on them. In 2011, nearly five decades after Sherman dealt him, Huff said, "I'll never forget that trade."

The Giants were a mess. The chase of Namath that winter went beyond keeping a young star in the NFL—it was a matter of keeping the Giants, with a frustrated fan base and a decayed roster, on top of New York's football hierarchy. The previous season, the Jets' Sonny Werblin had outmaneuvered them for rookie Ohio State running back Matt Snell, who had been drafted by both teams. It helped that Snell's parents lived on Long Island and that Jets backfield coach Clive Rush had been an assistant with the Buckeyes—it also helped that the $30,000 bonus the Jets would pay was a good bit more than the $5,000 reportedly offered by the Giants. But it was the details that won

Snell over. A week before the 1964 draft, Werblin invited the parents of several New York–area prospects to a Jets game, chauffeuring them in limousines to the Polo Grounds. On a freezing day, Werblin noticed Snell's parents shivering in the stands, and had hot chocolates sent over. Snell first met Werblin when Werblin traveled to Columbus after the draft, and Snell told him then, "Thanks for taking care of my folks." The Giants, meanwhile, sent Tim Mara, one of the owners' sons, to visit Snell, who was insulted that the team had not bothered to send a higher ranking team official. Snell signed with the Jets, and was the 1964 AFL Rookie of the Year.

While the Giants were still undeniably the football power-house in New York, they were staunchly against ceding any corner of New York to the Jets. They wanted Werblin and his upstarts gone. In 1963, according to Buffalo owner Ralph Wilson, a proposal had been floated that would have ended the AFL-NFL war and resulted in a merger. But, Wilson pointed out, "the strongest place of resistance to peace, namely New York. This is the town of John V. and Wellington Mara, owners of the wealthy Giants, and of Pete Rozelle, the NFL commissioner." Rozelle, still a new commissioner eager to please the Maras, showed such strong support for the Giants' founders that he even publicly forsook his manners by offering Werblin nothing more than a cold shoulder. Rozelle "means to continue the fight, even at Toots Shor's or '21.' At social events of the sports world, he turns his back on Werblin." In addition to Snell the Giants were also outbid the previous year by the Jets for quarterback Mike Taliaferro and lineman Dave Herman.

Anticipation for Namath in New York built while Giants were at the lowest point in franchise history. The general haughtiness of the Maras, and the overall disdain the NFL seemed to have for fans and media, was now a serious liability. As Maury Allen of the *New York Post* wrote, "The Giants had the town to themselves for many years. They had won championships and developed a hard-core following. The Giants always sold out, so they acted as if they didn't need the fans or the press. Suddenly, with Namath's appearance on the scene, the press didn't need them. The Giants were the Establishment team and suddenly nobody cared about the Establishment."

....

If the Giants had come to represent the Establishment in football, then the team with whom they shared a home field—the Yankees— was something altogether grander: they were the Emperors, the Establishment team in the nation's Establishment sport. From the late 1950s into the 60s, there was no question that professional foot- ball, packaged into neat timeslots each weekend with accompanying betting lines and wide television exposure, had made great inroads in popularity, and expositions hailing the arrival of King Football while signaling the impending demise of baseball filled many a column inch in the nation's newspapers. Football was the wave of the future. The truly hip might have been testing basketball or even hockey, but for much of the nation, baseball was still at the fore, still the national pastime. In the early 60s, no team had dominated the game, nearly to the point of removing fun and interest from the entire endeavor, quite like the Yankees.

The Yankees' manhandling of the American League had been thorough. They first won the American League pennant, behind the slugging of Babe Ruth, in 1921, and would win the American League 29 times in the next 44 years (the team with the second-most pen- nants in that span, Detroit, had just four). "Fans take it for granted that the Yanks will be in every series, as if they're merely exercising the divine right of kings," Chicago columnist John Carmichael wrote in late 1964. "They're a law unto themselves in Major League baseball." While repeatedly accepting those championships was their expected duty, utter resentment was spawned in more neutral corners.

In August 1964, the American League held its annual midseason meeting on a Monday in Chicago, during which little more than routine business was covered. The following day, beginning at 7:30 a.m., A.L. president Joe Cronin began phoning owners with shocking news, informing them of a proposed sale of 80 percent of the New

York Yankees' stock to the Columbia Broadcasting System. The price would be $11.2 million, and Cronin demanded almost immediate votes on the matter. He was unable (or, perhaps unwilling) to get in touch with loose-cannon Kansas City A's owner Charles O. Finley, who claimed he'd been in his Chicago office sipping coffee when Cronin allegedly called. Instead, a written copy of the proposed Yankees-CBS sale was hand delivered later to Finley, and when he called Cronin, irate over the sale and the fact that it had not been discussed at the league meeting, he was told that his vote didn't matter anyway, because only seven votes were needed for approval, and all seven had been delivered. Besides Finley, the Chicago White Sox also objected, and voted "no" on the deal. "It's a hell of a way to run a league," White Sox owner Arthur Allyn said. "I don't like to be called at 11:45 about something and be asked to approve it in three hours. I understand the subject was under discussion in the league office last Saturday, and we had plenty of opportunity to discuss it at our league meeting Monday. I know Joe Cronin is put out with me because I told him so. He can get mad all he wants because I'm just a little bit madder."

The bungling of the Yankees sale among A.L. owners was only the beginning. While Finley and Allyn very publicly slammed the Yankees and Cronin, the implications of the deal began to set in. Already in recent years, baseball had undergone a flurry of franchise movement that disrupted the game's long-accepted order. The sweetheart stadium deals moving teams got in their new locales left the impression that loyalty no longer mattered where economics were involved. The move of the Giants and Dodgers to the West Coast had devastated fans in New York in 1958, and the move of the A's from Philadelphia to Kansas City had been similarly surprising and upsetting. Before that, the Braves had gone from Boston to Milwaukee, and the Browns went from St. Louis to Baltimore, where they became the Orioles. Just after, in 1960, the Senators left Washington for Minnesota to become the Twins. The American League added two expansion teams (and collected the corresponding millions in expansion fees) in Los Angeles and Washington in 1961, and the N.L. expanded to include the New

York Mets and Houston Colt .45s (and their expansion payments) in 1962. After 1954, then, half of baseball's twenty teams in both leagues had either moved or been installed as expansion units. In every case, baseball's owners got richer as a result. The capper came in 1964, when, despite strong support from fans in Milwaukee, the Braves announced they would be moving to Atlanta.

"Baseball is a commercial venture," wrote the *New Yorker*'s Roger Angell, warning of the consequences of a bottom-line focus. "But it is one of such perfect equipoise that millions of us every year can unembarrassedly surrender ourselves to its unique and absorbing joys. The ability to find beauty and involvement in artificial commercial constructions is essential to most of us in the modern world; it is the life-giving naïveté. But naïveté is not gullibility, and those who persistently alter baseball for their quick and selfish purposes will find, I believe, that they are the owners of teams without a following and of a sport devoid of passion."

For many fans, seeing the Yankees go from a two-man ownership group (Dan Topping and Del Webb, who would stay in charge until the network decided when and if to buy them out) who interacted with fans, to an arm of the CBS org chart placed an apt punctuation mark on a game already proving to be dollar-oriented. The backlash came quickly. The case raised the issue of baseball's standing anti-trust exemption, a congressional blessing that the sport clung to and that hinged on the definition of baseball as a public entertainment, rather than as a business venture. News of the deal rattled through both houses of Congress, with promised investigations and increased scrutiny of the antitrust exemption. Rep. Emanuel Celler warned that, under the influence of television, there was the "danger that pro team sports, like wrestling today, may degenerate into exhibitions rather than bona fide athletic contests." Rep. Henry S. Reuss of Wisconsin—already no fan of baseball's magnates as he was attempting to block the move of the Braves—said flatly, "Baseball has lost its antitrust exemption." Even the Russians chimed in to dig at the capitalist pigs running American sports: "The sensational sale of the New York Yankees to the Columbia

Broadcasting System is another proof that some sports are being turned into an appendix of commercial television," official state paper *Izvestia* wrote.

Judge Roy Hofheinz, president of the Houston Colt .45s, announced that "the day CBS finally purchases the Yankees will be the blackest day for baseball since the Black Sox scandal." *Boston Globe* columnist Harold Kaese pointed out that any semblance of fairness was wiped out by the deal. "Is it indeed a sport," Kaese wondered, "when a club like Washington, whose net revenue in 1963 was about $1.5 million, now has to compete against one that is owned by a corporation whose net revenue was $564 million, or nearly 400 times greater?" Columnist Arthur Daley wrote, "The carpetbaggers and the quick-buck men have taken over a game that once had true sportsmen at the controls. The baseball phase of it is incidental. . . . The dollar sign is beginning to obscure the standings of the teams." For all the indignity and heartfelt lamentations, though, nothing really changed.

On November 2, the *New York Post* reported: "There is no indication that baseball commissioner Ford Frick or the Justice Dept. will do anything to halt the sale." Indeed, they didn't and on November 3, the most Establishment team in the most Establishment sport became a subsidiary of the Columbia Broadcasting System.

. . . .

As the CBS sale was being announced in August, Topping and Webb—still technically in charge—were coming to another decision: manager Yogi Berra would be fired at the end of the year. The Yankees were struggling, playing uninspired baseball, and sitting at third in the American League, 4½ games behind the Orioles. Berra, so popular as a player, had been a cornerstone in a shakeup at the top of the organization before the season, with manager Ralph Houk bumped up to the position of general manager and Berra taking over as the field manager after 18 seasons as a player. In doing so, the Yankees hoped that Berra's charm with the fans and press would counterbalance the newcomer Mets, whose popularity stemmed largely from their own quirky and quotable manager, former Yankees boss Casey Stengel. But that plan flopped. Houk was a tough-but-fair manager who earned respect, but players did not get behind their former teammate Berra as a manager. Milton Gross of the *Post* reported that players viewed Berra, "as a joke. The front office didn't laugh." Gross quoted one player as saying, "Respect Yogi? I don't guess we did as much as Ralph. Some of the guys resented him." The Yankees still had a good enough team to win the not-so-daunting American League, even without much help from Berra. Veterans like Elston Howard (.318 batting average), Mickey Mantle (35 home runs, 111 RBIs) and Roger Maris (.281 average, 26 homers) didn't need a strong managerial hand to figure out how to win. They did need some pitching help, though, and when Houk acquired hard-throwing Cuban reliever Pedro Ramos on September 5, the Yankees won 20 of their final 27 games, enough to hold off the White Sox and Orioles to capture the American League.

Entering the World Series that year, the Yankees' situation with Berra put them in a bind. Strangely enough, the N.L. champion Cardinals were in a similar situation. St. Louis was a lost cause by mid-August, and team owner Gussie Busch determined Johnny Keane would be fired after the season. Keane, certain something was amiss, drafted a letter of resignation that he kept at the ready for what he figured was his inevitable firing. But the Cardinals went 28–11 to close the season, capitalizing on a late-season, ten-game losing streak by the Phillies and a stretch of four losses in five games by Cincinnati to eke out an improbable pennant. The World Series itself was a classic—the Cardinals won in seven games as pitcher Bob Gibson dominated—but the proceedings were overshadowed entirely by the backroom dealings involving both managers. Busch was prepared to make amends with Keane, but at the Cardinals' postseason press conference, Keane sat down and handed Busch the resignation letter, embarrassing the owner on the spot.

The Yankees stuck by their earlier decision and let Berra go the day after the series ended, offering him a vague "consulting" job. The die was cast: Keane had already been picked to take over as Yankees

Berra had failed. They'd won the pennant in 1964, but the Yankees still lost ground at the turnstiles, bringing the fewest fans to Yankee Stadium since World War II was on. In 1961 the Yankees had attracted 1,747,725 fans. That dropped below 1.5 million the following year and, in 1964, it fell all the way to 1,305,638—a 25 percent fall over four seasons. The disillusionment with the Yankees was not just a media construction, nor was it connected to the team's performance on the field. They were losing paying customers even as they were piling up pennants.

That winter, Houk talked freely about changes needed on the Yankees roster. They needed depth and youth, but the Yankees' minor-league affiliates were uncharacteristically dry of talent, and the players on hand were mediocre. An offseason of trade rumors both real and imagined all fell away, unrealized. The 1965 Opening Day lineup was the same the Yankees had used for the bulk of 1964. Not only did the Yankees essentially stay the same as a team, but they gave raises to that set of players. The Yankees payroll blossomed to more than $850,000 between 1964 and '65, a baseball record. Mantle was tops at $100,000, but Maris was making $72,000, with Elston Howard and Whitey Ford making $65,000 each (and each turning thirty-six in 1965). In the NFL, Allie Sherman was a target of Giants fans because he did too much dumping of aging veterans. For the Yankees, Houk was a target because he did too little.

There was nothing tangible to explain the souring of Yankees fans—no scandal, no plunge in the standings, no unwise transactions. The Yankees spent much of that winter ruminating on a simple question: why doesn't anyone like us? The answer they came up with was absurd. *The television broadcasts!* Of course. The Yankees fired iconic broadcaster Mel Allen, who had been calling Yankee games for twenty-five years, and hired chatty and affable former catcher Joe Garagiola to replace him. They had been unable to generate positive attention in the newspapers with Berra on board, so their solution was to win back fans with a joke-cracking broadcaster.

At the press conference at Toots Shor's announcing Garagiola's hiring, Houk was almost embarrassingly concerned with the Yankees' public relations problems. He tried to play up the theme of the franchise's newfound good nature. "Down at 745 Fifth Ave., the Yankees command post," the *Sporting News* reported, "Ralph Houk and his swivel chair commandos are falling all over each other patching up the over-all image of the organization from the players to the ticket-takers. . . . In brief, watching games at Yankee Stadium next season wouldn't be like watching a game in a bank vault." As evidence, Houk said, the team would lift the ban that prevented fans from carrying banners, a tradition at Mets games that had caught on quickly. "We're not a bunch of stuffed shirts," Houk said. "We want folks to come to our ballpark and enjoy themselves. Baseball ought to be fun for the customers and we're going to try our darnedest to make it that way in the future."

A new broadcaster and relaxed rules on signage, though, hardly qualified as a team trying its darnedest. Writer Leonard Koppett observed: "One of the falsest assumptions stems from a habit of the Yankee mind: arrogance. Not until the Yankees shed the self-imposed blinders of belief in their own omnipotence will they be able to see their problems clearly. The first source of Yankee problems is the way of thinking that says, 'We've decided that this is how it ought to be,'—and then confidently expects other people or the universe as a whole to follow smoothly along the path the Yankees have outlined. . . . Can the Yankees regenerate interest? That, fundamentally, is Houk's job now. Houk is a man of exceptional ability and his big asset up to now has been that he understands so well how baseball minds work. The question is, can he understand that tickets are sold to fans, and that it is the fans' mind the Yankees must reach?"

CHAPTER 4

"What's the matter, rookie?"

ON THE WEEKEND BEFORE JANUARY 25, 1965, three weeks after Sonny Werblin officially made him the highest paid athlete in American sports history and just after his introduction to the New York media at Toots Shor's, Joe Namath was dancing. He had eaten dinner at the 21 Club, the swanky Manhattan restaurant, with Werblin in the evening, then decided to catch up with friends to unwind a bit more at the Western-themed Dudes N' Dolls, one of his favorite East Side hangouts. Namath was seated at a table, deeply involved in telling a story as he sipped a Grand Marnier, waving his hands wildly when he caught the snifter and spilled his drink. He called to the waitress ("Hey, Miss America!") and asked her to bring him another drink. "Give us another table cloth," he added. "Give us another everything." After sizing up a woman at the next table, Namath made quick conversation and extended his hand, taking her to the dance floor. Once his partner started moving Namath, one observer noted, "stayed right with her, snapping his fingers, shaking his pelvis like Elvis, moving his shoulders. All eyes were on him, not the girl." Under normal circumstances, it would have been no surprise that Namath could keep pace on a Manhattan dance floor on a winter night. Though Namath had arrived at Alabama from Beaver Falls as a notably shy kid in 1961, he quickly came out of his shell and gained a reputation. The *Atlanta Journal*'s Furman Bisher wrote of him during his senior year, "Joe's a swinger, as they say. He's got credentials all over Tuscaloosa to prove it." But these circumstances were not normal. Namath was doing his dancing on a right knee that was scheduled to be scrubbed up, sliced open and surgically repaired at Lenox Hill hospital in a matter of hours. "Go, Joe baby, go," yelled Al Hassan, Namath's oldest childhood friend, who had come to New York to be Namath's business manager. "He's moving like he hasn't got a care in the world. Here he is about to go in the hospital and he's having a ball."

The ball ended Monday morning as Namath was wheeled in for surgery. Dr. James Nicholas explained to Namath what was going to happen, and for good luck, Nicholas's mother gave Namath a medal bearing the likeness of St. Jude. When Namath was told that St. Jude was the patron saint of lost causes he thought, *"Wait a minute, lost causes? I'd rather think of him as the patron saint of difficult tasks."* But Dr. Nicholas was among the best in his field, and he quickly went to work on the knee, making a small, crescent-shaped incision just below the kneecap and removing the medial meniscus, which had been torn and, in the aftermath of the tear, had curled up and jammed the joint. That prevented Namath from extending his leg without pain. The meniscus sits between the thigh bone and the shin, and acts as a sort of shock absorber for the knee. Removing it entirely would relieve Namath of immediate pain, but would leave him susceptible to long-term knee trouble as the bones ground against each other. Modern protocol for an athlete like Namath would be to only remove the torn part of the meniscus, leaving as much as possible in place, but it might not have mattered in Namath's case, because Nicholas reported that Namath's meniscus was not just torn, but shredded, likely from the three months he spent playing on the knee after the original injury occurred in October.

After the operation, when Namath awoke, he was greeted by the commands of Dr. Nicholas, holding his right ankle and ordering Namath to lift the very leg that had just been sliced open. It would be crucial for healing, Nicholas explained, to build up the muscles around Namath's knee as quickly as possible. All in all, Dr. Nicholas told his patient, things went well, and he expected that Namath would be able to play pro football for four years. "Thank you, Lord," Namath thought to himself. "I get a chance to play pro football for *four years*."

Sonny Werblin was not about to miss a chance to exploit the fascination with Namath's knee. Namath had not thrown a single pro pass, but Werblin had been saying all along that he was banking on Namath not just because of his ability with a football, but because of the way he naturally attracted attention. Namath's knee surgery was covered by the local press, by television, by *Time* magazine (which featured a detailed diagram of Namath's meniscus), by *Sports Illustrated*, by *Life* magazine. "The hip line in New York," one writer joked, "became, 'Sorry I can't make your party, Sybil, but I'm going to the tapping of Joe Namath's knee.'" During his two weeks of recovery, cameramen from the city's papers filed in to take pictures of a convalescing Namath forcing a smile, often accompanied by a winsome nurse, and on the day of his release from the hospital, the *New York Times* did a story on the letters he had been receiving from admiring fans, mainly female. "Most girls are Beatle crazy. But I have gone Joe Namath crazy," wrote one. A high-school girl wrote to tell him, "I'm writing you in civics class and the teacher just caught me." The most intricate came from Texas: "I'm 19 years old, considered quite beautiful, have a marvelous figure and a nice personality. I am hereby inviting you to escort me to the Junior Prom of the University of Texas, all expenses paid. Daddy will fly you down and home in the company plane."

Namath responded: "That's sure a wonderful invitation. I can't make it, though. I already have a date that day."

As the *Times* noted, "Apparently it is great to be young, to be a Jet and to have had a knee operation."

Namath's "swinger" status was not limited to his good looks and groovy dancing. When he arrived in Manhattan, Namath truly wanted to be part of the scene. (He did briefly return to Tuscaloosa after his knee surgery to attend classes, but admitted he spent little time in those

classes—his degree was no longer a priority.) While it was custom-
ary for Jets players to live near Shea Stadium, usually on Long Island,
Namath had not come to New York to be a suburbanite. That was
fine by Werblin, who really didn't want Namath to be out of the lime-
light in some sleepy bedroom community. "I couldn't believe the city,"
Namath later remembered. "I was from Beaver Falls, Pa., a small town,
and had gone to college at the University of Alabama in Tuscaloosa.
Being in New York was magical, like being led around by the spirits."
Werblin's friend, Joe Hirsch, was, at Werblin's urging, tasked with helping Namath acclimate to the city. The two took an apartment on the
16th floor of the Yorkshire Towers on 86th Street and Second Avenue,
and Namath was stunned by the price: $360 per month, plus $40 to
park the famed green Continental convertible (which was beginning
to look like an unwise choice for Manhattan's tight quarters). Back in
Alabama, Namath had been living in a three-bedroom house for $115
per month. And the parking was free. After a little more than a year,
though, Hirsch and Namath would move to a penthouse apartment
on East 76th Street, this one going for $500 per month. Its opulence
became part of Namath's swinger legend, and one visitor wrote that the
place was reflective of Namath, "who is reputed to be something of a
hedonist's hedonist." He paid $25,000 to have it decorated, and among
its features were a wall-to-wall six-inch-thick llama-hair rug, furniture
upholstered in zebra with snow leopard pillows, gold fixtures and two
large paintings of Namath in action. "I guess it wound up a little over
the top," Namath said.

....

Back in late November of 1964, even before the Jets officially drafted
Namath, Werblin made an appearance in the Jets' locker room at
Shea Stadium. He knew the upcoming AFL draft and the subsequent
negotiations with the incoming rookies would be unnerving to the
veterans already on the team. With the bidding war between the AFL
and NFL, he stated publicly that it would take somewhere between
$600,000 and $1 million to sign the team's draft picks, an astounding

amount considering the Jets' incoming rookies had signed for $140,000 worth of bonuses the previous year. But Werblin's forecast would prove correct, as three of the top five 1965 picks alone—Namath, Heisman Trophy winning Notre Dame quarterback John Huarte, and versatile back Bob Schweickert—signed for more than $700,000 combined. Weeb Ewbank, a known tightwad who had grown up on an Indiana farm during the Depression, had been in the professional ranks for fifteen years, and knew that the numbers Werblin was discussing were both unheard of on one hand, and accurate on the other. "We don't have a budget," Ewbank said. "People tell us we shouldn't go crazy and we ask them how far crazy is, and they don't know."

All over football, established players grumbled over the kind of money draftees were being promised. Their gripes were justified, too, because even proven players had modest salaries. Receiver Don Maynard, for example, was among the league leaders in receiving yardage and touchdowns in 1964, but was slated to make $17,000 for the 1965 season. He was among the highest paid players on the Jets roster. Still, Maynard went back to Texas each offseason to work as a teacher, and was also a master plumber, to supplement his income. Most Jets, in fact, worked offseason jobs. Running back Bill Mathis worked for investment firm Bear Stearns, linebacker Ray Abruzzese was a bartender, running back Matt Snell had a construction business, linebacker Larry Grantham worked in a bank. These were husbands and fathers with families to support. How would it look to have an untested guy—a few of them, even—in his early twenties making a six-figure salary? How would it look to have three incoming rookies essentially combining to be paid the same amount as the entire rest of the team?

"This," Werblin told his players in the locker room, "is the year of the big bonus." Werblin stated that for the AFL to survive and for the players already in the league to prosper, it needed to add stars and would have to overpay those stars as they came out of college. He tried to assure the Jets that, once the draft picks were signed, the veterans would get raises. After Werblin was through, Grantham (the banker, fittingly) stood up and told his teammates that the bonus craze was not Werblin's doing, adding, "Fellows, I guess it's our hard luck to have been born five years too soon." Grantham explained that they should not confuse salaries and bonuses, which were, "an economic accident of the time." Grantham himself quickly realized that valued players like himself would stand to gain—he agreed to a healthy new contract with Ewbank before Namath's deal was made official.

Illinois linebacker Dick Butkus, drafted by both leagues and rumored to have gotten a $200,000 bonus from the NFL's Bears, said, "This is a players' market. It won't last, but you can't blame the boys for getting it while the getting is good." But resentment was everywhere, and though Butkus was one of several players to reap the benefit of the happy economic accident, it was Namath and his $427,000 contract who became the most convenient target. Even as he wished Namath well, Redskins quarterback Sonny Jurgensen said, "You know it gives a player an odd feeling to go out there on the field to play with or against a guy who has no pro experience and is getting $100,000 for one year. Meanwhile, a guy has been in the league 10 years and played well gets only maybe $18,000." Cleveland owner Art Modell—whose quarterback, Frank Ryan, said that if Namath was getting $400,000, he should be getting $1 million—called Namath's contract "ludicrous" at the NFL's winter meeting, and added that it represented, "a great harm to sports." Particularly vocal in his response was Dick Wood, the incumbent Jets starting quarterback. Acknowledging that the news of Namath's deal, "hit like a bombshell," Wood said he would be dissatisfied if the Jets simply came in and handed Namath the starting role. "I still can't believe anybody's worth 400-grand," Wood said, "not even me, my wife says." It would soon be irrelevant for Wood, who was dealt from the Jets to the Raiders before training camp started.

But in the spring of 1965, as Namath's knee healed and training camp approached, the backlash from the rest of football settled, and it was only the backlash from within the Jets that concerned Namath. The size of Namath's contract was the main issue, but not the only one. The publicity that Werblin had sought for Namath also registered with his Jets teammates, who wondered whether a rookie should have been thrust onto magazine covers and newspaper spreads, and whether Namath should have so eagerly accepted so much attention. The frequent dinners with Werblin and the perception that Namath was the owner's pet project didn't help, either. Once Namath's knee had healed, he and Werblin seemed inseparable. At a party in 1965, after listening to Werblin sing Namath's praises over cocktails, one woman commented, "It sounds like he is talking about a prize stud." Her escort assured her, "That is just about it."

In July, at Jets training camp at Peekskill Military Academy in upstate New York, Namath would finally have to confront his teammates, most of whom he'd not met. In the center of campus, fittingly, there stood a hanging tree, marked by a bronze plaque that read, "In Honor Of The Tree Upon Which was Hanged Jan. 27, 1776 An American Who Was Employed As A Spy By The British." (One wag commented, "The Continentals didn't fool around.") There was a sense that Namath might be a good candidate for the tree, if Jets veterans had their way. Rookie hazing was nothing new in pro sports, but, then, there had never been a rookie like Namath before. Naively hopeful, Namath headed to Peekskill guided by the outlook that if he played well, no one would care how much money he made. "In professional ball," Namath said, "a man is paid to do a job, and as long as he can do it, there never will be any dissension." On the hot July day on which the Jets were supposed to arrive at Peekskill, players filtered in throughout the afternoon, well ahead of the 6 p.m. deadline for arrival. As evening approached, though, the veterans took note that Namath had not yet shown up, and had gathered in a driveway to keep an eye out, pausing their conversations to check each incoming car to see if it carried Namath. 5 p.m. 5:15. 5:30. No Namath. *Was Werblin's $400,000 stud going to start his career a late arrival for camp?* At 5:55, in the car of a friend, Namath finally rolled up, causing one veteran to grouse, "I don't see why he's so early. He's got five minutes to go." Another conceded that, "At least he's left that big green car behind."

Some teammates were able to put Namath and his contract into the big picture, and see how he could benefit the team in general.

But for most Jets, Namath entered his first training camp wearing a bull's eye. "There were some that were eager to see him," lineman John Schmitt said. "There were some guys that were pissed-off to see him." So Namath was tested. In drills, he was nudged and pushed. He would wear the red "no-hit" jersey that quarterbacks were given, but would find himself taking shots from defensive linemen and linebackers, anyway. Ewbank only haphazardly reeled in the veterans. After a rookie scrimmage against the Patriots early in camp, Namath was excused from running because of his knee. "What's the matter, rookie?" one Jet yelled. "You too good to run? Your money weighing you down?" But Namath did his best to keep his cool. On Rookie Night, every Jets newcomer was required to sing his school's fight song, loudly and enthusiastically. Namath had barely begun, "Yea, Alabama!" when some veterans broke in and began drowning him out, singing "There's No Business Like Show Business." Namath handled it well, smiling smugly. "It was a good gag," he said. In the first week of camp, *Sports Illustrated* released an issue featuring Namath's photo on the cover, standing in the middle of Times Square with the headline, "Football Goes Show Biz." Namath was somewhat embarrassed to find that, one day after practice, a copy of the magazine had been placed in the locker of every Jet. This seemed to be the perfect recipe for further alienation of his teammates. Instead, thirty-two-year-old right tackle Sherman Plunkett, one of the most respected and—at 6–4 and about 300 pounds—biggest of the Jets, looked at the photo, then at Namath and smiled. "Broaaadd-way!" he boomed. "Broaaadd-way Joe!" There was laughter. That earned Namath a bit more passage among his teammates, and earned him the Broadway Joe nickname that defined him.

But the key moment for Namath might have come just before the start of the season during a players-only meeting called by Mike Hudock, the Jets' center and offensive captain, and Dainard Paulson, the defensive captain. Around the locker room, several veterans discussed the events of training camp and went over some of the keys for a successful upcoming season. Hudock looked around and asked if anyone had something to add. "I had to say something," Namath recalled. Namath reminded his fellow Jets that they were, in fact, on the same team. "I'm not just in this for the money," he said. He wanted to win. They did not need to like him, they did not need to approve of his relationship with Werblin, and they did not need to endorse the image that he'd earned off the field. But none of that could be allowed to spill onto the field. If anyone had a problem with him, Namath said, now was the time to address it, not when the season was going. He would be willing to go outside and fight whomever had a problem with him.

No one spoke up. There was still resentment after that, but at least the hazing ended.

....

Even more than his demeanor, it was Namath's sheer skill level that broke through the hardened attitudes of his teammates and earned him a measure of respect. After his first go-round in training camp, a 15-minute passing drill, Jets defensive back Marshall Starks remarked, "He's got it. He can't miss." As a receiver, Don Maynard also recognized it immediately. He bore the bruises on his torso that spoke to the power of Namath's passes, was wowed by his accuracy and, in his discussions with Namath, got a deep sense of his new quarterback's intelligence about the game. Namath and Maynard were not close friends—Maynard was a Texan with a quirky personality whose preferred drink was whole milk, not exactly a natural running mate for a swinger like Namath—but the two formed a fast rapport on the field. That was, in part, self-interest. Maynard had blazing speed, and had been with New York's AFL team since its inception, but by his own count, played with twenty-five quarterbacks in his pro career, and only Namath could take advantage of his deep-route ability. The struggle to find a franchise quarterback had been the curse of the Titans and now the Jets. If Namath could be as good as advertised, or even close, Maynard knew he would be a beneficiary. "I'll help make you a better quarterback," Maynard often told him, "and you're gonna make me a great receiver."

But Maynard also took time to get a better understanding of Namath, something few of his teammates or members of the media had done. Before his rookie year, when Namath began wearing low-cut white shoes, the perception was that he was doing so to be flashy and grab more publicity. In fact, Namath later explained, it was penny-pinching Weeb Ewbank who ordered the white shoes, because he had grown frustrated by the endless rolls of white tape Namath had been wasting to cover his black cleats, a superstition dating back to his days at Alabama (the one game Namath had failed to tape his shoes was during his senior year against North Carolina State—the game he suffered his knee injury). "It was assumed that if you played ball, you tried to emulate the legendary Johnny Unitas with his crew cut and black high-tops," Maynard observed. "But Joe didn't seem interested in emulating anybody. A lot of folks assumed that Namath's disregard for football tradition was just another calculated ploy to get more attention. So were his brash comments, his flashy shirts, and his constant presence on the party circuit." Maynard, similarly, had dealt with a good bit of derision when he'd arrived in the city because of his affinity for belt buckles and cowboy boots. He kept wearing them, though, because that's who he was—he was from Texas, and he wasn't going to change just because he was thousands of miles away. He found a similar mindset in Namath. For many, Namath was, and still is, a symbol of deep cultural rebellion that was taking place in the 1960s, but Maynard did not see it that way. "Those white shoes were ridiculous looking, but I had to give it to him," Maynard later wrote, "he was letting everybody know that he wasn't changing for anybody, and if you don't like it, well, you can stuff it in your pipe. His white shoes were no more an act of rebellion than my cowboy boots were. I was being myself, and Joe was being Joe."

Still, over the course of training camp, it was clear that, for all his talent, Namath was a rookie, one who had not played regularly in almost a year and who'd had knee surgery just months earlier. His arm was impressive, but the speed of pro football and the sophistication of the defenses overwhelmed him. There was speculation that publicity alone would force the Jets to make Namath their starter from the get-go—the New York Daily News reported, "There is a feeling among many who have followed the Jets closely that Ewbank (and prez Sonny Werblin) had long ago decided on Namath as the No. 1 quarterback." That was only half-true. Werblin wanted Namath on the field as quickly as possible, but Ewbank knew he needed a little more time to adjust. And Ewbank had to at least keep the appearance of competition going, putting rookie John Huarte and second-year man Mike Taliaferro in the mix for the top spot. Huarte spent the start of camp in Chicago, though, working with the college All-Stars in preparation for their annual scrimmage against the NFL champs. Because of that, Huarte did not arrive in Peekskill until early August and never quite got caught up. He was waived in September. It looked like Namath would beat out Taliaferro for the starting role coming out of camp until a disastrous performance near the end of the preseason in late August. Namath played the first half and led the Jets to just three points, as 11 of the 13 passes he threw fell incomplete. Taliaferro had been much better, and Ewbank almost had no choice but to put Namath on the bench, or else the entire quarterback competition would have been a sham. From Werblin's point of view, though, even with Namath on the bench, business was booming: the Jets sold 38,000 season tickets ahead of the opener in Houston on September 11, pretty good for a team whose average home attendance had been 42,710 the previous year.

Ewbank went with Taliaferro in the Jets' opening loss in Houston, and when the team came back for their season debut at Shea Stadium, the crowd of 53,658 was disappointed to find Taliaferro again as the starter against the Chiefs. Under a hail of boos and chants of "We want Joe!" Ewbank pulled Taliaferro and inserted Namath. He hit Maynard for a 37-yard, fourth-quarter scoring pass, the Jets' only touchdown in a 14–10 loss, but his importance to the franchise was highlighted when he took a hard hit from a pair of Chiefs defensive linemen near the Jets' sideline. Namath was slow to get up and Ewbank, in a mild panic, rushed over. "Joe, Joe, are you all right?" Namath lifted his head slowly. "I'm all right," he said, "but how's Sonny taking it?" Ewbank put Namath into the starting lineup, though he continued to play Taliaferro, too. With the Jets off to an 0–4–1 start, and Namath coming off of a 5-for-21 performance in a tie against Oakland, Ewbank tried to cover for his flailing young passer. "I think Namath is worrying too much," he told reporters. "He's got the world on his shoulders. Everyone thinks Joe should get a touchdown every time he throws, and as a result he's pressing. But this is normal. A lot of things are new to him. That's why there are no great rookie quarterbacks. We knew it would be this way. Eventually, this will all pay dividends."

At the end of October, the Jets started a four-game winning streak in which Namath began to feel more comfortable calling plays in the huddle and handling the speed of the oncoming rush in the pocket. In the last game of the streak, Namath set a franchise record with four touchdowns in a blowout win over the Oilers. For the first time, football observers were speculating that the Jets had actually made a wise move in paying Namath $427,000. Under a headline, "Namath Has Proved That Price Was Right," an article in the *New York Times* proclaimed, "Namath has become a professional football rarity—a successful rookie quarterback." Despite splitting time with Taliaferro, Namath finished with 2,220 yards on the season and threw 18 touchdowns, which tied for fourth in the AFL. His passer rating (68.7) was third in the league, and for his efforts, he was named the AFL's Rookie of the Year. Namath, though, was more concerned about the fact that the Jets had wound up just 5–8–1. "OK, so they voted me Rookie of the Year," he said. "What can it mean?" Equally important was that Namath was still wrestling with the perception that he was more contract than quarterback. He knew it. "I want to be known as a football player," he said. "Not as a $400,000 quarterback."

CHAPTER 5
Ten Million Lunatics

THE LASTING IMAGE OF JOHN V. Lindsay in the 1965 mayoral race is that of the celebrity campaigner, handsome and fit, wearing a dress shirt with rolled-up sleeves in a downtrodden city neighborhood surrounded by smiling children of different races. Or striding on Rockaway Beach, laughing with Sammy Davis Jr. Or dancing on an outdoor stage with Liza Minnelli. There was a time in the campaign, former city treasurer Roy Goodman remembered, when Lindsay broke all protocols and went shirtless with both voters and press cameras present. "One day he went to Coney Island," Goodman said, "and there was kind of a rough-and-tumble group assembled. He got up on the high board and did a perfect swan dive with his rather unique grace. People couldn't imagine the Mayor of New York would be willing to strip to the waist and get into a bathing suit." Certainly, no one was eager to imagine a shirtless, cannon-balling version of incumbent Mayor Bob Wagner.

But Lindsay was building a campaign of cool. He had ideas for New York, true, but for some, those hardly mattered. When comedian Phyllis Diller spoke on Lindsay's behalf at a Long Island beach club, she said, "I don't know what the hell John is talking about, this fusion mess. All I know is I'm on his wagon wherever the hell it's going." Boxers Sugar Ray Robinson and Jose Torres, actor Henry Fonda,

Broadway star Ethel Merman, writer Norman Mailer—they all were part of Lindsay's campaign cast. This was exactly how Lindsay wanted to be presented, as a bright light whose wagon was *different* from those uninspiring, cigar-chomping little men in horn-rimmed spectacles who controlled city politics. The Lindsay folks so took to the sentiment expressed by Murray Kempton in the *World-Telegram*—"He is fresh and everyone else is tired"—that it was adopted as the campaign slogan, plastered throughout the summer of 1965 on six-foot-high billboards above a photo of a grinning Lindsay striding down the street.

That image belies the reality, though. Getting elected mayor of New York is no easy business, even for a well-known congressman who appears on *What's My Line?* and rubs elbows with stars—particularly for a Republican. As clean-cut and well-coiffed as Lindsay was, in order to win a municipal office, he would have to get his hands dirty and would have to privately (at least, as privately as possible) compromise the high ideals he preached publicly. In Robert Price, he had a cunning campaign manager willing to wade in the deep muck of campaign deal-making. The first challenge was how to assemble a ticket (Lindsay would need to run with a candidate for City Council president, and a comptroller). Following the example of his Republican hero, Fiorello LaGuardia, Lindsay attempted to piece together a "fusion ticket" that included him at the top as a Republican, followed by a Democrat for comptroller and a Liberal for City Council president. It would help, too, if that Democrat were Jewish, because as a tall, blue-eyed WASP, the thinking was that Lindsay would need help courting the critical Jewish vote, which was heavily Democratic. It was pure ethnic pandering, the kind Lindsay would deplore when playing the part of the morally pure crusader but that Lindsay the politician accepted as necessary. (Obviously comfortable with religious pandering, Lindsay kept three yarmulkes on hand during the campaign and slipped one on whenever the situation even remotely called for it.)

Abe Beame, who was Wagner's comptroller but had frequently split with the mayor over fiscal issues, was approached about joining with Lindsay. He, like most approached by Lindsay's people, turned down the offer, unwilling to reject Mayor Wagner and the Democrats. With few options, Lindsay finally chose Housing and Redevelopment Board chief Milton Mollen for his comptroller candidate, bestowing the ticket with the very sort of dull bureaucrat Lindsay was promising to eradicate from city politics. It was only in April, a month before he declared as a candidate, that Lindsay himself was in Congress speaking about housing issues and read a report harshly critical of Mollen into the congressional record in Washington. And now Lindsay somehow wanted Mollen on his citywide ticket? I.D. Robbins, a Reform Democrat who had considered a run for mayor in 1965, said that Mollen had "miserably botched" his job and called him, "the least effectual person in the Wagner administration." Price was said to have defended the pick with some cynical double-talk: "We already have the good government people. Now we are looking for the bad government people."

The message from Lindsay seemed to be that good government could be sacrificed for political utility. Murray Kempton, disappointed, reviewed his description of the candidate as "fresh." That assessment had come, he wrote, "before Congressman Lindsay decided to begin our municipal rebirth by borrowing his candidate for Comptroller from Mayor Wagner. So it must be amended to say that Congressman Lindsay is not only fresh but, when necessary, he can be downright impudent."

But back-room politics were for the chattering classes. Lindsay was in this race, win or lose, to make his mark as Mr. City, and that meant hitting the streets. Although Wagner was expected to seek a fourth term, and frequently spoke as though he was to be the candidate, he had not yet firmly announced his intentions. Lindsay, carrying the "City in Crisis" mantle, made clear he was running his campaign as the antidote to the lax Wagnerian mind-set that had allowed New York to crumble. The Lindsay campaign set up shop in the Roosevelt Hotel on 42nd Street, and just a few days later, Price was explaining that there would be a nonpartisan Lindsay office in all seventy-six of New York's assembly districts, manned mostly by young volunteers. When it was pointed out to Price that, when running for president in 1960, Republican

Richard Nixon had set up 100 storefronts in the New York City and still got drubbed by John F. Kennedy, Price replied, "Lindsay is not Nixon." Indeed not. Over the course of the race, the Lindsay campaign would establish 117 storefronts and employ a small army of 30,000 volunteers.

Lindsay, though, still had the challenge of showing New York that not only was he was not Nixon, he should not even be associated with Nixon's party. In Congress, Lindsay's liberal voting record had made him an outcast among his peers, and his 1964 stand against the very conservative platform adopted by the Republicans under the aegis of presidential candidate Barry Goldwater had put him further out of the GOP picture. Lindsay's stands were contradictory to most Republicans, but they made sense to him as a progressive Republican carrying a mantle that went back to Abraham Lincoln, Teddy Roosevelt, and LaGuardia, who had himself been elected mayor only by subjugating his Republicanism (with initial help from the rampant corruption in the administration of his Democratic predecessor) under the cover of a fusion ticket. But Lindsay had a problem that LaGuardia did not: he *looked* like a Republican. Wagner had seized on that immediately, labeling Lindsay, "the Park Ave. candidate," even though Lindsay had been reared by a self-made father.

To combat what the *New York Times* called, "a widespread and rather inaccurate assumption among both politicians and voters that Lindsay is the wealthy scion of an aristocratic old New York family," Lindsay first sought to eradicate ties to Republicans that could be used against him by Democrats. After the Lindsay announcement, Republican National Committee chairman Ray Bliss—searching for any sort of good news for his downtrodden, post-Goldwater GOP—was ecstatic and pledged the national party's assistance. But Lindsay would be in an odd position if he accepted manna from the very cohorts who had left him isolated the previous year, as a *Post* editorial saw it: "If those same cohorts now exultantly endorse his candidacy, that is not because they have had a sudden change of heart. There is little evidence that they are ready to embrace the Lindsay brand of liberalism. But they will be delighted to use him as a front for a GOP comeback. Will Mr. Lindsay lend himself to such purposes?" The answer came quickly. He would not. In the first weeks of his campaign, Lindsay turned down help from the national committee, causing Wagner to quip to reporters, "It looks as though Mr. Lindsay is afraid of being Blisskrieged."

Lindsay declined offers of help from Nixon and Rep. Gerald Ford of Michigan, and caused a minor ruckus when he said in a press conference that he would not even seek help from former President Dwight D. Eisenhower, in whose administration Lindsay had worked. (Eisenhower had played the part of Wagner in the 1960 Presidential election, representing the "tired" Establishment, while John F. Kennedy was the "fresh" alternative.) An even bigger tussle came over the role of Governor Rockefeller, who had given $500,000 as a loan to help get Lindsay started in his run for mayor, only to have Lindsay shun the governor during the campaign. This infuriated Rockefeller and forever colored the relationship between the two. Rockefeller Chief of Staff Al Marshall would say of the Rockefeller donation: "There was a danger when he 'lent' you money. He always felt that Lindsay was an ungrateful son of a bitch." But Lindsay was serious about giving the impression that he was not beholden to Republicans outside the city. Lindsay's press releases never referenced his party affiliation, nor did his billboards. "I'm running as Lindsay," he said. "As Fiorello LaGuardia said, there is no Republican way or Democratic way to clean the streets."

Lindsay began a series of walking tours, often in the areas of the city hardest hit by poverty and crime. The tours offered him a chance to further shed the patrician perception of him, allowing him to show his compassion and sense of humor. In Congress and during his time in the attorney general's office, Lindsay had been a champion of the civil rights movement, but having supported bills in Washington was not enough to get his name circulating among the city's black and Latino population—a largely ignored segment of the electorate from which he thought he could peel normally Democratic votes. In late May, Lindsay was in the staunchly Democratic Bronx, standing in front of a butcher shop on 170th Street. A shopper approached him, cut through the crowd of media and campaign workers around him and took his hand. "You really want this job," she asked earnestly, "of taking care of 10 million lunatics?" Lindsay laughed and said, "I really do." As he shook hands with workers and shoppers, he stepped unwittingly into a beauty shop, where women sat, in curlers and underneath dryers. There was squealing and hollering at the intrusion, and Lindsay shouted, "Let's get out of here," to the crowd behind him, adding, "I've never been so scared in my life."

And so it went. Lindsay visited a Fulton Street tenement in the Bedford-Stuyvesant section of Brooklyn, viewing one woman's dilapidated apartment and promising a war on slums. He marched in the Puerto Rican Day parade, doing his best to address a Puerto Rican audience in his fumbling, limited Spanish. He did fifteen hours of campaigning that day, winding up in the Crown Heights section of Brooklyn with what he called pub crawling—campaigning without media attention by showing up at bars late in the evening, and letting word-of-mouth spread among voters in the wake of his appearance. At the Monterey Club, Lindsay danced the jerk, the twist, the cha-cha, and the monkey, before moving on to two other pubs, where the bartenders stopped the music and invited patrons to welcome, "The next Mayor of New York," to the establishment. He got warm greetings, but never lost sight of the fact that he was campaigning and not boozing. As one campaign employee noted, "Lindsay seemed to be doing more glass-holding than drinking." On June 7, a humid day with temperatures in the mid-80s, the sweaty candidate yanked down his tie and walked around Harlem, addressing a few dozen Baptist clergymen on 145th Street before touring the neighborhood. One woman on Eighth Avenue, near a pawn shop, told him, "Listen, this place is in terrible shape. We're afraid to walk. We want you to clean up this place." Lindsay replied, "I'm going to help you."

Three days later, on June 10, it was Lindsay himself who got some help. Wagner, citing the loss of his wife to lung cancer and the desire to spend more time with his sons, announced at City Hall that he was withdrawing from consideration for a fourth term as the city's mayor. The decision, he told the city, "is irrevocable and final."

....

Lindsay might not have beaten Wagner. As strong and likeable a candidate as he was, and as much as New York was in crisis, Lindsay might not have been able to withstand the measured discipline of an experienced candidate like Wagner, a known Democrat whose tenure had several failings but who had avoided scandal and had the backing of unions, liberals, and the large swath of voters who would punch the Democratic ticket without even considering an alternative. But with Wagner out, Lindsay was no longer the scrappy underdog. He now had the highest profile of any candidate in the race. Once afraid of having gotten too late a start on the trail, Lindsay now had an enormous head start on his rival, mostly because he had no rival. The Democrats would have to hold a competitive primary in mid-September and did not have much in terms of political talent behind Wagner, who had dominated the party's structure in the city for twelve years. The two leading candidates to emerge were Wagner's No. 2, City Council president Paul Screvane, and Abe Beame, who rebuffed Lindsay's advances to join his fusion ticket. Neither Screvane nor Beame was inspiring, and for three months after Wagner's withdrawal from the race, the two would sling charges at each other while Lindsay, with no real primary threat, could continue making an impression with his retail campaigning tours.

Worse for the Democrats, Wagner's absence opened the way for Lindsay to court the powerful Liberal Party, which had not backed a Republican for mayor since 1949 and had grown increasingly lashed to Democrats. In fact, the Liberals were under pressure to join with Lindsay. The group prided itself on independence, but had refused to back Republicans like Gov. Rockefeller or Sen. Javits, even when each was more liberal than his Democratic opponent, putting the party perilously close to earning a label as just another cog in New York's Democratic machine. After Wagner's withdrawal, Lindsay pressed party chairman Timothy Costello and vice chair Alex Rose for the Liberal endorsement, and on June 28, he got it, with Costello joining his ticket (he would run for City Council president). Lindsay's prospects no longer seemed far-fetched.

Throughout June, though, word arose that a third dimension would be added to the mayoral campaign: William F. Buckley, the thirty-nine-year-old writer and editor of the right-wing *National Review* was to enter the race as a Conservative candidate. This was a bad circumstance for Lindsay, for a few reasons. Against Beame (who was fifty-nine and just 5-foot-2) or Screvane (who was fifty), Lindsay had the market cornered on height, intelligence, and youthful good looks. But Buckley, too, was tall, handsome and young, with the added advantage of a deeper intelligence and a much sharper wit than Lindsay—Buckley was not one of the gaggle of "tired" political hacks roasted on Lindsay campaign posters. Additionally, stopping Lindsay, an apostate Republican in Buckley's eyes, was his only reason for running. Lindsay was an ideal foil for Buckley, who had the ability to deliver memorable rhetorical thumps, the kind of shots that cut down Lindsay's stature and lofty rhetoric. Even the way he pronounced the name, "Lindsay," came with a certain disdain. In his Connecticut drawl, the name stretched for three syllables: "Linnnnnnd-see-ay." When told that Lindsay had said that his book, *God and Man at Yale*, was, "not very well-written," Buckley sharply replied, "How could he tell?" On another occasion, Buckley zinged, "It is a relief when John Lindsay rises from banality, only to arrive at fatuity."

The last feature of Buckley's campaign that was dangerous for Lindsay was that he had no expectation of winning, and was free to speak bluntly without fear of upsetting the various voting blocs that required maintenance in order to have a serious chance at the mayoralty. After his entry into the race, Buckley held a press conference that can only be described as unique. He was asked a serious question about his motivation for getting into the race, specifically whether he was there simply to cause as much discomfort as possible to Lindsay. "No," Buckley said, "I am in the campaign to get the most votes I can get, consistent with maintaining the excellence of my position, so the decision, of course, is up to the people, not me."

That question was rapidly followed by, "Do you want to be Mayor, sir?"

At this, Buckley paused, breathed deep and looked into the distance. "I've never considered it," he said.

"Do you think you have any chance of winning?" Buckley was asked.

"No," he said, flatly.

"How many votes do you expect to get, conservatively speaking?"

"Conservatively speaking," he answered, "one."

Buckley did get more serious as a candidate as the race went on, but even as he espoused remedies for the city that were somewhere between brilliant, bizarre, and offensive (moving out all heroin addicts *en masse* from the city, building a bike-lane bridge over Second Avenue from Harlem to downtown, legalizing gambling) it was his contrast against Lindsay that defined his campaign. "It must also be said that no one could have been more majestically suited for spoiling Lindsay's campaign," wrote Norman Mailer, a liberal who supported Lindsay, but who remained friends with Buckley. "Buckley's personality is the highest Camp we are ever going to find in a Mayoralty. No other actor on earth can project simultaneous hints that he is in the act of playing Commodore of the Yacht Club, Joseph Goebbels, Robert Mitchum, Maverick, Savonarola, the nice prep-school kid next door, and the snows of yesteryear. If he didn't talk about politics—if he was just the most Camp gun ever to walk out of *Gunsmoke*, I'd give up Saturday nights to watch him."

Aside from poking at Lindsay's personality and intelligence, the one issue on which Buckley most consistently and effectively struck at Lindsay was his adamant support of a revamped civilian review board to handle complaints against police, generally centered around use of excessive force and brutality. Buckley held fast to the conservative view that police should be unfettered in fighting crime, and that the liberals' approach to the issue of law-and-order boiled down to unproductive coddling of the minority communities. That outlook rang true among whites who were hostile to the advancements made by the civil rights movement, and those who were just plain racist. Buckley himself was not necessarily a racist, but his rhetoric reached those who were. Even before Buckley's formal introduction into the campaign, Lindsay's presence seemed to inspire an aggressive posture by rank-and-file right-wing picketeers. Once Buckley was officially in, though, his personal pillories of Lindsay inspired even more aggression. There's no evidence that Buckley ordered his acolytes to set upon Lindsay, and it's probable that some incidents were overblown. But as the summer wore on, Lindsay appearances began to attract unwanted and unruly hecklers sporting orange "Buckley" buttons.

Those hecklers were out in the Bronx on July 3, shouting, "Vote for Buckley!" "We don't want a review board," and, "Vote for Lindsay for more crime in the streets." It was around that time, too, that several phone calls were received at Lindsay's Roosevelt Hotel headquarters, with only a male voice saying, "John Lindsay must be killed. We have to kill him." Kent Courtney, chairman of the Conservative Society of America, sent out a mass mailing from New Orleans declaring that Lindsay was pro-Communist and pro-socialist. (Buckley disavowed Courtney by calling him a "kook.") But Lindsay, who had not anticipated an attack from the right, also played up his victimization at the hands of Buckley followers, portraying Buckley as in cahoots with right-wing extremists, the ostensible leader of the kooks. In September, Price called *World-Telegram* reporter Woody Klein to inform him that some of Buckley's colleagues had smashed windows at Lindsay outposts in Brooklyn and Queens. Klein asked, "How do I know this is true?" Price responded, "Because I'm telling you." Buckley denied having any knowledge of broken windows, but Klein also reported on the death threats, and the fact that the threats had been considered credible enough to warrant a police detail for Lindsay. Later, near the end of the campaign, the Buckley-ites appeared at a Lindsay speech delivered on Wall Street, all but drowning out the candidate because of the jeering. Lindsay described that crowd as, "one of the most hostile he had encountered in nearly six months campaigning."

In September, Beame beat out Screvane for the Democratic nomination. Screvane had been a considerable favorite, with the backing of Mayor Wagner, but he ran a poor campaign and Wagner's political stock apparently had fallen so far as to be more hindrance than help. Beame's victory created some problems for Lindsay, though. He had arranged his campaign on the "City in Crisis" theme, and that crisis had to be traced back to Wagner to resonate most effectively. First Wagner himself withdrew, now his hand-picked successor, Screvane, had lost. Lindsay was without a straw man to pummel. Nor did it help that Beame was Jewish, one of Lindsay's prized voter targets. Shifting from Wagner's faults, the Lindsay campaign turned attention to the fact that Beame had gotten the Democratic nomination primarily because of three influential party bosses: Rep. Adam Clayton Powell Jr. in Harlem, Charles Buckley in the Bronx, and Stanley Steingut in Brooklyn. Railing against machine politics and "bossism" went back to the Tammany Hall politics of old New York, but even in the 1960s, the appearance of running while in the pocket of party masters was dangerous ground.

In the late-summer days around the primary, Lindsay reached his high-water mark. His summer of campaigning in the outer boroughs had raised his profile, and polls showed him no longer as the underdog, but building a lead. Two days after the primary, though, the *New York Times* staff, unable to reach a contract agreement with management, went on strike, and most other papers around the city walked out in solidarity. This was an especially harsh blow for the Lindsay campaign, which had hoped to sharpen the charges of bossism on Beame, while continuing the strategy of mostly ignoring Buckley's jousts. Without newspapers, the only forum for Lindsay was the four scheduled televised debates, and though Lindsay was eager to face Beame head-on, he was not eager to be seated alongside Buckley. With good reason. Lindsay presented well when working off a script, but he was not the debater that Buckley was (few were), and in a live setting, Buckley often left Lindsay holding his tongue and visibly angry. During one debate, Lindsay said he'd taken on the Democratic machine entirely alone, causing Buckley to laugh and comment, "I wish I could run alone with a million bucks and with the press engraving my every word on

Mt. Rushmore—run with the Siamese twins and a rump Republican party and the press and (radio host) Barry Gray!"

By the time the newspaper strike had been settled and the presses were rolling, Lindsay's aura had been tarnished. In the *Post*, Joseph Kraft wrote that Buckley had made Lindsay look like, "the Sheriff of Nottingham more than Robin Hood," and that Lindsay, "was neither funny nor clever. Worse still, it became clear that he had a nasty temper. Far from emerging as a cool, distant, Olympian figure, a fit object for incense, Lindsay was made to look just like everybody else—perplexed and harassed."

In the last desperate weeks before the election, the campaign turned increasingly shrill and ugly. A *Herald-Tribune* poll in early October showed Lindsay trailing Beame by a 44.3–36.9 percent margin, as Buckley (11.2 percent) picked up strength. Lindsay attempted to turn the tables on the Buckley picketeers who had been staking out his speeches by linking them first to both overt and implied racism, then tying them strongly to Buckley. In late October, on a taped show, *Ladies of the Press*, Lindsay said, "Bill Buckley's candidacy is an act of vengeance by the ultra-right for my refusal last year to support Goldwater. In the streets, it's translated into a very, very extremist business. It brings out the worst in people that I've been able to see . . . people carrying Buckley banners and calling me, 'Judas,' 'nigger-lover,' 'Commie,' and 'pinko' . . . I didn't go into this business for safety or security but I do think this is a radical right thing."

As the November 2 election neared, Lindsay willingly gave up the high road. He ran a series of television ads that, essentially, laid at Beame's feet the city's skyrocketing crime rate, the rise in heroin addiction, failures in the hospital system and decaying schools: "Does anyone believe that Comptroller Beame's City Hall has done enough?" Lindsay asked as the tagline to one TV ad. That begged the question, of course, of just how much responsibility a comptroller who'd often broken with Mayor Wagner actually had over city problems like drug addiction and crime rates. Lindsay did sink lower, too, running radio ads that portrayed Beame as responsible for, "making New York the heroin capital of the world." Beame also had pointed out that Lindsay had once asked him to be on his ticket, only to have Lindsay lie publicly by denying it. When asked about a Lindsay request for an added debate, Beame chided, "I find it personally distasteful to share a platform with you."

But the campaign devolved into a deeper and more disturbing silliness when race and religion were brought to the fore just ahead of Election Day. Buckley came first, reminding a group of largely Catholic conservative whites in Queens that he was a Catholic like them, and Lindsay was a "white Protestant" who would not stand up to the likes of black Harlem Rep. Adam Clayton Powell. The following day, Lindsay, while being careful not to label Buckley himself a racist, told reporters that, "in the streets, the Buckley campaign becomes a racist campaign," and warning that "the city is a powder keg and Buckley is doing his best to light the fuse." Shortly thereafter, Lindsay running mate Timothy Costello said at a news conference that based on Buckley's views on the poor and on minority groups, a vote for Buckley, who was a Catholic, would be, "an anti-Catholic vote." An upset Buckley promised to file a formal complaint with the Fair Campaign Practice Committee. Beame, as though upset at being left out of the parade of candidates making bungling and awkward religious remarks, took issue with the Presbytery of New York, which had issued a statement not endorsing any specific candidate, but merely supporting change in City Hall. Beame interpreted that as an endorsement of Lindsay, saying, "official religious appeals from pulpits for votes is repugnant to everything I have been taught this country stands for." For good measure, the Lindsay campaign (Senator Jacob Javits, actually) compared Buckley's plans to ship out addicts to Nazi concentration camps.

It was a mess. When the three candidates squared off for a debate four days before the election in a 16th floor CBS studio, all had some form of dirty-campaigning grievances to air. Beame said in his opening statement, "I have been faced with a strange and sinister form of attack. . . . Their campaigns have gone off on a strange road, a one-way road of innuendo, accusation and an appeal to base prejudice." To open his appearance, Buckley said, "I am apparently involved in so many conspiracies that it takes an accountant to keep track of them." Lindsay, meanwhile, presented himself as besieged on both sides, saying (rather illogically) that Beame represented Wagnerism, and that his campaign was, "aided and abetted by the radical right, Mr. Buckley's candidacy from Connecticut is a candidacy which is designed to defeat me and therefore to perpetuate machine power and control in New York City."

Despite the late and desperate scrambling by Lindsay, and despite the disintegration of the entire race into a muddle of racial and religious offenses from all sides, the influential *Daily News* poll showed a narrow victory for Lindsay heading into Election Night: 42.0 percent for Lindsay, 40.0 percent for Beame, and 18.2 percent for Buckley. Instead, when heading into the booth, a large group of voters had second thoughts about casting a ballot for Buckley, and the bulk of those changeovers went to Lindsay. Early returns showed a tight race, with Beame even holding a lead as midnight approached, and Lindsay preparing to deliver a concession speech. But Lindsay surged late (particularly among Jewish voters) and wound up topping Beame in what was dubbed the city's tightest mayoral election in twenty-five years, 43.3–39.5 percent. Buckley polled at 12.9 percent. In a telling example of how Lindsay's personal campaigning ultimately carried the day, his fusion ticket running mates—Costello and Mollen—both lost.

A study of how, exactly, Lindsay had managed to win showed that, though he did not have overwhelming success with any one demographic group, he was able to create enough appeal to chisel votes away from Beame's totals, and the result of that chiseling was enough for his margin of victory. He could also, ironically, thank his nemesis Buckley. Post-election analysis for WCBS showed that Buckley had strong support among Catholics, primarily Italians and Irish. Traditionally, Democrats count on those votes. "Conservatives," political columnist John Leo wrote, "will have to live with the possibility that they put Mr. Lindsay in office."

In the wake of the election, the *New York Times* asked in a headline, "Can Lindsay Now Make Good?" Lindsay won, but Democrats won just about every other seat in city government. "So, it must be admitted," the story read, "a Republican-Liberal Mayor starts out from a lonely base." That brought to mind another pertinent question, asked months earlier of Lindsay by the woman on 170th Street. "You really want this job," she'd asked, "taking care of 10 million lunatics?"

CHAPTER 6

Meet the Mets

THE YANKEES' PROBLEM WITH FANS in New York was simpler than they were willing to admit. It had come along even before the sale to CBS amplified the team's already staid corporate image, before the unsavory managerial roulette after the 1964 World Series that left Yogi Berra embittered and the St Louis interloper Johnny Keane at the head of the defending A.L. champs, before the lame grasp at self-humanization that was to somehow come from new broadcaster Joe Garagiola. There was a new team in the city: The Mets, the expansion franchise given to New York to begin play in 1962, filling the hole left by the departure of the Giants and the Dodgers in 1958. Logically speaking, this club should not have been a tremendous threat to the Yankees' spot on the New York sports totem pole. The Yankees were a great team that won all the time. They were packed with stars. They were paid nearly a million dollars as a group. The Mets, on the other hand, stunk. From the beginning, they stunk and they knew they would stink.

Baseball was in an expansionist wave in the early 1960s. The American League added Washington and Los Angeles in 1961, and after the expansion draft for those two teams had been too generous in the eyes of some, the National League tightened its expansion draft rules, limiting the two new clubs—the Mets and Colt .45s—to just fifteen available players on each of the other eight rosters, allowing teams to stash their best youngsters in the minor leagues. After an owners meeting in which the 1961 expansion draft rules were laid out, Houston general manager Paul Richards met with reporters and said, "Gentlemen, we've just been fucked." The Mets and .45s were left to pick from raw kids with limited futures on one extreme, and broken-down remnants on the other extreme. The best the Mets could do was at least find familiar exiles from the Dodgers and Giants, and picked up two ex-Dodgers—pitcher Roger Craig and infielder Charlie Neal—who were among the team's best players in its first year. The Mets also featured cameos from Brooklyn favorites like Don Zimmer, Clem Labine, and Gil Hodges. But actual talent was scarce. The owner of the team Joan Whitney Payson (sister of *Herald-Tribune* publisher Jock Whitney), had been an avid Giants fan and minority owner of the team and had funded the Mets' expansion bid because she wanted to bring the National League back to the city. Before the inaugural game in 1962, not entirely familiar with her new roster, she looked for positives in a conversation with influential sportswriter Dick Young of the *Daily News.* "Young told me not to expect anything good at all," she explained. "I said, oh, couldn't we beat out the Cubs and Phillies? They weren't particularly good clubs, you know. He said absolutely not. So I said to him, 'Well, can't we please expect to finish ahead of the other new team, Houston?' He said, 'No, I told you to expect nothing.' So I said, 'All right then, I'll settle for 10th place.'" The Mets finished 1962 with a record of 40–120, the second-worst in N.L. history. They were not just in 10th place, but 60 games behind Payson's old Giants, and 18 games behind the ninth-place Cubs. Young had prepared her for last place and, she said, "I certainly was not disappointed."

The Mets had a gift, though, which no draft could have provided, and the gift came, coincidentally, thanks to the Yankees: they were given Casey Stengel as their manager. Stengel had spent twelve years as the manager of the Yankees, starting in 1949, and in that time he won ten pennants. He had the most enviable talent pool in baseball with which to work, but Stengel also had the ideal personality for handling a team like the Yankees in a market like New York. He had been an outfielder for Brooklyn for six seasons in the Deadball Era, and was later with the New York Giants for three years during the 1920s. He understood the challenges of playing in New York and had played for two of the managerial icons of the sport—Wilbert Robinson with the Dodgers (who were sometimes called the Robins in Stengel's playing days because they were so identified with their manager) and John McGraw with the Giants. Stengel was a disciplinarian, but had a keen knowledge of when to drive his men and when to loosen up.

Mickey Mantle recalled a story from his early days with the Yankees, when he would frequently get up to no good with teammates and fellow stars Whitey Ford and Billy Martin, a trio Stengel called, "the dead-end kids." One afternoon at Yankee Stadium, after the three had violated some team rule, Stengel stood before the whole bench and "raged at the three of them." They were out too late, they were drinking, they were flouting the rules, and Stengel dressed them down in front of their teammates. When Stengel had finished, he turned to the other Yankees. "I want the rest of you to remember something," he said. "These three guys are carrying the load on this ball club. Some of the rest of you are drinking milk shakes and going to bed at eight o'clock every night, you ain't doing a thing for me!" Mantle always appreciated the balance Stengel was able to strike. "He was like a father to me," Mantle said. "And I mean that."

The newborn Mets certainly needed a father figure, but more important was Stengel's ability to charm fans and the media. Though sometimes cantankerous, he did not treat the local writers as enemies, and he was not the controlling paranoiac that many of his colleagues were. He understood the individual writers, and he knew knew how their papers operated and the ways he could add color to their daily stories. He had an encyclopedia of good-old-days stories always at the ready, and had a unique ability to peregrinate through the English language as he told them, sprinkled with his favorite phrase, "You can look it up" (which was actually an invitation to *not* look it up). The writers covering the team called it, "Stengelese," and headline writers called him "Old Perfesser." He also had a legendary hollow leg, never losing his wits despite his propensity to drink. Sportswriter John Lardner once wrote of Stengel, "He can talk all day and all night, on any track, wet or dry." One reason the Yankee reputation had been so degraded could be traced directly back to the shabby treatment the franchise had given Stengel in 1960, a few months after his seventieth birthday. Throughout the season, Stengel had been asked what his future was, if he was ready to retire. His response, in Stengelese: "Well, I made up my mind, but I made it up both ways." The Yankees, though, had already made it up more definitively. Shortly after the team lost that year's World Series, Dan Topping had a press conference at the Savoy-Hilton Hotel to announce the retirement of Stengel.

Topping made the mistake, though, of inviting Stengel to his own retirement. The Yankee owner expected Stengel to bid his good morrows to his writer friends and step meekly from the spotlight. Instead, Stengel sat with a drink and, when asked about his retirement, said rather directly, "I was told my services no longer were desired. . . . They say they need a new manager for a new system and a new organization. They don't want the old way." Stengel was asked if he was fired. "Quit, fired, quit, discharged, use whatever you damn please. I don't care. You don't see me crying, do you?" Topping had claimed that the Yankees were instituting a new policy of sending employees into retirement at age seventy, but few were buying it (the team did force out general manager George Weiss, too, and he was only sixty-five). "From a public relations standpoint," Arthur Daley wrote in the *New York Times*, "the Yankees have done great damage to themselves. They may have done the same from a baseall standpoint, especially if Weiss is to follow Casey into exile. It's a shabby way to treat the man who has not only brought them glory, but also has given their dynasty firmer footing than it ever had."

When Payson and the Mets got up and running, the team hired Weiss to take over the personnel side—he was made team president— and Stengel was coaxed (with minimal resistance) out of his Southern

California retirement to return to New York as a manager. He grasped completely the notion that he was not coming back to put any dynasties on firm footing. He was managing the Mets. For this team, existence was all that mattered. Stengel spent his first Mets spring training in 1962 waiting for Weiss, who had been brilliant working the trade block with the Yankees, to make some sort of swap that would brighten the Mets' outlook. But Weiss was unable to pull of any such deal. Stengel got the picture. As he sat putting together a batting order, Stengel said, solemnly, "I thought other things were going to happen before I had to make this lineup." When he rattled off the names to the Mets' press agent, Stengel said ruefully, "You better write down that lineup so I'll remember."

Just before the season began, Stengel was asked where the Mets would finish. He looked at the schedule. "In Chicago," he said.

. . . .

The early years of the Mets proved a fascinating study in human nature, upending long-held tenets of professional sports. The initial surge of support received by the Mets was a natural result of the return of National League baseball to New York City. It could be expected that, once curiosity waned, the Mets would need to show some measure of improvement in order to maintain support. For a team like the Yankees, who understood (as most did) fan support strictly as a function of success, the Mets could not have possibly been considered a detriment to their own attendance or prestige. So it came as a surprise that, in that first season played in the squalorous Polo Grounds as the team awaited its new ballpark at Flushing Meadows, the Mets were a historically bad team that still managed to bring in a respectable number of fans. They drew 922,530 on the year, which rated sixth in the National League, though still 571,044 behind the Yankees. The head-scratcher came in the team's second season, when they were only slightly better—51 wins instead of 40—but saw their attendance rise to 1,080,108 fans (fourth-most in the N.L.), despite still playing in the Polo Grounds after the opening of Shea Stadium had to be pushed back a year because of labor disputes, bad weather, and other delays. With the Mets firmly planted in 10th and the Yankees winning 104 games and easily taking the 1963 A.L. pennant, the Yankees' attendance advantage was sliced to 228,812 fans.

It was Stengel who received the bulk of the credit for the Mets' performance at the box office, and with good reason. Stengel understood that, for a team as bad as the Mets, he would be the show. Sure, there were some recognizable players to add interest—thirty-six-year-old Dodger hero Duke Snider joined the team in 1963, as did eccentric outfielder Jimmy Piersall—but they could not perform anymore. Stengel morphed into pure performance. He was to be the wise old clown, disarming potential critics with a feigned grandfatherly helplessness. He would smilingly glad-hand fans, ask their names and, young or old, leave them tickled with some bit of wisdom. He met one twelve-year-old in spring training, and Stengel gave him an autograph, saying loudly, "Give me your address. We'll sign you for the Mets. A bonus, too. We don't fool around." Stengel was even better with the aged. Robert Lipsyte, who cut his sportswriting teeth covering the early Mets, recalled a time when a fan in his sixties approached Stengel in Houston, telling Stengel he had pitched against him when both were minor leaguers decades before in Kankakee. "Why sure," Stengel exclaimed. "The old fireballer himself, why I was sure glad when you quit that league, did you make me look bad, why, I could never hit you a-tall." When Lipsyte approached Stengel later to ask whether he truly remembered the man, Stengel just shrugged before the question was even posed. Writer Harold Rosenthal chronicled a trip with the Mets that covered 6,240 miles, from Milwaukee to Houston to Los Angeles and up to San Francisco. Rosenthal noted that, "Stengel was not only selling tickets, but selling the game like no one since Ruth in these initial managerial appearances." When a double-header against the Giants sold nearly 40,000 tickets, the team's PR man said of Stengel's drawing power, "I ain't never seen anything like it. It's the greatest since Ruth."

Most important to the Stengel aura was the relationship he developed with the press, and the approach those writers took when presenting the team to the public. There developed a tacit under-standing among Stengel, the team, the press and the fans. No matter how bad the Mets were, the local writers would not bash them—and, for the most part, they went easy on Stengel despite his tendency to sleep on the bench and inability to remember the last names of the bulk of his players. This was in part out of reporters' self-inter-est. When the Giants and Dodgers left, they took away the need for about two dozen beat writers at the various papers that served New York. The introduction of the Mets brought back at least ten of those jobs, and if the papers printed stories hammering the team and its players, interest (and perhaps the beat jobs) would disappear. It helped, too, that Stengel was at his most colorful when sitting with reporters, killing time on team flights, drinking in hotel bars until the early morning and giving them ample copy by dosing out stories during rainouts. There was no doubting that the Mets were bad, and Stengel did not whitewash that fact. He spoke in general terms, though, giving obvious analysis like, "Our hitting is lousy," or, "My infielders aren't throwing the ball straight," or, "We're letting the other fellows hit the ball over buildings too much." But, as Dick Young wrote, "Rarely does Stengel single out an individual by name for critical exposure, and if it is done, you can bet it is done for a purpose, and that purpose is not to protect Stengel. The Old Man, if he criticizes anyone, criticizes himself as often as not."

More than the manager and the media, though, the fans were the story of the early days of the Mets. Many hours and gallons of newspa-per ink were spent contemplating the motivations and mind-set of the typical Mets rooter, a group that Young tagged, "The New Breed." This was a team beyond last place. They did nothing well. In their first sea-son, the Mets finished 10th in batting (.240), 10th in earned-run aver-age (5.04) and 10th in fielding (210 errors), then finished 10th again in all three categories in their second season, during which their batting average dropped all the way to .219. The Mets started 1962 by losing the first nine games in franchise history, and in 1963, they improved only slightly—they started 0–8 before getting their first win. They had a fifteen-game losing streak snapped with a win on July 15, 1963, and started a losing streak of eleven games three days later.

But there had to be something special about the individual who could back a team like this. "I have a son," the barman Toots Shor said, "and I make him watch the Mets. I want him to know life. . . . It's a history lesson. He'll understand the Depression when they teach it to him in school." The Mets' best-loved player was first baseman Marv Throneberry, a journeyman infielder who hit 16 homers for the Mets in 1962 but was better known for his ability to botch a rundown, turn a routine pop fly into an adventure saga and run with such enthusiasm on base hits that he'd miss stepping on the bag altogether. Such were the Mets that his exploits earned him the moniker, "Marvelous Marv." (When Throneberry did a commercial for Lite Beer in 1976, his punchline was, "I'm kinda worried. Because if I do for Lite Beer what I did for baseball, I'm afraid their sales might go down.") Throneberry took his foibles in stride, though, and the reporters covering the team gave him the Good Guy award in 1962, with a large silver tray as the prize. "I don't know if you should hand it to him or mail it to him," Stengel quipped. "If you hand it to him, he's liable to drop it."

But Mets fans kept showing up, and no matter how far behind their team was—and they were down often, by much—they continued to have an almost perverse faith that victory was possible. The essence of Mets fans lay not in the sum of their losses, but in the joy derived from those moments when things, against all reasonable supposition, went well. Rooting at the Polo Grounds was an inclusive act, and denizens of the bleacher seats were not the detached observers that attended most big-league games. They were as much a part of what was going on as the pitchers and batters and fielders. One of the great early traditions of Mets fans were the giant banners, unfurled as one would a flag or a bed sheet, on which would be scrawled some cryptic or offbeat message. As a former Yankee executive, Mets president George Weiss initially tried to stop the practice, but protestations from fans and media proved too strong, and he relented. The tradition flourished. One read: "M is for Mighty; E is for Exciting; T is for Terrific; S is for So Lovable." Another:

"We don't want to set the world on fire—we just want to finish ninth." In appreciation of husky young outfielder Ron Swoboda, another sign claimed: "Swoboda is Stronger Than Dirt." After Ed Kranepool, a publicized prospect who first appeared with the Mets at age seventeen, got off to a .180 start at the plate in 1964, a banner popped up wondering, "Is Ed Kranepool Over the Hill?" Kranepool was nineteen at the time.

Pondering the curiosity that was the Mets fan, early in 1963, Lipsyte took a psychoanalytical angle, putting the Metophile up against the typical Yankees supporter. (He even quoted anthropologist Dr. Margaret Mead, who said, "It's something like tribal rites.") The Yankees fan, one psychoanalyst told him, identifies with "The Establishment." She explained: "The Yankee symbol is a top hat and just the name 'Yankees' brings up images of founding fathers and New England aristocracy. The Mets must mean metropolitan area, a polyglot melting pot. And I've noticed on ads this year that they have a picture of a baseball with a man's face superimposed, Mr. Met—kind of a John Q. Public character." Lipsyte wrote, "The Metophile syndrome, say psychologists, is defiance of authority. It is present in almost every ego that is not involved in the higher echelons of General Motors, the Seventh Fleet or Washington affairs. Translated into pure Metophilian, this means that life beats us nine games out of 10, but the 10th game is a beautiful blue-eyed creation worth waiting through a losing streak for." And Lipsyte probably delivered the best description of the average Mets fan of the era: "The Metophile is a dreamer. He believes that one day he will punch that arrogant foreman at the plant square on his fat nose; that he will get in the last word with his wife; that he will win the Irish sweepstakes; that the Mets will start a winning streak."

And, of course, the absurdity of the Mets only exasperated the Yankees all the more, especially when the Mets finally moved out of the Polo Grounds tenement and into the spacious Shea Stadium in 1964. The Mets won only 53 games to finish in tenth again that year, compared with a pennant and 99 wins for the Yankees, and still brought in 1,732,597 fans—426,959 more than the Yankees. "The Mets, then, have not really competed with the Yankees—a fact the harried Yankees find hard to understand," Leonard Koppett explained in the *Times*. "The Mets simply filled a vacuum the Yankees had long since created. Baseball, around the Mets, is fun."

. . . .

Throughout the 1964 season, speculation held that Casey Stengel, at seventy-four years old, would finally retire. He shrugged off such talk, though, insisting he was not certain. "How do I know where I'll be next year?" he said. "Lots of people my age are dead." In the end, Stengel did come back, almost out of pure pride. It had been rumored that the Mets were hoping Stengel would retire so they could bring in Alvin Dark, deposed Giants manager and star shortstop of the Giants' great teams of the 1950s. Stengel was determined not to be put out to pasture (particularly not on account of a Giant, egads), and the Mets had learned enough from the mistake the Yankees had made in forcing Stengel out in 1960 to repeat it. When, with a week left in the 1964 season, Stengel decided he wanted to manage again in 1965, the Mets had little choice but to bring him back. Weiss did add a player/coach Stengel knew a few things about: Yogi Berra himself, let go in yet another Yankees PR screwup.

And Berra did inject a small bit of life into a 1965 Mets season that was, for once, not a catastrophe right from the first pitch. For the first time, the Mets actually won more than two of their first ten games, and in late April, they were perilously close to being a .500 team, at 6–7. Berra had hung up his catcher's mitt after the 1963 season with the Yankees, once he was made manager, but on May 4, 1965, Stengel inserted Berra behind the plate, and he was a key cog in a 2–1 win over the Phillies. Berra called a complete-game, 11-strikeout win for pitcher Al Jackson, and scored a run with two hits in three at bats. That meant Berra had, according to *Post* reporter Maury Allen, "a .500 lifetime batting average in the National League, a winning run scored and a hell of a lot of fun." When Allen asked Berra if he had been nervous, Berra said, "Only when I got to second base. I haven't been there in a while."

Alas, baseball around the Mets in 1965 would have some of its fun sapped soon thereafter. On May 10, when the Mets prepared to play Army in an exhibition game in Cooperstown, New York, Stengel slipped, fell, and broke his wrist. That night, at Essex House—the hotel on Central Park where he lived during the season—Stengel told the gathered newspapermen, "You're lettin' on like I'm dying. I ain't dyin'. I don't need no cane to walk. Nobody sees me fainting." Stengel, though, probably did need a cane, especially with the schedule he was keeping. On July 22, he was presented with a scroll by Mayor Wagner, honoring his seventy-fifth birthday, which would come the following week, and July 23 was declared, "Casey Stengel Day" in New York. He celebrated Old-Timers day on July 24, which was (quite naturally) followed by a party at Toots Shor's. After the party at Shor's, Stengel went out to the Long Island home of a Mets employee, and planned to sleep there because it was just a few minutes from Shea Stadium and there was a double-header the next day. Stengel stumbled getting out of the car, fell, and broke his hip. Stengel would be laid up for at least three weeks, and in the interim, coach Wes Westrum took over as manager. But it was obvious that the demands of managing had gotten to be too much for Stengel. Stengel finally retired, on August 30, 1965, saying at a press conference, "I didn't do as well as I expected with this club, that is, getting out of last place. . . . I didn't think it would take so long. If you don't think you're gonna win tomorrow, you oughtn't to manage." When Stengel took his place at the dais for the retirement announcement, he did, in fact, walk with a cane.

Having Stengel off the stage probably should have been a good thing for the Yankees. But in the wake of Berra's firing, virtually nothing went right for the Bombers. To start 1965, oft-injured star outfielder Roger Maris was hurt again, knee problems that chronically sapped Mickey Mantle flared up early, and thirty-six-year-old catcher Elston Howard, arguably the one irreplaceable player on the Yankees, needed surgery to remove a bone chip in his right elbow. On May 2, the Yankees were swept in a double-header that featured Art Lopez in right field for Maris, Johnny Blanchard (who was hitting .147 and would be traded the next day) behind the plate for Howard, and Phil Linz at third base for Clete Boyer. Orioles third-base coach Billy Hunter said, "That was a hell of a Yankee club out there. It looked like Toledo." The Yankees were in eighth place, and while Houk kept predicting a rebound, others were less certain. Owner Calvin Griffith of the Twins said, "Trouble? They're in a GD lot of trouble. They look over the hill. I would say we're all sitting in on the death watch. . . . They don't have it anymore. That's for certain."

The Yankees never got healthy. Even after Howard returned, he batted only .233. Maris broke a bone in his hand in June, had surgery in September, and finished an injury-plagued year in which he hit .239 in just forty-six games. Shortstop Tony Kubek injured his shoulder in a collision in April, and suffered pain thereafter, limiting him to a .219 average. After the season, he went to the Mayo Clinic and the diagnosis was a surprise: Kubek had nerve damage on his spinal column, and retired at age thirty. Pitcher Jim Bouton, a phenom the previous two seasons, working 520 innings and going 39–20, suffered from a dead arm and went 4–15. It was a stunning run of bad luck paired with the inevitable impact of age, compounded by the fact that the Yankees no longer had the steady supply of farm prospects that allowed them to replace aging superstars. They finished 1965 at 77–85 and in sixth place, their worst finish since 1925.

There was also the matter of Keane himself, who just never found a way to mesh with his players. They might not have respected Berra in 1964, but they sure missed him in '65—Berra had gone right along with the notion that, as a veteran club, the Yankees did not need much day-to-day discipline, that they could be trusted without curfews and that they could police themselves. Keane was not wired that way. He was mild-mannered and devoutly Christian, though decidedly capable of an ill-advised outburst. Giving him the reins of the Yankees, Bouton said, "was like putting Billy Graham in charge of the Hell's Angels." Houk knew that, so closely removed from the Berra fiasco, the Yankees could not again change managers after just one season, so Keane stayed on for 1966. Houk gave Keane virtually no new players, and Keane came unhinged. Less than a month into the 1966 season, reports surfaced that Keane, "chewed the help out," and that, "Keane's unprecedented postgame harangue triggered more rumors." Shortly thereafter, with the Yankees mired in last place and bearing a 4–16 record, Keane was fired. Houk, with few palatable options, stepped down from the general manager's chair and went back to managing.

Not much changed, however. In the early 1960s, the Yankees had been frustrated by declining attendance that came despite success of the club on the field—they were the Establishment team, as Robert Lipsyte wrote, and because of that, their unparalleled success only bred resentment among baseball fans. By the mid-1960s, too much success was no longer a problem. The Yankees fell to tenth place in the middle of September, and stayed there through the end of the season, earning their first last-place finish since 1912. But they were not yet done with the public relations fumbles. On September 22, the Yankees faced the White Sox in a rescheduled game on a drizzly Thursday afternoon. It was a funereal scene, as only 413 fans showed up. Broadcaster Red Barber, who had been in place for thirteen years, was calling the game, and asked the cameras to pan out over the empty seats in the venerable old stadium. The program director, though, would not do it, so Barber simply said, "I don't know what the paid attendance is today, but whatever it is, it is the smallest crowd in the history of Yankee Stadium . . . and this small crowd is the story, not the ballgame." Five days later, it was reported that Barber, having angered CBS executives with his discussion of the poor attendance, had been fired.

The Mets managed to pull out of the tenth-place cellar in the National League and finish ninth, just one more disgrace for the Yankees.

Before vacating the manager's office at Yankee Stadium, which also happened to be the office used by Allie Sherman, coach of the NFL's Giants, Houk scribbled a missive: "Dear Allie: Please get this place back in shape. I've left you a tough job. Best, Ralph."

The Giants would finish 1–12–1 in 1966.

CHAPTER 7

The Fun City Has a Fun Mayor

It was December 27, 1965, and John Lindsay was still four days from officially becoming the 103rd mayor of New York. In the triumphant weeks after the November election, Lindsay had dappled hope around the cob-webbed corners of city government, promising bold changes and bringing imagination to a job that, by Lindsay's estimation, Robert Wagner had allowed to grow stale and impotent. Acknowledging the "City in Crisis" theme that he had hammered in order to get elected, Lindsay now outlined his view of what he called the Proud City, seeking to make participation in city government more exciting, with changes both big and small. He promised a series of Little City Halls throughout the great expanse of New York, manned by local people and authorized to handle the day-to-day issues of the neighborhoods. He would consolidate city agencies and streamline city government by cutting back the 235 committees already in existence. He was in contact with a California computer company as he sought to utilize technology to address city problems. He pledged a drive to bring new companies and new jobs to the city, while keeping companies already in New York from leaving. He vowed a war on the overwhelming sulfur-dioxide pollution that was burning the eyes and throats of New Yorkers, reaching record highs in the winter of 1964–65 (and spawning a favorite Lindsay joke: "I'm from New York and I don't trust air that I can't see.") He made a symbolic gesture to the burgeoning budget deficit left by Wagner by cutting his own salary from $50,000 to $45,000 and suggesting others in his administration follow suit.

Lindsay populated his administration with young and forward-thinking staff members, taking after the approach of his mentor, former US Attorney General Herbert Brownell, who had hired Lindsay into his office when he was only thirty-three. Lindsay hoped to give city government the kind of swagger usually associated with Washington DC. "I want young guys to feel that being a deputy commissioner is as attractive, as big a challenge, as assistant secretary of state," Lindsay said. He shook up the whitest department in the city, the fire department, by making Robert Lowery the first black fire commissioner in the city's history. He had thirty-three-year-old deputy mayor Robert Price by his side, and added young idealists like thirty-four-year-old parks commissioner Thomas Hoving; thirty-year old newspaperman Barry Gottehrer as an assistant; lawyer and assistant Jay Kriegel, who was twenty-four and had been near the top of his class at Harvard Law; and another administrative assistant, Sid Davidoff, who was twenty-six when he was made an assistant buildings commissioner. Dubbed (somewhat scornfully) the "Kiddie Corps," these were not experienced hands when it came to city government, and for Lindsay, that was the point—he was looking for fresh outlooks. Davidoff later recalled that a reporter asked him what, at such a young age, qualified him to be a buildings commissioner, and he responded, "I've lived in buildings all my life." When Lindsay was in the process of offering the job of press secretary to Woody Klein, who was an award-winning investigative reporter with the *World-Telegram & Sun*, he asked Klein his age. When Klein told him he was thirty-five, Lindsay said, "A little old for this Administration, but I think I can use you."

Lindsay was committed to changing the way City Hall did business, and he thought its dealings with the various city unions would be an important part of that change. Under Wagner, union chiefs had developed a cozy relationship with the mayor's office, a tradition that went back to 1958, when Wagner signed an order that gave municipal unions the right to collectively bargain. This was good politics for a Democrat like Wagner, who needed unions to churn out votes in order to maintain his hold on power. Typically, Wagner would meet directly with union leaders and hammer out agreements in back rooms. But Lindsay found the practice distasteful and felt that unions should be level headed in what they ask of the city—it was the city in which they also live and work, after all. As much positivity and new blood as Lindsay was bringing to the office, he was also dealing with the yoke of debt left from the end of the Wagner years—an estimated $312 million deficit for the fiscal year that would stretch into 1966. After winning the election, Lindsay had said he was "acting as a receiver in bankruptcy" by taking over as mayor. Lindsay was counting on the civic-mindedness of the unions to smooth future negotiations, eliminating the unwieldy rituals in which Wagner and the unions had long indulged.

Then Lindsay ran up against Mike Quill, union president and one of the government's most unwieldy ritualists. Quill was an Irishman who, as a teenager, fought in the Irish Civil War with the hardline faction of the Irish Republican Army that refused to accept partition of the country and make peace with the British. He had also been involved in the Irish labor movement, but he was blackballed as a rebel and an agitator, and, in his early twenties, he sailed to the United States. After a series of stops, Quill secured work on the New York City subways. Within a few years, Quill began organizing the subway laborers, blending his fiery passion for the rights of workers with wit, charm and a mellifluous Irish brogue. He had a receptive audience—transit system workers were largely Irish and putting in 84-hour weeks under miserable conditions, without so much as a day off for church. In 1934, Quill and three fellow workers founded the Transport Workers Union.

Three decades later, though, Quill was sixty and had lost the lean-and-hungry look of his youth, now living in a high-rise apartment on Central Park. His brogue was still thick but more caustic than mellifluous. He had suffered a number of heart attacks and slept at night with an oxygen tank by his bed. He wore thick horn-rimmed glasses, almost always appeared with a hat and black topcoat, getting around with help from a blackthorn shillelagh. Though he could be reasonable in private conversation, Quill was always loudly combative in his role as union chief, and his slipping health only made him crankier. That was a problem for Lindsay. The Transport Workers Union contract was set to expire at midnight on December 31, 1965 (Quill generously pushed the deadline to 5 a.m. in order to get New Year's Eve revelers home safely), and without a new deal in place, there would be a strike on New Year's Day. That would shut down a transportation system that carried 4.5 million subway riders and 1.5 million bus riders each day, bringing the city to a paralyzing halt.

In the post-election glow, Lindsay failed to recognize just how real the potential for a strike was. But then, few did. After the election Lindsay did not feel it was his place to get his hands dirty with the negotiations—in keeping with the way he felt labor dealings should come down, Lindsay held that the TWU should deal with the Transit Authority directly, and the mayor should only get involved when necessary. Lindsay also was not yet mayor. Robert Price had reached out to Quill a few times, but there was no hint of a resolution. Wagner himself, still the mayor, acknowledged in the papers that he should be the one working to secure a transit deal. Generally, Lindsay did not feel much of a threat from a possible strike because it was illegal for the transit workers to walk off the job. Under the 1947 Condon-Wadlin Act, strikes by municipal workers were prohibited, and union leaders who led strikes in violation of the Act would be jailed. Most press reports painted the TWU situation as nothing particularly new. Transit contracts came up every two years, and without fail, each negotiation would start with Quill making outlandish demands, blustering and bantering (the *New York Times* called him, "the banshee of the subway system") before finally agreeing to a deal. There were no obvious indications that this time would be different.

But there were several key differences this time. First, Quill had long been the head of a union that was primarily Irish, but as blacks from the South and Puerto Rican immigrants began taking jobs in the transit department, that ethnic hegemony deteriorated and created internal conflict. Quill needed a big win in this negotiation—and perhaps even to lead a strike—to solidify the membership and keep his power consolidated. Second, Quill's failing health led many to conclude that this contract would be his "last hurrah," and he wanted to go out with something memorable. Because of his relationship with Wagner, Quill had never actually led a strike, but he still had some IRA rebel in him, and what better way to secure his legacy than by leading the 34,000-member Local 100 on a strike that choked the entire city? A third factor was Wagner. It was true that Wagner was still in charge and had an obligation to work at marshalling a settlement, but he had, for a six-month period heading into the election, listened to Lindsay bash his administration relentlessly. Wagner had nothing at stake. He planned a trip to Acapulco that would start at 9 a.m. on December 30, thirty-nine hours before the TWU contract would expire. At one point, a Lindsay aide called an aide for Wagner to plan for TWU negotiations, and was told, "Wagner's going to Mexico. You fuckers can deal with Quill yourself."

Maybe most important in paving the way to a strike, though, was Quill's outright hostility toward Lindsay. They were about as different as possible. Quill was short, bald, Irish-Catholic to his core and "a raving Anglophobe." Lindsay was a tall, handsome Ivy Leaguer who had written his thesis on Oliver Cromwell, the seventeenth-century English commander whose brutal anti-Catholic tactics long made him the most hated man in Irish history. ("I was fascinated by him because of his constant internal clashes," Lindsay explained. "He was always bumping into himself. The experience has not been entirely unfamiliar to me as a congressman and then as mayor.") Jimmy Breslin wrote of the two, "Quill is from the other side. He speaks in a brogue and he learned his first labor in the Dublin transit lock-out of 1913. . . . Mike Quill is a man of the past. John Lindsay . . . was young and tall and thin and with hair falling down onto his forehead. His speech is out of Yale and the theater district. Lindsay is a man of tomorrow, when there could be a chance to try to become the President of the United States.

John Lindsay looked at Quill and he saw the past. And Mike Quill looked at Lindsay and he saw the Church of England."

Quill began the bargaining process in November by presenting the Transit Authority (which was already running a deficit) with seventy-six contract demands that he termed, "very modest requests," including a four-day work week, an average pay increase of 30 percent and half-pay on retirement after twenty-five years. The Transit Authority first estimated the deal at $250 million, but revised that to $680 million, leading the chairman of the TA to say, "There can be little fruitful negotiations under such circumstances." That was understandable: The cost of the previous TWU contract was $38.6 million. It was obvious to anyone that Quill's demand of a 1,700 percent increase was not to be taken seriously, and on December 1, Lindsay sent Quill a telegram saying he would only get involved, "when it is evident that both parties are prepared to engage in good-faith collective bargaining." Quill seized on the telegram, presenting it as a slap in the face to his union and launching his first personal attacks on the mayor-elect. He called Lindsay, "an ungracious sourpuss," adding that the telegram was "that of a coward," and "the height of stupidity." When told that Lindsay stands by his telegram, Quill said, "He can stand on it, sit on it or do anything else with it that is handy." Quill broke off talks at that point, blaming Lindsay, who, of course, was not even mayor yet.

Quill continued to harangue Lindsay for most of December, needling him by intentionally mispronouncing his name as "Lind-es-ley," and seeming to delight in causing him embarrassment. But Lindsay did not really give much weight to Quill's strike threat. At least, not until Monday, December 27. It was then that Lindsay, for the first time, personally sat in with the TWU and the Transit Authority, showing up at 11:30 in the morning for a negotiating session at the Americana Hotel on 53rd Street. Lindsay met with the Transit Authority representatives and the mediators before finally logging an official meeting with Quill and representatives of the TWU. The meeting was brief, and afterward, Lindsay "seemed to suddenly grow tense," according to Woody Klein. It was as if the weight and seriousness of a transit strike, and how intimidating this process of labor negotiations really was, finally hit him that afternoon. Lindsay paused for a newspaper photo with Quill, and Klein noted, "his mood had become somber." Exiting the hotel, Lindsay slouched into the waiting back seat of a limousine and looked, silently, out the window. "This is going to be a bitch," he finally said.

....

Lindsay was sworn in as the mayor on New Year's Eve, arranging a small private ceremony at City Hall just after 6 p.m. so that his wife and four children could witness the event. It was only a brief respite from the agony of negotiations with Quill and the TWU, which had not been going well with the midnight deadline looming. Lindsay joined the talks, but when he suggested, "The union has waited till the 11th hour," Quill became visibly angry. "You wanted the job and you're here for the duration," Quill said. "Why don't you grow up and stop being a juvenile? That's a lie that we waited until the last hour." Quill stormed out shortly thereafter and, meeting with the press, referred to the soon-to-be mayor as, "That pipsqueak Lindsay."

As midnight approached, Lindsay stood behind a table in a corner of the ballroom at the Americana Hotel. To his right were the members of the Transit Authority, who had offered the union a meager package based on a 3.2 percent raise, which was in line with the federally recommended labor guidelines put into place by President Johnson. To his left was Quill, sitting with members of the union's executive committee. Elsewhere around the room stood hundreds of other union officials. Lindsay sought to appeal to the union members, leaning on rah-rah New York rhetoric. "I call upon you and all of your members not to walk out on your city," he told them. "This is a city which is on its knees. We have obligations. You have an obligation to your members. I have an obligation to eight million people. . . . I am inheriting a bankrupt city with a multitude of problems. I therefore call upon you in the public interest to respect the city in which you live and all of its eight million inhabitants." Recounting the meeting, Breslin wrote that Lindsay had lost the union men, "the first time he spoke to them.

'Distinguished New Yorkers,' Lindsay had started. The workers looked around to see who he was talking to."

Quill was not one to be lectured by Lindsay, particularly not in front of his members and certainly not when he'd already decided that his union was going on strike, one way or another. Quill told Lindsay that he did not believe the city was in such bad shape, or that it was bankrupt. He told him to stop campaigning, and that the election was over. "We are not going to stay here all night," Quill said. Then he stood up, looked at the clock and said, "It is after midnight. And I tell you as the Mayor of New York that there is a transit strike. As far as I'm concerned, the strike is as good as on." With that, Quill walked out, leading the rest of the union delegation with him.

What followed was part comedy, part tragedy. After the breakup of the talks at the Americana, Lindsay and his staff went to City Hall, arriving at about 1:40 a.m., where they discovered, to their amazement, that the place had been entirely cleaned out. Wagner's people had left nothing behind—the *Times* reported that, "There were no paper clips, no mimeograph or carbon paper, no scissors, all the things necessary to run a City Hall." There were only some old pencil stubs. In his office, Lindsay fumbled helplessly with the "Call Director," a box on his desk designed to manage incoming and outgoing calls, and was not able to master the device until an expert from the New York Telephone Company was sent to explain it. Several of the staff members found corners of City Hall in which to curl up for some sleep, but Lindsay did not finally stretch himself out for a brief nap until 5:15 a.m. New Year's Day fell on a Saturday, and the city awoke to a transit system that had gone silent. The massive, five-hour, five-borough tour that had been planned for Lindsay's inauguration—billed, "the showiest since George Washington was sworn in here as the first President in 1789"— was canceled because of the shutdown, and Lindsay was instead inaugurated on the steps of City Hall in front of 2,500 onlookers. Lindsay, who spent much of the day altering his speech to reflect the strike, got his loudest and most sustained applause when he addressed the TWU walkout, calling it, "an act of defiance against eight million people," and saying, "I shall not permit the public interest to be flouted, no matter how severe the threat."

The severity of the threat, though, would not really be apparent until the first working day of the transit strike, which came on Monday, January 3. Though Quill had come down from his outsize demands over the weekend, he was still seeking a package worth $180 million, well out of the city's range, which Lindsay had privately pegged at about $50 million for two years. With six million riders having lost their mode of transportation, and with a normal rush hour commute already dense with automobile traffic, Lindsay tried to brace the city for a shock. He warned drivers not to take cars into the city, and implored city employers to allow workers to stay at home without penalty. Again, Lindsay was appealing to civic pride, this time among employers, and would ultimately find little there. By one estimate, once the first weekend passed, the strike would cost the city $100 million per day. Hoping to set an example for his fellow citizens, Lindsay walked. In a press conference, Lindsay said, "This is a fun and exciting city even when it's a struck city." As columnist Dick Schaap wrote sarcastically, "Not long after the transit strike began the other day, Mayor John V. Lindsay went on radio and television to announce that New York is a fun city. He certainly has a wonderful sense of humor. A little while later, Lindsay cheerfully walked four miles from his hotel room to City Hall, a gesture which proved that the fun city had a fun mayor."

Soon, though, the strike took a harrowing turn. The state Supreme Court ruled that Quill and his committee had not shown that they had reasons to strike, and the court ruled the TWU walkout was illegal. On January 4, Quill was arrested right at his negotiating seat at the Americana. Before being hauled off to the jail on W. 37th Street, though, Quill shouted to the television cameras, "The judge can drop dead in his black robes and we would not call off the strike. We will defy the injunction and go to jail." But Quill was at the jail at about 2:15 p.m. when he suddenly grew pale and stopped breathing, his head falling forward. Quill was treated with oxygen and revived, then taken to Bellevue Hospital in serious condition with congestive heart failure.

Douglas MacMahon, one of Quill's deputies, took over at the bargaining table for the TWU, but Quill still directed negotiations, and MacMahon proved no friendlier to Lindsay than his boss had been. During a rally of transit workers downtown, as the strike made its way into its second week, MacMahon publicly termed Lindsay's negotiating skill "amateurish," and added, "It was a sad day when Bob Wagner left this town. This guy [Lindsay] doesn't know what the hell he's doing." There was even an effigy of Lindsay hung from a rope. When told of MacMahon's comments, Lindsay was furious. "I have rarely seen him as angry," Woody Klein remembered. "His face was expressionless, his jaw taut, his hands nervously twirling a pencil between them." Lindsay tried to pull himself together with some humor, calling his twin brother, David, on the telephone and telling him with a laugh, "Hey, Dave, they just hung a guy in effigy outside of City Hall. He looks like you!"

After MacMahon's rally, Lindsay, clearly frustrated, made a cryptic and assertive speech to the press. He laid out the reasonable steps his administration had taken to help resolve the strike, and put the legal nuances of the situation into historical context. But most notably, he condemned the shadowy structure of interests—all such interests, not just labor—that any New York mayor must navigate in order to achieve anything. Lindsay wanted to stand on the principle that got him elected, and New York would have to change the way it did business. "The government of this city will not capitulate before the lawless demands of a single power group," he said. "It will not allow the power-brokers in our city, or any special interest, to dictate to this city the terms under which it will exist in New York. The paramount issue confronting us today is whether New York City can be intimidated. I say it cannot and will not." For days, news reporters lined up to press Lindsay and Woody Klein to name these "power brokers." Klein, who was not in favor of the tone of Lindsay's speech to begin with, responded, "They know!"

While the public posturing continued, privately, the sides were moving closer to a deal as pressure mounted to bring the strike to an end. For much of the strike, it was Quill and the TWU who took the blame. But as the stalemate wore on, the focus shifted to the inability of

Lindsay to close a deal. One Monday rush hour lasted from 4:30 a.m. to after 11 a.m. New Yorkers were out of patience. Writer A.M. Rosenthal commented that the city was not even angry about the strike anymore—it was just worn out, in need of, "a rest and a shave." Stories about the city's resilience were no longer of much comfort. "[New York] was not terribly interested in being told how well it reacted in a crisis or how shared cabs and hitchhikers had made it so nice and home-towny, and one more story about Mayor Lindsay beating his own time walking to City Hall so vigorously might well have started a grass roots movement to bring back Vincent Impelliteri," Rosenthal wrote. It was, perhaps, in that spirit of exhaustion that Lindsay's team closed out the negotiations. Having waited out the TWU for nearly two weeks, the city finally urged a mediated resolution. Though the mediators put forth a package worth a little more than $43 million, the deal the city eventually agreed upon went to an announced total of $52 million over two years, which would represent an increase of about $14 million from the deal agreed to in 1963. But it would later be reported by the union that the deal actually was worth more than $61 million, a "record-setting" total and about a 70 percent increase from the previous contract.

Lindsay had shown some grit during the proceedings, but in the end, he also showed his inexperience. His faith in the civic-mindedness of union members was thoroughly unwarranted, and his dedication to a different kind of collective bargaining had yielded a bad deal for the city and put forth a blueprint for other municipal unions to follow. Two years later, political columnist Edward O'Neill wrote that the TWU in 1966 "is conceded to have set the standards which every other city union leader . . . has had to match or surpass in order to stay in control of his union. Since the TWU settlement, every other city accord—police, fire, hospital, teachers and welfare—has worn the 'record' label." Quill, fittingly, was delighted by the final agreement. After three weeks in the hospital, Quill held a press conference on January 25, back at the Americana Hotel, appearing in good health and surprisingly pleasant. He even had a kind word for Lindsay, acknowledging that the strike was not his fault because he was, "new at the job," and saying that once he grasped the seriousness of the standoff, Lindsay, "did everything he could to end the strike."

Three days later, Quill was lying in bed. His wife noticed that he didn't quite look right. He had no pulse. He had suffered another heart attack in his sleep. If he had approached the TWU's most recent contract as his "last hurrah," he was right. Quill was dead.

. . . .

For John Lindsay, the experience of his first weeks on the job, dealing with Quill and the TWU, would linger throughout his first term. He had rallied New Yorkers behind him, gotten the bulk of the city's newspaper editorials to batter Quill's tactics, and displayed remarkable energy and dedication to the fight against the union's extortionate demands. Yet he still lost. He could make angry speeches about power brokers, but if there was a lesson to be gleaned from January 1966 it was that the power brokers were much more deeply embedded than Lindsay could have known. Sharp rhetoric and fresh faces were not going to be enough to dislodge decades of established order, not when the city's government was made up of 300,000 employees whose agendas mostly concerned keeping their own jobs.

Worse for Lindsay was that, coming out of the transit strike, it was clear he had virtually no allies in any sphere of the political structure. His interaction with Quill and the TWU showed just how little he understood rank-and-file unionists. The mayor had gotten no transitional advice from Wagner, who punched out without leaving Lindsay so much as a stapler in his office desk. Lindsay had no friends in City Hall's other wings, either. When he was elected in November, the two other members of his fusion ticket lost, and Lindsay instead was stuck with two staunch machine Democrats, City Council President Frank O'Connor and Comptroller Mario Procaccino, neither of whom had much incentive to help a Republican mayor.

Nationally, though President Lyndon Johnson had made cities one of the focal points of his administration, and Johnson had sent labor czar Willard Wirtz to New York to help Lindsay, Wirtz mostly advised that Johnson remain on the sidelines of the strike. There was some personal respect between Lindsay and Johnson, but they were members of different parties, and Johnson was not eager to help a rising young Republican star long mentioned as a potential 1968 presidential challenger. After the settlement, LBJ took potshots at Lindsay, criticizing the package for being too generous to the union and not within federal anti-inflation guidelines. Democratic Senator Bobby Kennedy, who always felt threatened by the comparisons many made between Lindsay and his brother, did insert himself into the transit strike, but only at the end, when it was clear a settlement was near. On the day of the deal, Kennedy came to New York and was greeted warmly by Lindsay in his office for forty minutes, before the two made a joint press appearance. Lindsay spoke to reporters first, praising Kennedy for being "concerned and helpful." Following Lindsay, Kennedy slammed the mayor, saying he should have asked for mediation earlier and that the strike was a "catastrophe." Dumbfounded by Kennedy's back-stabbing, Lindsay said to his press aide, "He's a real operator, isn't he?"

Probably most disturbing for Lindsay was the lack of backing and guidance he got from the two most prominent members of his own party operating in New York. Senator Jacob Javits, one of Lindsay's few allies, did not get very involved, spending much of the strike touring Vietnam and sizing up the possibility of an escalating Southeast Asian war (the United States was not in danger of getting "bogged down in a land war" in the area, he concluded). And the bitterness between Lindsay and Governor Nelson Rockefeller only ramped up with the transit strike and grew deeper when the mayor and governor had to work out a new city budget for 1966–67 that would address the problems and shortfalls left by Wagner. Lindsay wanted to increase his budget by $500 million but got only $283 million in the end. The city was granted the ability to levy its own personal income tax, on both residents and commuters, and the legislature would eventually push the transit fare from 15 cents to 20 cents. More taxes and higher subway fares were not entirely Lindsay's doing, but in the minds of New Yorkers, the mayor would take the blame. The goodwill he built up among his constituents during the 1965 campaign was quickly being frittered away. Lindsay, who could be aggravatingly self-righteous, was caught in a seemingly endless tug-of-war with Rockefeller, who could be relentlessly vindictive. "It's personal," one aide told the *Times* about the rift. "No one really knows why, but they've just never gotten along with each other." Harry O'Donnell, press secretary at different times for both Rockefeller and Lindsay, recalled a time when Lindsay visited Rockefeller's personal residence on Fifth Avenue to iron out their political differences. When Lindsay called the aide later and was asked how the meeting went, Lindsay said, "Oh, we never got into politics. We were discussing architecture and got in an argument."

Writer and Lindsay friend Nat Hentoff spoke with a Reform Democrat early in 1966 who summed up the initial impression of Lindsay: "I voted for him, and so did my wife, but I have a lot of regrets now. . . . I've also been disappointed—amazed, really—at the attitude of Lindsay and some of those immediately around him. I mean self-righteousness, arrogance, claims to omniscience. He comes on as if he's bearing the white man's burden. . . . What bothers me about Lindsay is his lack of humility in trying to conquer that monster. He doesn't seem to know what he doesn't know."

. . . .

When Dick Schaap echoed in his column Lindsay's comment that New York was a fun city at the outset of the transit strike, he did so out of pure irony. But the mayor, unbowed, seized the phrase back, finding in those two words the essence of what he'd hoped to do with New York. It had become a difficult place in which to live and work, and for all the widely varying challenges Lindsay would be forced to deal with in his tenure, he unquestionably kept his focus on his vision of a city in which New Yorkers took pride in what was around them and were given a sense that they were living in a moving, evolving city that invited them to participate in that movement and be part of that evolution. He could never fully strip the Fun City moniker of sarcasm in some corners, but the notion of Fun City was genuine to him.

Thomas Hoving, his first Parks Commissioner, was among those who immediately grasped Lindsay's vision. Hoving was innovative, spastically roaming the city in shirtsleeves on a motorcycle, tallying ways to upend the "hideous concrete and asphalt WPA-Mussolini" style that marked most city parks. He most likely took it as a compliment when former Parks Commissioner Robert Moses referred to him as a "recreational leftist." On a visit to a public pool in July 1966, Hoving slipped into the changing room, came out in a bathing suit and leapt into the water. When a lifeguard protested that the pool was only for kids, Hoving shouted, "I'm the Parks Commissioner, I'm testing the water!" He was the first commissioner to shut down Central Park to automobile traffic on weekends, giving the park over to cyclists and pedestrians. He knew that returning Central Park—a forbidding space amid a rise in muggings and other crime—to the citizens of New York was necessary in order to provide a respite from ugly realities of city living and restore a sense of community. He spurred a renewed pride in the park by hosting massive "Hoving Happenings," which included a party for 20,000 children in Sheep Meadow, a viewing party for a late-night meteor shower, kite-flyings, and a Gay 1890s party that drew 35,000 revelers. Arguably Hoving's most important contribution, though, was his commitment to "vest-pocket parks," the beautification of small, abandoned city spaces that so often were overlooked. Hoving had a vision of installing 1,000 vest-pocket parks in New York, giving citizens small green spaces to break up city blocks. An op-ed published after Hoving's death in 2009 remembered, "Mr. Hoving recognized that [pocket parks] offered the city not only 'lungs' and a respite from noise, but opportunities for collective action by the surrounding communities whose help he enlisted in reclaiming the land. He believed that the communal act of making these spaces of quiet itself promoted harmony."

The Lindsay administration governed with more in mind than budgets and voting blocs. There was an attempt to integrate the needs of citizens on a micro level with the way City Hall operated on a macro level. Lindsay's effectiveness in doing so can be debated, but his sincerity cannot. Lindsay's team gave careful consideration to the preservation and creation of green spaces, not only in Central Park and the nooks and crannies of Manhattan, but on Staten Island and in Brooklyn, and eventually in underused places like Roosevelt Island in the East River. He modernized urban planning, authorizing a commission that produced a report, formally titled "The Threatened City" but more commonly known as the Paley Report, proposing a grand rethinking of city planning under the auspices of a group dedicated to addressing such, "offenses to the eye as depressingly blank architecture, arid street scenes and baleful housing conditions." Not long thereafter, the city's Urban Design Group was formed.

Lindsay sought to return New York to its position as a cultural beacon for the nation and the world. He wanted to attack the seedy wasteland that Times Square had become, with adult theaters loudly advertising such features as "My Bare Lady" and "The Dirty Girls," which had led acclaimed preacher Billy Graham to comment, "I couldn't believe that such things existed in America. Everything was packed with emotion—sex everywhere, pornography everywhere." There was still legitimate theater in the area, but it had been wiped out by high rents, and where eighty theaters dotted Times Square in 1926, by early 1967, there were fewer than thirty. James L. Marcus, an assistant to Mayor Lindsay who would later be embroiled in a kickback scandal, said that too many visitors to New York went only to the United Nations, and that Times Square should have its status restored as, "a showcase for the American people." Lindsay formally created a Special Theater District in Times Square, aiming to incentivize builders of office buildings in the area to include ground-level theaters. Certainly, Lindsay's commitment to a "fun city" had its limitations. When a lounge called the Crystal Room up on 54th Street began employing topless waitresses, Lindsay cracked down and outlawed the practice. "It has no cultural value, no artistic value," he said. "It's not burlesque; it's not even bad burlesque."

Lindsay also pushed New York back into the film business with the creation of his Mayor's Office of Film, Theatre, and Broadcasting. The goal had been to generate revenue and bring New York back into the fold of major American storytelling, which had gone with the Giants and Dodgers to California. Lindsay cut through the vast strands of red tape that had prevented movies from being shot on location in New York, making filming in the city allowable with the acquisition of just one permit, cutting back fees and taxes and providing a police detail unit to aid in the process. He also removed the long-held rights of censorship the city had imposed on directors who might make New York look bad. Lindsay felt there should be no trepidation in showing the city as it actually was, warts and all. When some officials attempted to block the 1966 filming of two movies—*Up the Down Staircase* and *You're a Big Boy Now*—Lindsay intervened and overruled them. The producers of *You're a Big Boy Now*, in a ceremony at City Hall to mark the new cooperation between the city and the movie industry, presented Lindsay with a leather-bound copy of the film's script. Lindsay, very theatrically, began flipping through it, and asked which role was his. Amid laughter, one film employee suggested, "Wouldn't you rather play Henry II?" The city films that resulted in the 1960s and 70s, like *The Out-of-Towners*, *Midnight Cowboy*, *Dog Day Afternoon*, and *The French Connection*, often highlighted gritty and stereotyped versions of New York, but they exposed filmgoers to some realities of the harsh life in urban America.

These were small changes in Lindsay's New York. They weren't union negotiations that were being watched at the state and national level, they weren't the racial politics that were bound to dominate any city of the era, they weren't the raising of taxes and subway fares. But the Fun City commitment had an impact nonetheless. Architect and writer James Sanders wrote that Lindsay's cultural initiatives represented, "a change in sensibility to pervasive—from the city as a place of function, in essence, to a place of pleasure—that today it surrounds us, almost invisibly, having quietly revolutionized the way we think about the meaning and purpose of New York and other American cities."

CHAPTER 8

White and Black and Redneck

IN THE BOOK HE WOULD later write with Dick Schaap—humbly titled, *I Can't Wait Till Tomorrow . . . 'Cause I Get Better Looking Every Day*—Joe Namath recalled an incident from training camp in 1965, his rookie year, in which some of the white veteran Jets were drinking with the younger guys, including a black player. According to Namath, one of the vets said to the black player, "You know, you're all right. You're a pretty good guy. I like you. You're a Negro, you know, but that Snell's a nigger." That would be Matt Snell, the Jets' top running back and 1964 Rookie of the Year. "Holy shit," Namath said, "don't start that shit."

The black player, agitated, said, "What do you mean, he's a nigger and I'm a Negro? What's that supposed to mean?" The next day, Snell got word of the incident and "was ready to explode." A team meeting eased the tension somewhat, and owner Sonny Werblin was called in to address the players, telling them, according to lineman Winston Hill (who is black), that, "there weren't but two indispensable people in the organization, Joe and Matt Snell." Anyone else who wanted to cause issues, rooted in racism or otherwise, could easily be shown the door. "We don't want any of that stuff here," Werblin said.

In the years immediately before Namath's arrival, the Jets' race problem was an open secret. There was an acknowledged "redneck"

faction of the team, made up of Southern players and led by Mississippi native Larry Grantham. All coach Weeb Ewbank could do was
give vague speeches about not tolerating racism, but like any coach,
he had little control over what went on behind the scenes. One story
from 1965 had Grantham, drunk in a bar near training camp in Peekskill, telling a group of black rookies who had stumbled into the place
to get the hell out, and "go find your own bar." A fight nearly ensued.
The white Jets, generally, were not made up of virulent racists, but the
team did reflect the patchwork of attitudes on race that could be found
throughout the nation. There would be outspoken bigots on the roster,
there would be suspicious-minded black players who reacted to those
bigots, there would be liberal-minded white players, and there would
be players of both races caught in the middle. Pro sports, unlike most
lines of work, smashed together stubborn-minded young men of greatly
differing social, geographic, and economic backgrounds. Locker rooms
were always in danger of being overrun by tension. As former offensive
lineman Sam DeLuca once commented, when asked what the team's
racial situation had been at the time, "Like the rest of the country was
in the sixties. Weeb tried to handle the situation, but could anyone handle it then? At the time, the entire country couldn't handle it."

(Grantham, it should be pointed out, made a concerted effort to
broaden his thinking on race, especially after he was made player rep by
the team. Known for his intelligence as much as his prejudice, in 1968,
Grantham won some respect by telling teammates, "Listen, I'm preju-
diced. I know it. I was brought up that way. . . . I'm hoping to change.
I'm trying.")

Namath had, in a way, a tangled relationship with race, if only
because he had such a simple outlook on the subject at a time when
it seemed to be complicating every crevice of American life, including—and maybe especially—sports. Namath just never thought much
about race. Growing up in Beaver Falls' Lower End and playing sports
year-round, Namath always had been around black kids his age, and
thought little of it. One of Namath's best childhood friends, Lynwood
Alford, was black. Phillies slugger Dick Allen, a black man who grew

up in Wampum, Pennsylvania, about ten miles from Namath's home in Beaver Falls, knew Namath (a star baseball player as a youth) since childhood. "We played a lot of ball together as kids," Allen said. "Joe never had any trouble, black or white. If you were his man, you were his man. That was it. We have been friends for a long time."

It was not until Namath left Pennsylvania for Alabama that he got a sense of the severity of the nation's racial divide. The university was all white when Namath arrived in 1961, and he was on hand in 1963 when Vivian Malone and James Hood, under the watch of the National Guard, bypassed Governor George Wallace's personal blockade and became the first black students to attend the school. In Tuscaloosa, surrounded by Southerners, Namath was shocked to find "water fountains for whites were painted white; there were different bathrooms for whites and blacks; blacks had to sit in the backs of buses and whites had to sit up front. I just couldn't understand it." In his freshman year at Alabama, Namath was also shocked to find that, when a teammate confused a black girl in a high school photo with Namath's girlfriend, he quickly was given the nickname, "Nigger Lover," which was shortened to just "Nigger." Probably his most farcical brush with the racial mania in Tuscaloosa at the time came when Namath was suspended by Bear Bryant for violating team rules (he had admitted to drinking) at the end of the 1963 season. When the school year began, Vivian Malone began to hear rumors that Namath actually had been suspended from the team for dating a black girl—and she was the only black girl on campus. "There were rumors that he dated a Negro girl, but he definitely hasn't dated me," Malone said. She said she had only seen Namath around campus once. "This guy and I have never even come close—never dated!" she continued. "I've heard the rumors (that he dated me), but I was surprised. It's so absurd." The racism rampant in Alabama troubled Namath, but he said, "They got to respect the way I felt and I think I might even have turned some of them around on a few things."

Namath was able to turn some teammates with the Jets around, too—or, at least, he (along with receiver George Sauer, son of the team's personnel director) had a hand in making the team more racially harmonious. Strange as it may be to consider, a professional sports team very often follows the same social rules as a tenth-grade class in a high school, in that players slip easily into cliques made up of other players most like themselves. As in a school, in no place do these cliques show themselves more blatantly than in the cafeteria. With the Jets at training camp, the pattern was predictable: a few black players would sit together at meals, and soon other black players would join them. There would then be a "black table" established for breakfast, lunch, and dinner. The same would happen with white Northerners and white Southerners, and factions within those factions would form, too. The cafeteria was not segregated by team mandate, of course, but social norms segregated it anyway.

But Namath would enter the dining room, easily stride up to an all-black table and start eating. Sauer or another white Jet might join him, and soon the all-black table would become just another table full of teammates. Jets beat writer Paul Zimmerman observed, "I've seen this happen too many times to assume it's accidental. The same thing on buses. I've seen Namath integrate a little knot of black players by his presence." Winston Hill, who had come to the Jets in 1963 and described black Jet players at that time as a "kind of lonely group," told Zimmerman that Namath made a difference. "You know Joe Namath probably did more than anyone to help race relations on the Jets," Hill said. "Joe Namath and George Sauer, actually, but I think Namath did the most. . . . Mainly, Joe just did it by being himself. The only way you can break down a situation like that is to have it come from within, from the leaders on the team."

In 1966, the Jets played their exhibition season opener against the Oilers, a game played at Legion Field in Birmingham, Alabama. It was to be a celebration of Namath among Crimson Tide fans. Namath knew well the racial lay of the land in Birmingham—just about every American had seen news coverage of the abuse and murder of civil rights workers in Alabama over the preceding few years. He and Hill eased potential tension with a joke, with Hill telling Ewbank that when they got to Alabama, he wanted to be Namath's roommate. It was tough enough to get a hotel that would accommodate the black Jets in Birmingham, but to have a white player and a black player together in one room? Ewbank was taken aback. "You want to what?" Ewbank said. "Hell, put us together, Coach," Namath said. "That'd be a lot of fun." Namath recalled later, "Weeb looked a little shook." Also during the 1966 season, lineman Sherman Plunkett, whom writer Dick Young dubbed, "the spokesman for the colored players," was thumbing through the team's program while sitting at his locker and came to the page that featured Jets cheerleaders. He called Sonny Werblin over. "Why," asked Plunkett, "aren't there any colored girls?" Werblin stammered trying to explain that the Jets merely brought the girls over from St. John's University, but there were not many black girls at the school and, Werblin said, "You go get pretty girls to go to St. John's and cheer." At that, Matt Snell bellowed, "Oh no, not him! His taste is awful!" and a potentially uncomfortable moment for Werblin turned to laughter.

....

Jackie Robinson of the Dodgers broke baseball's color line in 1947, becoming the first black player to participate in the Major Leagues. Baseball had long been a bastion of racial segregation, with Negro League stars left out of the American and National leagues, but Robinson's courage in integrating the sport was supposed to open a new era for baseball, one in which talented black players could sign with teams and be given the same chance to earn their way to the big money of the majors. Now, the floodgates would be open, and players would be judged on ability, not skin color. If the rest of the nation was not yet integrated, at least its most popular sport would be. That's how it was supposed to work, at least. But in baseball, in all major sports and in the nation at large, a harsh truth had settled in among black citizens: Integration was not synonymous with equality.

In March 1960, thirteen years after baseball was integrated, *Sports Illustrated* did a 7,000-word story titled, "The Private World of the Negro Ballplayer." In it, writer Robert Boyle gave his largely white audience a titillating look into the hierarchy and lingo (he explained mysterious terms like "mullion" and "hog-cutter") of black players, as well as the special struggles of players coming from Latin America, who had no frame of reference for the kind of treatment and segregation they faced in much of the nation, especially the South, where teams trained in the spring and had minor-league affiliates. Boyle painted a serious and stark picture on the nature of race relations in American sports, namely, that there were not many relations to be had. Black players, Boyle found, stuck together. Latin players did the same. So did whites. Many teams might have been integrated, but, as with the Jets, integration did not mean the elimination of racial factions. "Negroes aren't supposed to stick together," Reds pitcher Brooks Lawrence told Boyle, "but the closest kind of adhesion I've ever known has been among Negro ballplayers."

Black players were frequently suspicious of white teammates, as well as the power structure that existed in the major American sports. There was a feeling that teams wanted only the best black players and could easily toss aside the rest. One player told Boyle that black players only have a shot if they were demonstrably better than their white rivals: "If two players are the same, and one is white and one is colored, and one has to go, nine out of 10 times the colored guy will be the guy." Especially troubling about that remark was the fact that, nine years later, when Jim Bouton (who is white) was writing his groundbreaking book, *Ball Four*, he found little had changed. "The situation of the Negro in baseball is not as equitable as it seems," Bouton wrote. "He still has to be better than his white counterparts to do as well. . . . There are a lot of Negro stars in the game. There aren't too many average Negro players. The obvious conclusion is that there is some kind of quota system. It stands to reason that if 19 of the top 30 hitters in the major leagues are black, as they were in 1968, then almost two-thirds of the hitters should be black. Obviously it's not that way at all."

For black athletes, coping with segregated services when playing in the South had become common, but over the course of the 1960s, athletes and their teams took stands against the practice of segregation and, frequently, they won. When the Braves were planning their transfer from Milwaukee to Atlanta in October 1964, slugger Hank Aaron—who had played in a segregated stadium in Atlanta as a minor leaguer—said, "I just won't step out on the field," if the Braves' new park were to be segregated. When the Braves made their debut at Atlanta Stadium in 1966, it was integrated. In January 1965, when the AFL was set to hold its postseason All-Star game at Tulane University, twenty-one black players (and several white players) threatened to boycott the game after arriving in New Orleans and being ignored by taxicabs, turned away at the entrance to bars, and denied reservations at restaurants throughout the city because of their race. AFL Commissioner Joe Foss acquiesced and moved the game to Houston. "Negro players run into problems in nearly every city," Foss said. "But I guess what went on in New Orleans was more than they could be expected to take."

But that sort of segregation was a surface problem and largely limited to the South. The more complex issue was that of structural racism, the kind that ran deep in the owners' boxes and managerial offices—and their all-white tenants—and left the black player feeling that he must "be better than his white counterparts." Certainly, there were individual owners whose racist beliefs had an impact on their teams. George Marshall of the NFL's Washington Redskins refused to sign black players, and once said, "We'll sign black players when the Harlem Globetrotters start signing whites." Marshall only relented in 1961 because he was building a new stadium on federal land and the Kennedy administration threatened action if the Redskins continued to exercise discriminatory practices. In Boston, Tom Yawkey was the last owner in baseball to bring up a black player, and he kept blatantly racist former big-leaguer Pinky Higgins on hand as manager, then as general manager in the late 1950s and early 1960s. In 1973, writer Al Hirshberg claimed Higgins had told him, "There'll be no niggers on this ballclub as long as I have anything to say about it." And there was Calvin Griffith, owner of the Senators when the team moved from Washington DC to Minnesota in 1961. Griffith explained in a speech to a white audience in 1978 why he moved the franchise: "I'll tell you why we came to Minnesota. It was when I found out you only had 15,000 blacks here. Black people don't go to ball games, but they'll fill up a rassling ring and put up such a chant it'll scare you to death. It's unbelievable. We came here because you've got good, hardworking, white people here."

In New York, the problem was no different. George Weiss had been fired from the Yankees along with Casey Stengel in 1960, and subsequently hired by the Mets. Though there was no question about his capability when it came to building a team, Weiss also had a reputation as a staunch racist. At a cocktail party while still running the Yankees, Weiss once supposedly said he would "never allow a black man to wear a Yankee uniform. Box holders from Westchester don't want that sort of crowd. They would be offended to have to sit with niggers." He brought that worldview with him to the Mets. In 1966, the Mets held the first pick in the draft, and most teams around baseball were salivating over the prospects of burly Arizona State slugger Reggie Jackson, who had signed on with the school as a football player but turned into a baseball star. (Jackson was also the first black player to suit up for the Sun Devils.) Pirates manager/executive Danny Murtaugh told the *Arizona Republic* that Jackson was "head and shoulders above everyone else." But not for the Mets. They instead chose catcher Steve Chilcott, on the advice of scout Bob Scheffing. According to Jackson's autobiography, before the draft, ASU coach Bobby Winkles sat him down and told him, "You're probably not gonna be the No. 1 pick. You're dating a Mexican girl, and the Mets think you will be a problem. They think you'll be a social problem because you are dating out of your race." Jackson was stunned. His girlfriend, at the time, was Juanita Campos, of Mexican descent. Jackson was part black, part Puerto Rican. His middle name was Martinez. He and Campos were not just dating, they were talking about marriage. Winkles knew there was nothing to be done. "You're colored, and they don't want that," he told Jackson.

In 1968, Jack Olsen wrote a scathing series for *Sports Illustrated* (which became a book) about the state of black athletes in the U.S.

and found that, "Black professional athletes say they are underpaid, shunted into certain stereotyped positions and treated like sub-humans by Paleolithic coaches who regard them as watermelon-eating idiots." Olsen highlighted racial tensions on the NFL's St. Louis Cardinals, a team that was severely segregated and, according to former Cardinal Dave Meggyesy, featured veteran linebacker Bill Koman, who once, "told me and anyone who would listen that 'niggers' were generally too dumb to play football, that pro clubs were giving 'niggers' a break by having them around." Meggysey also pointed out that, in the 1960s, "very few blacks hold positions that are thought to require a great deal of intelligence rather than a great deal of strength—positions such as linebacker, offensive guard and quarterback." One example was the case of college star Gene Washington, who had been a promising quarterback at Stanford in 1966 but, when it became clear he had a shot at a pro football career, asked his coaches to switch him to wide receiver in 1967, because he knew black players did not play quarterback in the pros. The first modern professional black starting quarterback did not take the field until the 1968 season, when Marlin Briscoe was under center for the injury-depleted Broncos. "I knew a black man had never played quarterback," Briscoe said. "I also knew there were those who could but got switched to flanker or defensive back. There had been prejudice." Briscoe's time as a starting passer was short-lived, though. He kicked around the NFL for eight more seasons, but not as a quarterback—he, too, got switched to flanker.

Amid those injustices, an underground movement grew to organize black athletes into a union that would grant active black players more power to address the issue of salary inequality. It didn't catch on, in the words of Cardinals first baseman Bill White, because, "If the Negro professional were to be separated from the main body of players, we'd be losing 20 years of hard progress since Jackie Robinson's entrance into the game. . . . This is why unions or 'black power' or 'player power' could do nothing but hurt us." But in addressing the union issue, players did voice concerns over the lack of post-career opportunities for blacks, who were almost universally shut out of coaching and front-office posts. It was in 1966 that the Celtics made Bill Russell, who still starred as a player, the first black head coach in major American sports. Baseball would not hire a black manager until 1974 (Frank Robinson, who made his debut with the Cleveland Indians in 1975), and the NFL, rather shamefully, would not install its first modern black head coach until 1989 (Art Shell with the Raiders). The NHL has never had a black head coach.

Former Dodger pitcher Joe Black, then an executive with Greyhound bus lines, said baseball—like other major sports—was ignoring its retiring black stars. "Fellows like Larry Doby, Don Newcombe and Roy Campanella, all ex-major league stars, have contacted the commissioner's office about the possibility of employment, but have received no response or recognition, whatsoever," Black said in 1967. "We have players qualified to every kind of job there is in the front office." But Black would have to wait. Baseball did not have a black general manager until the Braves hired Bill Lucas in 1976.

. . . .

While Joe Namath was trying to heal the Jets' racial divide, he was also looking to do something about their historically woeful place in the standings. A sign planted at Shea Stadium early in the 1966 season was an indication that he just might be on his way to accomplishing that. The sign was something more expected at a game featuring the Mets and their New Breed fans, and was somewhat out of place for the Jets, but reflected the fascinating turns that had taken place in football. In June of 1966, the NFL and AFL called a truce in their war and agreed to a merger. The league would be called the National Football League, and would be divided into the American Football Conference and the National Football Conference. The schedules would not yet be interlocked, but that would come in 1970. In the interim, the teams would hold one combined draft (draftees said good-bye to those Namath-esque bonuses) and the league champs would meet in what was being called the Super Bowl. That lent a special excitement to the early part of the 1966 season for the Jets, who won all of their exhibition games, even with Namath mostly hobbled and dealing with bursitis in his left knee, then got off to a 4–0–1 regular-season start. In the NFL, former Giants assistant Vince Lombardi had coached defending champion Green Bay to a 6–1 mark. The hopeful sign read: "Bring on the Packers."

Namath was sensational. In the Jets' undefeated first five games, he threw for 1,056 yards and nine touchdowns, looking much more comfortable in the pocket than he had as a rookie. "With that added year of experience, Joe is now able to exploit his ability," Jets assistant coach Jack Donaldson said. "As a passer, he could become one of the greatest the pros have ever seen." Playing in Boston in Week 4, the Jets were lethargic and got behind, 24–7. The 27,000 Patriots fans were letting Namath have it, hollering at him relentlessly from the stands. Namath smiled and put his hand to his ear, cupping it as if to encourage more hostility. He was hearing it from the Boston bench, too, which reminded him that he was supposed to be worth $400,000 but sure was not playing like it. Namath rallied the Jets with 17 points in the final quarter, pulling out the tie. He'd rather have the win, of course but the outcome made Namath smile. "There is nothing I enjoy better than to show up those who belittle me," he said.

It was during this period of sustained success that media coverage of Namath shifted noticeably. As a rookie, the bulk of the stories on Namath were devoted to the $400,000-quarterback angle—his talent, the pressure, the banged-up knee, the gamble the Jets were taking. There were some adulating stories playing up Namath's swinger credentials, including one interview that Namath did with the *Post*'s Milton Gross in training camp, in which he was asked about women and said, "I love them all. A filly with brown hair is all right. So is one with black hair. But blondes, they come first." Now in his sophomore season, the contract was old news. Writers flocked to Joe to hear more about these blondes. One of those blondes, the voluptuous actress Mamie Van Doren, recalled that Namath could be obsessed with what was written about him. Earlier in 1966, while the two were having a fling, Namath was lounging in a hotel room with Van Doren in South

Florida, when a friend of Namath's stopped by with a stack of newspapers. Namath took the papers and put them into piles on the hotel room floor. "It was a kind of giant scrapbook of newspapers from all over the country," Van Doren remembered. "During the time we were there, Joe carefully read all of them, scrutinizing all his press minutely for a few hours every day."

Now, press attention was on the Broadway Joe lifestyle, what one writer was already calling, "the Joe Namath legend." And he loved it. Namath stayed out late. He drank. He liked women, and lots of them. A *Sports Illustrated* feature from October 1966, titled, "The Sweet Life of Swinging Joe," described Namath out at a Manhattan bar in the wee hours, spotting, "foxes," and "studying the defensive tendencies of New York's off-duty secretaries, stewardesses, dancers, nurses, bunnies, actresses, shopgirls—all of the people who make life stimulating for a bachelor." One national story claimed, with notably vague attribution, that, "Someone said that she had seen him in the Copa late one night, grinning into a mirror and saying fondly, 'Joe, Joe, you're the most beautiful thing in the world!'" It didn't matter whether he'd actually said it. Once it was published, it just fed into the fantasy of Namath as a playboy Narcissus, dazzling those who glimpsed him, even himself. Namath let reporters and photographers into his absurdly decorated penthouse, llama rug and all, the symbol of his Upper East Side bachelorhood. Even the stodgy *Sporting News* ran a story in 1966 about Namath's pad, probably the only time in the publication's history it quoted an interior designer. "You'll notice the color motif, including curtains in both the living room and dining room, is black and white," Allan Kirk, who had also designed apartments for Frank Sinatra and Dean Martin, told the venerable weekly.

But things turned quickly for Namath. In the season's sixth game, the Jets went on the road to play Houston, a team they'd clobbered, 52–13, in their first meeting in Week 2, with Namath going for five touchdowns. The Jets had never won in Houston, but their early success had them pegged as 4½-point favorites. Some on the coaching staff were nervous about the game. The Oilers were not that bad a team, and the offensive line had done a nice job the first time around against Houston defensive lineman Ernie Ladd, who stood 6–9 and weighed 315 pounds, and would become a pro wrestler after his football days. Before the second Houston meeting, Namath said of him, "Ernie Ladd, he got me so hard once last year that I couldn't talk." The coaches' trepidation was justified. When the game started, the Jets looked out of sorts. They fumbled on the first possession. Then Namath threw three interceptions, and the Oilers took advantage, building a 17–0 lead. Weeb Ewbank, exasperated, looked to his players with about two minutes to go in the half. "Anyone have anything?" he said. No answer.

The Jets were being blown out in the second half when Ladd was able to break through the line and flatten Namath. He took a few seconds to get up. "Yeah, I thought about staying down," he said. With four interceptions, Namath turned in the worst performance of his brief career, and the final score (24–0) marked the first time the Jets had been shut out since 1963. Namath said it was the first time his team had been shut out since junior high.

In the locker room after the game, Namath was sullen. Before the media session began, one of the assistant coaches had ranted about players, "drinking and running around." It didn't take much to decode what he was really saying—*Namath* was drinking and running around. That ticked him off. "This isn't high school," Namath later said. Angry and in pain, the crew of New York reporters bore in with questions. Namath, all too willing to preen late at night for reporters giving him positive publicity, had trouble with the press when his performance went sour. He could not explain why the Houston game had gone so badly, and he really didn't want to. "Bad day," one reporter suggested to Namath. "Yeah, bad day." Another reporter tried: "The interceptions were tough." Namath simply repeated, "Yeah, the interceptions were tough." Jimmy Cannon, long-tenured syndicated columnist, was not going to accept Namath's stonewalling. Cannon had once been among the finest sportswriters in the country, but by the mid-1960s, his star had faded, and one colleague called him, "a crabby, opinionated, lonely, middle-aged, 'sportswriter' railing incessantly at most younger writers, all liberals and black militants." Cannon asked Namath how he could be so good one week, and awful the next. He asked about the interceptions. He wanted to know what happened, and kept at Namath until he cracked. Namath knew what Cannon was driving at. "I was up all night," Namath said sarcastically. "Booze and broads, that's why I played so lousy. That's what it was. That's what you wanted to hear, wasn't it?" Namath wasn't serious, of course. But Maury Allen recalled that, "Namath said it and Cannon wrote it. Maybe both of them did a service to sports and journalism. Now it was out in the open."

On the plane home after the game, Namath was calmer. But his knees were killing him. He knew the right knee would need more surgery. The bursitis in the left knee was worse than most knew. He had just played the nineteenth game of his career but, as a cramp shot through his "good leg" causing him to abruptly stand up in the aisle of the cabin and walk it off, he was having doubts about just how long he would be a professional quarterback. He grabbed the arm of a reporter who was working on a story about him for the *Saturday Evening Post*. "I'm so racked up," Namath said. "This is the first time in my life I've ever thought about quitting football." The writer asked if he was serious, and when Namath said he was, the writer asked if he could include that in his story. "I don't give a damn," Namath said.

The following week, the Jets returned home to Shea Stadium, where they built a 21–17 lead that they clung to in the final minutes of the game, but finally lost when the Raiders scored a touchdown on a fourth-down goal-line play with two seconds remaining, giving the Jets a 24–21 loss. As he was coming off the field, one ticked-off fan threw coffee on Namath. It got worse the following week, when the Jets played Buffalo on October 30, still holding onto first place at 4–2–1. Namath had another awful day, throwing five interceptions as the Jets fell behind, 30–3, before rallying to bring the final score to 33–23. Prior to that game, Namath had heard the occasional taunt from the home crowd, but it was in the Buffalo loss that the Shea Stadium partisans turned against him, full-throttle, even calling for Ewbank to put in

Mike Taliaferro. This time, he was a bit more accommodating toward the press. Namath was asked if he'd ever had that sort of treatment before, and joked, "I used to get booed by my family every time I came home."

If Jimmy Cannon had been making connections between Namath's struggles and his after-hours lifestyle after the first loss in Houston, and if the home fans had turned on Namath, too, the rest of the media was now ready to pile on, with the Jets wobbling through a Namath-led losing streak. Call it swinger backlash. In the wake of the Buffalo loss, Gene Ward of the *Daily News* cited an overheard conversation at Shea Stadium in which one fan said, "I've never seen him look worse. He must have been out drinking all night." For Ward, that was the price Namath could be expected to have to pay for so freely publicizing his off-field activities. "He was a sitting duck for the abuse of fans because of the playboy image he has created—the penthouse pad, the sharp clothes, the posh drinking hangouts and the cuddly dolls. The high, white football shoes he wears scream his rugged individualism and his penchant for nonconformity. A pro football star can live the Golden Boy life in the flashspots, but on the football field he'd better be sensational. Being adequate, or even good, isn't enough. He must be great, game after game, or New York's peculiar breed of fans is going to go on tearing him apart."

The Jets had a week off after the Buffalo loss, and Ewbank decided the team needed a break. He gave them three days to forget about football. Namath, now with both knees in pain and acknowledging he wanted more surgery after the season, went to Puerto Rico, taking the advice of Dr. Nicholas, who had told him, "get away and relax." Ewbank, of course, would not stop thinking about football. He used the bye week to remind reporters that Namath was still only twenty-three, still learning his way in the league. Ewbank had never quite been comfortable with the level of exposure Namath was getting in the press, something over which he and Sonny Werblin clashed. Speaking at the Jets' weekly luncheon, Ewbank lamented the overwrought coverage of Namath, almost pleading with reporters to ease up. "Joe or any other quarterback in his second year of pro football has too much to learn," he said. "There's too much pressure. Just let the kid develop normally. Don't put him on a pedestal and let everybody chop him down."

The time off did not help much. The Jets lost again to Buffalo in their first game back, and followed a win over the Dolphins with two more losses and a tie to drop their record to 5–6–2. Namath still could not get his passes under control, throwing seven interceptions during a two-game trip to the West Coast in December. The Jets, and Namath, did finish on a high note, beating Boston (which was playing for the AFC East championship and a spot in the playoffs) by a 38–28 margin on December 17, a game that saw Namath throw for 287 yards on 14-for-21 passing, with three touchdowns and no interceptions. It was the kind of win that gave a glimpse of what the Jets might yet become— Namath threw two touchdowns to veteran speedster Don Maynard, another to Sauer and Jets running backs Matt Snell and Emerson Boozer added touchdowns, too. Like Namath, Sauer and Boozer were just twenty-three, and Snell was twenty-five. Namath led the league in passing in 1966, with 3,379 yards (533 yards ahead of the runner-up), but he logged a whopping 27 interceptions, also a league-high.

But Namath was back under Dr. Nicholas's knife after the season. He had more cartilage removed from his bad right knee and had what amounted to ACL surgery, pulling parts of tendons from elsewhere in his leg and using them to tighten the joint. There was not quite as much hoopla around this surgery as there had been around the one two years earlier, with national magazines parading through for photos and interviews. But on January 4, 1967, Namath declared from his bed at Lenox Hill Hospital: "It feels great, it's ahead of schedule. There's no pain, I'll be leaving here a week early, I'll be able to toss a football in February, play golf in March and start running in April."

And he'd be able to shed the restrictive hospital life for his off-season haunts down South. "Once released from the hospital," it was reported, "he will make a beeline for Miami to pursue his recovery from his operation and from the monastic life of the last 10 days."

CHAPTER 9

"I think we're going to have a riot"

ON A WEEKEND NIGHT IN February 1966, William Hawley, a retired private security guard, was in his usual spot, working at Joe's Place, a black bar in Harlem, at Amsterdam and 125th Street. It was a quiet evening, with only fifteen patrons in the place at about midnight, when a white police sergeant entered the bar. This wasn't new. Just the previous night, a cop had given Hawley a summons for not having enough soap and towels in the bathroom. Hawley was told this visit was just a routine inspection, but he was skeptical. Two more officers, one patrolman and one captain, slinked into the bar. A fourth joined them shortly thereafter. Music was playing and some customers were bobbing their heads, prompting the sergeant to remind Hawley that New York's cabaret laws forbade dancing. "They're not dancing," Hawley said. "They're just snapping their fingers and moving their heads to the music." As the cops scoped the place, the patrolman mentioned to the sergeant that some female impersonators had been arrested in the bar not long before, and made the suggestion that they check for transvestites. The sergeant approved. The patrolman approached a table, where a few women were seated. He told one, thirty-year-old Gertrude Williams—a married mother of two who lived a block away—to show identification. She had none. The patrolman took Williams by the arm, leading her to a kitchen area, where he told her to "prove she was a woman." Shocked and terrified, she partially undressed in front of him. When Williams returned from the kitchen, she looked dazed, like she might cry. The patrolman was behind her, grinning.

Word of the incident spread. Westley Williams, Gertrude's husband, confronted the police, who ignored him. "I was hurting," he said. "I couldn't do nothing. I can't fight the law." Soon after, the Harlem branch of the Congress of Racial Equality (CORE) filed a complaint to Mayor Lindsay and the police commissioner, Howard Leary, who had three of the officers transferred. There was a protest of the incident, in which one CORE member carried a sign reading, "Protect Our Women from Vicious Animals in Uniform." But there was no formal punishment. For blacks in places like Harlem, these outrages at the hands of police were all too common, as was the feeling of helplessness Westley Williams described. There was no recourse.

There long had been a call among New York's minorities and liberal whites to change the way the police department disciplined officers accused of excessive force and other abuses. As it stood, charges against police were heard by a three-member panel of cops who would mete out punishment for offending officers. But few punishments were ever actually handed out. The perception that no members of a police panel were ever going to keep their colleagues in line persisted, especially among blacks. The most notable case came in November 1964, when New York police Lt. Thomas Gilligan was exonerated by the board in the shooting death of black fifteen-year-old James Powell in July, an incident that had set off six days of rioting in Harlem and Brooklyn. Gilligan had been cleared by a grand jury, and the review board's pass meant that he would be free to rejoin the force without a trace of punishment. The decision outraged black leaders and heightened calls for a new review board, manned not by police but by citizens. Civil rights activist Rev. Milton Galamison said, "No one is yelling for Gilligan's neck. The fact the Negro community has no faith in the department's review board will always cast a shadow on his claims of innocence, whereas if an objective body had exonerated him there would be instant mutual acceptance."

During the 1965 election, Lindsay had taken a strong stand in favor of a civilian review board, and he owed his mayoral victory, in part, to his ability to pluck votes from the black and Latino communities with promises to address their concerns about police behavior. Those communities were decidedly fed up with what they saw as deep-seated racism in the NYPD, which was dominated by white cops—of seventy-nine precinct commanders on the force, just one was black, and only three out of more than 400 captains were black. The lack of influential minorities within the department was a sticking point, and Lindsay felt he had to act. But putting the review board in the hands of civilians was anathema to the cops, because it would expose them to the judgment of a group that could not possibly comprehend the difficulty of their jobs. Cops argued, too, that fear of going before a civilian review board would inhibit them from doing their jobs decisively when under fire, putting the communities at greater risk. And there was the undertone of discrimination in the argument—the creation of a civilian review board would amount to an implicit acknowledgement that white cops were employing racism when working in black neighborhoods. "The 1965 campaign in a real sense was run against the police force," said former Lindsay chief of staff Jay Kriegel. "Not that we thought they were racists, but that the department was old and tired, and badly in need of modernization. But institutionalized racism was an important issue—the problem of brutality and the lack of minorities on the force. The cop on the street took it all as a criticism of himself."

Shortly after taking office, Lindsay took action on the review board. He replaced police chief Vincent Broderick (an opponent of the civilian review board) with Howard Leary of Philadelphia, where a civilian review board had been implemented. In February, in order to mitigate opposition from the NYPD, Lindsay seized on a middle path that he felt could please all sides in the review board argument: Add four citizens to the three-member board, and have the seven-person panel reach non-binding recommendations for punishment to be passed along to the commissioner and implemented at his discretion. That arrangement would give citizens a greater voice but ultimately leave responsilbility for discipline with the department. It was a typical Lindsay solution, simultaneously a reasonable compromise, and one that failed to take the political temperature of the situation. James Farmer, the civil rights leader who was the director of CORE, insisted on a board entirely outside the control of the police, saying Lindsay's proposal was, "right, but not right enough unfortunately." On the opposite side, officer John Cassese, the president of the 27,000-member Patrolmen's Benevolent Association (PBA), was not impressed by the nuances of Lindsay's proposal. The PBA sued to halt the review board, and sought to put the question to a referendum in that November's election.

Cassese went after Lindsay for playing to minorities, and, rather amazingly, suggested that the adoption of a civilian review in New York would spread and eventually lead to all of America turning Communist. "Russia should send a medal to the City of New York and say, 'Thank you for accomplishing what I haven't been able to do for these many years,'" Cassese said. "Russia, if they want to take over any country, they have to immobilize the Police Department and knock out the religion of the country. You put in a police review board throughout the country, you immobilize the police force." As the civilian review board issue gained increased attention throughout the spring and into the summer, Cassese grew more and more virulent. The PBA fought the board in court, but also managed to get the issue put on the ballot as a referendum question for that November's election. Lindsay built a long list of bipartisan endorsements for the board, including gubernatorial candidates Nelson Rockefeller and City Council President Frank O'Connor, as well as Lindsay's former mayoral foe, Abe Beame, and Senators Javits and (reluctantly) Kennedy. One who opposed the board, notably, was Comptroller Mario Procaccino.

But the PBA continued its attacks. Cassese's thinly veiled racism even lost its thin veil. "I'm sick and tired of giving in to minority groups with their whims and their gripes and their shouting," he said. Lindsay had put forth a common-sense proposal with widespread support, but

Cassese's ability to play on racist and Communist fears was proving powerful. Polls showed the board proposal having little popular support. "The PBA has turned loose something that has turned into a bit of a monster," Lindsay said, almost dumbfounded. When the PBA began running an ad in newspapers and on billboards, showing a young white woman looking frightened as she considers entering a subway station on a dark street, with the headline, "The civilian review board must be stopped! Her life . . . your life . . . may depend on it," Lindsay was much sharper. "The only thing it didn't show was a gang of Negroes about to attack her," Lindsay said. "It was a vulgar, obscene advertisement if I've ever seen one." Stepping up efforts to save the board, Lindsay tried to link the passage of the board in the referendum to possible race riots in New York, telling Cassese and PBA communications chief Norman Frank during a breakfast at Gracie Mansion that, "If anything happened in New York, if there was a blowup, they would be responsible." As writer Tamar Jacoby later noted, "Abandoning all hope of winning over uncertain white voters, the mayor tried to bully them with threats of looming race riots, helping in effect to legitimize violent disorders. Nothing could have been more likely to alienate middle-class whites."

. . . .

An issue like that of the civilian review board in New York highlighted one of the paradoxes that was settling over the nationwide drive for civil rights. Everyone could agree that Jim Crow laws were outdated and insulting, but civil rights laws helping Southern blacks only made blacks in Northern American cities more acutely aware that there was no drive on to help them. Washington could secure a black man's right to vote, but it could not eradicate the stubborn reluctance of white homeowners to share their streets with black neighbors or of white employers to hire black workers or of white policemen to show kindness in black neighborhoods. If the problem of racial relations had developed into a serious and ugly undercurrent in the world of sports—including in the locker room of Joe Namath's Jets and in the front office of baseball's Yankees and Mets in New York—then in the nation in general, urban racial issues were no longer mere undercurrents. They were developing into explosions. The South was undergoing forced change, but the Northern (and Western) ghettoes were not, and frustration began to build. When that frustration blew up, it took the form of an urban riot. New York had gotten a glimpse of that in Harlem in 1964, and Los Angeles felt it full bore in the summer of 1965, when the Watts riots raged for five days, leaving 34 dead, 1,032 injured and causing $40 million worth of property damage as looters chanted, "Burn, baby, burn!"

For Lindsay, the plight of minorities and the treatment they received at the hands of their government would be a defining issue. It had been Lindsay's first responsibility as a professional in Washington, working on civil rights legislation with Attorney General Herbert Brownell. It was a focus for Lindsay during his time as a congressman, when he criticized President Kennedy for paying too much lip service to the plight of blacks without following through with action, and when he helped to guide civil rights legislation to passage on the House floor. Lindsay actively courted the traditionally Democratic black and Puerto Rican vote in the mayoral race. His frequent junkets into the tenements and ghettoes throughout the city during his campaign were viewed with skepticism as they were happening, but Lindsay wanted to follow through on the promises he made to help those places. If he was to become Mr. City and brandish his presidential bona fides, he would have to do so by showing progress on race, the most difficult urban problem facing America.

Lindsay, though, like many liberals of the era, underestimated the scope of the city's issues. What was happening in America's cities went well beyond racism, well beyond politics and well beyond the 1960s— there were economic, technological, and demographic forces at work that no urban mayor could reverse, even if he had significantly more political backing than the bare support Lindsay had. The problem had begun with the migration of Southern blacks, with labor skills mostly limited to sharecropping, to Northern cities. The first wave of such movement took place in the years around World War I, when Northern factory employment was plentiful, but ground to a halt with the Great

Depression. After World War II, blacks again began heading north. In 1940, New York's black population was just 6 percent, and that grew to 9 percent in 1950. In 1960, it was up to 14 percent, and reached 20 percent by 1968. That was happening in other cities, too, but New York was unique in that it also took in the bulk of immigrants from Puerto Rico. Poor, agrarian residents of the island were encouraged to come to the mainland for jobs, and the population of Puerto Ricans in America rose from 69,967 in the 1940s to 887,662 in the 1960s. About 85 percent of those were in New York.

These new arrivals came for jobs and opportunity, but found a city that was changing. Automobile ownership grew 44 percent in the decade from 1955–1965, a development that freed Americans, allowing them to live farther from their places of employment and making them less dependent on proximity to systems of public transportation. In 1956, the federal government authorized the paving of 41,000 miles of roads to develop the Interstate Highway System, which meant that those who owned cars could live 20 or 30 miles away from their workplaces and still have a relatively easy commute. Members of the (mostly white) middle class, with good jobs that enabled them to afford a car and a house, left the city in droves for fast-growing suburbs, taking their property-tax payments with them. Companies, too, left the city, seeking to rid themselves of the high overhead that came with pricey rents, taxes, and the hassles of traffic. New York was especially hit, as 76,000 manufacturing jobs—which provided a bedrock of decent wages for unskilled workers—left the city in a five-year period from 1959–64.

Put it all together, and New York in the 1960s was left with a departing middle class, a declining tax base, a rise in unskilled minority workers, and a paucity of jobs for those workers. This was taking place during the implementation of President Johnson's "Great Society" program, which expanded the social safety net. In New York, that meant welfare, and a lot of it. The welfare rolls in New York tripled from 330,000 to 1 million recipients over the course of the 1960s, draining the city budget and adding to the stock of racial animosity among those whites who viewed black and Puerto Rican newcomers as social-handout carpetbaggers, heading north to city ghettoes in order to collect easy welfare money. A rise in drug addiction, particularly to heroin, and the grinding poverty of city slums, fueled a stark rise in crime. In Lindsay's first year in office, violent crime in New York (homicide, rape, robbery, and assault) nearly doubled, from 27,014 violations to 49,158. That was, in part, because of better reporting methods, but it also reflected the reality of increased crime. It was robbery that was most to blame for the sharp rise, going from 8,904 incidents in 1965 to 23,539 in 1966, a shocking jump of 264 percent.

The relative connectedness and causes of these numbers can be, and were, debated. But they were very much taken as a whole by Northern whites at the time, who viewed cities like New York through the prism of race. The calculus seemed simple: minorities had moved in and now there was urban decay where there had been none. It didn't matter that the decay might have come with or without the new minority population. Northern whites were adamant about keeping black and white neighborhoods separate. In 1963, under the headline "What Northerners Really Think of Negroes," the *Saturday Evening Post* ran a poll based on 500 in-depth interviews, all of which came to the conclusion that "the white North is no more ready to accept genuine integration and real racial equality than the deep South." The poll found that 33 percent of Northerners felt race was the top issue in the nation (the most of any category, ahead of 22 percent for foreign policy issues) and that 63 percent approved of President Kennedy's civil rights programs. But the poll also found that 43 percent of Northerners believed whites were either innately superior to blacks or superior because of education, and reported that 77 percent believed whites should have the right to refuse to sell a house to a black family. One poll respondent said blacks are "human beings just like the rest of us, but I wouldn't want one living next door."

A year after the *Post*'s poll, the *New York Times* ran a poll gauging the racial views of white city residents, and found that 54 percent thought the civil rights movement of the time was moving too fast, and that 70 percent felt that it would be at least ten years before blacks and whites could live together. One retired woman on Riverside Drive told the pollsters that "Negroes are asking for the whole world on a silver platter." A housewife from Brooklyn was quoted as saying, "If they were educated, quiet people, they wouldn't bother me. But if I saw them moving in, it would bother me. I wouldn't want to live in a colored neighborhood." Another woman, described as "well-to-do" and living on the West Side with her stockbroker husband, admitted that she liked blacks less than other people, giving in to her liberal guilt by adding: "But I don't like myself for saying it."

....

There was some irony in a poll by the nation's paper of record suggesting that the civil rights drive was moving too fast. For an increasing portion of black society, the view was quite the opposite: civil rights were not coming fast enough. By 1966, the development of radical movements of blacks that had no (and wanted no) connection to the nonviolent discipline of Martin Luther King had matured, primarily in major cities. New York was ahead of most cities in this regard. In 1959, news of militant black philosophy first appeared in the mass media. It was then that a black reporter named Louis Lomax approached Mike Wallace, a young reporter and anchor for a show called *News Beat* on Channel 13 in New York. Lomax told Wallace of the Black Muslims, strict religious followers of a man named Elijah Muhammad, whose top preacher, Malcom X, was gaining a powerful following in Harlem. These were not agitators for voting rights. They did not aspire to integration. "They were separatists," Wallace recalled. "They wanted to separate, separate the blacks from the whites in this country." The views of the Black Muslims had never before been put to a largely white mainstream audience. Lomax and Wallace created what would become an influential documentary, *The Hate that Hate Produced*, which aired in the city but was widely reported on by newspapers and magazines in the weeks and months that followed.

In one exchange with Malcolm X, Lomax asked whether his church taught that the white man is evil. Malcolm responded, "You can go to any small Muslim child and ask him where is hell or who is the devil and he wouldn't tell you that hell is down in the ground or that the devil is something invisible that you can't see. He'll tell you hell is right where he has been catching it and he'll tell you the one who is responsible for him having received this hell is the devil." Lomax asked whether this devil was the white man. "Yes," Malcolm said. This was shocking to white viewers, who also heard Malcolm's claims that the Nation of Islam had 250,000 followers nationwide. The group was downplayed by more moderate black civil rights leaders at the time, but Lomax's reporting pointed out that prominent politicians had found it necessary to court favor with the Black Muslims, including Manhattan Borough President Hulan Jack and entrenched Harlem Rep. Adam Clayton Powell. The message was clear: white New Yorkers might not have heard of the Black Muslims, but they had influence over important black figures.

For four years after Lomax's program aired, New York's media gave glimpses into the state of Malcolm X and the Black Muslims. But Malcom's path was altered drastically in December of 1963 when, after a speech at the Manhattan Center, he called the assassination of President Kennedy a case of, "the chickens coming home to roost"—in other words, the violence perpetrated by Kennedy's administration in places like Vietnam, Africa, and the South had inspired a violent society, of which Kennedy had now become a victim. Muhammad suspended Malcolm and publicly repudiated his statement. This was a difficult blow for Malcolm, who traveled to Africa and the Middle East during his suspension, and had an awakening there, after which he returned to America determined to stop preaching Elijah Muhammad's anti-white vitriol and to focus on reconnecting black Americans with their African roots. Malcolm also began to spread the word of some startling facts he'd learned about Muhammad: he had fathered several children with young secretaries who worked for the church, violating the church's strict forbiddance of fornication and shattering Malcolm's respect for the Black Muslim leader. He knew that was inviting trouble, knew well Muhammad's capacity for violence. In early February, he told a reporter, "My death has been ordered by the higher-ups in the Muslim movement." On February 21, 1965, while speaking at the Audubon Ballroom in Harlem, Malcolm X was murdered in broad daylight in front of 400 followers.

His assassination, and the November 1965 release of an autobiography constructed by Alex Haley from taped interviews, heightened Malcolm X's influence. Through Haley's book, Malcolm was able to articulate the frustration and despair that comes with the realization that, as a black citizen in the United States, there would not be much of a future. The book was very much about the spiritual changes Malcolm went through, but it exposed more readers to the secular, political philosophy of black separatism. One of the book's admirers was Stokely Carmichael, a native of Trinidad who moved to Harlem when he was eleven. Carmichael, twenty-five, was a recent graduate of Howard University who was inspired by Malcolm X when, in May of 1966, he helped push aside the leadership of the Student Non-violent Coordinating Committee, one of the primary organizations for both black and white young people seeking to be involved in the civil rights movement. (The SNCC was generally just called "Snick.") One of Carmichael's first acts after taking charge of SNCC was to rid it of white liberals, whom he felt were paternalistic toward blacks. One profile of Carmichael summed him up as having "so successfully called attention to the growing spirit of black consciousness among American Negroes that some have begun to describe him as a new Malcolm X." Carmichael rejected the notion of what Martin Luther King called, "striped power—black and white together," and boiled down his radical new approach to the two words he shouted at a rally during a march in Mississippi in June 1966, two words that dramatically changed the course of the civil rights movement: Black Power.

At a press conference in July, Carmichael was asked to define what black power meant. He said it did not mean violence against whites, but, rather, "Black power means that black people have to politically get together to organize themselves so that they can speak from a position of power and strength rather than a position of weakness." But Carmichael sought alliances with radical black organizations, and commented that he supported urban rioters. In stark contrast to King, Carmichael said bluntly that blacks should defend themselves when attacked, adding, "I am not opposed to violence." This new leaning toward violence was played up and sensationalized in the mostly white press. In a *Time* magazine piece on "The New Racism," a white civil rights activist was quoted as saying that black power "doesn't necessarily have anything to do with black supremacy or hating whites, but it can go sour in that way." In a July *New York Post* column, writer Pete Hamill asked a young black man in Harlem about black power, and Hamill claimed he said: "This time next year, you don't even get here 'less you got a passport. Harlem be a nation then. All the Jew bastards be gone. We gonna own the stores, we gonna have our own polices, and everything else. You come up here then, you gonna be killed. Your women come through in a car, you never see them again. Blood gonna flow, whitey."

A *Newsweek* poll showed a frustrating reality: in the summer of 1966, attitudes and outlooks on race had barely changed since 1963. In fact, after national civil rights laws were passed in both 1964 and 1965—the pinnacle of the movement—the push for civil rights effectively stalled. For whites, Carmichael's call for Black Power in the wake of those bills smacked of ingratitude. Seventy percent of whites polled said that blacks were "trying to move too fast." About 63 percent of whites felt that all demonstrations were harmful, which was up from 50 percent in 1963. And the magazine found sharp differences between attitudes of wealthy white liberals living in the suburbs (57 percent of whom supported civil rights demonstrators) and poor whites living in cities (only 24 percent of whom supported those demonstrations). One article summed up the poll's findings: "'Tolerance flowers in the suburbs,' but shrinks among poor whites of the city, who feel even more abandoned by Government than do Negroes."

Black power established its strongest bases of support in cities, but white city residents were racially resentful, and even scared. Lindsay was right about the importance of race in urban life, but he was wrong to assume that granting justice to blacks was all that was required to fix

the issues. In the cities, racial lines—among both black and white—
were hardening.

·········

In 1979, Stanford psychologists Merrill Carlsmith and Craig Anderson
published findings in which they showed, scientifically, what many
knew to be true instinctually: "There is good evidence for a monotoni-
cally increasing relationship between temperature and the probability
of a riot." For tension-wracked sections of cities, extended periods of
summer heat were especially dangerous, and the fact that Southern
California was in the midst of a heat wave in August 1965 when the
Watts riots broke out was held as one reason for the length and severity of that tragedy. This was bad news for New York in July 1966, as
a stagnant weather pattern lingered overhead, one that would pound
the city with wilting air. On July 13, the temperature in New York
hit 101 degrees, the eighth straight day that thermometers topped 90
degrees. One prediction held that that it would be "the hottest July
recorded by the city, and this may become the hottest summer city residents have ever had to swelter through." When citizens swelter, they
are more likely to untether from the norms of their surroundings, and
more likely to engage in riots as a result.

The norms were melting, particularly in East New York and surrounding neighborhoods like Brownsville and Bedford-Stuyvesant.
This was the distant eastern corner of New York, the kind of Brooklyn
neighborhoods that Manhattanites hardly knew existed. Barry Gottehrer, a Lindsay aide who had been the editor of the *Herald-Tribune*'s
series, "City in Crisis", described the area as "an abandoned neighborhood, with one of the highest rates of infant mortality, drug abuse, abandoned buildings and welfare, and the lowest employment in the city."
This was the kind of place that was boiling over, and as the heat wave
simmered throughout much of the nation, July riots had broken out on
Chicago's West Side and in Cleveland's Hough neighborhood, where
violence was not quelled for four days, and needed the intrusion of the
National Guard. In Brooklyn, all the ingredients for similar outbursts

were in place. In the early part of July, sporadic and random violence broke out. On July 8, after a softball game in Bedford-Stuyvesant, an argument between Puerto Rican and black teams led to a six-hour brawl involving 100 youths. Three days later, there was more violence between blacks and Puerto Ricans, with three fight participants suffering knife wounds and a fourth who was shot. Neighbors complained to a Lindsay envoy that there were no lights in the parks, that the public washrooms were always locked, and that there might need to be a curfew to ward off youth violence. One twelve-year-old tugged at the envoy's pant leg and said, "Put some sand in the sandbox," pointing to a bare concrete pit that contained only empty cans and torn clothing.

In nearby East New York, more serious conflicts were developing, as the black–Puerto Rican tensions were joined by a white, largely Italian population. The epicenter was a small triangular traffic island where Livonia and New Lots avenues met, which happened to be where black, Puerto Rican, and white neighborhoods intersected. The train station at the end of the New Lots line was a flashpoint, and local women of all races complained to police that racial harassment at the station was so intolerable, they would not go in or out without a male escort. On a hot Thursday night, July 14, a group of white teenagers tossed a trash can into the streetside window of a black grocery store owner on Hendrix Street in East New York. Three nights later, a black youth was struck by a bullet in the back, and three Puerto Ricans were knifed in the open. The night after that, a Monday, a black woman was shot in the hip. The violence between blacks and Puerto Ricans living in three tenements on Alabama Ave.—despite the police putting the tenements under 24-hour guard—caused 200 of about 220 residents to abruptly leave. The black tenants blamed the problems on outside Puerto Ricans seeking to keep the neighborhood roiled, and the Puerto Ricans blamed Black Muslims. One Alabama Avenue tenant, Kizy Samuels, summing up the mood as moving men removed her furniture, said, "I don't know where I'm going but I'm going to get out of here."

On July 21, East New York began to unravel. At about 5 p.m. that evening, a three-year-old boy was wounded by a stray bullet, and gangs of young blacks began strolling the streets, vandalizing. Angry locals on the roofs of buildings hurled bottles, bricks and tire jacks at passing police cars below. Groups of white, Puerto Rican, and black teenagers clashed repeatedly. After the shooting, Lindsay arrived in Brooklyn with police commissioner Howard Leary. He met first with a group of concerned minorities, who called themselves the Council for a Better East New York. After hearing their complaints, Lindsay went back outside and waded into a crowd of white picketers on the Livonia-New Lots traffic island, who claimed they were representing SPONGE (an acronym for the Society for the Prevention of Niggers Getting Everything). There, he was booed and hooted, with one picketer yelling to him, "Go back to Africa, Lindsay! And take your niggers with you!" Lindsay held his resolve, found members of the white crowd who were calm enough to talk and took a small group to a bar and pizzeria called Frank's. While, outside, the shouts of, "Two, four, six, eight! We don't want to integrate!" continued, Lindsay listened to grievances. Even as he suffered insults during the talk at Frank's, Lindsay kept his jaw firm and told the whites that a full riot in East New York would be devastating to everyone. He promised that the city would bring attention and services to the area. There was suspicion of the mayor's motives, but a measure of respect had been won. As Lindsay was leaving Frank's at about 9:30, one white kid said, "I still hate his guts, but he's sure got balls."

Lindsay, feeling the situation was eased, finally left Brooklyn at 10 p.m., hopping into a patrol car for a ride back to City Hall. Thirty minutes later, he was back in Manhattan, and took a call from Gottehrer: come back to Brooklyn. Things had deteriorated. There had been a shooting. An eleven-year-old named Eric Dean had been walking with his aunt and fifteen-year-old sister, and when he got to Ashford and Dumont, about 200 yards from Frank's restaurant, a round of six shots pierced the hectic night. Dean tried to run back to his home, but collapsed in the gutter. He had been hit by a bullet from .25-caliber pistol. He was dead. Immediately, rumors swirled—Dean had been killed by the police, he had been killed by SPONGE, he had been killed by Puerto Ricans. (A black teenager later was arrested but acquitted for the shooting.) An angry group of young blacks, armed with clubs and bottles, faced off with the SPONGE picketers. "I think we're going to have a riot," Leary said. Newspapermen and television cameras were on hand as Leary's men swarmed the area, lending a surreal quality to the deteriorating scene. Lindsay toured the neighborhood briefly, then headed to Ashford Street, to spend a few minutes with Dean's grieving family. (Dean's mother was on welfare and could not afford to bury her son, so Lindsay and some of his aides later paid $450 out of their own pockets to have Dean given a proper burial.) Meanwhile, 1,000 policemen and 100 patrol cars had been brought to the area, and across the city, officers were ordered to hold for possible riot duty in East New York. But the heavy presence of police somehow kept order. It was 12:30 when Lindsay finally left. By 2 a.m., some calm had been restored, but heading into the weekend, the police stayed put.

Over the days that followed, scuffles broke out in East New York, but it appeared the potential for a riot had been defused. The size of the police squadron helped maintain the calm, but so did the restraint shown by police as tensions had been mounting. In both L.A. and Cleveland, as well as in Harlem in 1964, riots had been born from relatively minor incidents that ignited after a fidgety member of the police unwisely discharged his weapon or swung his night stick, driving mobs to violence. Leary, who had just come aboard from Philadelphia in February, had been a pioneer in the tactic of engaging a heavy police presence but with an emphasis on restraint. During the crisis in East New York, the *New York Times* reported, the police did not once fire their guns. Lincoln Lynch, an associate director for CORE in New York, told the paper that the attitude of police had gotten noticeably different, and said, "The new reasonableness on the part of the police will achieve much more in the ghetto than will brute force." But, as with the civilian additions to the police review board, the rank-and-file cops were not enthused by what they saw as lenient methods from

Lindsay and Leary. "The police did not like it," press secretary Woody Klein wrote, "but they followed orders."

The trouble in East New York was a revelation for the Lindsay administration. Wagner had been so disengaged from the far-off trouble spots of the city that it was doubtful they could be easily returned into the folds of city life, and the young new tenants of City Hall had precious little experience in dealing with the issues of those areas. There was self-congratulation that a riot had been averted, but residents did not necessarily feel safer and the methods of the neophyte administration were called into question. In order to help calm the white sections of East New York, one aide had accepted help from the Gallo brothers, notable Brooklyn mobsters. They had clout in Brooklyn, the thinking went, and however despicable their business interests might be, they had the power to prevent chaos. One story had Joey Gallo overhearing a young Italian saying he was going to "knock off some of those fucking niggers" and Gallo scolding him to stop talking that way. Refer to them as "colored people," Gallo said. When the young man muttered, "I still think they're fucking niggers!" Gallo supposedly slammed him against the wall and left him unconscious, announcing, "I said they are *colored people*." Not everyone was happy about having mobsters working with the city in a crusade for racial tolerance, however. The Brooklyn district attorney had a grand jury look into the matter, though no charges were filed.

In August, Lindsay was back in East New York and Brownsville, on another campaign-style walking tour. He had made "visible" government one of his hallmarks, but for residents in the area, the salient point was that nothing had changed. The sandboxes were still empty. Charles Koslow, owner of a kosher butcher shop that had been vandalized, said in the aftermath of the skirmishes, "Look at my store now. A wreck. Mayor Lindsay? Mayor Lindsay? I got him in hell, I got him in hell—and I never cursed anyone before." Woody Klein knew that Lindsay could be seen on the streets all he wanted, but eventually, people were going to want more. "What can it help, this walking?" said Bertha Zampas, a shoe store owner at Blake and Williams Avenue.

"He says hello and he goes away." Another store owner said, "What we need here is a stronger police force, not deals with gangsters. Let Mayor Lindsay come here at night and see how people are afraid to walk out of the house."

....

Nationally, momentum was against a healing of the racial divide, as nonviolence gave way to black power and drove away white support. The humiliating 1964 electoral defeat suffered by Barry Goldwater and the Republicans had political observers standing over the grave of American conservatism, but just two years later, things had swung back. The November 1966 elections were a major repudiation of Johnson's liberal Great Society programs. With a record 56 million midterm voters, the Republicans gained forty-seven seats in the House of Representatives, added three senators, and won eight governorships, including Ronald Reagan in California; Nelson Rockefeller's brother, Winthrop Rockefeller, in Arkansas; Claude Kirk, the first Republican to win in Florida since Reconstruction; and Spiro Agnew in Maryland. Segregationists Lester Maddox in Georgia and Lurleen Wallace (the wife of George Wallace, who had been term-limited) in Alabama won governorships. This was a repudiation of the rise of radicals. Edward Brooke, a Republican from Massachusetts, became the first popularly elected black US Senator, in part because of his assertion that, "A vote for me is a vote against Stokely Carmichael."

In New York, the referendum on Lindsay's changes to the police review board was summed up in the *Daily News* headline: "Board Is Clobbered." The paper called the result "a stunning personal defeat to the Mayor, but also revealed a pronounced white backlash." Lindsay's board had been able to win in Manhattan, but the margins in the other four boroughs (it was 2-to-1 in the Bronx and Brooklyn, with ethnically mixed populations; and in Queens and Staten Island, with more middle-class white populations, the margin was 5-to-2 and 6-to-1, respectively) showed just how disenchanted New Yorkers outside of Manhattan already were with the hopeful new Mayor. Rockefeller had retained the governorship of the state, but even that was glum news for Lindsay—it meant that he would continue to have an enemy in Albany, as well as send Frank O'Connor, who was less Lindsay-friendly than Rockefeller—back to his City Council presidency. Remarking on the mayor's woes, columnist Edward O'Neill wrote, "What was that somebody was saying about this being a Fun City?"

Lindsay's powerlessness to fix urban racial issues was laid bare by the trouncing of his civilian review board, and though race would remain an issue of great personal interest to Lindsay, there was little he could do about it in a mayoral context. From there, Lindsay's civil rights policy mostly would be limited to the success he'd won in East New York—defusing potential riots. There was a move on to bring the civil rights movement into the nation's cities, but with fear of black power, that would have trouble gaining traction. At the end of 1966, America would move on, from the domestic issue of race to the international issue of war.

CHAPTER 10

No Quarrel with Them Vietcong

ERNIE TERRELL WAS ANNOYED. HE had been in an office at Madison Square Garden since noon, and nearly an hour had passed. Terrell was the heavyweight champion of the World Boxing Association, a splinter group that had refused to recognize the widely accepted heavyweight champion, Muhammad Ali, in 1965 because of a contract technicality. Now it was late December 1966, and after a previous failed attempt, Terrell would finally get a bout against Ali, which would take place in February in Houston. Terrell had known Ali for years—he was twenty-seven, Ali would shortly turn twenty-five—going back to their days coming up as amateurs competing in Golden Gloves tournaments. For him, Ali was and always would be Cassius Clay, the loquacious kid from Louisville who was not much of a heavy puncher but whose speed and intelligence made him a unique challenge among typically lumbering heavyweights. Word came that Ali had reached Kennedy Airport, but was stuck in traffic. Terrell joked with some reporters and broadcasters about the portion of his life that had been devoted to waiting for Ali. It was about that time that Ali burst into the office, flanked by three of his Black Muslim bodyguards.

It had been a strange year for Ali. In February, his draft status for the Vietnam War had been changed by the selective service board in his hometown of Louisville from 1F, unfit for service because of insufficient intelligence, to 1A, which meant he would be eligible for a call-up at any time. Ali's reaction was emotional. He had been given the news while he was meeting with reporters, and his initial response was, "Why me? Why me?" The change in status made him angry, he said, because for the previous two years, the draft board had caused him "international embarrassment" by keeping him out of the military because he wasn't smart enough. "Why did they let me be considered a nut, an illiterate for two years?" he asked. He would appeal the decision, and would find as many possible ways to challenge it as he could come up with. Exasperated, Ali was asked about Vietnam. He didn't know much about it. He was asked about the Vietcong. He didn't know much about them, either. But he did say, in a quote that would be tattooed on his legacy, "I ain't got no quarrel with them Vietcong." It was an unfortunate utterance, and though Ali would apologize, it did not seem to matter—the backlash from the exclusively white and mostly hawkish cadre of columnists that anchored the country's sports sections had already been registered. Red Smith, one of the most widely read sportswriters and an ardent Ali critic, commented that, "Cassius makes as sorry a spectacle as those unwashed punks who picket and demonstrate against the war."

Even before his draft-status rant, the bulk of the media covering Ali had moved from bemused by brash young challenger Cassius Clay, to tepid toward new champion Clay/Ali, to outright hostile toward Muhammad Ali. When he burst into the national consciousness years earlier, Ali's self-aggrandizement could be forgiven as the braggart ramblings of a deft entertainer, but arbiters of thought in the sports world could not forgive Ali's conversion to Black Muslimism in 1964, nor his insistence that he no longer be called Cassius Clay. His declaration, after a visit to Africa, that, "I'm not no American, I'm a black man," put Ali on the forefront of the same black separatist bent that would irrevocably alter the civil rights movement. In the view of most columnists, it was one thing for black separatism to spread through the nation's ghettoes and gain a hearing on college campuses, but it was quite another for the heavyweight boxing champion of the world to shun the pre-dominantly white nation that paid him so handsomely. After his con-version, virtually no newspaper would refer to him as Muhammad Ali, only mentioning the name parenthetically. New York's Jimmy Cannon, who had elicited the booze-and-broads comment from Namath, com-pared Ali and the Black Muslims to German boxer Max Schmeling and the Nazis. Pulitzer Prize–winning *Los Angeles Times* columnist Jim Murray recalled a conversation that had Ali insisting on being called Muhammad Ali, and asking Murray, "How's come you always call me by my slave name?" To which Murray responded, "Well, you can call me by my slave name, Cassius. JIM."

When he arrived for the press conference in New York with Terrell, Ali already was simmering. Terrell would be a solid challenger, stand-ing 6-foot-6 with an 82-inch reach, a 39–4 record and a reputation for toughness—he had never been knocked down as a pro. Most experts thought he had the most legitimate shot of any contender to beat Ali. This was a nice change. Ali had fought five times in 1966, the most title defenses in a year by any champ since 1941, but had mostly fought second-class opponents, and critics compared Ali's slate of challengers to Joe Louis's run of suspect foes in the 1940s, known as the "bum-of-the-month-club." Ali was eager to see Terrell because he was one of the few heavyweight contenders in his prime, but moreover, because Terrell was among those who continued to publicly call him Cassius Clay.

When the two were interviewed by Howard Cosell at the Garden, things took an ugly turn. Terrell casually referred to Ali as Clay. When Ali asked Terrell why he continued to call him Clay, Terrell said, "Because that's your name, it says so here on the publicity paper." Ali grew incensed. "Why do you call me Clay?" he screamed. "You know my right name is Muhammad Ali. It takes an Uncle Tom Negro to call me by my slave name." At one point, the exchange got so heated that Ali and Terrell leaned in toward each other, just a few feet away. "Back off of me, man!" Ali said. When Terrell moved closer, Ali shoved him, a violation of pre-fight decorum. During the ensuing standoff (Cosell kept talking through the scuffle), Ali took another swipe at Terrell.

When Ali stormed out, Terrell seemed stunned, as were the gathered media members. No one was quite sure whether Ali was engaging in a publicity stunt, or if his eyeball-shaking anger was legitimate. In a later interview with Cosell, Ali said he was serious. "I don't like him for his actions and the way he was insisting on calling me Cassius Clay. . . . Whenever this is discussed, it's serious. I don't play with the religion or the name." Terrell shook his head and repeatedly said, "He's just an idiot."

The world found out just how serious Ali's anger was when the Terrell bout got underway on February 6. Ali eased into the fight for the first two rounds, but in the third, he was accused of "thumbing" Terrell in the eye, a dirty tactic that can blind an opponent temporarily and cause long-term damage. Terrell would require surgery for a blow-out fracture under his left eye. Years later, Terrell recalled: "What he did was grab me around the neck and started poking his thumb in my eye until he broke a vein in my eye. One eye was following him around and the eye he broke the vein in was standing in one spot." With Terrell partially blinded, Ali went after him, delivering a pounding that one writer called, "a vicious demonstration of savagery." In the eighth round, Sam Saxon, one of the Black Muslims who first introduced Ali to the sect and who was now seated in Ali's corner, began shouting, "What's my name?" It was a line Ali had used when beating Floyd Patterson in 1965, when Patterson also called Ali by his given name. That, though, was mostly a publicity put-on for Ali. With Terrell, it was different. He'd injured his eyes, then began taunting and screaming, "What's my name?" as he knocked around the bloodied and wobbling Terrell. Ali told Terrell, "I'm gonna mess you up." He called him an "Uncle Tom nigger," Ali scaled back the verbal attack after the eighth, but Terrell refused to be knocked down, and simply took a hammering for all fifteen rounds. In the press conference after Ali was declared the winner, Ali called Terrell a dog. The normally measured *New York Times* columnist Arthur Daley wrote that Ali had indulged in "racist hate," noting that "about all that Clay achieved was to keep destroying the image he once had of being the likeable charm boy. . . . Ever sharper grow the divisions in Clay's split personality. The more he improves as a fighter the more apparent becomes his retrogression as a man. It's a pity."

A little more than a week later, Ali was back in New York, arriving in Fun City to sign a contract for another fight, this time against thirty-four-year-old Zora Folley, a father of eight who was the No. 1 contender in 1958, but was now working in Chandler, Arizona. Ali was obviously chastened by the outcry after his treatment of Terrell, and had apologized for "making the ring into a speaking rostrum." Now, Ali spoke kindly: "That Folley's such a nice, sweet old man, eight little kids, calls me Muhammad Ali, thanks me all the time for giving him a chance. How'm I ever gonna get mad at him and build up this fight?" For New York, there was no trouble with build-up—the fight would be the first for the heavyweight title to be held at Madison Square Garden in sixteen years, and surely the last at the building's current location on Eighth Avenue between 49th and 50th streets. After years of delay, a new, modern $43 million Madison Square Garden built on top of Penn Station at 33rd Street and Eighth Avenue was scheduled to open around the end of the year. Having Ali put on a title fight, even against a sweet old tomato can like Folley, made good sense. The soon-to-be demolished Garden had been the most significant stage during what was a golden era for boxing. Joe Louis made his Madison Square Garden debut at age twenty-two, defended his title seven times there, and ended his career when he was KO'd by Rocky Marciano in 1951. Henry Armstrong, who for a few months in 1938 held championships in three different weight classes simultaneously, was a regular on the marquee, and the Garden was where Sugar Ray Robinson (Ali's hero) had made his professional debut in 1940, his first of twenty-five fights at the Garden over twenty-two years, including two of his six famed bouts against Jake LaMotta.

But New York as a boxing town had gone the way of New York as a town of fedoras, gimlets, and Joe DiMaggio. By 1960, television had sapped much of the appeal of live boxing, and the focus of televised fights—emphasizing hard-punching, bloody brawls over refined boxing skill—drained the sport. There were repeated scandals involving organized crime that chipped away at public faith in boxing's legitimacy, and when, in a 1962 bout at Madison Square Garden, Emile Griffith pummeled Benny "Kid" Paret into a nine-day coma that led to his death, orphaning his two-year-old son and widowing his pregnant wife, a hue-and-cry over the savagery of boxing and a clamor for its prohibition was raised from the halls of the Vatican to governors' mansions to local city councils. In 1965 and '66, a series of small but vicious riots broke out during second-tier fights at Madison Square Garden. Describing the perpetrators who ripped out rows of seats and pipes, and hurled them toward the ring, Dick Young wrote, "You saw men become beasts." Such incidents left boxing at Madison Square Garden stale and diminished as a sport. When the new Garden opened, it would be two rising sports—basketball and hockey—that would carry the building, with boxing on the East Coast moving to the casinos of Atlantic City.

But the Garden had been the capital of boxing's universe, and it should be bade farewell by Ali, the sport's reigning king. His bout with Folley would be only the third fight in the Garden for Ali, including the 1960 Golden Gloves championship he won as an amateur before achieving fame in the 1960 Rome Olympics. He obviously had some regrets about not having fought in New York more often, especially with his own career so uncertain. After signing his contract, Ali left Les Champs restaurant on 40th Street and wandered up Fifth Avenue, saying, "Love New York. Always something to do. You can go to any kind of restaurant, always find a movie, or just walk around and look at people and traffic; that's fun, too." He was beset by autograph seekers near St. Patrick's Cathedral, which, one observer noted, "made him truly happy."

Six days before his fight with Folley, Ali was in a jubilant mood. He was holding afternoon workouts in the gym underneath Madison Square Garden, where boxers would train in the days before a fight. He'd had a packed-house, open-to-the public workout in front of 240 fans with his sparring partner, Jimmy Ellis, and was delighted when Sugar Ray Robinson stopped by. "The greatest fighter who ever lived," the PA announcer claimed. Ali smiled and turned to the crowd: "Next to me." At the workout, he was also introduced to a twenty-three-year-old fighter from Philadelphia he'd heard a little about named Joe Frazier. Ali stopped to chat with Frazier, who told him, "I thought you were much larger. You look pretty small to me." Ali smiled and responded, "If you even dreamed about fighting me, you'd be in big trouble." When Ali showed up for his workout the next day, though, he was much more somber. The previous night, he had been told that his number had been drawn in the draft, and he would have to report. "You could tell, that was on his mind more than anything else," said Dave Anderson, who was covering Ali for the *New York Times*. "Everyone assumed that once he was called, he was going to go and do his two years in the Army and come back. But that day—he didn't come out and say it, he implied it—he let it be known, he was not going to take that step forward. He was going to let himself get arrested instead of going to the Army. So that fight became, is this the last time Ali is going to be out there?"

Ali went off as a 6-to-1 favorite (according to the *Daily News*; the *Times* had him at 5-to-1) on March 22 against Folley, and if he was concerned about working up enough anger to go after Folley, he was probably right. He mostly danced around Folley for three rounds, with only a few worthy exchanges between the two, and it wasn't until Ali's manager, Herbert Muhammad (Elijah's son), told him to, "stop playin'" that Ali knocked Folley with two sharp rights to the jaw that put him on the canvas at 1:48 of the seventh round. The blow that felled Folley was hardly resounding—a "six-inch punch" it was called. After the fight, Ali was sedate, and where he had called Terrell a dog in Houston, in New York, he calmly called Folley, "a respectable man." But attention immediately turned to what was next for Ali, whose future now seemed much bigger than boxing. "I've left the sports pages," he said. "I've gone onto the front pages." Reminded that he was facing the draft call the following month, Ali said, "If I thought that going to war would help 22 million Negroes get freedom, justice and equality, you would not have to draft me. I would join."

On the day after Ali's fight with Folley, a headline on Page 2 of the *Daily News* read: "Death Hits New Highs As War's Pace Rises." The story, with a dateline of Saigon, led with news of 2,092 American casualties (including 211 dead) in Vietnam in the previous week. That was a record, beating the old casualty mark, set three weeks earlier, by more than 25 percent.

A month later, at a little before 8 a.m. on April 28, Ali entered the Federal Customs House in Houston, where, along with forty-five other young men, he was given a battery of medical and physical tests over a five-hour period. When it came time to take the symbolic one step forward that signifies induction, Ali refused. The US Government announced it would begin criminal proceedings against Ali. He was stripped of his championships. An editorial in the *New York Times* worried about the psychological effect that Ali's decision would have on blacks across the country. "Clay," in the opinion of the editors, "may become a new symbol and rallying point for opposition to the draft and the Vietnam War. In Harlem, the nation's largest Negro ghetto, there were indications at week's end that Clay's refusal to be drafted was creating considerable emotional impact, particularly among the young."

. . . .

In the mid-1960s, the fellow celebrity to whom Ali was most often compared was Joe Namath. It's obvious enough why: Ali and Namath were both at the top of the sporting world in terms of talent, they were both handsome, notably individualistic, and possessing of the kind of personalities that made the old-guard establishment steam under the collar—so much so that each had a secret file at the FBI. But, below the surface, Ali and Namath could not have been more different. Ali's dedication to his religious beliefs, no matter the nature of those beliefs, and his commitment to justice for black Americans required a level of self-sacrifice that was never asked of Namath. Ask Ali at different times from 1966–67 and he'd claim that he'd lost between $3 million and $8 million in endorsement money. Namath and Ali preened for the television cameras, but the circumstances in which Ali came up forced him to develop as a three-dimensional person, where Namath (early in his life, at least) was strictly 2-D, constructed in large part out of the same, flat material that Sonny Werblin had used to create celebrities in Hollywood and music. Ali was dedicated to a cause. Namath was dedicated to, in his words, "girls, clothes and good times, and I don't need more to enjoy myself."

But Namath and Ali had something else in common in that each had been the targets of superpatriots railing over his draft status. During training camp before his rookie year, in 1965, Namath was slated to go before the draft board in Beaver Falls in August. Because the Jets were in camp, his papers were transferred to the board at Peekskill, New York, where Namath was given a temporary reprieve—Peekskill would not be calling him in August, which meant that he would again be transferred, this time to New York City. At the time, the draft was exempting married men, but when it was suggested to Namath that he get married in order to avoid being drafted, he joked, "I'd rather fight those Reds in Vietnam than get married. Too many pretty girls in this world." Namath finally went before the board for an examination downtown on September 15, and if his flippant comment about marriage did not aggravate the nation's staunch armchair generals before, his appearance at the board did. Namath showed up at 7:20 a.m., a seldom-seen hour for him, wearing shades and taking a hasty breakfast: an apple. Photographers outside the induction center asked him to remove his sunglasses, and when Namath refused, an argument ensued. Namath's shades stayed on. So the photo of Namath that ran with the stories about his five-hour exam that would determine whether he would be hauled off to fight for his country 9,000 miles away featured Namath with an apple in his jaw and shades covering his eyes.

Once inside, Army doctors especially prodded Namath's surgically repaired knee. A decision on his status was expected about two week after his original exam, but because of the sensitivity of Namath's case as a celebrity and the obvious problems with his knee, he was brought in for further examination. On October 8, without notification of the press, Namath went to Harkness Pavilion, one of the top hospitals in

New York, where he was examined by renowned orthopedist Dr. Frank E. Stinchfield, for whom Namath was but a B-List celeb. Stinchfield had been sent by Harry Truman to Saudi Arabia to consult on treatment for King Ibu Saud, and had also done knee surgery on Sonny Werblin's friend, movie producer Samuel Goldwyn. By the time the Army was ready to release its determination on Namath's status in 1965, he had taken over the Jets' starting job and was on his way to a Rookie of the Year award. His success on the field made it all the harder for the Army to put forth its conclusion: Namath would be listed as 4F, deferred from the draft based on the condition of his knee, a knee that was apparently healthy enough to allow him to star as a quarterback but not as a rank-and-file private.

Girding for an onslaught of criticism, a 500-word memo went out to members of Congress, "in view of the anticipated public reaction," according to the Army's chief legislative liaison. The memo conceded that Namath's status, "may seem illogical," but pointed out, "When playing professional football, it must be presumed that J. Namath does so with the counsel and preparation of doctors and trainers. In the military service, these conditions would not necessarily be present." The memo pointed out that Namath's knee could imperil both himself and his comrades in the heat of war. But moreover, the memo catalogued just how banged-up Namath's knee was, even after his first surgery: the medial meniscus had been removed, his anterior cruciate ligament was torn and he had a tear in the lateral meniscus. The extent of damage that combination of injuries represented was difficult for the layperson to understand, but any one of those injuries would have a modern athlete under the knife for surgery immediately, and laid up for months. Those who were incredulous that a quarterback like Namath couldn't perform as a soldier were missing the point. With that knee, it was a miracle he *could* perform as a football player.

In January 1966, Rep. Paul Rogers of Florida read a letter on the floor of the House of Representatives from an angry father in his district, whose son had also suffered cartilage and ligament injuries to his knee, as well as multiple broken noses, chronic bronchial infections and a painful bone spur in his arm, but was still inducted into the Army and was just then fighting in Vietnam. The father called Namath's deferment, "the most asinine action of the year." A House committee took up an investigation of the matter, and a general tightening of deferment standards, across all Selective Service boards, followed thereafter. The *Times* reported in February that "big-name athletes are beginning to feel the pressure of stepped-up draft calls caused by the war in Vietnam." Namath was listed as one whose status could be imperiled. The paper noted that Cassius Clay had already seen his draft status change, and that stars like tennis' Arthur Ashe and incoming Kansas City Chiefs rookie Mike Garrett were also looking at possible induction under changing draft guidelines.

Namath's status never changed, though. As hard as it was to play through the pain caused by his knee, he always would appreciate the irony. Decades later, Namath would say, "It's a trade-off. Heck, if I didn't get my knee hurt in my senior year at Alabama, what might have happened? I know darn well what would've happened. I would've been drafted into the military. I had a few physicals for the military, but I was rejected because I had a bad knee. I would've been putting guys at risk. I just accept the way it turned out and thank God a whole lot for giving me a chance to play."

....

On the very day in February 1966 that Ali was informed of his changed draft status, a bit of political drama unfolded at a hearing of Senate Foreign Relations Committee in Washington, broadcast across the country on television, seemingly creating a starting point for a national debate on the issue of the war. For more than six hours four-star General Maxwell Taylor—an adviser to President Johnson on the war—sat, facing questions from Senators. Taylor had staked his reputation on the war in Vietnam, and told the 19-member committee that the Americans did not need to add to their 200,000-troop force in the war, but only needed to step up their bombing campaign in North Vietnam, emphasizing that the North Vietnamese were losing 17,000 men per month in casualties and defections. At that rate the Vietcong would be out of fighters by the end of 1966. The tide of the war, Taylor assured the committee, was "decidedly" ours.

A handful of senators, though, was deeply skeptical of Taylor's rosy outlook, and the tenor of the session showed that opposition to the US involvement in Vietnam, widely seen to that point as the domain of flag-burning hippies and bored college intellectuals, had gone mainstream. Sen. William Fulbright of Arkansas offered tough questioning to Taylor, indulging in a speech about the horrors of the US strategy of mass bombing, which was killing civilians. "I don't see the moral distinction," Fulbright said, "between killing children and women with bombs and disemboweling with a knife because a knife is all you have." It was William Morse of Oregon who had the tensest exchanges with Taylor. Morse suggested that Americans would soon "repudiate" the way the United States was conducting the war in Vietnam, to which Taylor responded, "That of course is good news to Hanoi." Morse shot back: "I know that's the smear argument you militarists give to those of us with an honest difference of opinion, but I don't intend to get down in the gutter with you." There was ringing applause in the hearing room.

As *Washington Star* political columnist Mary McGrory wrote, Taylor "had failed to convince the dubious that this is a limited war with limited objectives." In the press the next day, the confrontation was laid out as one of Doves vs. Hawks. Those of a dovish inclination who were quietly skeptical about the war now had cause to be more vocal. Cultural battle lines had been drawn. For the Hawks, the other side was made up of Red-loving, yellow-tinged traitors. For the Doves, the other side consisted of bloodthirsty warmongers. While black power was alienating whites and splintering the civil rights movement, the war in Vietnam was superseding it in attention. A Gallup poll conducted in October 1965 showed that 27 percent of the country listed civil rights as the most important issue facing the nation, with Vietnam at 19 percent. Less than a year later, in September 1966, Vietnam surpassed race relations, by a whopping margin of 56 percent to 24 percent, as the most important issue for the nation.

New York was both a central stage and a barometer for the strength of the anti-war movement—in May 1964, the first major student protest of the war took place when hundreds of students held a rally near Columbia University, and marched from Times Square to the United Nations to voice their opposition to US involvement in Vietnam. The number swelled to 12,000 protestors when a major march up Fifth Avenue was held in the city in October 1965, one which saw a quart of red paint hurled at the vanguard of the march, followed by a pelting of eggs, apples, and according to one account, "the curses of spectators who lined the sidewalk six deep at places." A little more than three weeks after Ali fought Folley at Madison Square Garden in the spring of 1967, another march was lined up for New York, this one slated to go from Central Park to the United Nations on April 15. by now, though, the protests had taken on a different tenor. As civil rights lost momentum, more radical black leaders like Stokely Carmichael and new CORE director Floyd McKissick latched on to Vietnam as a matter of racial injustice. The numbers backed up that assertion: by the summer of 1966, 18.3 percent of the Army's combat deaths had been black soldiers, while only 13.3 percent of the troops were black and only about 10 percent of the nation's population was black. Blacks were dying disproportionately in the war. McKissick, in fact, blamed the racial battles that took place in places like Brooklyn and Cleveland in 1966, on "widespread frustration and anger toward the war." The protest movement won over another influential follower in late 1966 and early 1967, when Martin Luther King Jr. finally began speaking out against the war—his original stand was that picking sides over Vietnam would only hurt the politics of the civil rights drive. King recognized that he had been behind Carmichael and McKissick in talking about Vietnam as a racial issue, and became increasingly outspoken in his disappointment that civil rights and the Great Society of President Johnson had been abandoned in favor of what he called the "obsession" with Vietnam.

But when King wanted to make his most definitive and pointed statement on the war, he went to New York. King had approached the group, Clergy and Laymen Concerned About Vietnam (CALCAV), seeking a forum. CALCAV arranged a speech at the historic and majestic Riverside Church in Morningside Heights, a soaring Gothic cathedral tucked between Harlem and the Upper West Side, a short way from the Hudson River. The church had been financed by John D. Rockefeller, father of Nelson, who was both a friend and a patron of King. It had a long tradition of social activism and pacifism, and during World War II its liberal and internationalist preacher Harry Emerson Fosdick spoke out against the war, a particularly unpopular stand at the time. It was a perfect place for King to deliver a speech that would highlight what he knew would be a major shift in the direction of his movement, and CALCAV had gone so far as to hire a publicist to spread word of the event. On the day of the speech, the church was so packed that additional folding chairs had to be set up to accommodate the crowd of 3,000, while more listened on loudspeakers set up outside. King wanted to leave no doubt about the content of his speech, and CALCAV printed 100,000 copies for distribution, including copies for all major American newspapers. King's title for the speech was "A Time to Break Silence," but it would become known as "Beyond Vietnam."

In his address, King painted the war as an injustice being forced upon the nation's poor. TheUnited States was, he said, "taking the black young men who had been crippled by our society and sending them eight thousand miles away to guarantee liberties in Southeast Asia which they had not found in southwest Georgia and East Harlem." He told of the hard questions he heard from young black men in the ghettoes of Chicago who advocated violence as a means of bringing change, and here he delivered his most scathing and controversial line: "They ask if our own nation wasn't using massive doses of violence to solve its problems, to bring about the changes it wanted. Their questions hit home, and I knew that I could never again raise my voice against the violence of the oppressed in the ghettos without having first spoken clearly to the greatest purveyor of violence in the world today—my own government." King knew the consequences of such inflammatory talk. He would lose the goodwill of President Johnson and political allies, and would lose standing among moderate Americans. He was pilloried in the press the next day, as he expected. In Chicago, the *Tribune* wrote in an editorial, "Communism commands more faith from King than free government, and the murderers and terrorists of the Viet Cong are paraded by him as the apostles of, 'justice and equality.'" Even the liberal *New York Times* scolded him for the "error" of connecting civil rights, poverty and the war: "Linking these hard, complex problems will lead not to solutions but to deeper confusion." The speech guaranteed King would lose the middle, but by that time the divisions between black and white, between hawk and dove, between liberal and conservative had grown so great, there really was no middle remaining.

When the 15th came, the newfound power of the anti-war demonstrators was on display. Led by King and Carmichael, as well as singer Harry Belafonte, pediatrician Dr. Benjamin Spock, and scientist Linus Pauling, who had won Nobel Prizes for his work in chemistry as well as his role as a peace activist, a crowd of somewhere between 125,000 (the police estimate) and 400,000 (King's estimate) gathered for the march and the rally at the United Nations, a group around 300 times bigger than the one that had marched in New York just eighteen months earlier. They burned draft cards—about 200 of them—and while some radicals toted North Vietnamese flags, most carried signs that read, "Stop the Bombing," "Children Are Not Born To Burn," and, "No Vietnamese Ever Called Me Nigger," before listening to King's speech in front of the United Nations. There again were eggs and red paint, but now, the sheer size and solemnity (there were fewer than ten arrests) of the anti-war crowd only made the hecklers look silly and futile. Mayor Lindsay was not ready to bring Vietnam into city politics, and issued a mild statement praising the performance of the police during the march.

In a hasty press conference the following day, though, King said that, given the previous year's riots, the escalation of the war and the intractable problems plaguing the nation's ghettoes, the coming summer of 1967 could be a dangerous one. He called cities in America, "powder kegs," and warned that New York and a handful of other cities would, "explode in racial violence this summer."

CHAPTER 11

Backlash

THE THREE SANITATION WORKERS SAT easily, coats off and caps doffed, at the John Haynes Bar, on Second Avenue and 89th Street, having left their large yellow truck double-parked outside on a late afternoon in December 1966. They were on what they were calling a ten-minute "coffee" break, but it sure looked like they were drinking on the job. Not a big surprise. The Sanitation Department had earned a reputation as the city's least efficient outfit, where workers bartered for medical disability vouchers and reportedly sabotaged their own trucks in order to avoid work. The head of the sanitation workers' union, John DeLury, was mostly concerned with the political power his men afforded him, so it behooved him to keep them placated. "DeLury," one advisor from the Wagner administration would explain, "decided that part of his job was protecting his men from doing any work." The trio could not have known that, outside, an unmarked city car was pulling up to the truck, carrying the Mayor of New York and Edward Kearing, the new commissioner of the Sanitation Department. Yes, their boss and *his* boss. The Mayor told Kearing to find the men who should be occupying the truck, and when Kearing located them in the bar and brought them out, they were stunned to see a smiling John V. Lindsay waiting for them. Lindsay didn't fly off the handle. Rather, he determined that their stammering discomfort would be punishment enough. "C'mon now," Lindsay said, "let's get out and clean up this city."

Lindsay's first year at the helm of the City of New York had been mostly overwhelmed by misfortunes beyond his control. He was handed a transit strike almost as a welcoming gift and found himself engulfed in a civilian-review-board controversy that he was slow to recognize and address. He inherited a budget that was unsustainable, kept afloat by his predecessor only by putting the city into debt, which left it to Lindsay to raise taxes and transit fares. But he had made mistakes, too. Lindsay had been harsh in his personal tone, too rigidly moralistic, and quick to lose his temper, while at the same time too naïve in his approach to nuts-and-bolts governance. He'd made no allies and, in fact, was losing them. His relationship with Rockefeller had deteriorated to the point that he had not even called Rockefeller to congratulate him on his win in the November election—Rockefeller took this as an indication that Lindsay had hoped he would lose to his Democratic challenger. Bob Price, who had run all of Lindsay's campaigns for Congress, was leaving to take a job with the Dreyfuss Corporation. The Price-Lindsay relationship thrived in a campaign setting, but when it came to running City Hall, Price was too controlling and Lindsay resented the perception that Price was pulling the strings. He was just one of many early departures for the Lindsay administration: Thomas Hoving left the parks department to take over the Metropolitan Museum, press secretary Woody Klein was replaced by Harry O'Donnell, and housing chief Charles Moerdler went back to practicing law. Lindsay found that recruiting sharp young talent into the exciting prospect of city government was much easier than keeping young talent in the frustrating drudgery that was the reality of city government.

He had not been able to keep many of his campaign promises. He had taken a special interest in sanitation in the city, but with limited results, and, in late 1966, a frightening curtain of smog had enveloped the city, lasting three days. Trash incinerators had been put out of use to help air quality, but New York was generating 7 million tons of trash, and landfills were nearly running out of space. The cityscape was still dotted with the rusted out frames of abandoned cars, and though 25,000 per year were removed, there always seemed to be more to replace them. He'd promised cleaner streets, but the city was still filthy. Lindsay had promised to reduce crime, but the crime rate had nearly doubled. He had promised to cut out $300 million in "fat" from the city budget, but instead the budget kept growing, and Standard and Poor's actually downgraded the city's bond rating. He'd promised to build a bridge to minority neighborhoods, but found that he was mostly walking that bridge alone—those minorities were not necessarily ready to trust their white fellow New Yorkers, and vice versa. Lindsay would not have disagreed with white residents who felt he had not made them a priority, but rather, he sought to explain that his approach was a necessary one. At one point, when Lindsay was walking through a mostly white area in Brooklyn, he was asked, "why all the taxes came out of white pockets only to be spent on black neighborhoods. 'We have three hundred years of neglect to pay for,' Lindsay said, and half the sidewalk audience was shuffling in impatience."

At the end of year one, Lindsay was a long way from earning that "Mr. City" tag that would springboard him to national recognition. He understood from the beginning that gaining a national footing would not be easy, and he frequently brushed off inquiries about his desire for higher office, but by the end of his first year, a poll showed that, already, 51 percent of New Yorkers disapproved of his performance. When Wagner left office after twelve years, his disapproval rating had been 53 percent—essentially the same portion of the city was disappointed in the fresh, new mayor as had been disappointed in his tired predecessor. Just after the massive Vietnam protest in April, Gallup released results of a poll it had taken of Republican county chairmen across the nation, asking their preferred candidate for the party's Presidential nomination the following year. Far ahead of the pack was defeated 1960 nominee Richard Nixon, who had the support of 1,227 chairmen. Second on the list was George Romney, governor of Michigan, picked by 341 chairmen, ahead of new California Governor Ronald Reagan. Fifth on the list was Nelson Rockefeller, who was firm in his insistence that he had no interest in trying for the presidency again after his failed 1964 bid. Way down at No. 9, with the support of just ten county chairmen, was New York City Mayor John V. Lindsay.

But 1967 provided some shot at redemption for Lindsay. King, it turned out, had been right about urban violence and the upcoming summer. The escalation in Vietnam grew more divisive, and in August, the *Times* ran a story pointing out that the US force in Vietnam would grow to 525,000 in less than a year, that 12,269 Americans were dead already and that, "Victory is not close at hand. It may be beyond reach." Alongside the spiraling war, racial divisions in American cities grew ever deeper, and the ghettoes became more violent. New York was always a city in peril, and gave the impression of not just on the brink of a riot, but on the brink of a full-scale race war. In October 1966, an ultra-right-wing group known as the Minutemen, a national organization whose New York contingent was mostly located in Queens, had been infiltrated and found to be holding an enormous stockpile of weapons that included bazookas and tons of ammunition that were to be used in a plot to bomb radical left camps, what the *Daily News* called, "the first time that the supersecret, ultraright organization has attempted a warlike act." One police spokesman said that the rise of militant whites, "is part of the white backlash, too." Meanwhile, militant blacks in the city were gaining strength, too. The Black Panther party, which saw American blacks as engaged in an armed struggle and had thrived on the West Coast, had arrived in New York, was accumulating an East Coast following and would soon take in the remnants of SNCC and make Stokely Carmichael their "prime minister." In June 1967, sixteen members of the Revolutionary Action Movement, a black militant group, were arrested and charged with a plot to assassinate moderate black leaders like Roy Wilkins of the NAACP and Whitney Young of the Urban League, as well as Senator Robert F. Kennedy. Police reported recovering 30 weapons, 1,000 rounds of ammunition, 275 packets of heroin and assorted explosives. Defendants—both for RAM and the Minutemen—insisted that the charges had been trumped up, and many were acquitted, but the steady stream of reports exposing violent plots among extremists created a very real sense of impending domestic war.

Lindsay was an easy target for backlash among whites who felt his lax treatment of looters and lawbreakers would only encourage future disturbances, and reinforced the perception that Lindsay was giving away the city to minorities. Bronx Rep. Paul Fino, a conservative Republican who served with Lindsay as part of New York's congressional delegation, did little to hide his distaste for Lindsay's high-minded Manhattan liberalism. In May 1967, Fino himself was on a ladder pulling off the burlap covering of a twenty-by-eight-foot billboard over the Willis Ave. Bridge, which connected Manhattan to his district. "Fun-City Line Ends Here!" the billboard's headline read, and, "Republicans of Bronx County Want No Fun Riots, Fun Taxes, Fun Crimes, Fun Mayor." As it was unveiled, a crowd of about fifty flag-waving supporters cheered. Some accused Fino of playing to his increasingly conservative base of Italian and Irish homeowners in the Bronx (he had been a moderate, and even somewhat liberal, when he first was elected to Congress), and there was a rumor that his split with the mayor came in 1965 when, after Lindsay's election, Fino had requested a law partner of his be made sanitation commissioner. Lindsay supposedly rejected the idea, and Fino would not forgive the slight. Whatever the provenance of their feud, Fino had little trouble plucking at the race issue to agitate his constituents.

Three weeks after the RAM arrests, riot season began in earnest. Riots broke out across the Hudson River from Manhattan in Newark, spreading to other New Jersey suburbs and leaving twenty-six dead. Amid reports of gunfire exchanges with snipers, perhaps outside agitators, the National Guard was called in, as Governor Richard J. Hughes declared the city in "open rebellion" and added that, "The line between the jungle and the law might as well be drawn here as any place in America." It was the worst rioting in the country since Watts in 1965, and remained so until another riot exploded in Detroit later in July, a five-day disaster that left more than forty dead and about 2,000 buildings destroyed, and an estimate of up to $75 million in property damage. By some counts there were as many as 150 race riots in the country in the summer of 1967, many concentrated at the end of July. But, for the most part, New York was spared. On July 27, under the headline "Cities in Turmoil" the front page of the *Washington Post* featured race-riot dispatches from places as varied as Phoenix, Chicago, Toledo, Englewood, New Jersey, and Saginaw, Michigan. There was a report from New York, too, where residents of Spanish Harlem had been fearing a riot among Latino youths after days of anti-police violence had broken out, leaving three dead. The NYPD, too, had been fearing that the unrest in Harlem would spread to other areas and thin out the ranks of the cops who had managed to keep the peace. But some well-timed rain cooled the situation and, as the *Post* reported, Lindsay got a "hero's reception" when he showed up that night. "Cheers of, 'Viva Lindsay!' went up as the unescorted Mayor hopped out of his car, coatless and with his shirtsleeves rolled up, to walk nearly a mile through the steaming slum streets," the report read.

That evening at a little after 5 p.m., President Johnson called Lindsay at his residence at Gracie Mansion, and opened by saying, "John, you know what I think of you. I've got to ask you to be the good American I know you to be." Johnson told Lindsay that he would be giving a speech that night and was likely to announce the formation of a seven- or nine-man commission (it wound up being eleven) to study the causes and potential remedies for the rioting that had been going on in the cities. "I want nothing but competence," Johnson told Lindsay on the phone, "and I want nothing but compassion and I want nothing but patriotism." Governor Otto Kerner of Illinois would be the chairman of the committee, but Johnson wanted Lindsay to be vice chairman. He rattled off some of the other candidates for the commission, and abruptly told Lindsay, "I don't want you to even consider thinking about it. I just want you to say, 'Yes, sir.'" To which Lindsay responded, "Yes, sir. I will. You ask it, I will do it."

The commission, it seemed, was his opportunity. Lindsay would have a national platform from which he could advocate for the saving of America's troubled urban areas. He could yet earn his Mr. City title.

....

The summer of 1967 was one of discontent for Joe Namath, who showed up at training camp with thick sideburns and a shaggy-headed new look, which caused coach Weeb Ewbank to sigh and request that Namath get himself trimmed up. (He didn't.) Much like John Lindsay, Namath had marched into Manhattan in 1965 as a guy who did not look much like his predecessors and certainly did not sound like them, but who carried a promise to shake up the established order nonetheless. His first two seasons quarterbacking the Jets didn't bring about much change, however. All told, New York had gone 11–14–3, and the good that Namath had done (37 touchdowns) was easily outweighed by the bad (42 interceptions).

The fascination with his swingin' lifestyle that had dominated in 1966 gave way to criticism of that very lifestyle, and doubts about whether a hard-drinking, fornicating star could ever be the anchor for a winning team. When he arrived in Charlotte for the Jets' fourth exhibition game of the summer on a Friday in late August, Namath was not in much of a mood to speak to anyone. The Jets bus rolled up to the team hotel, and when Namath emerged, *Charlotte Observer* columnist Mel Derrick asked for an interview. Namath attempted to blow him off, but when Derrick persisted, Namath finally said, "All right, but no stupid questions. Y'all understand?" Derrick was just a few minutes into his questions when he apparently offended Namath's stupid-question ban. "How do you relax in the offseason?" Derrick had asked. Namath walked away. That night, Namath was a guest of the Charlotte Sportsman's Club, at a $500-a-ticket fundraiser, and arrived in a lace-front shirt with a pinch of chewing tobacco in his gums and a steady line of tumblers of Scotch on his lips. He made an off-color remark about Auburn, spoke of the "indignities heaped upon him by the scurrilous New York press," and finally got around to berating the Jets for their decision to release defensive back and Namath friend Ray

Abruzzese in favor of Henry King, whom Namath called—entirely without irony—"some rich rookie." When approached for autographs by local kids, Namath signed, "Best wishes, J.W. Smith." *Houston Chronicle* Oilers reporter Wells Twombly wrote that, "Possibly the last Southern city to be so honored by a guest was Atlanta, which once had Gen. William T. Sherman banging on its gates."

Three weeks earlier, when the Jets were wrapping up their practice sessions in sweltering heat at Peekskill, Namath had gotten bad news about his brother, Bob, who had been struck with sudden paralysis in his legs. That had special significance to Namath's mother, Rose, whose brother had the same symptom years earlier before he died suddenly. Upset, Namath went to Ewbank to ask for time off. Ewbank reminded Namath that the team was to begin its exhibition slate the next night, and that he should probably stay right where he was. Namath brooded. He had dinner with his teammates, a gray meal of chewy roast beef and runny potatoes. He was fed up. He left, and made the ninety-minute drive to Manhattan. Namath did not return until noon the next day, where he found a crowd of disgruntled teammates.

Namath did have family concerns to deal with, but on that night, he had chosen to deal with those concerns by skipping out on training camp and getting together with his lawyer, Mike Bite, and American Basketball Association guard Art Heyman, formerly of the Knicks and part owner of the Bishop's Perch bar on the East Side. The trio was at a dingy bar called the Open End on First Avenue near 76th Street (next door to Heyman's place), and they were undeniably loaded. In the morning's wee hours, *Time* magazine sports editor Charles Parmiter also came into the bar, and from there, accounts varied. Parmiter attempted ask the star quarterback why he was not at training camp, but Namath was in no mood for questioning. In Namath's version of the story, Namath brushed him aside and went to another part of the bar. Parmiter told a different story, though, in which an enraged Namath shouted, "I don't need you $100-a-week-creeps going around writing about me," before he hit Parmiter, slammed his head into a cigarette machine and held him in a headlock for at least ten minutes.

Parmiter would later sue Namath, and Namath, claiming innocence, would countersue for defamation of character—in his suit, Namath also denied any "dislike" of reporters, saying he, "enjoyed consistently good relations with the press generally, and have been on cordial terms with sportswriters." Tell that to the folks in Charlotte.

But upon his return to Peekskill, his tussle with Parmiter was not Namath's primary problem. The anger of his teammates was. Namath had figured he would catch an earful and the usual $50 bed-check fine from Ewbank, a price he was willing to pay in order to get out of Peekskill for the night. (Ewbank was not so lenient, though, fining Namath $250.) He had not considered the reaction of his fellow Jets, however. Namath was struck by their disappointment. The exhibition game in Bridgeport, Connecticut, could not have gone much better, a 55–10 rout of the Patriots, with Namath getting his first action since the previous winter's knee surgery. It was after the game that Namath had to fess up, first to Ewbank and more important, to the other Jets, who could not be particularly sympathetic after seeing quotes from Sonny Werblin in the *New York Times* the next day, saying that, sure, Namath should be fined, "But you can't treat him the same as everyone else because he's not the same. He's a superstar. You have to compare him with the DiMaggios, the Mantles and the Ruths." (They'd probably be even less enthused if they'd learned that, later that summer, Werblin actually rewarded Namath with a secret contract extension that would add three more years and $105,000 to the ongoing $427,000 deal.) Werblin's protection of his precious star was an act that was wearing thin among players, not to mention Jets coaches. But Werblin and Ewbank had a working relationship when it came to Namath—Ewbank had 100 percent control over him on the field, but Namath's off-field exploits were the province of Werblin, whose PR instincts told him that for a star, there was no such thing as bad publicity, even if the star was literally beating up the press.

Veteran guard Sam DeLuca, a well-respected spokesman in the locker room and the offensive captain, approached Namath and said, "We want to talk to you. We have a right to know why you left." Namath was humbled. "I'm sorry," he told them. "I didn't realize this would have such a serious effect on you guys." He explained that he left because he was upset for personal reasons, and that he had not skipped out on camp to pursue more prurient ambitions. That didn't necessarily make it right, but it was more acceptable. "He convinced us that he believed he had a valid reason for leaving, and that it had to do with his family, that he wasn't just running off for a date," DeLuca later explained. "Whether it really was a valid reason, whether he was right, was unimportant. The fact that he believed it, that was important. That's what we wanted to hear from him."

The passing of Namath's AWOL adventure, though, didn't pull the 1967 Jets entirely out of turmoil. In what was a bad bit of foreshadowing, DeLuca tore ligaments in his right knee in the exhibition game in Charlotte. This was a big blow to the offensive line, as DeLuca was an anchor for the unit that had been entrusted with keeping Namath and his bum knee from a weekly pummeling. DeLuca was lost for the season, and at age thirty-two, he never recovered enough to play again. In the same game, Namath's backup, Mike Taliaferro, broke his right collarbone, knocking him out for the bulk of the year. In the season opener, on September 10 at Buffalo, cornerback Cornell Gordon went out with a knee injury, and his inexperienced replacement, Solomon Brannan, was burned for a key touchdown as the Jets blew a 17–0 fourth-quarter lead to lose, 20–17. Worse, star running back Matt Snell tore cartilage in his knee in the opener and would be out two months. In Snell's absence, second-year back Emerson Boozer stepped in and grew into a star himself, racking up 13 touchdowns in eight weeks. But in the first game of November, Boozer suffered, according to Dr. Nicholas, a "blown-out knee" which was about as bad a knee injury as a player could have. Boozer tore both ligaments, both cartilages and broke part of his knee cap. Nicholas would later call his reconstruction of Boozer's knee the surgery of which he was proudest.

The injuries were frustrating, but impressively, the Jets were able to withstand the blows. After the loss to the Bills, they won three straight, managed a tie against Houston (Namath threw six interceptions in that game) and won four of their next five to sit in first place in the AFL's Eastern Division, at 7–2–1, a game ahead of Houston. Despite that start, a simmering rumor popped up again: that the Jets would replace Ewbank with Packers autocrat and former Giants assistant Vince Lombardi, who would take over as coach and general manager with a partial ownership interest in the team. As for Ewbank? "He'll be kicked upstairs, win or lose," one NFL source said anonymously. If Namath sometimes chafed under Ewbank, pairing him with Lombardi would have been an unparalleled spectacle.

As for Ewbank's Jets, Namath was not immune to the wave of injuries. Without Boozer, and with Snell less than 100 percent, the Jets had no running game, creating an invitation to opposing defenses to blitz at will. In Week 7, in a win over the Patriots, Namath had his ankle rolled over by 270-pound Patriots defensive lineman Houston Antwine, an injury that had hobbled Namath so badly that Howard Cosell had reported Namath would not play in the next game. (He did.) In Week 11, Namath sprained his right thumb, which prevented him from gripping the ball tightly and testing Kansas City's stingy pass defense in Week 12, when Namath was also battling a virus that pushed his temperature to 101 degrees. In Week 13, playing against a Raiders team that he had said employed "dirty tactics," Namath suffered a fractured cheekbone. He had been hit in the face by a forearm from defensive lineman Ike Lassiter, and hurled to the ground so hard that his helmet spun off by his nemesis, Ben Davidson, the 6-foot-7 defensive end with a sharp tongue and a corned-beef face punctuated by a neat, red handlebar mustache. Namath, unwilling to give the Raiders the satisfaction of knowing the pain they'd caused him, showed up in front of the press at dinner the evening after the game, smiling and fully decked out in a green blazer, a white turtleneck shirt with French cuffs and a pair of dark sunglasses tucked into his shaggy hair. When asked about the cheek injury, Namath dodged, telling reporters, "I bit into a bad steak, a hard steak, in the morning."

There was no denying that Namath was hurting, though. For all the personnel losses the Jets suffered that year, they could not withstand a banged-up Namath. He didn't miss a game, but as the season ground on, he would deal with more and more pain. After establishing their first-place lead through ten games, the Jets suffered three straight losses in Weeks 11, 12, and 13. They entered the final week of the season in San Diego with a chance to pull into a tie with the Oilers, but when Houston beat Miami to close the year, the Jets' win over the Chargers was rendered useless. The Jets set a franchise mark for wins, at 8–5–1, but for the second straight year, they would start strong but fizzle and miss the playoffs.

Namath's numbers had been impressive. He broke the AFL's record for passing yardage before the season finale and wound up with 4,007 yards, the first quarterback in either league to top the 4,000-yard mark. He threw 26 touchdowns, second in the league, but he also threw 28 interceptions, most in the league. And, just as the preseason had been marred by Namath's August escape from Peekskill, it was an incident in December 1967 that affected how his Jets teammates viewed the capricious quarterback on whom their fortunes rested. That came in the Denver game, in Week 11, the beginning of the unraveling of the Jets' season. Earlier in the year, Jets defensive end Gerry Philbin later recalled, there had been a game in which Namath had shown up ten minutes before kickoff, looking so unkempt, "You could tell he had been out all night." But the Jets had won. Against the Broncos, a team with 18 rookies, a moribund 2–10 record and losses in 14 of their previous 16 road games, Namath and the Jets were 14-point favorites, and better yet, Denver quarterback Steve Tensi had been in traction as late as Thursday because of back spasms. But when Namath showed up at Shea Stadium that day, he was in far worse shape than Tensi. He reeked. His teammates knew he had been out with Werblin the previous night. "I saw a situation where Joe came straight from being out with Sonny, drinking all night, into a game on Sunday," Matt Snell later told Namath biographer Mark Kriegel. "He had to get in the sauna. You could just smell the booze. You knew it wasn't going to be good for him. But sometimes he played better. And sometimes he didn't. Sometimes he threw five interceptions." On this day, it would be four interceptions, in a game played on a sloppy, cold field drenched with rain. The Broncos won, 33–24, and the Jets lost their hold on first place in the East Division, and from there the Jets would complete their collapse. Losses in their next two games knocked them out of the race with Houston.

Werblin would later deny that he had kept Namath out late, explaining that he had dinner with Namath, Namath's father, and Namath's date, but that Namath and his date left while Werblin stayed with Namath's father. But that didn't matter. The perception among the players had hardened. "There were two sets of rules that were created," Philbin said. "One for Joe, one for everybody else." For the Jets to move forward, change was needed.

·········

On the morning of December 28, 1967, Red Holzman—a native Brooklyner who had grown up the son of a tailor in the Ocean Hill-Brownsville section—drove his blue Chevy Impala from his home in Cedarhurst on Long Island to the Midtown Tunnel and into Manhattan's Garment District. As he drove, he scrolled through the list of players on the roster of the New York Knicks. There were twelve altogether, but eight of them he knew particularly well, having personally studied and advocated for them as draftees as part of his eight years as the Knicks' chief scout. There was star big man Willis Reed from Grambling State, second-year scoring forward out of Michigan Cazzie Russell, point guard Howard Komives of Bowling Green, shooting guard Dick Van Arsdale from Indiana, DePaul guard Emmette Bryant and rookies Walt "Clyde" Frazier from Southern Illinois and Phil Jackson from North Dakota. It was, Holzman knew, a talented group.

There was one peculiar standout on the roster, a player so good as a collegian at Princeton that Holzman only needed to see him once to know he could be a superstar, and didn't scout him again thereafter: swingman Bill Bradley. Just before the 1965 draft, Lakers coach Fred Schaus had said of Bradley, a three-time All-American who had averaged more than 30 points as both a junior and senior, "He is the most exciting player to come out of college since Oscar Robertson and Jerry West." The Knicks had territorial rights over Bradley, and exercised them. But Bradley bucked expectations, not to mention a lucrative basketball career, and chose to accept a two-year stint at Oxford on a Rhodes scholarship, to prepare for a law career. When his time at Oxford was up, the Knicks persuaded him to put off lawyering for a bit and play in the NBA. He had, though, been a disappointment to Knicks fans who expected him to be the high-scoring savior he was in in college. Instead, in the 1967–68 season, Bradley averaged just 8.0 points in 45 games.

Holzman had been disappointed that, in previous years, the players he pushed the team to draft had been so utterly unable to become consistent winners. Well, it would now be his job to fix that. The day before, Holzman had been named coach of the Knicks following the dismissal of Dick McGuire. It was a job Holzman never really wanted. He had been perfectly happy as a scout, still very much a part of the game without having to put up with the pressure of head coaching. Holzman had undergone the rigors of running a pro team before, working four years as the head coach of the Hawks before he was fired. He didn't need that again. But the Knicks were 15–22. If he did not take the head coaching job, Holzman figured, the organization would move to the next guy on the list and hire him, and if they did that, they'd probably hire a new scout, too.

Holzman had an aw-shucks, self-deprecating humor about him, and wasn't comfortable in the spotlight. When he was told by a reporter that he dressed like it was 1956, Holzman didn't disagree, and said, "I have nine suits, all Brooks Brothers, all ordered by phone, all the same style and color. It's simpler that way." When another reporter visited his home for an interview, he noted the paneling in one of Holzman's rooms and asked what kind of wood it was. Holzman shrugged. "It's wood," he said. "Wood's wood." His postgame cocktail: beer, in a paper cup, with ice. But Holzman couldn't be so laid-back if he was going to coach. He'd have to toughen up. If he didn't, he would be challenged by the players. Holzman had earned a reputation for strictness mixed with humor in his tenure with the Hawks. At halftime of one sloppy game in 1953–54, Holzman pulled out a picture of his infant daughter, and showed it around the locker room, proudly commenting, "Isn't she pretty?" His bewildered players agreed she was. "Well, you guys are going to kill her if you keep playing this way. I'll get fired and I won't be able to feed her."

The Knicks had been given too much slack by McGuire and had developed a reputation as overpaid, spoiled underachievers. On that first morning of Holzman's tenure, Van Arsdale and Komives strolled in a few minutes late for practice. They had stopped off at Nedick's, a fast-food spot nearby, for doughnuts and coffee. Holzman fined them $10 each. The pair protested—a few minutes late had never before warranted a fine—but Holzman stood firm, and his message was received. He would be holding players accountable, even on the little things. There would be no eating in the locker room, before or during a game. Families and friends, who too often turned the late part of Knicks practice sessions into minor jamborees of snapping cameras and crying babies, would be banned from practices. "I mean business," Holzman told his players, "and I want to start school straight." The Knicks responded to Holzman's tighter grip, and went on a six-game winning streak that brought them within four games of .500 in early January.

Holzman, though, was not the first new guy to make an appearance among the coaching ranks of major New York sports franchises in late 1967. It would be months before the Mets would open the 1968 season, but while the Red Sox and Cardinals were battling for the '67 World Series crown in October, the Mets were busily recruiting a new manager—former Dodgers great Gil Hodges, who had a brief hitch with the newfangled Mets at the end of his playing days. After Casey Stengel's retirement, Wes Westrum was given the managerial job, but like the Knicks and Dick McGuire, there was not much discipline or accountability under Westrum. "He was always second-guessing everybody," catcher Jerry Grote said, "so we didn't have a whole lot of respect for him." The Mets were ready to shed their gig as the perennial sad-sack, but after a brief interlude in ninth place in 1966, they'd fallen back to 10th in 1967, and Westrum resigned with eleven games to go in the season. Attendance, which had been so encouraging in those early and futile Mets seasons, had waned, down more than 367,000, forcing the Mets to do something utterly un-Mets-like. They went after Hodges, who had another year on his contract and was having some success in Washington, where he had pulled the Senators (an expansion team in 1961) from the bottom of the American League to sixth in 1967. When the Mets slipped in to steal Hodges, the Washington press was outraged. Veteran columnist Shirley Povich labeled it, "the rape of the Washington Senators by the New York Mets," and deemed the Senators, "helpless against baseball's code of the jungle, the honorless system that condones this form of wife-stealing." Povich might have been a bit extreme in his view of the Hodges affair, but the point registered: the Mets, so long lovable in their haplessness, made the kind of cold, Machiavellian play for Hodges that one might expect from the Yankees.

Hodges was sharply different from Westrum—quiet but self-assured, baseball savvy, described by former player Frank Howard as "a very dapper ex-Marine—shoes were shined, pants were pressed, clean shaven every day." That also made Hodges sharply different from the garrulous and besotted Stengel. He was, unlike the Ol' Perfesser, short on small talk, pleasantries and late-night pow-wows. But New Yorkers knew him, and he knew New Yorkers. It wasn't easy for Hodges to leave behind what he had been building in Washington, but he had played eleven years and earned eight All-Star selections as a player in Brooklyn. He still lived there with his wife, Joan, his son, Gil Jr., and his three daughters, and had interests in bowling alleys in the area. When Hodges was discussing the Mets offer with Joe Pignatano, his friend and a coach on his staff, Pignatano told him, "Gil, we busted our butts in Washington. This club is getting close to becoming a team that can fight for the pennant."

To which Hodges replied, "Joe, we're going *home*."

CHAPTER 12

"Nothing but garbage and rats"

By the outset of 1968, John Lindsay was gaining the increased national footing he had sought when he decided to run for mayor in 1965. The biennial brinksmanship that had traditionally marked negotiations between the Transit Authority and the Transport Workers Union had been avoided. Mediator Theodore Kheel, who had a close-up view of Lindsay's disastrous performance in his negotiations with Mike Quill, said that, this time, the mayor, "handled himself perfectly," and added that "the difference between this Lindsay and the Lindsay of the 1966 transit dispute is like the difference between day and night." Lindsay was honing his message, too, as the spokesman for American cities. As mayor, he had mostly refrained from comment on national politics, but in the wake of the massive Central Park-to-the-UN anti-war march in April 1967, Lindsay began making the same connection that Martin Luther King, Muhammad Ali, and Stokely Carmichael had all been making—that the Vietnam War was not just a moral problem, it was a problem of fiscal priorities, and thus, a problem of cities and slums and race. He appeared on *Meet the Press* on New Year's Eve 1967, and told the national audience that if more federal money could not be found to support American cities, "the obligations the United States feels it has in Vietnam and elsewhere ought to be re-examined." Lindsay explained, "Possibly the most serious international issue that faces the country is the deterioration of the American cities. . . . Whatever must be done should be done in order to put the needs of the cities as a matter of first priority."

Lindsay's position on the Kerner Commission gave him a platform on the urban crisis, and few had the intimate experience with the crisis that he had. But Lindsay's vision for the commission was significantly different from that of President Johnson, who expected the resulting report to be a mealy, fact-finding affair that mostly focused on quelling paranoid fears of white Americans, who were largely concerned that the 1967 riots in Detroit, Newark, and elsewhere had been pre-planned and coordinated by outside agitators. The commission had been definitive on that—there was no evidence of outside agitation—and it was one of the few bits of information that was allowed to be leaked to the media from the commission's closed summer hearings. Polls showed that an overwhelming majority of white Americans, fueled by specious media reports and the rhetoric of the extremes, believed that the riots had been organized by a central group. Black militant leaders spoke the language of nationwide rebellion, and put the riots into that context, while many white officials legitimized rumors that the same riot-starters who had been seen in Newark had been seen in Detroit, and in Chicago, and in Watts, and so on.

In Newark, Captain Charles Kinney, part of a police squad that had studied the riot, created a stir by insisting it had been instigated by Communist conspirators "desirous of changing the form of government in America." They took their cues, Kinney said, "right from Peking, and it's coming from China by way of Canada." That's what President Johnson wanted from the Kerner Commission: findings that would hush conspiracy theorists like Kinney, and little more. He wanted recommendations that would not require a significant financial commitment from the federal government, whose budget was sinking under the weight of the Vietnam costs. Rather than aiming their report at Washington, Johnson wanted to see the Kerner commissioners keep their focus on simple steps that could be taken by mayors and governors.

But Lindsay had bigger things in mind than quelling white angst and protecting the war in Vietnam. He was distressed that the commission could not expect much resistance to Johnson from the low-key Otto Kerner. (Once a dynamic protector of civil rights, Kerner was now a spent force politically and had announced in January he would not run for a third term as Illinois governor for personal reasons.) As the Kerner Commission moved toward its deadline for releasing a report, at the beginning of March, Lindsay quietly seized control of the group, along with young Democratic Senator Fred Harris of Oklahoma. The two had been the most invested and the most diligent in fact-finding. Throughout the summer and fall of 1967, Lindsay and Harris made tours of different riot-torn cities, avoiding the media and local officials when possible, instead focusing on those who were at the center of the turmoil. They went to Cleveland, where the Hough riots had required National Guard assistance in 1966. They went to Cincinnati at the end of August, where they met alone with a group of black nationalists, who, "frankly informed [them] of the group's dedication to the destruction of American society as now constituted." In Milwaukee, Harris and Lindsay spent a day in a barbershop in a black section of the city. Harris later recalled that, when asked whether they faced discrimination, blacks in the barbershop couldn't really answer. "Turned out, the reason was, that they didn't see any white people," Harris recalled. "That's how segregated Milwaukee was."

Johnson was being kept abreast of what was happening on the Commission, and was angry. After all, no president in the past century had overseen more progress on civil rights and poverty than Johnson had, but now he worried that the Kerner Commission would say nothing to reflect that record and, worse, that a damning report would ultimately tarnish his legacy. A memo he received in January, as the report was being written, contained information passed secretly to the White House, beginning with: "John Lindsay has taken effective control of the Commission. A majority now accepts Lindsay's thesis that the cities are in a state of war, a $40 to $50 billion program is essential, the cities' expenditures should be comparable with the outlays for Space and Vietnam." It was bad enough that Lindsay had gotten the commission to include an enormous request for federal aid, but the memo noted that Richard Nixon, the strongest GOP challenger to Johnson in the upcoming 1968 election, planned to take the same position as the Kerner Commission report—putting Johnson in the uncomfortable position of potentially repudiating his own commission, one his opponent supported.

At one point in the run-up to the report's release, Harris, with another senator, had to go to the Oval Office to meet with Johnson briefly on a separate errand. As he shook Harris's hand, Johnson said, "I'm surprised to see you up, Fred." When Harris wondered what he meant, Johnson replied, "I heard old John Lindsay had you down and had his foot on your neck." To counter Lindsay's recalcitrance, Johnson administration officials worked up a strategy to keep Lindsay from being too personally critical of Johnson—they created a list of potentially embarrassing issues that had come up with New York City's misuse of federal Housing and Urban Development funds, and stood ready to use it against Lindsay, but only as, "retaliation to unfriendly Lindsay statements."

Lindsay, unfazed, went on the offensive. He and his staff would write the introduction and summation of report, which would have the most immediate impact and would ultimately frame its contents. Lindsay, finally, was where he wanted to be: directing national urban policy, in a visible and significant capacity. He was not quite angling to run for the presidency, but Johnson suspected he was, and a Harris Poll taken in the fall of 1967 showed that Lindsay would beat Johnson in a head-to-head matchup for the White House in 1968. Even setting his sights lower, Lindsay was well positioned as a vice-presidential running mate for a Midwestern moderate like Michigan Governor George Romney or a Californian like Richard Nixon, who was far to the right of Lindsay politically, but was pragmatic enough to put that difference aside if necessary. Romney's campaign, though, was foundering and the liberal Republican backup plan should Romney collapse—a third crack at the nomination for Nelson Rockefeller—would obviously not include Lindsay. In early January, Lindsay did an eighty-minute interview with the *Washington Post*, in which he assailed the "lethargy" that Americans displayed in dealing with the city problem. "I don't think the country gives the appearance at the moment of being ready to take up the burden," Lindsay said. "I find this extremely troubling." As if nudging his fellow committee members to strong action, he also said, "What is needed is not a bunch of promises, but a very honest statement of what we resolve to do, and that we will leave no stone unturned." In February, he said the upcoming report "will make all Americans uncomfortable," and that a five-year national program to curb riots would be laid out. Aware that the president was trying to undermine him, Lindsay got more aggressive in attacking Johnson on Vietnam, calling the administration's policy "bankrupt" and saying Johnson had, "ignored or bungled," opportunities for peace.

When the Kerner Commission report (officially titled the National Advisory Commission on Civil Disorders) was released, it was, in fact, uncomfortable. Lindsay had originally been given a twenty-seven-page document that was to provide the overview of the report, but at the eleventh hour, he had cut it to two pages, expressing an unmistakable sense of urgency that would grab attention. The report itself was blunt, attempting to gird Americans to the grim facts baring what cities had become. There were distressing statistics: one in five black Americans "lives in squalor and deprivation in ghetto neighborhoods"; that the majority of the 14,000 rat-bite cases in the United States in 1965 happened in ghettoes; that black unemployment rates were double those of whites; and that black infant mortality rates for babies from one month to twelve months old were triple those of whites. The report did not blame the riots on those who had done the rioting, but instead pointed to institutionalized white racism. The report blamed the white news media, which too often reported on the ghettoes only when they were in flames. It blamed a vague "climate that tends to encourage violence," stemming from the images of nonviolent protests met with, "white terrorism," perpetrated by authorities in the South during the civil rights movement. "What white Americans have never fully understood—but what the Negro can never forget—is that white society is deeply implicated in the ghetto," one passage went. "White institutions created it, white institutions maintain it, and white society condones it."

The report also advocated for a massive redistribution of wealth as the major remedy to the problem, including a higher minimum wage; the addition of one million government jobs; an increase in welfare benefits; and boosting government programs in education, health care, and housing. It was estimated that the full implementation of the commission's plans would cost $2 billion *per month*. Many objected that the burden for the riots had been placed on whites who had done no rioting themselves, but still, the power of the report resonated. It quickly became a best-seller, as Bantam Books sold more than one million paperback copies of the report in its first month. While it was, in its entirety, 426 pages, it was one sentence from Lindsay's summary that stuck with most readers. (Provenance of the sentence has been debated—Lindsay aides Peter Goldmark and Jay Kriegel have been given credit for the line, but it was Jack Rosenthal, later a Pulitzer Prize–winning journalist who edited the report's opening, and has a claim to it.) "This," the report stated, "is our basic conclusion: Our Nation is moving toward two societies, one black, one white—separate and unequal."

....

President Johnson had troubles. While he was attempting to manipulate the Kerner Commission report, he also was fending off a rare primary challenge of an incumbent president by anti-war Senator Eugene McCarthy of Minnesota. In early February, the *Christian Science Monitor* ran a poll of political writers in all fifty states, and found that Johnson was "definitely vulnerable" in twenty-eight states—those states carried 279 electoral-college votes, nine more than would be needed to win the presidency. On February 2, the front page of the *New York Daily News* featured what would become the photo that most encapsulated the savagery of the Vietnam War, showing South Vietnamese police chief Nguyen Ngoc Loan in rolled-up shirtsleeves, casually putting a bullet in the brain of a still-standing, handcuffed suspected member of the Vietcong from

Just minutes into his tenure as Mayor of New York, John Lindsay had a crisis on his hands—the city's transit workers went on a strike that would last nearly two weeks. Lindsay tried to set an example by walking, saying that his strolls were indicative of a "fun city." Here, he walks to City Hall, accompanied by boxer Sugar Ray Robinson. (AP Photo/Anthony Camerano)

By 1966, fiery Transport Workers Union president Michael J. Quill was looking for his "last hurrah." He got it, antagonizing Lindsay by calling him a "pipsqueak," and saying the judge who sentenced him to jail could "die in his black robes." Shortly after the strike was ended, Quill died. (AP Photo)

By the end of the 1967 season, Joe Namath had racked up more than 4,000 yards passing, a record, and brought the Jets to their first-ever winning record. But his off-field activities kept him from gaining the trust of teammates, who voted him sixth on the Jets' team MVP balloting. (AP Photo)

On March 1, 1969, a Yankee era ended when outfielder Mickey Mantle decided he would not play anymore, and retired. He received a plaque memorializing his achievements at Yankee Stadium in June 1969, with Joe DiMaggio looking on. Mantle's retirement broke a string of Yankees stars that went back from DiMaggio to Babe Ruth. (AP Photo/Marty Lederhandler)

In a way, Joe Namath took on Mickey Mantle's persona as the top rascal on the New York sports scene. Mantle retired as Namath was ascending, but the two became fast friends, even forming an employment agency, "Mantle Men and Namath Girls, Inc.," in August 1969. (AP Photo)

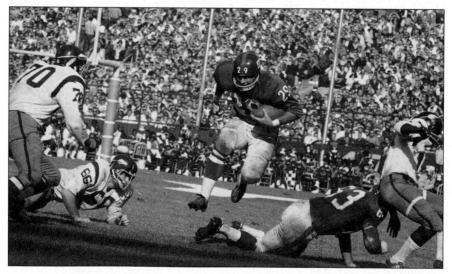

Linebacker Sam Huff (70), playing here for Washington against the Giants, had a bitter separation from the Giants before the 1964 season. Huff went on to play five more NFL seasons, and his departure was a catalyst for the Giants' collapse in the mid-60s—after winning 11 games in 1963, the Giants won 10 games combined over the next three seasons. (AP Photo)

Coach Allie Sherman inherited a dynasty when he took over as Giants coach. But as his players aged, Sherman made a series of unpopular trades, and was serenaded with chants of "Good-bye, Al-lie!" by home fans at Yankees Stadium, before he was finally let go in September 1969. (AP Photo)

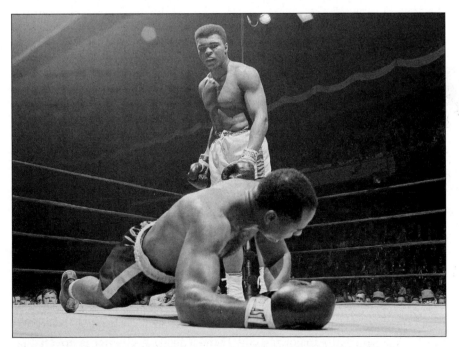

Muhammad Ali's last fight before he was scheduled to be drafted into the Vietnam War took place at Madison Square Garden on March 22, 1967. He faced thirty-four-year-old Zora Folley, whom he called "such a nice, sweet old man," and knocked him out in the seventh round. (AP Photo)

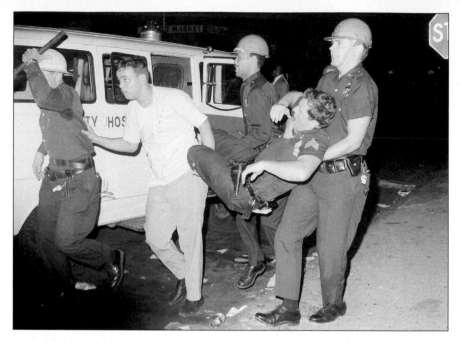

Relative to the rest of the country, New York City avoided the large-scale race riots that became commonplace during the late 60s. In September 1967, a small outbreak took place in Brooklyn after the shooting of a black fourteen-year-old. Two officers were injured, including Sgt. George Hartigan (above) but police quelled the potential riot peaceably. (AP Photo/LB)

New York police employed a policy of restraint in riot situations, one reason the city avoided a major tragedy. Here, a suspected looter is arrested on the night of Dr. Martin Luther King's assassination. Where Chicago Mayor Richard Daley ordered his officers to shoot looters, Lindsay, pointing out that most looters were teenagers, famously said, "We are not going to shoot children in New York City." (AP Photo)

On April 4, 1968, the night that Dr. Martin Luther King was killed, riots hit several cities across the US. In New York, though, the worst damage was limited to looting in Times Square. Here, police arrest a suspect after a shoe store was looted. (AP Photo/Marty Lederhandler)

Unhappy at the prospect of Robert Wagner winning the Democratic nomination for mayor and even unhappier about Comptroller Mario Procaccino, writer Norman Mailer (right) entered the race, with Jimmy Breslin (left) as his running mate. The two attracted 5 percent of the vote. (AP Photo)

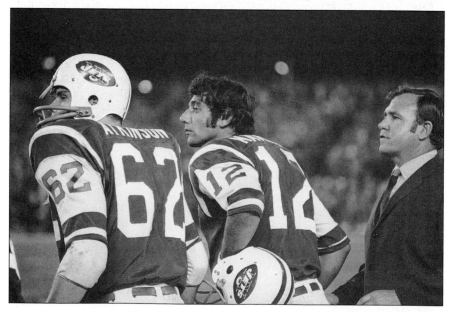

One teammate who was critical of Namath and his lifestyle in 1970 was middle linebacker Al Atkinson (62), an important cog for the Jets' defense during the 1968 season. The two were side-by-side in more peaceable times, on the sideline during an October game at Shea Stadium in 1969. (AP Photo)

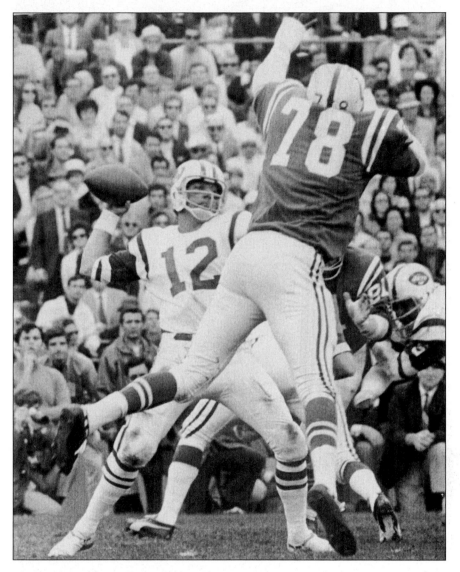

"A football player who's real good doesn't have to talk," said enormous Colts defensive lineman Bubba Smith (78) of Joe Namath during Super Bowl week in 1969. But Namath's talking seemed to give the Jets a psychological advantage that pushed them to an incredible 16-7 upset win. (AP Photo/File)

Over the course of their time in New York, Joe Namath and John Lindsay went through huge swings of public approval and disdain. In the wake of Super Bowl III, Namath was on an upswing, while Lindsay, here giving Namath a medallion recognizing the Jets' triumph, was at a low point. (AP Photo)

In February 1969, Namath played in a celebrity golf tournament in California. He had begun to grow back his Fu Manchu mustache by then, and very willingly posed for a publicity photo to highlight it. (AP Photo)

Whatever controversy Joe Namath might have gotten into with his teammates, after the Super Bowl III win, they were more supportive. Emerson Boozer (right) joined Pete Lammons and Bill Mathis to model clothing on the set of Namath's short-lived talk show in December 1969. (AP Photo/Harry Harris)

Pitcher Nolan Ryan came on in relief in Game 3 of the 1969 National League playoffs against the Braves, the first-ever postseason baseball game at Shea Stadium, and held on for a 7-4 win that sent the Mets to the World Series. Catcher Jerry Grote joined Ryan on the mound to celebrate. (AP Photo/File)

In a dryer moment, Mayor Lindsay congratulated Mets catcher Jerry Grote following the Mets' win over the Braves in the National League playoff. Later, Grote would be among the players dousing Lindsay with champagne in front of television cameras. Lindsay latched onto the Mets' run in his re-election bid. (AP Photo)

The interior of Bachelors III, the Upper East Side bar owned, in part, by Joe Namath. In the summer of 1969, when the NFL tried to force Namath to sell his stake in the bar because it was frequented by gamblers and underworld figures, Namath refused and briefly retired, before relenting. (AP Photo)

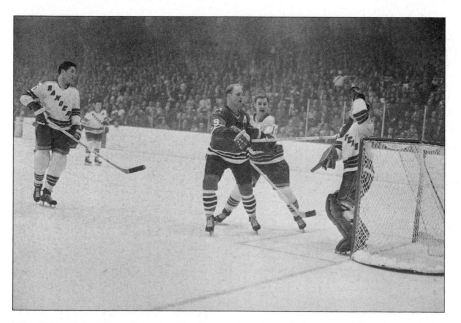

The New Madison Square Garden opened in February 1968, and its two primary tenants enjoyed breakthrough seasons. The Rangers, above, had their best winning percentage since World War II in 1967-68. (They are shown here playing a Stanley Cup semifinal series in Chicago.) Two years later, the Knicks were NBA champions. (AP Photo)

Forward Bill Bradley, shown during his first workout with the Knicks in December 1967, arrived from Princeton via a two-year stint at Oxford, where he was a Rhodes Scholar. Bradley never became the high-scoring star many expected, but he was a valuable role player for the Knicks' champions. (AP Photo)

Bill Russell (6) and the Celtics were one of the main obstacles for the Knicks in the Eastern Conference, and eliminated them from the playoffs in 1969. But Russell retired after that season, opening the way for the Knicks in the East. (AP Photo/A.E. Maloof)

A vicious Shea Stadium wind forced Joe Namath into one of his worst performances in the 1969 AFL divisional playoff game, a 13-6 loss to Kansas City
in which Namath completed just 14 of 40 passes, with three interceptions.
Namath would play eight more seasons, but never reached the playoffs again.
(AP Photo)

point-blank range, at the outset of the bloody Tet Offensive. On February 27, CBS anchorman Walter Cronkite, just back in New York after visiting Vietnam, told his audience, "To say that we are mired in stalemate seems the only realistic, yet unsatisfactory, conclusion." To which, legend has it, Johnson said, "If I've lost Cronkite, I've lost America."

For Lindsay, the outset of his own February crisis was considerably milder. In the same February 2 edition of the *Daily News*, back on page 64, under the Orphan Annie comic strip, the paper reported that the city's talks with the Uniformed Sanitationmen's Association (USA) had progressed to the point where the sides were "very close" to a deal. This was good news, because the sanitation contract was one of a handful that the Lindsay administration was struggling to wrap up, and it had technically expired back on June 30, 1967. That morning, about 7,000 sanitation workers gathered at City Hall Plaza. Sixty-three-year-old USA president John DeLury addressed the crowd, telling his union they'd reached a proposed agreement that would include a $400 wage increase, and that the decision to accept or to strike would, by union rules, be made on a mail-in vote. It would not be so simple, though. DeLury miscalculated the mood of his union. The rank-and-file was rebellious, fed up with a general lack of respect as "trashmen" and, more important, with Lindsay himself. It was the mayor, after all, who delighted in the story about pulling sanitation men out of a bar, who was leading a crusade against the filth of the city that necessarily made sanitation workers look incompetent, who had pushed an increase in productivity by, according to DeLury's statistics, 26.6 percent, while forcing unprotected workers into dangerous slum areas. The USA was bent on striking. DeLury was booed by the workers, and pelted with eggs. As he stepped off the sound truck from which he had been speaking, he was "cursed and pummeled before being conducted away by policemen."

When a beleaguered DeLury entered City Hall to talk with Lindsay and arrange the details of a settlement, the deal that had been "very close" collapsed. DeLury changed terms—he wanted a wage increase of $600, retroactive to the end of the last contract. Lindsay was stunned.

He issued DeLury a flat, "No," on the new proposal. DeLury's demands were untenable. There would be a strike.

After the smooth handling of the TWU negotiations, Lindsay now had another major municipal-worker strike on his hands. He'd weathered others—from teachers in the previous fall, from welfare workers before that—but this was different. Short breaks in welfare delivery and even in schooling could be withstood. The snarled traffic of the transit strike was an immense test for New Yorkers, but it was a test of patience and resolve. A garbage strike threatened to bring the chaos of filth, stench and health hazard. There had been a sanitation strike in 1960 (DeLury was booed by his raucous members in that one, too), but it had lasted just two days. In that short span, though, 16,000 tons of garbage had piled up on New York's streets. There were more residents creating more trash now, around 10,000 tons per day. DeLury, unlike Quill before him, was not much interested in the revolutionary nature of being a strike leader. He was a political creature, more concerned with exercising the clout his 10,000-member union had in Democratic elections in the city than in unionist idealism. New York State had recently passed the Taylor Law, replacing the Condon-Wadlin Act that had proved so toothless in the TWU strike, and provided that a leader of a municipal strike would be locked up for an automatic fifteen-day sentence. Teacher's union president Albert Shanker had done his time the previous fall, and now DeLury's membership pushed him to do the same. DeLury was arrested five days into the strike. As he was led into the jail, he was greeted by a brass band playing "When Johnny Comes Marching Home Again," and a crowd of supportive workers. Victor Gotbaum, director of the local municipal unions, said, "If you don't go to jail, you don't have credentials."

From the outset of the strike, Lindsay engaged in strong rhetoric, and employed a resoluteness that gave weight to his words. He said the USA's approach had been one of "blackmail, brute force and muscle" and using his old playbook, he appealed to the civic pride of city residents. "Now is the time and here is the place," he said, "for the city to determine what it is made of; whether it will bow to unlawful force or whether it will resist with all the strength and courage that eight million people can find within themselves." For Lindsay, the sanitation strike provided a chance to win back some control over the fat settlements to which every city union seemed to feel entitled. New Yorkers would not stand for striking garbage men for long. After two days of the strike, Lindsay toured the garbage-strewn streets and warned that there would be a health crisis if the strike were not ended in four or five days.

The following day, the scene was more intolerable. The *New York Times* reported that "the refuse spilled over onto the sidewalks and into the street gutters. In some places the mounds were higher than the automobiles parked at the curbs. Pedestrians had to walk gingerly along the walks to avoid slipping on banana peels and other discarded foods." Strong winter winds were not helping, spreading the stench and sending loose trash swirling into the streets. Elsewhere, striking workers had fired shots at the Brooklyn home of a non-striking sanitation foreman. In Queens, a glacier of trash had caught on fire and caused a five-alarm blaze, damaging four houses. Said one resident, interviewed on television, "You can't go down no one avenue without seeing nothing but garbage and rats." Lindsay, sticking with his principle of government visibility in times of crisis, roamed streets in all parts of the city. He was in Harlem when he caught sight of a large, moldy mattress. As he inspected it, a young boy asked him, "Hey, Mayor, you think you're gonna win next year?" Lindsay, with the 1969 mayoral election far from his consciousness, responded with irritation, "What's your trouble, boy?" When the kid said, "I ain't got no problem," Lindsay collected himself, smiled, touched the boy's shoulder and said, "Well, if you don't have any, let me tell you mine."

Lindsay's biggest problem was that he had no effective way to combat the USA. He'd wanted to get other city employees—firemen, highway workers, hospital drivers—to help with the removal of garbage to at least temper the growing crisis, but they, too, were union employees, and would not cross the sanitation picket line. On February 8, with stray dogs and cats scavenging on the sidewalks, sewers backed up and warnings of a growing rat infestation, the Board of Health declared a citywide state of emergency for the first time since 1931, when it had been acting on a polio scare. There had been not yet been an outbreak of disease, but Health Commissioner Edward O'Rourke said in a press conference, "There's no need to wait until somebody dies, comes down with typhoid fever, breaks his neck falling over a pile of garbage, burns to death in a fire or comes down with dysentery or hepatitis." With his options exhausted, Lindsay swallowed hard and turned to Rockefeller, hoping the governor would employ National Guard troops to remove the refuse. Lindsay wisely framed the request in the context of the Guard's role in other cities. Where places like Los Angeles, Chicago, and Newark used troops to suppress riots, in New York, they'd be used to alleviate a health crisis. Good PR, there.

Rockefeller, though, was not impressed by the logic. The presence of the National Guard on the streets of New York City might incite violence in vulnerable areas, and using the Guard to break the sanitation picket line would probably lead to a wider strike. Besides, it just wasn't the National Guard's duty to pick up trash. "You can't move garbage with bayonets," Rockefeller said in a press conference. He agreed to get involved on the negotiating side, but he was guided by dual motivations: he would bolster his national presidential profile by rescuing the situation, and would simultaneously humiliate Lindsay. Rockefeller got DeLury out of jail and, with a new panel of mediators, worked out a deal under which the USA would accept a $425 increase, just $25 above the original deal. Even that, though, was too much for Lindsay, who held strong on the $400 agreement. Lindsay, aides told reporters, was, "incensed" and New Yorkers got a sampling of that anger later that night, when he made a radio address from Gracie Mansion and microphones broadcast him using profanity as he told an aide to shut the door. "I had hoped the governor would join me in combating the extortionist demands of the sanitation union," Lindsay said. "I deeply regret that he has chosen not to do so."

Rockefeller then tried a run around Lindsay, telling the sanitation men that they could go back to work under their new agreement because he would assume control over the Sanitation Department on a temporary basis—a stunning and unprecedented state takeover of a city department that hit at the basic notion of home rule for the city.

On February 11, after nine days, New York's sanitation trucks were fired up again and the difficult task of clearing out nearly 100,000 tons of trash over the course of a bitterly cold day was begun. But the Rockefeller-Lindsay battle was ongoing. Rockefeller's maneuver drew outrage, not only from New York City residents but from all over the state and the nation. After the announcement of the settlement, the *Times* labeled the deal, "The Governor's Surrender." The *Daily News* was a bit more colorful: "Sellout! Complete el foldo!" Fellow Republicans with presidential ambitions piled on, too. California Governor Ronald Reagan said Rockefeller was "treading on pretty thin ice when he tries to run the major cities." Nixon said, "To acquiesce to this type of blackmail is to invite repetition not only in New York, but in every great city in America." Romney said he would have sent in National Guard troops. The state legislature, keenly aware which way the public-relations wind was blowing, backed Lindsay and refused to approve the governor's Sanitation Department takeover.

The situation became an utter embarrassment to Rockefeller, as well as to DeLury, who would eventually accept mediation (a dread fate for city union leaders) that left his men with a fifteen-month contract in which they'd receive the agreed-upon $400 increase for the first six months, and just nine months at $425. Lindsay emerged triumphant, though he suffered some bruises, too. As City Hall columnist Edward O'Neill wrote, Lindsay was facing an "incongruity" in the wake of the garbage strike. He had given more in union concessions than any other mayor in the city's history, but union leaders were stridently against him and, "In fact, they'll oppose him to a man if he seeks reelection." The bitterness of his relationship with Rockefeller, too, hurt Lindsay's public image. The rumored behind-the-scenes brawling between the two was no longer a rumor, and no longer behind the scenes. "There's nothing secret about it now," wrote columnist James Desmond, in the days after the strike was settled. "The two are locked in a grim struggle for control of the Republican Party."

Even before New York's strike was settled, sanitation men in another major US city walked off the job—in Memphis, where about

1,000 workers, all of whom were black, refused to report to work until demands of higher wages and better conditions were met. An angry Mayor Henry Loeb told strikers, "This is not New York. Nobody can break the law. You are putting my back against the wall and I am not going to budge." That strike would drag on for two months, and gained national attention when Martin Luther King went to the city to support strikers in late March and early April.

....

A few days after the end of the sanitation strike, New York marked a milestone: the new $43 million Madison Square Garden was set to open after a mammoth construction undertaking whose plans were originally laid out in 1960. The project had been bumped back multiple times and dogged by controversy—to build the new Garden, the Beaux-Arts masterpiece that Penn Station had been was razed, and the ensuing outcry of architects and citizenry led to the establishment of the New York City Landmarks Preservation Commission in 1965. But the new arena was part of a remaking of the area, which had only one office building erected since World War II. Now, there would be a 29-story office tower adjacent to the Garden at Two Penn Plaza, and another 52-story, 1.8 million square-foot building planned for just north of the arena. In fact, the entire lower portion of Manhattan, from Midtown down to Battery Park, was experiencing a staggering office-tower construction boom that had begun under Wagner but accelerated under Lindsay. In 1967, a postwar record of 7.8 million square feet of office space was built, which would increase to another 8.8 million square feet in 1968, 10.2 million square feet in 1969 and 14.3 million square feet in 1970. In the final year of the boom, according to the city's Economic Development Administrator, New York accounted for 25 percent of all commercial development in the United States.

The boom provided jobs and opportunities, but it was not universally loved—it was also dirty, too focused on areas that were already well-off and causing too much crowding. "Size can mean healthy growth or cancer," said architect Percival Goodman. "In New York, it's become cancer." In August of 1968, construction would begin on the pet project of financier David Rockefeller (Nelson's brother), the twin towers of the World Trade Center. Those, too, were controversial. In May 1968, a group known as the Committee for a Reasonable World Trade Center ran a nearly full-page ad in the *New York Times*, claiming that the 1,350-foot towers should be no taller than 900 feet because they would interfere with television signals and that the towers would make navigating the area by air so dangerous that, "airline pilots feel the risk is unjustified." To emphasize the point, the ad featured an artist's rendition of the towers, with an airplane poised to fly into them.

The opening of the Garden was not without controversy. It was spacious, and among the benefits of the new layout was supposed to be completely unobstructed views, because the mezzanine section was set back within the lower bowl and the roof was held up by cables—at 425 feet, it was the largest cable-supported roof in the country—eliminating the need for support posts. But when the NBA opened the building with a double-header of Celtics vs. Pistons followed by Knicks vs. Rockets, those seated in the first row of the mezzanine found that the six-inch brown metal railing actually did obstruct their view. They also found that there were no restrooms or concession stands on the mezzanine level, and would have to take five escalators down to the nearest ones. The first game was delayed by thirty minutes because the metal basket stanchions had not been wrapped with rubber, and once it got underway, the crowd found that the large electric scoreboard was not working, and the only way to know the time and score was to listen to the PA announcer. It was worse for Rangers fans attending NHL games, where those in the mezzanine were unable to see plays at the goal, and those with high-priced seats near mid-ice could not see into the corners. A week after the NBA debut, upset Rangers fans showed up at the second Garden NHL game and were given yellow hand-bills with the headline, "Obstructed View," and asking, "Will (Rangers executive) Bill Jennings pay your chiropractor bill?" and, "Does he supply periscopes?" After that display, Garden Chairman Irving Mitchell Felt held a press conference and promised to fix the issues that had plagued the building's opening. "The obstructions sicken us," he said. "You're damn right they do."

A more profound controversy darkened the opening of the arena. On February 16, the New York Athletic Club was scheduled to hold its annual indoor track meet, the oldest in the country, at the Garden. It would be the 100th anniversary of the first meet, and the NYAC was preparing a gala celebration. But in December, Dr. Harry Edwards of San Jose State, who was organizing a black boycott of the upcoming Olympic Games in Mexico, held a press conference in New York, proposing black athletes skip out on the NYAC event, too. This would be considered something of a trial run for the action on the Olympics.

The boycott of the Garden event was a relatively easy sell to black athletes, because the NYAC was demonstrably racist, prohibiting black and Jewish members. The matter had been co-opted by the likes of radical SNCC-Black Panther activist H. Rap Brown, who was asked what should be done if the NYAC went ahead and held the track meet. "I think Madison Square Garden should be either burned down or blown up," he said. Edwards was a more thoughtful militant, and, speaking to *Times* columnist Robert Lipsyte, said he understood that the coming Olympic boycott would be tougher because the issues—race, war, oppression— were wider and more complex. But he was determined that sports was the appropriate forum in which to make these points on behalf of blacks. "It seems as though the only way we can reach a lot of the people is by showing them that all is not well in the locker room," Edwards said. "No one attempts to change anything he's not in love with, and the Negro loves his country, fights for it in war and runs for it. The tragedy here is that the country the Negro loves doesn't love him back." When the track meet went off, there were threats, but no one blew up the Garden. The meet got second billing. The success of the boycott was the headline. The mystified crowd of 15,000 saw only nine black athletes compete while, outside, there were, as Lipsyte described it, almost 2,000, "demonstrators in black combat boots and dark glasses surging around the arena, Cause groupies screaming for murder in the February night."

For the building's regular NBA and NHL tenants, controversies faded and opening-week bugs were smoothed out. What's more, the two teams seemed to like playing in their new home. The bigger building allowed the Rangers, who had been forced onto a shrunken rink at the old Garden, to have regulation-size ice, which allowed the team to play, according to star Rod Gilbert, "better position hockey." The Rangers went 13–5–1 after the building opened, including an 8–3 record at home. They finished 39–23–12 in the newly expanded NHL, which doubled from six to twelve teams, earning their best record since 1942. The Knicks seemed to benefit, too, winning their first four games at the new Garden, and closing out with a 9–4 record in their final 13 home games, playoffs included. There was special excitement around this version of the Knicks, who had rallied under Holzman to finish 43–39, their first winning season since 1959. They lost their playoff series to Philadelphia, but took the powerful Sixers to six games and lost one, on the road, in double-overtime. "They will be right up there next year," Philadelphia star Wilt Chamberlain said, "fighting with us." Bradley had a rough first year, but he was still only twenty-four. Leading scorer Willis Reed was twenty-five. One of the league's top rookies, Walt Frazier, was just twenty-two and might have been Rookie of the Year if not for an early-season ankle injury. Frazier had also taken a cue from teammate Dick Barnett, and begun to wear, "sharp, bright suits, ties, coats, flowing breast pocket handkerchiefs," and $80-per-pair alligator shoes. Frazier liked wearing wide-brimmed hats so much that teammate Nate Bowman began calling him, "Clyde," after Warren Beatty's natty version of Clyde Barrow in the movie, *Bonnie and Clyde*. But, Frazier pointed out, "I had my hat before the movie came out."

CHAPTER 13
Of Riot, Revolt, and Hair

ON MARCH 31, 1968, A gallup Poll showed President Lyndon Johnson in an approval-ratings freefall. Not only was Senator Eugene McCarthy challenging him within his own party, but New York Senator Robert F. Kennedy clouded the picture by entering the race for the Democratic nomination, too. Johnson had been vice president under John F. Kennedy, but Johnson was far from friendly with the second Kennedy. For LBJ and RFK, there was nothing but overt and mutual disdain. Johnson's approval rating was 36 percent, lowest of his presidency and a full twelve points lower than it had been three months before. Just 26 percent approved of his handling of the Vietnam War, down from 39 percent in January. Johnson announced in a hasty Rose Garden press conference that he would address the nation on television that night, about Vietnam and "actions" he was planning, but he was cagey when pressed for details. In front of the camera that night, he did speak almost entirely about Vietnam, and announced a near-cessation of US bombing in order to clear the way for peace talks. But it was what he said near the end of the speech that reverberated around the nation: "I shall not seek, and I will not accept, the nomination of my party for another term as your president." Just like that, Johnson had scheduled his own release from the vise grip of the presidency. He was out of that November's presidential contest. The vacuum would be filled by

Kennedy, McCarthy or Johnson's vice president, Hubert Humphrey for the Democrats, and Richard Nixon for the Republicans, challenged by unannounced quasi-candidacies from Nelson Rockefeller on his left and Ronald Reagan on his right. Committed urbanists still hoped that John Lindsay would enter the fray, but he continued to insist that 1968 would not be his year.

Later that week, Lindsay and President Johnson were at St. Patrick's Cathedral on Fifth Avenue, along with about 5,000 other dignitaries—including Senator Kennedy, Jackie Onassis, former Mayor Robert Wagner, and Senator Jacob Javits—to witness the Rev. Terence Cooke installed as the seventh archbishop of New York. It was a Thursday, April 4, and that night, the mayor and Mary Lindsay went to the Alvin Theater on 52nd Street for the opening of the musical, "The Education of H*Y*M*A*N K*A*P*L*A*N." Mary tended to be strict about her dates with her husband. There was no city business allowed. Lindsay was to be interrupted if only there was an emergency. So, when, a little after 8:30, Ernest Latty, one of the mayor's security men, quietly slipped down the aisle to Lindsay's seat and handed him a note, he knew it was important. When he opened it, he grasped just how important: Martin Luther King had been shot dead in Memphis. Lindsay quickly left his seat and strode out of the theater.

Barry Gottehrer, who had been with the mayor during the black-white-Puerto Rican strife of 1966, heard about King and immediately headed up to Harlem, fearing the worst. After East New York, Gottehrer had developed a unique role within the Lindsay administration, serving as a troubleshooter and cooler. He was, nominally, the head of the Urban Action Task Force, but what that meant in real terms was that he would spend his evenings befriending and developing relationships with reputed mobsters, ultra-Zionists, gamblers, student radicals, black militants, and chip-on-the-shoulder kids. These were his point people, the ones he knew he could seek out if a neighborhood showed incipient signs of trouble. Gottehrer estimated the city had about 200 teenagers on the city payroll in twenty different areas, kids he could call on if an area came close to the tipping point of rioting and looting. Among his closest allies was a man calling himself Allah, born Clarence Smith, who was the head of the Five Percent Nation, so named because its members believed that 10 percent of the population actively kept 85 percent of the population ignorant, and it would be the remaining 5 percent who would save civilization. Allah had also spent part of 1965 in a prison for the criminally insane. Gottehrer's was a controversial program, but the near-riots summer of 1966 and another disturbance in Crown Heights the year after had taught Lindsay and his staff the value of having a street-level knowledge of the mores, characters and personal politics that shaped neighborhoods and could turn latent animosity into kinetic chaos. The UATF sought out that street-level knowledge, and bartered for it. "We were accused of paying off criminals for their good behavior, of paying petty criminals, dope peddlers and numbers runners for cutting us in on their action," Gottehrer later recalled. But the program was not about money: "We wanted peace. We didn't want what was happening in other cities to happen in our city."

After King's murder, Gottehrer knew where he was heading: the Glamour Inn, a black bar on Seventh Avenue in Harlem where he'd often meet Allah, a place that served as a headquarters for his operations. When he'd arrived, Gottehrer was struck by the surreal scene that was already developing around Harlem. Calm before the storm, perhaps. On a typical night in Harlem, record stores would have speakers hung above their doors, and would blare various styles of music into the streets. On this night, though, the record stores were playing recordings of the speeches of King throughout Harlem, the boom of his voice and his halting cadences bounding over the sidewalks. "King's presence was so palpable, you half expected to see him moving through the crowd that spilled on the streets," Gottehrer would write. Lindsay had gone back to Gracie Mansion after leaving the theater, and almost as if by instinct, got into a car with an aide and a police detective, headed for Harlem. By then, crowds were building. There were 4,000 angry residents in the streets. King's voice was still rolling from record-store speakers. The wail of fire sirens whirled, responding to alarms, some real and some false, and the din occasionally was punctuated by the glass of a storefront being smashed.

It was 10:40 p.m. when Lindsay arrived, stepping out of the limousine onto a simmering 125th Street. It did not take long for Allah and the Five Percenters to locate and surround him, giving the mayor a protective barrier. Lindsay, his 6-foot-4 frame and pale skin standing out distinctly in the crowd, expressed sympathy to some of the locals, picked up a bullhorn and shouted to those gathered, "If I lead you down the street, will you be quiet with me? Let's go together." Gottehrer thought, "Jesus, this is just the night for someone to take a shot at him." But even in the midst of the crowd's tumult, Lindsay was cheered. "You're the greatest mayor there ever was in this city," Allah told him. "You come here to see the people before the riot, not after the riot." Still, there was anger among those in the crowd, and concern about Lindsay's safety in those circumstances. Leonard DeChamps, head of Harlem CORE, rushed toward Lindsay and told him, slightly panicked, "John, I don't think you should come up here now, because the situation is too tense." DeChamps turned to two black men next to Lindsay and said, "Get him out of here!" Lindsay, after about thirty minutes on the street and a little more than an hour in Harlem, was hustled back into a car and taken back to Gracie Mansion.

Lindsay returned to Harlem a few hours later, this time staying in his car and viewing the scene. It was quiet. He ordered the Sanitation Department into Harlem to clean up the debris, to make the neighborhood appear as undisturbed as possible. There was no looting, no more fire alarms. The streets were mostly clear. New York had held. In the days that followed, the city gave residents organized outlets for grief. There were official demonstrations, memorial services and speeches planned—Dr. Benjamin Spock, singer Richie Havens and actor Ossie Davis highlighted a four-hour rally in Central Park that drew about 8,000, Floyd McKissick spoke before 2,500 in the Garment District, two other memorials convened at the United Nations. City government and schools, along with many businesses, were shut down on the Monday after King's murder. According to the *Post*, there had been 95 arrests on the first night of disturbances, 80 in Harlem and 15 in Brooklyn. Most of those arrested were looters charged with malicious mischief and disorderly conduct. There were some complaints about the restraint the NYPD showed in allowing the looting, but Commissioner Howard Leary said, "Sixty percent of the looters were under sixteen. What were we supposed to do, shoot the next Martin Luther King?" A total of fifty people in black neighborhoods had been treated at local hospitals and discharged with minor injuries. One man died of a stab wound, but a police spokesman said it was not the result of a racial attack. Five patrolmen were injured by bottles and other thrown items.

Across the country, though, city ghettoes were aflame, as 55,000 National Guardsmen and federal troops were engaged nationally in riot duty by the end of the weekend after King's murder. Relative to the damage and death seen in the riots of 1965–67, the toll was not as bad as might be expected, offering some validation of the policy of police restraint, which Leary had used in New York and other departments had begun to employ. In all, the riots had cost thirty-nine lives nationwide, fewer deaths than the forty-three seen in the 1967 Detroit riots alone. An *Associated Press* study done after the riots determined that rather than reaching for tanks and riot gear, "Authorities relied instead on manpower administered quickly and in heavy doses." Detroit used that approach in 1968, and there were only two deaths. But not all cities fared that well. President Johnson ordered 13,600 troops into fire-ravaged Washington DC, the largest occupation of an American city since the Civil War, and riots there left almost $30 million in damage. Chicago's South and West sides were devastated, too, as almost 12,000 troops joined the police in actively battling rioters. When the city was pacified, eleven civilians had been killed, all black and as young as sixteen years old. Asked about calling in the Guard, Lindsay said, "Troops. The hell with troops. You can't wall yourself in and call out troops. You can't sit behind a wall during one of these things. Get out and go someplace. There is no other place for you to be."

Chicago Mayor Richard Daley would prove to be a serious contrast to Lindsay. After the riots in Chicago, Daley was outraged by a story in the *Sun-Times* that asserted Chicago police had been given no uniform instructions on how to deal with looters and rioters. Daley wanted to make his directives in riot situations clear. "I have conferred with the superintendent of police this morning and I gave him the following instructions, which I thought were instructions on the night of the 5th that were not carried out," Daley said at a press conference. "I said to him very emphatically and very definitely that [he should issue an order] immediately and under his signature to shoot to kill any arsonist or anyone with a Molotov cocktail in his hand in Chicago because they're potential murderers, and to issue a police order to shoot to maim or cripple any arsonists and looters—arsonists to kill and looters to maim and detain." When asked about Daley's pronouncement, Lindsay uttered three sentences on which, columnist James Wechsler wrote, he "may have staked his political life." Lindsay stated: "We happen to think that protection of life is more important than protecting property or anything else. . . . We are not going to turn disorder into chaos, through the unprincipled use of armed force. In short, we are not going to shoot children in New York City." The risk, of course, was in the possibility that sometime in the near future, New York would be struck by its own riot, and Lindsay's walks through the ghettoes then would be demeaned as, "the futile pilgrimages of a soft-headed 'do-gooder' who lacked any authentic comprehension of the real world." But Lindsay stuck by his principles and came off looking heroic next to Daley.

It was the finest moment of Lindsay's mayoralty. He had built up personal capital with his outreach to the city's worst neighborhoods, and though he had not necessarily been able to bring about quality-of-life changes in those areas, his efforts engendered goodwill, and that goodwill paid him back in early April 1968. The rest of the nation endured a week of violence, but New York had mostly quiet, meaningful remembrance of King. The policy of restraint enacted by the NYPD had been exemplary. Additionally, in the wake of the riots, frustration over federal inaction on the recommendations of the Kerner Commission report resurfaced as an issue, and Lindsay was credited for being right about national lethargy on America's urban crisis. He'd also still carried the glow from the perception that he'd been victorious in the sanitation strike. Lindsay was now a popular national figure, appearing on the cover of the May 24 issue of *Life* magazine next to the headline, "The Lindsay Style," and featuring a quote from an aide that said, "He's given the city some hope. . . . There's a better feeling about the city; it's hard to put your finger on just what it is, but it's there."

The May 27 cover of *New York* magazine featured a faux campaign button with Lindsay's smiling mug square in the middle, surrounded by the words, "Lindsay for President." The story acknowledged it was a long shot, quoting a, "Lindsay man," saying that his political advisers had looked into his presidential prospects and determined his only chance in 1968 was through a deadlocked GOP convention. Still, Lindsay was a wanted man in Republican circles. He had made a trip to California in late 1967, where he delivered several speeches, met with Reagan, and appeared on television with Los Angeles Mayor Sam Yorty. He was in Oregon in February, delivering an address to the state's Republican Lincoln Day Dinner gathering, and making several speeches to college students. He was slated to speak at a fundraiser in Pittsburgh, and, in June, would deliver speeches to the GOP conventions in North Dakota and Minnesota—where he would find, to his bemused embarrassment, a "Lindsay for President" office had opened in Duluth.

Lindsay waved off his presidential ambitions. "I'm really concerned about this city," he said. "Some people thought the country was going conservative, but now we have the issuance of the riots commission report, which ruffled a few people, and then there was Dr. King's death and what happened afterwards. Many people are now aroused about the urban problems."

. . . .

In the Sunday edition of the *New York Times*, way back on April 29, 1956, Columbia University president Grayson Kirk published an essay concerning the benefits and challenges of the urban university. Columbia occupied a special place in that context, one of just a handful of first-rate American colleges entirely located in an urban setting.

Columbia had moved from Midtown to a bluff on the Upper West Side in 1896, the Hudson River to its west and Harlem to its east. "The city and its colleges and universities," Kirk wrote, "are not for the scholar who would be sheltered. Here the questing student cannot help being part of the cosmopolitan scene to the degree that his intellectual curiosity warrants. Whether he wills it or not, it is impossible for him to be insulated from the activity around him." Almost exactly a dozen years later, Kirk's sentiment would be borne out, by students with more of a questing nature than the unfortunate school president could have imagined.

On the afternoon of April 23, 1968, about 300 members of the radical group Students for a Democratic Society (SDS) went to Hamilton Hall on the campus of Columbia and set up a barricade of the office of acting Dean Henry Coleman, who was told he was being taken hostage. The students had a list of demands they wanted the university to meet. One was the removal of the university from membership in the Institute for Defense Analyses, a mostly clandestine weapons think-tank associated with the Defense Department, which handed out various assignments to twelve participating colleges around the country. Columbia was one. Another demand was the cessation of construction on an $11.6 million gymnasium the school had planned to put on a park located at 113th Street and Morningside Drive. The park itself, which was mostly barren and sometimes dangerous, was not of consequence, but it was what the park represented that mattered: an alleged pattern of racist real estate maneuvers taken by the university, especially during Kirk's tenure, infringing on the Harlem neighborhood around Columbia and angering minority Harlem residents. Novelist Thomas Gallagher, who lived on 116th and Riverside Drive, said, "In my opinion, the university administration is as ruthless as any landlord we have in the city." Columbia had been buying up property in surrounding areas when it became available, and had evicted more than 7,000 Harlem residents from those properties over the preceding decade. Columbia's SDS chapter was taking a stand on behalf of the cosmopolitan scene around it.

The origins of the SDS had gone back to 1962, a part of what was being called the New Left, a loose set of groups born from the rubble of the old American Communist and socialist organizations that had been decimated by the wave of anti-Red furor at the start of the Cold War. The collegiate aspect of the New Left gained focus at the University of California in Berkeley, where a small but committed group of students protesting the school's limitations on their ability to organize and speak out gained momentum and became the Berkeley Free Speech movement in 1964. Alongside the student political movement developed a counterculture that rejected societal norms of dress, behavior and even language—student protest and the counterculture had different origins in the early 1960s, and only later in the decade became intertwined. The word, "hippie" first appeared in the *New York Times* in a 1964 story about Greenwich Village live-audience storyteller Jean Shepherd (later to gain fame as author of a nostalgic holiday memoir, *A Christmas Story*), who was speaking about the crowds who would come to watch him perform when he said, "It's funny, you can't tell much about a gang by looking at them, by what they wear. You find the squarest people with beards carrying guitars. And the little old grandmother from Circleville can really be a hippie." In introducing the concept of a hippie, Shepherd acknowledged that what exactly, constituted a hippie was open to interpretation. But for much of Middle America, it would be summed up by Ronald Reagan, who had used outrage over student protests and the growth of counterculture at Berkeley to help win election in California in 1966. "We have some hippies in California," Reagan famously said. "For those of you who don't know what a hippie is, he's a fellow who dresses like Tarzan, has hair like Jane, and smells like Cheetah." It was simplistic (and erroneous) to conflate student activists legitimately disillusioned by the behavior of their governments and universities with counterculture radicals who tested society's limits on drug use and sexual freedom, but for a conservative governor of a massive state like California, putting any form of youth revolt into the same box was useful.

The spread of student protests very often mimicked the development and tactics of the civil rights movement. Taking from the sit-in concept of black Southern protestors, student groups began holding anti-war "teach-ins" at the University of Michigan in the mid-1960s, and soon after, teach-ins were regular happenings all over the country, spreading to high schools and far-flung places like Tokyo, Rio de Janeiro, and Amsterdam. That spring, political writer James Reston was critical of the teach-in wave for its lack of critical balance when it came to the war: "These nocturnal marathons have not been debates at all, but anti-Administration demonstrations disguised as 'teaching' and in many cases backed by propaganda of a most vicious nature." Responding to Reston's assertion, Columbia anthropology professor Marvin Harris said that professors of opposing views are invited to teach-ins, but most often don't want to spend their time staying up all night. That, he insisted, was a failure of critical thinking. "Many Americans," Harris wrote, "are sleeping at night only because they are inadequately informed about Vietnam."

But as the civil rights movement gave up nonviolence and turned militant, and as opposition to the Vietnam War went mainstream, radical student groups were empowered (or perhaps pressured) to follow the lead of SNCC and CORE, and take a more forceful approach in the conflict with the university power apparatus. In the midst of the Washington DC riots that followed King's murder, Stokely Carmichael had announced, "Now that they've taken Dr. King off, it's time to end this nonviolence bullshit." Teach-ins were about as nonviolent as it gets. They increasingly seemed flimsy exercises in academic self-congratulation. The student movement was ripe for a more serious and direct blow against the Establishment.

Columbia, with its dual and completely unrelated offenses—the school participated in military-industrial research to support the Vietnam War, and was pushing its footprint into Harlem—was a perfect target, a place for a group of mostly white students with radical aspirations to lash out at the Ivy League university on behalf of the mostly black surrounding population and North Vietnamese peasants. Their limitations, though, were obvious from the start. These were mostly middle- and upper-class post-adolescents after all, with little experience in

violent or nonviolent protest, and who had varying levels of commitment to the cause. Shortly after it started, the seizure of Hamilton Hall
was co-opted by black student groups, including many non-Columbia
students, members of Harlem CORE and SNCC honchos Carmichael
and H. Rap Brown, who pushed past police and campus officials into
the building. "We're going to let Columbia know," Brown said after
meeting with the students, "that if they don't deal with the brothers
inside, they're going to deal with the brothers on the street." The black
students essentially evicted the white instigators, taking Hamilton Hall
for themselves. David Anderson, a black twenty-four-year-old senior,
explained of his group, the Student Afro-American Society, "Our organization is in liaison with the community and not with white leftist
radicals. This is why, although the demonstration against the gym was
organized by SDS, we threw them out."

The white students fanned out to Fayerweather and Avery halls,
then moved to the Low Library and Mathematics Hall. They took
control of the office of Kirk himself. But the moderate Columbia students, who greatly outnumbered the demonstrators, decried the "anar-
chy" of the situation and a group of athletes threatened to bull into the
buildings to remove the protestors themselves. In the initial stages of
the standoff, Lindsay was credited with preventing bloodshed, because
he held sway within both camps. Demonstrators described Lindsay
as, "a great guy," "a swinger," and "the people's man." On the other
side, one athlete credited Lindsay for "keeping down the violence and
keeping the university's good name intact." Still, the strikes were an
annoyance for most Columbia students. Basketball coach Jack Rohan
had to warn a group of about 250 athletes against a counterstrike. "I
don't think the answer is to start to smash people around," he said.
"If you're willing to take part in mob violence, then I take pity on you
and pity on this university." Eventually, there was violence. At 2:30
a.m. on April 30, after much deliberation on the part of university
officials, a force of about 1,000 policemen moved into the campus at
the administration's request, in what the student newspaper termed, "a
brutal bloody show of strength." Over the course of three hours, they

cleared out all five buildings, making 712 arrests and leaving at least 148 injured.

There was some hypocrisy in that the student actions were not much different than those taken by ghetto residents in the much-publicized riots of the previous five years—there was protest, vandalism, theft, and anti-authority violence—but when such incidents took place within the leafy sanctuary of the college campus, they were labeled protests, not riots. At New York's State Psychological Association annual convention in Manhattan that May, local professors wrung their hands with concern over what had led these impressionable college students to such dramatic action. "President Johnson invoked personal conscience to justify violence in Vietnam," one Columbia psychoanalyst stated. "These students, too, are fighting for power, pure and simple, just as the President is." That, of course, was the same explanation often given by black leaders to explain ghetto riots. But, given conditions in the ghetto, the anger behind those riots made sense. What, though, were campus radicals after? Paul Jacobs, co-founder of *Mother Jones* and an old-school leftist, diminished the student motivations, saying, "We were rejecting a Depression; they're rejecting affluence." Sociologist Daniel Bell said, "At best, the New Left is all heart. At worst, it is no mind."

Meanwhile, parents who had sent their rosy-cheeked boys and girls off to college in the fall only to have them return as shaggy dissidents by Christmas break naturally had questions. Norman Vincent Peale, conservative minister and author of *The Power of Positive Thinking*, blamed renowned pediatrician Dr. Benjamin Spock, whose book, *Baby and Child Care*, first appeared in 1946 and had been a become the bible of American parenting, advocating a staunch attentiveness to a child's needs. Maybe too staunch. Peale looked around at the children reared under Spock's directives, who were reaching their early adulthood here in the mid-to-late 1960s, and saw sexual permissiveness, rampant drug use and rebellion. Peale said in a sermon that the state of America's youth was evidence that, "the U.S. was paying the price of two generations that followed the Dr. Spock baby plan of instant gratification of needs." Dr. Spock also had become one of the first and most vocal opponents to the Vietnam War, making him an easy target for conservatives, but on September 23, 1968, *Newsweek* caught on to Peale's criticisms and published a cover featuring a baby holding a flower, wearing buttons on his onesie reading, "Don't Trust Anyone Over 7," "Kindergarten Power," and, "Down With Mom." The cover banner said: "Is Dr. Spock to Blame?"

And there were those who thought the country's young folks just needed a makeover. In February, a mysterious billboard popped up—2,000 in total, in 48 states, plus another 5,000 wall posters—featuring the face of a llama-coiffed, beaded adolescent on a yellow background. In bright red lettering, the billboard implored: "BEAUTIFY AMERICA, Get a haircut."

....

Few Americans in the 1960s knew more about the perils and misperceptions that could come from an even slightly unkempt 'do quite like Joe Namath. One letter Namath received had the greeting, "Sir: Get a haircut, you bum!" and visiting stadiums were usually decorated with at least one sign imploring him to visit his local barber. The nation's preoccupation with hair as a matter of personal identification bordered on the psychotic, and Namath was just a symbol of that dementia. In early 1967, John F. Kennedy Jr., just six years old, appeared in photos with his sideburns grown out, and caused such a stir, it was reported, "the repercussions have been felt all over Manhattan's Upper East Side. Next month, Des Moines." (Repeat: He was *six*.) Later that year, a suit was settled between the family of a sixteen-year-old student and a teacher in San Diego who had given the student a haircut using, "cattle clippers." In early 1968 in Deerfield, Illinois, a parent sued the local school district for $310,000 in damages in the wake of the suspension of his fifteen-year-old son during midterm exams because his hair was too long. At the same time in Norwalk, Connecticut, fifty-three boys were summarily suspended at McMahon High School, with the Director of Secondary Education explaining, "We aren't anxious to see boys' hair becoming as long as girls. We are simply holding the line." All of this long-lockedness had economic consequences—a meeting of the Association of Master Barbers in Anaheim, California, lamented their collective financial reports, concluding that local hair cutteries had seen a 14 percent drop in revenues the previous year.

Barber inactivity was less of a problem in the sporting world, where there was widespread hippie/radical backlash. An NCAA convention in Los Angeles in early 1969 was almost entirely dominated by the question of whether an athlete could be stripped of a scholarship because of his haircut, which to black coaches present seemed aimed particularly at Afro haircuts. "This looks like a slap at the black athlete," one black NCAA delegate said. Nebraska coach Bob Devaney, torn on the issue, said he didn't know what he'd do if his players showed up looking, "like Joe Namath of the Jets. Joe seemed to pass all right. We try to discourage it, but as subtly as possible." After the 1968 baseball season, White Sox general manager Ed Short won (only briefly, it turned out) a leaguewide ban on beards, goatees, mustaches, and "excessive" sideburns. "This is just another step," one columnist wrote, "in a campaign to drain the baseball player of all individuality." Short said his concern was, "to keep the proper image of major league players before the young fan especially." Namath, somewhat taken aback by major league baseball's position, said, "That's ridiculous." He would later expand: "Who tells the children it's bad? Parents—they're the ones at fault, because they tell their child that mustaches and long hair are only worn by freaks. Where else does a kid get the idea that mustaches shouldn't be worn and that a man can't have more than a crewcut? As soon as that child looks at our history books and sees all that hair on our forefathers, he's gonna wonder what the hell kind of history we've *had*."

Namath was always miscast as a hippie, his long hair mistaken for a social statement rather than the simple matter of style that it was. He fit some concepts of hippie-dom—he'd disavowed his Catholicism, he was sexually promiscuous, he didn't accept orders blindly, he liked beads. But he had little in common with Columbia protestors or Village drug users or West Coast flower children. When asked if he were a rebel, Namath scoffed. "That's not true," he said. "If I don't believe in something, though, I'm not gonna go along with it: it has nothing to do with being anti-establishment or whatever; it's just that if it's not right for me, then I can't go along with it. I'm not trying to fight society—I'm just trying to be myself." Namath, like Lindsay, had a special ability to appeal to seemingly opposing camps. Reston wrote about him, "He defies both the people who hate playboys and the people who hate bullyboys. He is something special: a long-haired hard-hat, the anti-hero of the sports world." Larry Merchant, a columnist for the *Post*, wrote, "Joe Namath is no hippie," but added that in his day and age, "a young person who questioned authority, religion and society's hypocrisy, and who didn't take a haircut every three weeks, was automatically hooked up with Allen Ginsberg, Haight-Asbury and dirty feet. Namath drove a Lincoln, lived in a penthouse, was a devout hedonist, affected Frank Sinatra's glass-in-hand insouciance, and would rather go one-on-one with Dick Butkus than sit in the mud for three days and listen to rock music. But America saw him as a hippie . . . and that was that. He was ranked alongside the Beatles, Bobby Dylan and Muhammad Ali as symbols of a decade's decadence."

But give Namath credit. Whatever the complaints about him, there was no one else that American guys wanted to emulate more. By the late 1960s, not only did wavy locks and sideburns become so de-hippified that high school sophomores were taking a stand on their hair, stores in New York were running up big business on a "face-falsies" fad. Yes, the thing for a respectable Manhattan fellow to do in 1968 was to stop by Hollywood Joe's Hairpiece Co. on Fifth Ave. and pick from an array of fake facial foliage options, all made with real human hair imported from Italy. One Brooklyn College student liked to be presentable at school during the day, but was in a rock band called the Brooklyn Dodgers at night, and explained, "We wouldn't be hired if we looked cleancut and normal." As one of the owners of Hollywood Joe's said, "After eight hours in the office, a guy is going to swing. The question is, is he going to swing like a yokel, or like a guy who's in?"

CHAPTER 14

"What kind of people are we?"

THERE HAD BEEN HINTS, IN late 1967 and early 1968, that something was not quite right with the Jets organization. A rumor had cropped up in January that the team was for sale, and that the surging Madison Square Garden company, its new building set to open, would buy the club. Or that NBC, following the lead of CBS's purchase of the Yankees, would purchase the AFL's flagship franchise. There was the persistent Vince Lombardi-to-the-Jets chatter, and further rumor that Oakland's Al Davis, former commissioner of the AFL, would be offered the job if Lombardi said no. But as the months passed, there were no announcements, the gossip was written off as idle and the top-line news of the Jets concerned, as usual, Namath and knee surgery. The twist this time was that Namath had surgery in March on tendons in his left knee, which thereafter could no longer be called his "good knee."

But if anything amounted to a major clue about the state of the Jets' front office, the attentive sports detective would have noticed that on May 19, a small, one-column news item appeared in the back of the *Daily News* sports section, between National League batting averages and the weekly bowling column. The two-paragraph article stated that Namath had agreed to a new contract with the Jets the previous day while golfing with Sonny Werblin in Florida. "Terms—salary and length—were not announced," the story read. This, surely, could not be the work of master PR puppeteer Sonny Werblin. Rumors had been floated that, when Namath and the team agreed to a new contract, it would be worth something like $1 million ("I mean, that's a nice round number," the *Post*'s Paul Zimmerman wrote. "Why not?") The dance, from there, would be well-choreographed: there would be an all-expenses paid shindig for reporters up at Toots Shor's, the press would prod and pull at Werblin and Namath for the contract details, they would offer only lip-locked smiles, and speculation on the price paid for Namath would, as it had in 1965, dominate. That was Werblin's style. He didn't aim for the twenty-four-point headline type that topped the Namath contract story, and he certainly didn't aim for Page 47.

On May 21, the real news was announced: Werblin was leaving the Jets. He was to be bought out of his 23 percent share by the other four owners, the men who had been silent partners in Werblin's football adventure dating back to their purchase of the Titans for $1 million from Harry Wismer in 1963. But the silent nature of those partners was part of the problem. They hadn't begrudged Werblin his theatrical PR maneuvers but they'd felt that they'd been frozen out of team decisions altogether. Don Lillis, who had 20 percent of the club and according to Dick Young, "more spirit than hair," would take over for Werblin as the public face of the team. "He didn't treat his partners like partners," Lillis said. "We were completely forgotten men. I don't want publicity, but hell, I do expect to have some fun. Well, it wasn't fun. All I was getting was a ticket to the game and a free lunch in the director's room. Hell, for the kind of money I had invested, you could buy a lot of tickets with the interest." Some reports suggested that there was jealousy, with Werblin getting all the headlines and national recognition. But Lillis said he took the job reluctantly. The other members of the ownership group were not of limelight-seeking backgrounds. Townsend Martin said he was not after headlines, "We just wanted to know what was happening before it happened." Phil Iselin admitted he would not want Werblin's duties because, "I am not a football man." Oilman Leon Hess, the wealthiest of the partners, not only was not seeking publicity, but actively sought to avoid it. Iselin's wife, Bette, said, "Leon Hess pays people to keep his name out of the papers." Further, Mrs. Iselin lamented the bump in what had been a longstanding friendship with Werblin and his wife. "He degraded us," she said. "He made us feel really like nothing. It became an intolerable situation for all of us. He hated the idea he had partners."

From Werblin's point of view, a venture like the Jets should be guided by one strong, empowered decision maker, supported by partners. The tension that had begun to unfold between he and his partners reached its peak when they found out he had signed Namath to a new contract back in the summer of 1967, without a word's notice to them. But even before that, Lillis had gone to Werblin and told him he wanted out of the Jets. "The others heard about it," Lillis said, "and they decided they wanted to sell, too." The partners were willing to sell to Werblin on a bargain basis of about a $7 million franchise valuation. Werblin offered to put $1.5 million down and pay the balance over seven years, but the other four wanted a lump sum. Werblin was not willing to mortgage his estate to keep the team. So he had to sell, and accepted $1.65 million.

On the following Friday, Werblin held a party at Luchow's, a German restaurant on 14th Street, and invited just about the entire New York sports press corps. It had been a tough four days for him, because not only had he sold off his beloved Jets, but, on the advice of his lawyers, he had not addressed the media until the deal was finished, and a gag order at a time like this for a media-friendly bon vivant like Werblin was torture. Now, surrounded by his press friends and sipping cocktails, he was wistful and still a touch angry. He had plenty of cause for bitterness. He had been the one to go to Tuscaloosa to recruit Namath in 1964, had hosted him at his vacation house in the Bahamas, had gone to Columbus to persuade Matt Snell to forsake the Giants and sign with the Jets, had arranged the television contract with NBC that had saved the American Football League. Now, this. Werblin revealed that in 1967, the time and angst he'd invested in the Jets had paid off, as the franchise made its first-ever profit, worth $180,000. "When we were a failure at the beginning, nobody came around," Werblin said. "The moment a profit appeared, we were running things by committee. You didn't see them in Kansas City when it was 14 below zero and your feet stuck to the metal floor. But the moment a profit appeared, we were running things by committee."

For Namath, this meant a significant change. Werblin had been his guide into both stardom and adulthood, but also his protector and enabler within the franchise—arguably to the detriment of the team. "Werblin treated Namath like an indulgent father who spared the rod and spoiled the child," Arthur Daley wrote. "The owner socialized with the athlete at times and undercut the authority of the coach." The new ownership announced they were keeping Weeb Ewbank as coach and general manager, and though it was not part of the announcement, the understanding was that Ewbank would be coaching on a playoffs-or-else basis. Lillis also made clear that he would stay clear of Namath off the field, but he expected more on it. For all his stats, Namath never had been voted the Jets MVP by his teammates. "The only way I'll get involved with Namath is to sit down and talk to him like a father, if I think it's necessary," Lillis said. "Everybody raves about his passing, but when your quarterback is fifth or sixth in a most-valuable-player vote of his own teammates, something is wrong. But whatever's wrong, it's not his haircut. . . . I don't think his long hair has anything to do with Namath's performance on the field. He'll never be unattractive to the gals, and we can't do away with gals."

Without Werblin as a buffer, Ewbank could be tougher on Namath. Now with more power but also more pressure, Ewbank would be tougher on everyone. He issued new rules, including barring reporters from the training room and forcing them out of the locker room an hour before the start of a game. Beat writer Larry Fox commented, "Werblin would have allowed writers in the huddle if he thought it would help publicize his team." Ewbank also pulled hard liquor from team flights, and said that beer would be only offered in rationed amounts. For Namath, it must have been clear that his friendship with the owner had caused unnecessary locker-room resentment. "Mr. Werblin is my friend," Namath said. "But he never pampered me—if you mean interfering with discipline. I have paid every single fine Coach Ewbank has asked for." Namath said Werblin's departure would make no difference to the team, and that he would be the same man he'd always been. When asked what kind of man that was, Namath thought about the question. He'd been a swinger when the Jets got off to good starts in 1966 and 1967. Then he'd turned combative grouch when things went sour and his lifestyle became a point of scrutiny. "Maybe it's bad to say this," he said, "but I might be a better football player if I didn't like to stay up and see so many late movies. But I can't change the way I am."

....

The Mets had left Florida and were in Palm Springs, California, for an exhibition game against the Phillies as they wrapped up training camp back in April when word came that Martin Luther King had been killed. There were only four black players on the team at the time—pitcher Al Jackson, infielder Ed Charles, and outfielders Tommy Agee and Cleon Jones—and the front office did not have much of a reputation for its forward-thinking on race. That fact, though, was easily lost in the handful of wracked emotional days between April 4 and Opening Day. There had been mixed signals coming from ineffectual baseball Commissioner William Eckert, a former Air Force general hired by team owners in 1965, who gave out no strict directives on how to handle the start of the season, which was scheduled for Monday, April 8. The owners had hired Eckert precisely because he would not give overly strong leadership, and would allow the teams to do as they wished. With the riots that blew up all over the country that weekend, Eckert left it up to individual teams to decide whether to push back Opening Day, and pick the date and time of their choosing for the postponement. It was chaotic, and in the public sphere, Eckert and baseball took a bruising. Still, for the four black Mets, the big picture was disturbing. Charles called Stokely Carmichael a "fool," and characterized his call for blacks to take guns into the streets, "One idiot trying to stir up other idiots." Agee, who was in his first season with the Mets after having been traded from the White Sox, worried about King's murder pushing more blacks toward militarism: "Some people were on the borderline, undecided which way to go—violence or non-violence. Which way do you think they'll go now?" Jackson worried about where the country would go next. "A man tries to do some good, like Martin Luther King," Jackson said. "He does good for black people and for white people. . . . Somebody doesn't agree with him, and gets a gun. And you say to yourself, 'My God, can a thing like this happen in this country?'"

Two months later, a thing like that did happen. Again. Just after midnight on June 5 in Los Angeles, Senator Bobby Kennedy, just forty-two years old and not even five years removed from the assassination of his brother, was celebrating his victory over Eugene McCarthy in the California primary, a critical win that could well have set him on a path toward the Democratic nomination. He'd given a victory statement at the Ambassador Hotel and, as he stepped from the podium, five shots from a small-caliber pistol rang out. Rosey Grier, the former Giants defensive tackle who was on hand with the campaign, was among those who wrestled the assailant—twenty-four-year-old Jordanian refugee Sirhan Sirhan—to the ground. Kennedy was rushed to the Good Samaritan Hospital, where doctors attempted to surgically remove the bullet fragments lodged in the Senator's brain. Kennedy was in intensive care for nearly twenty hours. But the surgery and the blood loss had been too much. He died. And the question was again relevant: *My God, can a thing like this happen in this country?*

In Harlem, resident Charles Blocker said, "I think the world is coming to an end. It looks like we're trying to kill each other off." A middle-aged woman on a Queens subway, dabbing tears into a handkerchief, told the *Post*, "I'm not sure I'm crying for Bobby or for all of us. Have we really become this horrible?" In Washington DC, picketers demonstrated outside the office of the National Rifle Association, calling for tighter gun-control laws. One sign read, "Who's next, John John?" John Lindsay had been woken up by an aide informing him of Kennedy's assassination before dawn on June 5, when he scribbled down some notes for what would be that afternoon's commencement address at Miss Porter's School in Farmington, Connecticut, where his daughter was graduating. What do you tell a group of aspiring young women on a day like that? Or at a time like this, when United Nations Secretary General U Thant had surveyed the war in Southeast Asia and announced, "I'm afraid we are entering today the first phase of World War III," and when the *New York Times* had looked at the anti-Soviet agitation of Marshal Tito in Yugoslavia and saw that he "could start World War III if he attacked." Two weeks earlier, word from Washington was that technicians were busily installing blue panic buttons in the office phones of every US Senator. Lindsay didn't have answers for the graduating girls, only questions. So he echoed Al Jackson. "What kind of country is this where something like this could happen?" he said. "What kind of people are we?"

Eight hundred miles west, in Chicago, the Mets were wrapping up a series against the Cubs on a Thursday afternoon—June 6—when they got word that Kennedy was dead. They would head out to the airport to travel for a weekend series in San Francisco, but before they left, manager Gil Hodges asked the media to leave the clubhouse so that he could address his team. Having apparently learned nothing from the mishandling of baseball's post-King assassination schedule, William Eckert was again descending into an utter bungling of the Kennedy tragedy. President Johnson had declared Sunday a national day of mourning, so the sensible thing for baseball to do would have been to cancel all games on that day. But this was a June weekend, and baseball was expecting a total crowd of 300,000 fans on Sunday alone. The owners did not want to give up that revenue. Several teams had their annual "Bat Day" planned, and you couldn't very well cancel Bat Day.

Eckert, meeting at the Americana Hotel in Manhattan with several league owners and executives for the annual baseball draft (at which the Mets, with the first pick, would pass on a catcher named Thurman Munson in favor of infielder Tim Foli), offered no resistance to their directives. Games would be played on Sunday. They would be canceled in New York and Washington on Saturday, out of respect for the two places affected by Kennedy's funeral procession. The rest of the league would have to push games back so they started after Kennedy's burial, scheduled for 5 p.m. That would force a postponement for the Cubs, because Wrigley Field had no lights. But the other games would go on once Kennedy was buried. Mets beat writer Joe Trimble summed up the crassness of the plan by noting, "It was nice of them to wait until the last shovelful of earth was deposited in the grave before yelling, 'Play ball!'"

In the Wrigley Field visiting clubhouse, Hodges told his players they had three choices. They could play on Saturday at 8 p.m. as the Giants were planning. They could vote not to play on the grounds that owners were not allowed to schedule night games on the day before a doubleheader, and the Mets were scheduled to play a doubleheader on Sunday. Or they could vote not to play at all out of respect for Kennedy. Hodges told them he would accept whatever their decision would be. First baseman Ed Kranepool, the Mets' player representative, said, "We're New Yorkers and he's our Senator. I think a lot of people in New York would be disappointed if we played this game." The vote was unanimous. The Mets would not play. In San Francisco, Giants owner Horace Stoneham was furious. Saturday was, of course, Bat Day at Candlestick Park. There were already 30,000–40,000 tickets sold. Stoneham stood to lose $80,000. Stoneham offered to start the game at 4 p.m., which, with the time difference, should still be after the funeral. If the Mets refused that proposal, they could be subject to a forfeit. When the Mets' flight landed in San Francisco, Hodges cleared the plane of reporters and trainers, and told his players of the 4 p.m. offer. He said the second vote, "took only 30 seconds." The Mets were firm. Forfeit or no, they would not play. "I'm very, very happy they voted that way," Hodges said. "I'm not a political individual at all but I have my feelings. This goes deeper than politics."

The Mets' stand was one of the few positive stories to come out of the weekend for Eckert and the league. At St. Patrick's Cathedral in New York on Friday, mourners—an estimated 120,000—stood in a line a mile long for hours to pay respects to Kennedy as he lay in state.

On Saturday, Lindsay declared a day of mourning in New York, and Kennedy's funeral was held in the afternoon. His coffin was placed on a train at Penn Station at about 1 p.m., but on the trip to Washington, mourners crowded the tracks and forced the train to slow down. Kennedy's body arrived after 9 p.m., five hours late. Baseball's plan to "honor" Kennedy by delaying start times until after his funeral was now blown, and four games started well ahead of the burial. "I keep pinching myself," said Marvin Miller, the head of the nascent players association, "and telling myself they just can't be this stupid." On Sunday, owners in Boston and Baltimore decided to observe the day of mourning and postponed their games. But other owners refused to give in. In Cincinnati, player representative and pitcher Milt Pappas quit his post and asked to be traded out of anger when Reds manager Dave Bristol pressured players to suit up for Saturday's game against the Cardinals. (He was dealt to Atlanta three days later.) In Houston, Rusty Staub and Bob Aspromonte of the Astros failed to appear for the Astros' game against the Pirates, and Maury Wills of Pittsburgh would not take the field, either, instead staying in the clubhouse training room. "This is an individual thing, not a team matter," Wills said. "You must let your conscience be your guide. I was out of uniform when Dr. King died and if I didn't respect Senator Kennedy's memory, too, I felt I would be hypocritical." *Post* columnist Milton Gross wrote that, "Baseball's conscience apparently lies in its cash register."

But for the Mets, the confrontation with the Stoneham's Giants was a bonding moment. The team was young—other than thirty-five-year-old infielder Ed Charles, the regular lineup was entirely twenty-five years old or younger, while the pitching staff was anchored by the 1–2 punch of ace Tom Seaver (who was twenty-three) and lefty Jerry Koosman (twenty-five). After three-and-a-half years of Ol' Perfesser Casey Stengel and two-and-a-half years of Wes Westrum, the Mets now had Hodges, who was serious about turning the team into a winner and instilling discipline. He even made his players wear coats and ties on the road. Dick Young of the *Daily News*, who helped to spearhead the coddling of the woebegone Mets in their early days, even supported taking a tougher line with the losing ways of the club, which had finished in last place five times in its existence, and next-to-last once. "Till now," Young wrote, "nobody has spanked the Mets, and maybe it's about time it started, or we are liable to have a spoiled brat on our hands, if we don't already."

But Hodges was a reserved personality and, early in his tenure, did not connect with the greenhorns on his roster. That changed after early June 1968. The players had made a stand, and Hodges (as well as the front office) had backed them completely. The Mets were still not quite seasoned enough to be a winner over 162 games, but they did go 16–14 that June, only the second winning month in the history of the franchise, and wound up with 73 wins, seven more than the previous team high. Early students of the Metophiles, who forecasted that fans would forsake the team when it became just another middle-of-the-road outfit, were wrong. The Mets were trying to win, and their attendance jumped by 216,000 fans.

. . . .

Shortly before Kennedy was shot, political writer Nick Thimmesch asked John Lindsay about the possibility of vying for a seat in the US Senate, either head-to-head against Kennedy in 1970 or in some other circumstance, should Kennedy wind up in the White House. Lindsay did not hide his distaste for the prospect of low-pressure Senate life: "No, I don't want to go to the United States Senate. I'd get the bends, the decompression, back in a legislative job." But after Kennedy's assassination, under New York law, Nelson Rockefeller would have to pick his replacement, and Lindsay was immediately tabbed by the press as the logical choice. The papers reported a reluctance on Rockefeller's part to go that route, though, because moving Lindsay out of City Hall would put the city in the hands of Democratic City Council president Frank O'Connor, who had lost a bitter gubernatorial fight to Rockefeller two years earlier, at least until the election of 1969. But Rockefeller's real angle was his long-shot bid for the Republican nomination, against the heavily favored Richard

Nixon. Lindsay confided to a friend, "I know what he's thinking. 'If I do make you Senator, would you still come up to New York this summer and walk through the ghettoes?' He's afraid there might be a riot while he's running for President and he wants me in the city to cool it for him."

Rockefeller knew he had to at least make the offer to Lindsay—he just couldn't be blunt about the fact that he didn't want Lindsay to accept it. And Lindsay didn't want to accept it, didn't want to abandon the city just when he'd finally seized momentum. Lindsay did, however, want to force Rockefeller to ask him so that he could turn him down. Publicly, Rockefeller had hailed Lindsay as an ideal candidate, but Lindsay had been careful to keep his comments vague. "I have a four-year contract with the people of New York," he said on June 10, "and I intend to fulfill that contract." As Lindsay recalled it, when he met secretly with Rockefeller on June 16, Rockefeller said, "Tell me why I should appoint you to the Senate, John."

"Nelson, you're starting wrong," Lindsay replied. You're inviting job applications. I don't do business that way. The stakes are high; we're grown up, we're not children. Are you making me an offer?"

"I've told you that you're my first choice."

"Then that's an offer."

"No it isn't."

"Okay. That's the end of the conversation on this subject."

If the private Lindsay-Rockefeller conference sounded juvenile, it came off the same way publicly. At the end of June, Rockefeller told reporters he would give Lindsay "prime consideration" but only "if he asks for it." Lindsay followed the next day by saying he would consider the post if it were offered, but he would not be the one doing the asking, "now or ever." And that was where it was left. The job of junior Senator from the State of New York was not determined by qualification or political calculation, but by stubborn egotism. *He has to ask for the job. No, he has to offer it first.* Rockefeller waited until after the GOP Convention, and in September, named Upstate liberal Republican Charles Goodell to fill Kennedy's seat.

But that wasn't the only brush with higher office Lindsay had in the heady days of the summer of 1968, flush with his brandished national credentials. As the early August Republican convention in Miami approached, Lindsay was looked upon as an ideal running mate, either for Nixon, or for some rebel faction that might step in and offer a late convention coup. Lindsay had told Nick Thimmesch he was not the vice presidential type. "There are robins and non-robins," Lindsay said. "I don't want to be a non-robin. There are two types of people: Those who are vice presidents and those who aren't. I wouldn't take the vice-presidency. If this job [the Mayor's] is the second-toughest in the country, why take on the third?" A Nixon-Lindsay ticket had the right amount of yin and yang, though. Nixon was a Westerner who was honing the Southern Strategy that had been the lone success of Barry Goldwater in 1964, taking advantage of the white reactionary vote to cull an entire bloc of states that had been off-limits to Republicans since Reconstruction. If Nixon's appeal in those places held, Lindsay could be used to attract votes in the urban centers of the Northeast and Midwest. There was also the matter of age and appearance. Calling Nixon-Lindsay a "dream ticket," *Washington Post* columnist Joseph Kraft evoked Murray Kempton's fresh-vs.-tired contrast. "At 46," he wrote, "Mayor Lindsay is physically young. . . . He is a fresh face. He also has the looks, manner and wideranging cultural interests of the new breed. He bridges the generational gap."

When the convention arrived on Monday August 5, despite Nixon's comfortable victories in the Republican primaries—he lost just one, in Massachusetts to Rockefeller—there was little predictability. That Saturday, fears that Nixon could not win a general election gripped both the left and right wings of the Republicans, with Rockefeller on the left and Ronald Reagan on the right seeking to coalesce into a Stop-Nixon faction. Reagan, though, was as hardheaded as Rockefeller. Both wanted to be the nominee to replace Nixon, and neither would yield, watering down the legitimacy of their challenge (which might not have worked anyway). Lindsay, meanwhile, was prepared for all eventualities. He had a staff of fifty with him on the ninth floor of the Americana

Hotel on Miami Beach, where the *New York Times* joked about his vague aspirations, saying he had established a, "Lindsay-for-Something headquarters." He was still mentioned as a darkhorse nominee if the Stop-Nixon group managed some success, but found that he was playing a much bigger role as a potential vice presidential candidate. On the first day of the convention, Lindsay gave a very liberal speech about Vietnam (calling it "deadly folly"), urban issues, polarization, and the need for Republicans to appeal to minorities. After hearing that, Mississippi chairman Clarke Reed said that Lindsay, "scares the hell out of us," and that if he were put on the ticket with Nixon, "I'd feel like we'd been shot down." Reagan, holding out hope of surprising Nixon, was going after Southern delegates, selling them on his conservative credentials and spreading the rumor that Nixon would pick Lindsay. He'd become a toxic choice as vice president. That, Lindsay would later claim, was the point. His overtly liberal speech was, "specifically designed to put everyone on notice where I stand," he said, "and thereby keep me off the ticket."

According to columnists Robert Novak and Rowland Evans, when Nixon and his advisors convened to pick a vice president, Lindsay was at the top of the list, with Rockefeller and Illinois' Charles Percy. Nixon crossed out Rockefeller, knowing he would not accept. "But the Southerners present, headed by [South Carolina Sen. Strom] Thurmond, took care of Percy and Lindsay." Instead, Nixon found what he thought would be a satisfactory compromise: little-known Maryland Governor Spiro Agnew, a conservative from a Shallow South state whose limited liberal credentials included having run to the left of segregationist Democrat George P. Mahoney in 1966. He'd quickly squandered those credentials. At the end of the riots that followed Martin Luther King's death—Baltimore was one of the hardest hit cities—Agnew met with prominent civil rights leaders, and proceeded to berate them as, "riot inciting, burn America down type of leaders," prompting one state senator to say, "He's a wolf in sheep's clothing." Nixon did call on Lindsay for help, though. He needed a liberal to give Agnew's seconding speech, and he wanted it to be Lindsay. Fellow liberal Republicans urged him not to, and proposed a floor fight to ward off Agnew's nomination. But Lindsay was visited in a trailer near the convention hall by his political mentor, Herbert Brownell, who told him it would be politically damaging to challenge for the vice presidency through a floor fight. Agnew was going to be nominated either way. Lindsay might as well get some benefit by seconding him. Coming from Brownell, the advice stuck. Lindsay gave the speech and refused to listen to further entreaties on a liberal revolt. That left Thurmond looking like the hero, while, according to one reporter, "Lindsay had passed up the chance to be the white knight of industrial-state Republicans."

By the end of the Republican convention, it was tough to gauge Lindsay's position. He had been forcefully liberal in his first speech, but the later drama around the Agnew seconding speech left the more lasting impression. He'd go back to New York, neither a senator nor a vice president, with a trove of unspent political capital among national Republicans that carried about as much value among City Hall types as Confederate money. A Miami columnist wrote, "It is doubtful if Lindsay will ever have a better chance nationally than he did here last week, and nothing came of it." Worse, Lindsay had sold out his principles to the party powers. He could, apparently, assail power brokers on the municipal level, but was happy to play power broker on national television. "You can understand Brownell, an opportunist, pushing Lindsay into it," Jimmy Breslin wrote. "But so many people still can't understand how Lindsay could do it. How he would walk onto the platform in Miami and spit at all of us in New York and begin to glorify the Spiro Agnews of the country."

CHAPTER 15

Confrontation

FROM THE BEGINNING, 1968 WAS a season of promise for the Jets. The relentless string of injuries that had marred 1967 had healed, and though Namath was now coming off his third knee surgery, he had gotten accustomed to dealing with constant pain. He would also have to deal with his strained relationship with Ewbank, who, with Werblin no longer around, had more clout. Don Lillis, who had taken over after Werblin's ouster, died just two months later of a heart ailment, and Phil Iselin, a dressmaker by trade, reluctantly moved into his role. Ewbank now had free rein with the roster, but he was also under tremendous pressure, aware that if he didn't win this time around, he would be out. He exercised his muscle from the beginning. When veteran lineman Sherman Plunkett, who had been with Ewbank in Baltimore all the way back in 1958 and had played in every game Ewbank coached with the Jets, showed up weighing 337 pounds, Ewbank fined him $15 per day until he got to 300 pounds. When Plunkett couldn't do it, he gave up and asked Ewbank to waive him, which paved the way for rookie Sam Walton to be the starter.

The larger problem was the contract of bruising running back Matt Snell, who had not been fully healthy in 1967 and was threatening Ewbank with a holdout. The Jets had used their top draft pick on fullback Lee White, and rather than acquiesce to Snell's demands, Ewbank put out trade feelers around the league for him. Ewbank had a reputation for seeking absolute control of player contracts, making sure that a team's salary structure stayed in line. And he was cheap. Receiver Don Maynard recalled that a salary negotiation with Ewbank would usually involve writing a desired salary figure on a piece of paper and pushing it across Ewbank's desk, who would write his own number, and push it back. The paper-pushing would continue until an agreement was reached, at which point, Ewbank would jump up, shake hands and tell the player not to tell his teammates how much he was making. "I won't, Weeb," Maynard once told him. "I'm just as ashamed of it as you are." The world was changing around Ewbank, though—Snell was represented by an agent from Probus Management, and there would be no scrawling of numbers on sheets of paper. After Week 2, when White injured his knee, Snell was signed.

The rest of the roster, though, was shaping up nicely over the course of the preseason. Snell's backfield mate, outside threat Emerson Boozer, was playing on a completely reconstructed right knee, but like Namath, injury was both curse and blessing—Boozer left the team for a six-month army hitch, but was sent back once the military saw how bad his knee was. The Jets had the best receiving group in the league, and maybe in all of football, with Maynard and George Sauer at receiver and Pete Lammons at tight end. The defense was loaded with players who were either in or just hitting their prime years—end Gerry Philbin, linebacker Al Atkinson, defensive backs Randy Beverly and Jim Hudson—and who, as a group, had developed a tough competitive edge. *Look* magazine's football preview had the Jets listed first in the AFL's East Division, with their archrival Raiders picked to win the West. And, in the big picture, after two shellackings of AFL teams by the NFL champ Packers in the Super Bowl, the junior league just might be making some progress. The leagues would not mesh their regular-season schedules until 1970, but in 1968 exhibitions, the AFL went 13–10 against the NFL, and the Jets beat both Atlanta and

Detroit. The previous preseason, the AFL had gone 3–13 against the NFL.

Namath was on the upswing, too. Rehab was behind him, and some new business prospects were ahead of him. He'd agreed to start a chain of three fast-food restaurants in Miami, called Broadway Joe's, with plans for a big expansion. He and two friends had bought an East Side bar on Lexington Avenue they would renovate and call Bachelors III, a safe haven where Namath could be both owner and best customer. Even when convalescing, Namath was ever an exemplary resident of Fun City—as part of his recovery from left knee surgery, he and friend Bobby Van got a tandem bicycle and rode it from his apartment over on First Avenue to Central Park ("We almost got killed ten times," Namath said), throwing a football around once they got there. Most significant was the change in training camp plans for that summer. At long last, the Jets could bid good riddance to Peekskill Military Academy, with its cramped, ramshackle rooms and barren campus. Now they would be training at Hofstra on Long Island, staying in a highrise dormitory. Though students were on break, there still was summer school. To the Jets, summer school at Hofstra meant one thing: coeds. When informed of that new reality, Namath said with interest: "Girls, right here on the campus? Is that so?" The Jets would come into the dining room each day around noon, and the young women would be prepared. "It's amazing," one Hofstra official said, "how the girls get up to get another straw for their Coke when the football players troop through. Some of those girls need two or three extra straws."

On more mundane topics, Namath was equally engaged. Discussing the season with sportswriter Larry Fox, Namath said, "I want it to be the best one I ever had. I think we can win it all, and if I have a halfway good season I know we'll do it. I have confidence now that I can do it. Last year, I thought I was ready and I wasn't. A championship. That's the whole thing. Everything else is incidental." But dating back to the end of 1967, an accepted theory about Namath had developed, and he was unable to shake it. In the aftermath of their disappointing three-game losing streak that December, the Jets had taken a vote on taken a vote on team MVP. Sauer was the winner. That would seem strange at first blush, with Namath setting a record and going over the 4,000-yard mark, but Sauer was a first-rate route-runner with great hands, and was the Jets' only first-team All-Pro. (Quarterback Daryle Lamonica, whose Raiders had gone 13–1, was first-team All-Pro and league MVP). The real problem for the Jets was not that their star quarterback lost out to Sauer, it was that he finished *sixth* in the balloting. Even as the magazine picked the Jets for the playoffs, *Look* noted, "When Jet men rate AFL's best quarterback, Joe Namath, only sixth most valuable member of [the] squad, a morale problem is obvious." Perhaps players had not been as forgiving of his training-camp disappearing act back in August 1967, or maybe they were still stung by Namath's late arrival and alleged drinking binge with Werblin before the crucial loss to lowly Denver on December 3. But the vote was held up as evidence that Namath was not respected by his teammates. Just ahead of the 1968 season, Hall of Famer Otto Graham said, "The Jets have never named Namath their Most Valuable Player. They voted him fourth once, but never higher. That's what his own team thinks of Broadway Joe."

At the outset of the Jets' exhibition schedule, in Houston in August, that narrative gained steam. Before facing the Oilers, Namath told Ewbank his knee was hurting and he would not play. Ewbank had not made the news public because, according to Namath, "he was too worried about the damn ticket sales and the Jets' percentage." As the team was going through its warmups, Namath and Ewbank were spotted in an argument—Ewbank wanted him to at least put on his uniform, but Namath refused, arguing it would make fans think he would be playing. As the game got underway, Namath was on the sideline, wearing a pinstriped suit. "Weeb wasn't happy," Namath explained, "and I wasn't happy." Dick Young of the *Daily News*, who was tight with Sonny Werblin, claimed the real source of the problem was that Werblin had paid Namath $3,000 per exhibition game, rather than the $100-$350 that league rules required, and Namath refused to take the field until the Jets honored that agreement. The story was denied by all involved but it was another black mark for Namath and his impact on Jets morale. Namath admitted, "That was one of the times I really hated Weeb."

Three days into the ensuing controversy, Namath was pictured in the papers in a publicity shot with diminutive tailor Hyman Rifkin, who was eagerly fitting Namath with a $5,000 fur coat. As ever with Namath, the photo spurred stories nationwide about how suddenly fashionable it had become for men to wear furs. An article in the *Atlanta Journal*'s fashion section read, "There is a fur coat to suit the personality of every man alive. . . . Acceptance of fur coats by public figures, such as Joe Namath, have paved their way to popularity." None of this was boosting Jets morale. While Namath was traipsing the catwalk, football writer William Wallace had a different idea: Trade him. Noting that, "crisis comes to Namath easily," Wallace cited Namath's "scant respect for the coach," and concluded, "It is unlikely that the Jets can ever win with Namath and Ewbank out of harmony."

But Ewbank had a different notion. He would empower Namath. At the tail end of the exhibition season, Jets players were urged by coaches to put aside Namath's issues, and give him increased responsibility. Make him captain. The vote came on the day before the season started. In Kansas City, when a reporter brought up the Otto Graham criticism, that his teammates didn't think much of him, Namath responded triumphantly, "I'll tell you what my own team thinks of me. They voted me offensive captain of the Jets one hour and 53 minutes ago. We voted in the locker room before practice." Namath, unaware his teammates had to be cajoled into the vote, said, "This is the greatest honor of my life."

. . . .

When John Lindsay returned from the Republican convention, there were two looming questions. First was whether he would run for Governor in 1970. Second was whether he would run for president in 1972. The *New York Times* reported that, upon getting back to City Hall, Lindsay received offers of help for a potential future campaign from Republican governors and senators, and that one of the popular parlor games of the week in Miami was forecasting a Lindsay vs. Ronald Reagan nomination fight in 1972, should Richard Nixon lose in November. When, at the end of August, Lindsay's mayoral counterpoint, Richard Daley of Chicago, again allowed his city to slip into chaos during the "police riot" against protestors at the Democratic Convention, Lindsay was further buoyed—every riot on Daley's shoot-to-kill watch was a reminder that New York City had managed to avoid large-scale violence. As for the 1969 mayoral race, that was of little concern here in August 1968. "Mr. Lindsay has private polls," the *Times* said, "that indicate he could easily win re-election as Mayor."

While Lindsay was making his name nationally, a stubborn problem developed locally, one that could be loosely linked to the Chicago convention violence, the Columbia University occupation in April and even the boycott of the New York Athletic Club track meet at Madison Square Garden in February. The common thread was a New Left notion called, "confrontation politics," an umbrella term for the use of stark confrontation as a way to force the nation's attention onto serious social problems. The ascendancy of television meant that, in order to capture the attention of the citizenry, the would-be agent for social change had to choreograph visual elements that would not only reach the widest possible audience, but would shock it. One scholar wrote that confrontation politics, "grows up through improvisation, and it has been improvised as a way of getting around the sense of futility which has usually beset American radicalism." Confrontation didn't require a Martin Luther King, didn't need a massive civil rights bills as a goal, didn't need think-tanks or policy wonks or white papers. It needed memorable, visual *action*. At the 1968 Olympics in Mexico City, in front of the largest worldwide audience in history, US track stars Tommie Smith and John Carlos raised black-gloved fists on the medal podium. That was drastically scaled-back from the boycott of all US black athletes that had been advocated at the NYAC meet, but still, Smith and Carlos were engaging in confrontation—the patriotic indignation offered in sports pages was evidence of a confrontation, exactly the response desired by Smith and Carlos. Confrontation politics could take the shape of Columbia students pushing their administration out of Harlem's real estate, or protestors getting their heads corrugated in Chicago in the name of ending the Vietnam War.

Or it could be a radical citizen takeover of a failing local school district. In 1967, as part of a pilot project in the decentralization of schools (a policy for which Lindsay and other liberals had long advocated) New York set up three experimental projects in which local parents would be given more control over schools. Lindsay, rather unwisely, picked three largely minority districts for the experiment: one in Harlem, one on the Lower East Side and one in the Ocean Hill-Brownsville section of Brooklyn, a troubled area not far from the New Lots train station that had been central to the 1966 Brooklyn racial disturbances. One of the prominent figures in the neighborhood was Father John Powis, an idealistic young white priest who looked at the situation in Ocean Hill-Brownsville and determined the area was in need of "a confrontation with a sick society." The decentralized schools could provide a platform for such a confrontation. As part of the project, a local board of Ocean Hill-Brownsville parents and residents was hastily put together, with eighteen-year school system veteran Rhody McCoy in charge. Among the first acts of McCoy and the board, taken in May, was to move out nineteen teachers and administrators. This was a stunning confrontation. The board claimed the teachers were not fired, just that they were no longer welcome at Ocean Hill-Brownsville and could report to the Board of Education for reassignment. Worse was that the teachers were essentially "reassigned" without cause. The only cause seemed to be that they were white.

The Ocean Hill board had not been explicitly granted the authority to make personnel changes, and could not "fire" anyone, since it did not really employ anyone. There was a formal process for the removal of teachers, one respected both by the Board of Education and by the powerful United Federation of Teachers, but here, there was no process. The teachers were just told to go elsewhere. For those who lived in the three experimental districts, this was a test. The removal of the teachers was obviously wrong, but now they'd see whether those who had established the decentralized districts were serious about giving local boards real control. Would they be backed by the Board of Education? By the city? There had been lip-service paid by Lindsay and others toward empowering neighborhoods. But there had been little action. For those seeking that action, the local board's decision became a rallying point—public education was a bedrock of American society, and if parents in the area couldn't have control over something as basic as the people who would teach their own children, then there was really no such thing as local control. The "decentralization" process would be seen by people in places like Ocean Hill-Brownsville as a sham designed to placate, not empower.

For the Lindsay administration, the political problem was thick. The board at Ocean Hill-Brownsville was mostly black. Eighteen of the nineteen teachers and personnel who were being ousted were white. Specifically, most were Jewish. In the larger picture, this summed up what was happening with public schools in the city (and the nation), and the teachers who taught in them. With increasing numbers of white parents sending kids to private schools, the percentage of minority students in New York public schools passed 50 percent—even though the combined minority population was only 27 percent. But there were still disappointingly few teachers who were minorities, fewer than 10 percent. Achievement by minority students lagged white students considerably, and for black parents in places like Ocean Hill-Brownsville, there were only two conclusions to be drawn from numbers like that: Either something was wrong with their kids, or something was wrong with the mostly white system that was failing to educate them.

For teachers, this was a period of national mobilization. Teachers had long been the most docile element on the labor spectrum, and had called for strikes just 35 times across the country in the period of 1956–66. But the erosion of local education funding had chipped away at conditions in schools, especially in cities, meaning larger class sizes and more perilous working environments. Meanwhile, the average mean salary of a teacher had, from 1939–67, risen 39.4 percent, while the average for the rest of the labor force had risen 114.2 percent. One teacher in Des Moines in 1968 asked rhetorically, "How would *you* like to work in a classroom with beat-up furniture, broken windows and filthy words smeared on the walls that an overworked janitorial staff hasn't gotten around to scrubbing off?" And this was *Des Moines*. There had been an average of 3.5 teacher strikes per year over a decade, but in 1967 alone, there were 100, including one in New York in September, which went for two-and-a-half weeks. On the eve of the 1968 school year, it was predicted there would be 300–400 teacher strikes nationally.

At the end of the 1967 strike, there had been a Board of Education meeting that presaged the 1968 trouble in Ocean Hill-Brownsville. A group of about 200 black parents and activists stormed into a Board meeting and threatened teachers who had walked off the job during the strike. To the parents attempting to make decentralization plans work, white teachers were obstructionist and did not want to see control of schools transferred to local hands. For white teachers, the atmosphere had become one of threats and, "increasingly 'hate whitey' in tone." Indeed, one leader of Brooklyn CORE said at the meeting, "Better have somebody to guard those teachers in our neighborhood from now on." Those sentiments—blacks who saw white teachers as obstruction-ist and white teachers who felt threatened—did not abate through the summer of 1968 until, at the start of the school year, with no resolution to the Ocean Hill-Brownsville teacher dismissals, UFT head Albert Shanker called a strike.

Lindsay was not well-equipped to handle this sort of confronta-tion. No mayor would be, but for Lindsay, two of his base constitu-encies were blacks and liberal Jews, and here they were, pitted against each other. The Lindsay playbook for municipal labor relations—cry extortion, shout angrily about the illegal strike against 8 million New Yorkers for a while, then get the mediators—did not apply here. The teachers were not after more money, and they were not fighting the city. They were fighting a group of minority parents who were fed up with poor school conditions. There were 57,000 teachers on one side, 1 million kids and their parents on the other. Good luck picking villains and heroes in that battle.

The union would call three strikes in total—the opening two-day strike, a second September strike lasting more than two weeks and a third strike in mid-October, which ran for five weeks. Blacks and white liberals excoriated Shanker and the UFT for what they viewed as a racist strike. Shanker, who had participated in civil rights marches in Selma and Birmingham in the 1960s, was stung by the criticism. Columnist Jimmy Breslin compared Shanker to George Wallace and Joseph McCarthy, and wrote that Shanker was "the worst public person I have seen in my time in the city of New York." Anti-Semitism on the other extreme was disturbing, too. One black Ocean Hill-Brownsville teacher read a poem, reportedly written by a student, addressed to Shanker that started, "Hey Jew Boy, with that yarmulke on your head; You pale-faced Jew boy—I wish you were dead." Because it was already employing non-union teachers, Ocean Hill-Brownsville remained operational during the strike, though it required a cordon of police to escort teachers through the picket lines, and to keep Black Panthers monitoring the schools from creating problems. Layer that against the scene, only five years earlier, when the National Guard was sent to the University of Alabama to escort Vivian Malone and James Hood past George Wallace, and it was clear how quickly the civil rights movement had been turned on its head. Now, the police were required for black and white teachers to enter mostly black schools.

Even after the strike was settled in November—mostly out of sheer exhaustion—Lindsay would not recover his reputation. He supported local control of schools, but not in the confrontational way the board of Ocean Hill-Brownsville had gone about it, and to black supporters, he had abandoned them. His criticism of Shanker and the UFT (which was two-thirds Jewish) was more politically damaging. To whites, it put him in the corner of black militants and anti-Semites, a devastating turn considering the city had about 2 million Jews. The defining moment of the strike for Lindsay came on October 15, when he visited the East Midwood Jewish Center in Flatbush in hopes of rationally explaining the ideas behind school decentralization, but found a raucous, chanting crowd of 1,700 that booed him so loudly during his remarks that the rabbi took the microphone and implored, "As Jews, you have no right to be in this synagogue, acting the way you are acting. Is this the exemplification of the Jewish faith?" To which the angry crowd hollered, "Yes!" Lindsay, shouting to make his points, "facial muscles twitching, one white-knuckled hand gripping the podium," was continually drowned out by the taunts. Finally, he and his wife exited from a back door, faced a crowd of 5,000 more angry protestors chanting, "Lindsay must go!" and with help from the police, was able to slip into his car as the crowd surged forth.

In the November 5 election, Richard Nixon defeated Hubert H. Humphrey by a sizable margin in the electoral college count, though by only 0.7 percent in the general balloting (George Wallace's American Independent Party managed 13.5 percent). That would rule out the hypothetical Lindsay-Reagan for the Republican nomination in 1972. No matter. By November, the Lindsay summer ascendancy felt ages ago. Now, Lindsay was just trying to hold New York together. "The question now," he said, "is whether we can continue to survive as a city."

....

There were, at least, the Jets. The first two games of the 1968 season seemed to validate the excitement around the roster. Kansas City had the best defense in the league, and the Chiefs were seven-point favorites in the opener, but it was the Jets' defense that ruled the day, holding Kansas City to four field goals and one punt-return touchdown in a 20–19 win. Namath showed maturity, too. With six minutes to play, the Jets got the ball on the 5-yard line, and Namath put together a patient, clutch 70-yard drive that chewed up the remainder of the clock and kept the Chiefs from bringing on their hammer of a kicker, Jan Stenerud, for a game-winning try. The Jets rolled over the Patriots in Week 2, and were expected to do the same against Buffalo in the third game of the year. The Bills were 0–3, had lost both starting quarterback Jack Kemp and backup Tom Flores to injuries, and were left with thirteenth-round draft pick Dan Darragh as the starter. The Jets were 19-point favorites.

Namath, though, threw five interceptions in the game, three of which were returned for touchdowns, and Buffalo won its only game of the season, 37–35. Defensive coordinator Walt Michaels, a tough, reserved coach well-respected for his innovations, understood just how good his defense could be. The Jets had allowed nine touchdowns in their first three games, with six coming either on special-teams break-downs or Namath interceptions. After the Buffalo game, he called Namath to the front of the team plane. Michaels was seething. Namath said, "I could feel the heat coming from that chair." Michaels reminded Namath that the Bills had been playing with a rookie quarterback. He reminded him that the Jets' defense was capable of winning games on its own. He reminded him that, in a game like that, he should not be making mistakes. It was, ultimately, the lesson that Namath was still struggling to learn. "If Joe has a fault, it's that he thinks he can complete anything," Ewbank said. Namath led the Jets to a Week 4 win over the previously undefeated Chargers, but when the rebuilding Broncos came to Shea Stadium on October 13 as 20-point underdogs, it was the Buffalo game all over again. Namath threw five interceptions, and the Jets fell to a lowly opponent, 21–13. After the game, Namath didn't hide his despondency. He asked reporters to leave him alone. "I've always talked with you fellows before, no matter what," he said, "but not this time, please. Just say I stink. I fucking stink."

The Jets were 3–2, and held an unconvincing first-place spot in the East Division. With Namath having thrown 12 interceptions, there was talk of replacing him with thirty-eight-year-old backup Babe Parilli, who had been a starter for the Patriots the previous season but was swapped for Jets backup Mike Taliaferro. This stretch by Namath seemed to be Parilli's chance, but Ewbank wouldn't hear of it. He was sticking with Namath. Taliaferro would not have been surprised. As he was packing up to leave New York, he had said, in frustration, "The only way I could have played here was if Joe Namath fell off a bar stool and hurt his knee." Namath had gotten the vote of confidence from his coach, but it was time for him to allow the entreaty from Walt Michaels to sink in. Watching film after the Denver loss, Namath saw how good his own defense was and thought, "Why not let those 11 do their thing and give them the shot to win some games for us?"

Namath was ready to put more faith in his fellow Jets. It was good timing, then, that the Tuesday after the Denver loss, defensive lineman Verlon Biggs showed up at practice with a ring of scruff on his chin and under his nose. He was growing a goatee, he reported, and, "I'm not shavin' it off till we win the division championship." Jim Hudson liked the idea. He was in, too. So was Cornell Gordon. Al Atkinson, George Sauer, John Elliott—several Jets from both the offense and defense would make the no-razor-till-title commitment. Namath, who at times had been such a catalyst for team camaraderie, and at others had been distant and separate, loved the idea. He would grow a Fu Manchu. He couldn't fault the defense for being angry with him after the Buffalo and Denver games. But Biggs's gesture, Namath later wrote, showed, "unity was more important than defense versus offense. . . . We were gonna get through this together."

The Jets gained momentum from there. They won three straight. They were 6–2, and predictions for a weak East Division were proving to be spot-on. The Oilers were coming to Shea on November 10, and though they were just 4–5, that was good enough for second place in the division. A win here would put Houston four losses behind the Jets with just five games to play, ensuring that the New Yorkers would need to win two more for the division crown. For added incentive, Ewbank decorated the bulletin board in the locker room. He put up a large copy of a check, made out to "Each Jet Player," in the amount of $25,000, the player share for the winning Super Bowl team. He also included a reminder of the travails of 1967, when Houston beat out the Jets in the final week of the year for the East championship. The Oilers sent a telegram then, reading: WE HAVE SAVED SECOND PLACE FOR YOU. Focused and motivated, the Jets took the sloppy field at Shea Stadium in a pouring rain and struck quickly. Undaunted by the weather, Namath completed strikes to Don Maynard for 19 yards and Sauer for 43, putting the ball on the 5-yard line. Bill Mathis plunged ahead for a touchdown, a total of five plays into the game. The Jets built a 13–0 lead before allowing a Houston score, but stifled the Oilers from there, taking a 26–7 victory that effectively—if not officially—ended the playoff chase.

Namath had been suppressing his instinct to sling deep passes into coverage and, instead, was attacking intelligently and conservatively. It had yielded wins, but now Namath was under fire for an entirely different reason: He wasn't throwing touchdown passes. In fact, he went six games without a TD, dating back to the September loss to Buffalo. Longtime AFL columnist Larry Felser blamed Ewbank's offense, writing, "This is the team with the greatest passer to emerge since Unitas, and with people like George Sauer, Don Maynard and Pete Lammons to catch him. It's like seeing Rocky Marciano stoop to pulling hair." He implored Ewbank to consider the fan, too, because when an offense like the Jets' goes mild, Felser wrote, "it's time to start questioning the entertainment value of your product." Namath could only shake his head. "That's a lot of baloney," he said. "It just shows how ignorant people are. What's the difference how you score? I don't care how many touchdown passes I've thrown. Man, let's talk about winning." That was the focus now among the Jets. In their two previous seasons, they had let great starts dissolve into miserable finishes, and in three seasons of the Ewbank-Namath combination, they'd gone 3–6–1 in December. Guarding against that kind of collapse, Ewbank stepped up discipline ahead of the Jets' annual Oakland-San Diego trek, getting players to agree to $5,000 fines for anyone who missed the 11 p.m. curfew.

Not that the Jets needed much incentive to focus. The Raiders were also 7–2, but that wasn't what mattered. In their short history, especially since the arrival of Namath, Oakland had developed into a hated rival. The previous year, of course, Namath had been the target of cheap shots from fearsome linemen Ike Lassiter and Ben Davidson, who had broken Namath's cheek on an especially egregious tackle. At the time, Davidson feigned ignorance on having injured Namath, but later, he said, "I'll admit that the Namath thing was not quite a spur of the moment. That was the result of some things he said in New York earlier in the week that a quarterback shouldn't say." One night after the Jets arrived, Ewbank and Namath happened to meet Raiders President Al Davis at the team hotel. "You know what he told Joe?" Ewbank reported. "He said, 'I can't tell you who it is, but there's a guy on our team who's promised to get you Sunday. You'd better be careful.' That's the kind of stuff you pull in high school." The Jets-Raiders meeting was emotionally charged from the outset. The Jets committed a team-record thirteen penalties for 145 yards in the game, three of them facemasks, which was more facemask penalties than the team had been called for in the first eight games combined. In the second half, with the Jets leading, 19–14, and Oakland driving deep into Jets territory, Jim Hudson was whistled for another facemask. That was it. He lost his temper, going after the referee, and was ejected from the game. As the fans hollered and hurled debris at him, Hudson raised his middle finger and saluted them. Still, the Jets managed to hold a 32–29 lead with 1:05 to play.

That, however, was when disaster struck both the Jets and NBC. The network was slated to show a movie, *Heidi*, at 7 p.m., and when the time came around, the decision was made to switch away from Jets-Raiders in favor of the movie. Outraged Jets fans flooded NBC with calls. Back in Oakland, Daryle Lamonica torched Jets rookie defensive back Mike D'Amato—Hudson's fill-in—with a touchdown pass to give Oakland the lead. The Jets, still with time to make a desperation drive to win, fumbled the ensuing kickoff. The Raiders recovered it and scored again. The Jets gave up two touchdowns in nine seconds and lost, 43–32. (The headline in the *Daily News* read: "Jets 32, Raiders 29, Heidi 14.") After the game, the Jets were stunned and furious with the referees. Walt Michaels was, according to one observer, "in a rage after the game. He had to be restrained from crashing the officials' dressing room." The Raiders, actually, agreed that Michaels' rage was justified. Tackle Harry Schuh, who was near Hudson when he was ejected, said that the ejecting referee actually was the bigger offender because, "When Hudson questioned the call, the official used the worst language I ever heard." Another Raider said, "I never heard so much arguing back and forth between players and officials."

As for NBC and *Heidi*, Namath later worked with Dick Cline, the man who was responsible for giving the order to switch away from Jets-Raiders. "I'm sorry," Cline told Namath. "Don't be," Namath replied, "we lost."

CHAPTER 16

"I'll guarantee you"

IN OCTOBER 1965, A $9 million plan was presented by New York City Sports Commissioner Ben Finney to place a glass dome on top of Shea Stadium. The dome would allow a section of stands in the outfield to be completed, adding 14,000 seats and increasing capacity for baseball games to 70,000. Casey Stengel thought it was a great idea. "It looks like it's gonna be the greatest sports center in the world," he said. Sonny Werblin, still Jets impresario at the time, concurred, calling it, "the biggest boon New York could have commercially." Rep. John Lindsay, candidate for Mayor, was in favor of the plan, "in principle." The plan went nowhere—Mets chairman M. Donald Grant opposed, and Shea Stadium could not be altered without Mets approval. When December 29, 1968, came around, 62,627 fans and a roster full of New York Jets sure would have liked to give Grant a good throttling. Of course, most New Yorkers wanted to give Lindsay a good throttling, too. In the final week of December, New York was hit with a sort of Arctic apocalypse, starting with a strike by fuel-oil workers that left as many as 200,000 homes without heat just as the weather turned its most frigid (it was 12 degrees on December 26). That crisis, combined with a flu epidemic and a shortage of blood transfusions at city hospitals spurred the Board of Health to declare the city in a "state of peril." Lindsay, though, had taken his family to the Bahamas for the holiday. Even the *New York Times* editorial page, ever supportive of Lindsay, tut-tutted, "Mayor Lindsay's place is in the New York, not the Bahamas."

At Shea Stadium, the weather had pummeled the turf. Even the tarp was useless, because it only covered the field itself, leaving the sidelines exposed and allowing water to seep in underneath along the edges of the field. After the deep freeze, there had been snow on Friday, then a melting rain on Saturday. The temperature fluctuation left the ground pliant in places, hard as concrete in others. But maybe the bigger issue on that day was the shortage of blood transfusions. After all, Sunday would be the AFL championship game, and as bad as the weather picture was, the blood-transfusion shortage might have been more perilous: The Oakland Raiders were coming to New York.

After the "Heidi game" loss to the Raiders in November, the Jets closed with four straight crushing wins, by an average of 19.3 points. These were good times for the Jets. They'd clinched the franchise's first-ever playoff spot on Thanksgiving, but Weeb Ewbank was able to keep his players focused for the remainder of the schedule. Namath, publicly skewered for finishing sixth in his own team's MVP balloting the previous year, was named the MVP of the AFL, and did so despite a drop in passing yardage of more than 20 percent—his interceptions fell from 28 to 17, and 10 of those 17 had come in the two dreadful games against Buffalo and Denver. The Jets had two weeks to rest before the league championship game, while the Oakland had to play Kansas City to settle a tie at the top of the Western Division, with both teams at 12–2. In the downtime, Namath spent an evening at the Biltmore Theater in Times Square, to check out the musical comedy, *Hair,* which had opened to great acclaim in April. His review was both harsh and obtuse: "I didn't like it," he said. "I know it got good reviews here and in London, but I just didn't like it." Meanwhile, the Raiders shocked the rest of the AFL with the way they clobbered Kansas City, 41–6, in their tiebreaker.

Now both teams were walking into an icy, puddly, 37-degree, half-melted, undomed Shea Stadium, with forty-mile-per-hour winds whipping off Flushing Bay and tearing the canvas covering from the bottom of the stands. "The wind here," Jets kicker Jim Turner warned, "is the worst in the league." So was the bad blood between the teams, particularly between the Raiders' voracious defensive ends, Ike Lassiter and Ben Davidson, and their pipsqueak prey, Joe Namath. Al Davis was so pleased by the 1967 hit in which Davidson had broken Namath's cheek that he had a photo of the play blown up in black-and-white, and hung in the Raider corporate office, Namath helplessly sprawled on the turf. The duo would be trouble again. Ewbank had been having trouble all season filling the right tackle spot, after Sherman Plunkett had been waived in training camp. Rookie Sam Walton had not proven up to the task of replacing him, so Ewbank was left to tinker with sliding backup guards into the spot and hoping for the best. From the first quarter, Lassiter and Davidson were keyed in on Namath. The Jets took a 10–0 lead early, but Lassiter had laid a hit on Namath that was so hard the quarterback needed smelling salts on the sideline. In the second quarter, in the middle of a pileup, the ring finger on Namath's left hand got crunched, so that, according to one account, "It was bent three ways." Raiders lineman Dan Birdwell stood over Namath, saw the finger and said with enthusiasm, "Hey, Joe, you broke your finger!" Namath had to have the finger popped back into place and taped to his middle finger. Just as bad: he had again jammed the thumb on his throwing hand, making the ball difficult to grip.

Namath took another hard hit when both Lassiter and Davidson converged on him near the end of the second quarter, and was again dazed. *Boston Globe* writer Will McDonough described it as "a tremendous belt to the head that put him in a fog for 30 minutes." By halftime, the Jets led, 13–10, but when they got to the locker room, a limping Namath was taken quickly to the training room, where he was ministered by Dr. Nicholas and trainer Jeff Snedeker. He was given painkilling shots in his knees, and xylocaine for his finger. But the bigger problem was that Namath was in more than a fog. He had a concussion. He didn't know where he was. Ewbank made his halftime speech to the rest of the team, and was approached by Nicholas. "You may have to go with Parilli," he told the coach. Ewbank went to the training room to see Namath. His quarterback was in bad shape. Ewbank said nothing, only made some inaudible noises, but Namath could see his fists were balled up. "Boy it felt like he was willing me back out there," Namath later said. Namath did, indeed get back out there. After the Raiders tied the game, Namath led an 80-yard drive against the wind, capped by a touchdown pass to Pete Lammons, putting the Jets back in front, 20–13, heading into the fourth quarter. There, visions of the Heidi game had to haunt the Jets—the Raiders put up 10 points in a span of twenty-three seconds, getting a field goal from George Blanda, followed by a wind-aided interception thrown by Namath to cornerback George Atkinson to set up a score. For the first time, the Jets trailed, down 23–20.

After the interception, Don Maynard told Namath he still could get a step on Atkinson when he needed it. Atkinson was talented (he made the AFL's Pro Bowl as a kick returner that year), but he was a rookie and the thirty-three-year-old Maynard had dominated him for ten catches and 228 yards in the teams' first meeting. Atkinson, Maynard told Namath, had been cheating up throughout the afternoon, figuring that with such wild gusts at Shea, the Jets would not attempt a deep pass. Namath took heed. With about eight minutes to play in the game, Namath warned his team in the huddle to be alert, because he might call an audible at the line for "60 G"—that is, a deep bomb to the goal line. From the Raiders 42-yard line, Namath dropped back and unleashed a high, spiraling bullet that the wind lifted, knocked to the left, then to the right and finally into the hands of Maynard, who had to swivel from his inside to his outside shoulder to make the catch, the momentum of the ball carrying him out of bounds at the Raider 6-yard line. On the following play, with 7:47 to go, Namath again dropped back to pass, but went through his progression of receivers, only to find his first two options draped by Raiders defenders. He turned to the right, though, and found Maynard in the back of the end zone for a touchdown.

The Raiders would get the ball back twice, but failed to score, the final drive ending on a botched pass to the flat from Daryle Lamonica, which was technically thrown backward and, thus, a fumble. The Jets recovered. By a score of 27–23, they were AFL champions. The 60 G throw Namath made to Maynard still resonates. "That pass from Namath to Maynard," *Times* beat writer Dave Anderson recalled, "That was always the greatest pass play I've ever seen. He had to throw it 75, 80 yards just to get it there, and in that crazy wind. That play, to me, defined that Jets team, that Jets era." The play was greater still when Namath's condition is taken into account. He later said he considered pulling out of the game. Ewbank—who had so much staked on this season—cried as his team carried him off, cried again when they gave him the game ball, and cried when they playfully put him, fully clothed, into a running shower. (He might have been crying, too, because his players injured his hip during the horseplay.)

Namath was asked about the matchup with the juggernaut Colts, who were 13–1 in the regular season and already clobbering the Browns in the NFL championship game when the Jets game ended. Namath didn't think they were so invincible, and pointed out that Lamonica, whom they'd just beaten was "a better quarterback" than NFL MVP Earl Morrall, who had been outstanding in filling in for the injured Johnny Unitas. "Miami is going to be fun," Namath said. "We're going to beat those guys, huh?" Namath asked Ewbank where the champagne was. Ewbank motioned toward the training room, which he'd made off-limits to the press before the season, and said, "In there. 25 cases." Namath nodded and said, "That should be enough."

Reporter Ken Nigro of the *Baltimore Sun* asked around for other players' thoughts on the Super Bowl. Kicker Jim Turner, "almost hysterically" according to Nigro, yelled, "Hell, you wait till we get hold of 'em! If you don't think we can beat the Colts, you get the hell out of here!" Lineman Winston Hill, meanwhile, was doing a radio interview and was asked whether the Jets were going to beat Baltimore. "Yes," he said, "we are."

. . . .

New York had six entries in major American team sports in 1965, '66, and '67—the Jets and Giants in football, the Mets and Yankees in baseball, the Rangers of the NHL and the NBA's Knicks—which meant they played a combined 18 total seasons in those three years. Only two of those seasons produced records better than .500: the 8–5–1 Jets in 1967, and the Rangers at 30–28–12 in 1966–67. Those Rangers made the playoffs and were swept. The Knicks backed into the playoffs, too, in 1966–67, with a 36–45 record, and were eliminated by losing three of four. Those were the only playoff games New York teams played in three seasons. The city had become a sports wasteland by 1968, when Namath and the young Jets, who were fresh while the Yankees and Giants were tired, reached their AFL ascendancy.

A glimmer of hope, though, also had been given by the Knicks the previous season after the hiring of Red Holzman, as they rallied behind their more disciplined, more innovative new coach to earn a playoff spot. In training camp, the Knicks were touted as championship contenders, a team that had shed its previous image as petulant and spoiled underachievers, one that was ready to restore a little pride the way the Jets had. It took only nineteen games to correct that notion. The team stumbled to a 6–13 record by late November, and when they were crushed by the Lakers, 130–109, to end a miserable road trip in which they lost five of six games, Holzman was so irate at his team's lack of effort, he fined each player $100. When the Knicks got back to New York, they were met by Irving Felt, head of Madison Square Garden, the Knicks' owner, who angrily bawled out the players. It looked like another season of disappointment, and beat reporter Leonard Koppett wrote that until management "comprehends what it has created by overpaying, overrating and overpublicizing its players in the hopes of selling season tickets, there is little hope for progress."

Within the team, it was clear that the problem began with their big men. The Knicks were trying to play Willis Reed and Walt Bellamy together. The two didn't much like each other and, worse, Reed felt he was a center but had to be moved to power forward to accommodate Bellamy. Reed was the Knicks' best player, the league's Rookie of the Year in 1965, and an All-Star every season. He ranked as Holzman's best find from his scouting days, passed over until the second round because teams were unsure what position he would play or whether his numbers were distorted because he played for Grambling State, an all-black college. At 6–9, Reed was undersize for a center, but he was powerfully built, renowned for his work ethic and a better player when he was inside, near the basket. Bellamy was perhaps as talented as any center in the league, a 6–11 behemoth who had averaged 31.6 points and 19.0 rebounds as a rookie in 1961–62, and was one of the few capable of matching star centers Wilt Chamberlain and Bill Russell. But Bellamy had a tendency to slack off in effort when he was playing against lesser opponents, and that unevenness bothered not only Holzman, but his teammates, too.

As the early part of the 1968-69 season pressed on, Holzman and Knicks general manager Ed Donovan determined to trade Bellamy. It wasn't easy—once word was out that Bellamy was available, teams around the NBA attempted to lowball the Knicks. But Holzman and Donovan knew the guy they wanted: Dave DeBusschere, a versatile forward who was a local hero in Detroit (he'd gone to the University of Detroit) but had been languishing with a bad team. After weeks of haggling, the Pistons finally consented to make the deal, but needed the Knicks to add guard Howard Komives in order to make the trade more palatable to fans who would not be happy to see DeBusschere shipped out.

Oddly enough, the Knicks were in Detroit on December 19 to play the Pistons when the trade was finalized. DeBusschere was in his home hanging a painting in his living room when he took the call from Piston general manager Ed Coil. Even odder—the painting was of DeBusschere, in his Pistons uniform, driving around an opponent in a game; the opponent was Walt Bellamy of the Knicks. When DeBusschere got the news, it was liberating. The pressure of trying to carry his undermanned hometown Pistons had worn on him, and the sting of having failed in a stint as a player-coach still lingered. The trade freed Holzman to tinker with his lineup, too, giving him a faster, more versatile team that could employ his pressing defense, with "Clyde" Frazier in at point guard and Reed back to his preferred center spot. Reed was thrilled. Asked about going back to playing center, he said, "It's like coming home, like being in a foreign country for a long, long time and then coming back to your old home town."

On the Knicks' first night with DeBusschere in the lineup, against the Pistons, everything went right. DeBusschere was active, helping the Knicks to a 12-point lead at halftime that grew to 24 in the third quarter and wound up a lopsided embarrassment in favor of the Knicks, 135–87. DeBusschere had a game-high 21 points, leading seven Knicks who scored in double-figures. The Pistons drew a crowd of about double their normal Friday-night draw, as the locals wanted a look at how the principals in the trade shaped up. According to one reporter, the crowd, "gave their decision when DeBusschere left the game with about 6 ½ minutes to go. They gave him a standing ovation. Bellamy, who fouled out two minutes later, got stony silence."

The DeBusschere trade remade the Knicks. On the day the Jets were taking the field in Miami for the Super Bowl, the Knicks were in the midst of an eight-game road trip, in San Diego. They were also in the midst of a stretch in which they won 16 out of 17 games and moved four games behind the Bullets for first place in the Eastern Division. "We had a lot of negativity that was holding us back before that trade," Frazier said. "That was a big moment for us. Willis and Walt did not get along, and it was affecting the whole team. There was bad chemistry. But we made the trade and that was the end of that animosity. That was when we really came together and took off from there."

. . . .

Fans would be excused if they'd failed to take note of the Knicks' success as the calendar turned over from 1968. That's because the first two weeks of 1969—not just in New York, but across the nation—belonged to Joe Willie Namath.

By this point of his career, Namath understood his relationship with the press. His first two seasons were consumed by Namath's willingness to open his swingin' booze-and-broads night life to every dumpy middle-aged national magazine writer who wanted to pass along to America the fawning images of Namath swimming the East Side bars as Jacques Cousteau would pass along the image of a spiny urchin on a coral reef. But Namath realized magazine writers would crop up for a spell, write something incendiary, then disappear, and all the while, a chorus of national columnists would chime in from afar with their disapproval of his words, actions or Fu Manchu mustache (which, he had shaved for a handsome $10,000 endorsement fee). Increasingly, Namath limited himself to New York writers, and named a few he trusted, including Dave Anderson. "We got along because I knew 10 guys like Joe Namath when I was growing up in Brooklyn," Anderson said. "So I was always straight with him. And, I'll tell you, in all the years I knew Joe, he might be the only athlete who never lied to me."

But so few writers were straight with Namath, or really knew him. He'd become a caricature to many. "There have been so many dumb things written about me—by so many people who haven't even talked to me—that it's just ridiculous, man," Namath would explain. "As far as football writers go, I don't think one of them really knows what's happening on the field. . . . Another thing that happens to almost every ballplayer is that quotes get jumbled up something fierce. Usually, even if reporters get the words right in a quote, they screw up the emphasis, and the next morning, you discover you've said something you just never said. In general, I think most sportswriters want to do a good job, and if they talk straight to me, I give them straight answers." But Namath found that most reporters only had their own self-interests in mind. "Mostly, I don't dig the press. Because the press doesn't care how much it hurts people like me, so long as there's a good headline. Look, I realize I wouldn't be where I am without the press, but after a while, you can't help getting annoyed over the bullshit papers print about you."

It was in that spirit that Namath arrived at the Galt Ocean Mile hotel in Fort Lauderdale on January 2, 1969. The Super Bowl was in its infancy—so new, Commissioner Pete Rozelle was still resisting calling the thing the "Super Bowl," though it was the accepted phrase among writers and fans—but it was unquestionably a media event, attracting hundreds of reporters and drawing television advertisers willing to pay

$135,000 per minute. The NFL's representative in the first two games had been Green Bay, and under the stern eye of Vince Lombardi, there was little chance that any Packer would make an impolitic utterance that would land in a headline. In the first Super Bowl in 1967, Kansas City defensive back Fred "The Hammer" Williamson found that his team was so intimidated by the NFL's Packers that they were like "zombies." Williamson took it upon himself to taunt the Packers with threats to "drop my Hammer," and belittled his opponents by comparing them to mundane AFL players. Later, Williamson explained, "They see me peacocking around, maybe they'll pick it up, maybe they'll start saying, 'Green Bay Packers? Sheeit.' Who cares if they didn't like me?" The Hammer, however, was knocked unconscious by a Packer running back and had to leave the game in the fourth quarter. The following year, the Raiders took the opposite tack against the Packers, plying them with kindness and wonder, or, as one Raiders official said, giving Green Bay "the great snow job." Even slick-haired Al Davis got into the act. "Imagine," he gushed, "us on the same field as the Green Bay Packers." Neither approach worked, however. The Packers beat the Chiefs, 35–10, and gently put away the Raiders, 33–14.

From the beginning, Namath was the show on Super Bowl week. It was fitting that the Jets' practice facility happened to be where the Yankees held spring training each year—a piece of tape with "Ewbank" written on it in crayon temporarily covered the Ralph Houk nameplate on the coach's office, and Namath was designated the same locker as Mickey Mantle. Much as Mantle, Namath had developed an ability to dominate surrounding conversations without having to do so as a conscious choice. He wasn't "Hammer" Williamson, peacocking for publicity, but if he was going to speak, he was going to speak the truth and not give the kind of clichés the Raiders had offered before the previous year's game. In fact, Namath was through with clichés altogether. He wasn't going to put on an air of false humility. Las Vegas gambling guru Jimmy "The Greek" Snyder set the betting line at 17 points, and in announcing it, "Proudly . . . noted that he publicly made Spiro T. Agnew the favorite to become Richard M. Nixon's running mate before Nixon was even nominated as the presidential candidate." When asked about Snyder's point spread, Namath slyly said, "I didn't know we were that bad of a team." Yeah, the Colts were good, but so were the Jets, Namath insisted. "I might sound like I'm boasting and bragging," Namath said, "and I am."

On the flight from New York to Florida, he vented about the pro- hibition of locker-room champagne in the AFL by the league commis- sioner, which had forced he and his teammates back into the training room. He was told it was to keep booze out of sight of kids watching on TV. Namath called out the league on its hypocrisy. Didn't the commis- sioner see Lassiter and Davidson knocking Namath loopy in the league championship? And some celebratory champagne is bad? "You know what the real image of football is, it's brutality," Namath said. "Why don't they tell kids like it is? Tell the kids that this guy is trying to hurt that guy and knock him out of the football game."

Namath's first official act of Super Bowl week was to sleep through the mandatory photo and media session, which was slated for 10 a.m. on Monday, incurring a $50 fine. Namath offered no apology: "I always sleep in the morning, that's the thing to do." That came after a Sunday night in which he tussled with Colts kicker Lou Michaels, who was no ordinary kicker—Michaels had been a defensive lineman earlier in his career, weighed 250 pounds and was the brother of Jets defensive coordinator Walt Michaels. Michaels spotted Namath with friends at Fazio's restaurant in Fort Lauderdale, introduced himself and, rather than getting a simple introduction in return, listened to Namath launch into a spiel about, "how the Jets were going to kick the shit out of our team." Michaels was taken aback. "I believe in that little thing called modesty," Michaels later said. "I asked him about that, and he said, 'That's not in my dictionary.' I don't know why he came on so strong." That probably had something to do with Namath's glass, tumbled full of Johnnie Walker Red, as Namath conceded. Michaels invited Namath to step outside, before the situation would be defused by fellow Colts and Jets at the bar. To make amends, Namath pulled out a $100 bill and bought the drinks for Michaels' table. On Tuesday, after Colts coach

Don Shula expressed his disappointment in Namath's statement that Raiders quarterback Daryle Lamonica was better than Earl Morrall, Namath, as he lay tanning poolside at the Galt Ocean Mile, reiterated that he actually thought the AFL had four or five quarterbacks better than Morrall. Heck, when asked about it earlier, he'd even said *Babe Parilli* was a better quarterback than Morrall, which meant that on the Jets, Morrall would be a third-stringer. Colts defensive linemen Billy Ray Smith and Bubba Smith scoffed, too. "When he gets a little older," Billy Ray said, "he'll get humility." Said his fellow Smith, Bubba: "A football player who's real good doesn't have to talk."

Even Morrall himself—an irreproachable gentleman and family man, thirty-four years old and a veteran of five pro teams (let go by Allie Sherman's Giants in the 1968 preseason), the year's most endearing story after taking over for Johnny Unitas and his injured arm—finally cracked and snapped back at Namath's Jets. "We have faced a lot better teams this season and come out all right," Morrall said. "They say we are big favorites. I don't see any reason why we shouldn't be." The gathered media had developed a Namath dependence, hanging on his words, breathlessly rushing back to their keyboards to clack out copy and send it back to their papers in Duluth or Des Moines or Denver. The problem for the Colts was that, as the week went on, they, too, were breathlessly hanging on Namath's words. He'd infiltrated their collective psyche.

It culminated in one final outrage, committed on the Thursday before the game, when Namath was invited to the Touchdown Club near the airport in Miami Springs to receive the group's award as the outstanding player in football. He popped out of the Galt Ocean Mile in a shiny green suit, and swung by the Jets' team barbeque, dabbling in some food and beer before putting some Johnnie Walker Red into a paper cup to sip as he was being driven to the Touchdown Club gathering. When Namath walked into the King Arthur's Room of the Miami Springs Villas, where the ceremony was being held, he was surprised to find a room packed with six hundred people. He'd been expecting a third of that. Standing at the podium to deliver a speech increasingly spiced with scotch, Namath acknowledged his coaches, going back to Larry Bruno in high school, Bear Bryant at Alabama, and now, Weeb Ewbank. He acknowledged Sonny Werblin and the current Jets owners. He paused repeatedly to slurp from his tumbler. "You fellows out there under twenty-one, this ginger ale is good stuff," he said. Namath thanked his teammates, then said, "You can be the greatest athlete in the world, but if you don't win those football games, it doesn't mean anything. And we're going to win Sunday, I'll guarantee you."

Namath kept rambling from there. Certainly, the sentence would not have struck many as all that incendiary. It was something he had been saying in one form or another since the AFL championship game, something his fellow Jets had been saying all along, too. No big deal. But, because it was Namath, because he phrased it *just so*, because a reporter from the *Miami Herald* happened to be there, and because the editor on the *Herald* copy desk that day knew how to blow a thing out of proportion, it would become the gasconade that defined Namath. The *Herald* was, in fact, the only paper to make much of Namath's statement, but every sportswriter with a travel budget was reading the Miami paper that week. It didn't take the rest of the Fourth Estate to catch on. It was more of the press bullshit he knew so well, more quotes and emphasis getting jumbled up something fierce in pursuit of a headline, but it would belong to Namath, forever.

We're going to win Sunday, I'll guarantee you.

CHAPTER 17

Light, Meaningless, Dippy and Lovely Few Days

Hours before Super Bowl III, Colts owner Carroll Rosenbloom paid a visit to Jets coach Weeb Ewbank. These were never easy meetings for Ewbank. He had worked for Rosenbloom as head coach of the Colts from 1954–1962, and when he had taken that job, as when he got the Jets job, Ewbank promised that he could get the Colts operating at a championship level in five seasons. That's exactly what he did in Baltimore, where the Colts won the 1958 championship, and backed it up with another championship in 1959. But after finishing .500 in two of three seasons after that, Rosenbloom let Ewbank go, a decision that pained both men. It stood as the only time Ewbank had been fired from a job, and it embittered him. Rosenbloom brought in thirty-three-year-old Don Shula to replace Ewbank, but he had never been certain Shula was any better than Ewbank, and Shula's teams had not won a championship, demonstrating an inability to win when the stakes were highest. Ewbank later recalled that once after a couple drinks, Rosenbloom's wife, Georgia, said to him, "Did Carroll ever tell you how sorry he is that he let you go?" When Ewbank said he had not, she replied, "Well, he's said it to me a lot of times."

Rosenbloom owned a house on Golden Beach near Fort Lauderdale and invited Ewbank and his wife, Lucy, to come by for a postgame party. *A party?* It obviously wasn't a routine Sunday evening cocktail gathering. No, Rosenbloom had already planned the *victory party* for his Colts. He did not think, Ewbank told Rosenbloom, he and Lucy would be making it. Ewbank let his players know the Colts' owner had a victory party planned before the game. Not that their sense of underdog outrage needed to be stoked any further. What had started as a 17-point gap in the betting line between the Colts and Jets grew to more than 20 points by game day. One survey of gathered reporters—there were 367 altogether—showed that 49 were picking the Colts to win, and only six had the Jets winning. Another poll of more than 200 writers showed just 23 supporting Namath and the Jets, and 18 of those were employed in and around New York. *Sports Illustrated*'s Tex Maule picked the Colts to win, 43–0. Jesse Outlar of the *Atlanta Constitution* was more conservative, picking Baltimore, 38–0.

Namath had spent the previous night the same way he had spent many nights in the two-week run-up to this game, sitting with what he called "the one-eyed monster"—the film projector—at the Galt Ocean Mile, picking apart what he saw of the Colts' defense. Whatever Namath's faults were as a player and a teammate, none of his coaches or fellow Jets could criticize how hard he worked at preparing for a game, analyzing an opponent, taking what he saw on film and applying it, real-time, once kickoff came. What he saw of the Colts, he liked. Baltimore's defense was its strong suit, having put up four shutouts on the season, allowing an average of just 10.3 points and giving up only nine passing touchdowns all year. (By way of comparison, the Jets had allowed 20.0 points per game, and 17 touchdown passes.) The Colts had a big defensive line, anchored by 6-foot-7 star Bubba Smith, but it was what Namath saw from their defensive backs that intrigued him most. They frequently used a safety blitz, bringing defenders from the back line forward to rush the quarterback. That left spots open in the middle of the field, and if Namath called for short, quick pass plays to those spots, the Jets could turn Baltimore's strength into a weakness. "I just prayed that the Colts would blitz us," Namath observed. "If they did, I figured, they were dead." Of course, Namath was not going to spend a perfectly good South Florida Saturday night in a suite of rooms by himself. His roommate, Jim Hudson, was married and was staying in a separate room with his wife. So, as Namath explained it, "I went out and got a bottle and grabbed this girl and brought her back to the hotel in Fort Lauderdale and we had a good time the whole night." Therapeutic, don't you know. "It's good for you," he said. "It loosens you up good for the game."

The Jets did the best they could to make Super Bowl day like any other game. There was a morning breakfast of steak and eggs at the hotel. There was Namath, ambling in with droopy eyes. Ewbank projected an easiness. It was a front. "I was calm," he said, "but my stomach wasn't." At the Miami Orange Bowl, officially, 75,377 fans were in place, and it was estimated that 60–70 million fans worldwide would be tuning in, either on television or radio. For Namath, it was a clash of his various realities—almost exactly four years ago, in this very stadium, he was a college kid with a bum knee, trying, and nearly succeeding, to rally Alabama from a big deficit against Texas. Now, Hudson, the quarterback of those Longhorns, was his roommate. Sauer and Lammons, his two short-route receiving targets, were on that Texas team, too. Sonny Werblin, who shoved a contract into Namath's hand shortly after Alabama's defeat was final, was in the crowd for the Super Bowl. When Namath took the field for the coin toss with the other team captains, there was Johnny Unitas, a fellow Pennsylvanian who had been his boyhood idol. Namath had even worn Johnny U's No. 19 in high school. Namath needed a deep breath.

The game didn't get off to the start the Jets had hoped. They picked up a first down, but were stifled from there and punted. On their first drive, the Colts moved easily on the Jet defense. Morrall found end John Mackey for a nineteen-yard play, and went to the ground game with Tom Matte and Jerry Hill, pushing quickly into New York territory. Another pass from Morrall got the Colts to the Jets nineteen-yard line, and early indications were that 43–0 might not be such a bad guess. But the Colts drive stalled from there, and Lou Michaels—who had more pressure on him, having been the guy who'd gone toe-to-toe with Namath a week earlier—stepped on for a 27-yard field-goal try. Wide right, no good. By the end of the first quarter, the teams had traded fruitless drives, before Baltimore caught a break. Sauer took a pass from Namath, was hit as he turned, and fumbled at the Jets' own 12 yard-line just before the first quarter elapsed. But as would so often happen on this day, it was the Jets who had fortune on their side. Rather than punching in for a Colts score, a Morrall pass was tipped by linebacker Al Atkinson, hit the shoulder pad of Colts receiver Tom Mitchell and fell into the arms of Jets defensive back Randy Beverly for an interception in the end zone.

It was an enormous momentum swing. By now, Namath's nerves had settled. He was still taking Walt Michaels's advice—*don't be making mistakes*. Patiently, Namath led the Jets on an 80-yard drive that used up 5:06 of the quarter, eschewing plays called in the huddle and instead making all of his play calls at the line of scrimmage, reading the defensive backs, waiting for that blitz. Namath attacked the weak side of the Colts defense with three straight handoffs to Matt Snell, and once the Colts adjusted to the running game, he attacked through the air, his mix of plays keeping Baltimore's vaunted defense off guard. When Snell scored from the 4-yard line and Jim Turner kicked the extra point, making the score 7–0, not only had the Jets taken the AFL's first lead in Super Bowl history, but they had wiped clean the aura of invulnerability that had cloaked the Colts defense. "I could hear them cursing themselves in their huddle," lineman John Schmitt would say.

That sequence set the tone for both Morrall and Namath. On the ensuing drive, Morrall got the Colts into field-goal position, but again, Michaels missed. With time winding down in the half, the Colts got a 58-yard run from Matte and moved the ball to the 15-yard line of the Jets. But Morrall, trying to find receiver Willie Richardson in the middle of the field, instead was intercepted by a diving Johnny Sample. On the last play of the first half, the Colts had the ball on the Jets' 41 and attempted a flea-flicker. It might have worked—Morrall had receiver Jimmy Orr wide open—but instead Hudson intercepted him. Morrall finished the half completing just five of his 15 passes, with three interceptions, and with the Jets leading, 7–0, the gathered crowd expected the Colts to come out with Unitas in the second half. Shula, though, surprisingly stuck with Morrall. It might not have mattered. The Colts fumbled on the first play of the half, giving the ball to the Jets at the 33. Namath was brilliant in the third quarter, sticking with the doctrine of patience. Even after the fumble, the Jets managed just eight yards, but Namath used up 4:17 off the clock to do it, and a Turner field goal put the Jets up, 10–0. Namath followed that with a 10-play drive that yielded another field goal, and used another 4:06. The Jets ran twenty-three plays in the third quarter. The Colts ran nine. Down 13–0, though, Shula did finally bring in Unitas. But it was too late. The Jets opened the fourth with a field goal and a 16–0 lead, and though Unitas rallied the Colts to a touchdown, the melting of the clock behind Namath's play calls and Snell's bruising runs was too much.

In the final seconds of the game, broadcaster Kyle Rote scanned the Colts sideline and said, "If you don't think that is a dejected Baltimore bench right now—what are their feelings? They were anywhere from 18- to 22-point favorites. They were ridiculing the Jets and the AFL. The Colts, called one of the greatest teams in the history of pro football." Once time expired, Namath and the Jets headed into the locker room to start what would be an extended postgame celebration. Namath, leaving the field, was caught by the surge of applause from the crowd and lifted his right arm as he hit the tunnel, extending his index finger in a "No. 1" sign. "If Namath made some money before this game," Rote wondered, "what's he gonna do after the game?"

Namath was named the game's MVP, but in the locker room, Snell (121 yards rushing, 40 receiving) and Sauer (eight catches, 133 yards) were getting equal credit—the Jets knew they would be the best weapons against the Colts' blitz, and Namath used them with near perfection. Snell had picked apart the left side of the Colts line, running away from Bubba Smith consistently. The Jets offensive line played its finest game. Shula conceded that "Namath's quickness took away our blitz. He beat our blitz more than we beat him." Namath was asked what he thought about the NFL-backing reporters who had written that the Jets had no chance. "I hope they eat their pencils and pads," he said. Jimmy "the Greek" Snyder, scrambling to excuse his 17-point opening betting line, pointed to the Colts' miscues and said, "If the Colts and Jets played again tomorrow, I would send out odds still making the Colts 11- or 12-point favorites." Veteran Oakland Raider George Blanda marveled not so much at Namath's on-field performance, but his media performance throughout Super Bowl week. "Namath psyched two teams," he said. "He psyched the Jets into believing they could win and he psyched the Colts into doubting they could win."

Packers lineman Jerry Kramer, who had played nine seasons under Vince Lombardi, said, "What a blow to clean living."

On the raucous bus ride back to the hotel in Fort Lauderdale, Ewbank had a moment of special satisfaction. Going up the old Route 1A, along the beach, the Jets passed the home of Carroll Rosenbloom. There was a blue-and-white tent outside, the expected headquarters for his victory party. But there was no rowdy party going on. Senator Ted Kennedy, Vice President Spiro Agnew, NFL Commissioner Pete Rozelle, all were invited guests of Rosenbloom. But the place was virtually empty. Ewbank just looked, saying nothing.

. . . .

New York City, at that moment, needed Joe Namath. Fun City had deteriorated to the point that the irony of the moniker wasn't even clever anymore, it was just heavy and sad. But then: Namath. "He comes with a Scotch in his hand at night and a football in the daytime and last season he gave New York the only lift the city has had in so many years it is hard to think of a comparison," Jimmy Breslin wrote. "And there is only one sport anymore that can change the tone of a city and there is only one player who can do it. His name is Joe Willie Namath and when he beat the Baltimore Colts he gave New York the kind of light, meaningless, dippy and lovely few days we had all but forgotten."

In the wake of the Jets' victory, Mayor Lindsay sent a telegram to Ewbank: "All of us are proud of you. Your smashing triumph is the greatest upset in the history of professional football. We are looking forward to welcoming you world champions back to New York City." When the Jets arrived at Kennedy Airport the following day, 500 fans were there to greet them, including Lindsay and new City Council President Francis X. Smith, along with a five-man band and a chorus of chants declaring, "We're No. 1!" The crowd was disappointed when the plane emptied. Namath was not aboard, having had stayed behind in Florida, where he would (begrudgingly) play in the AFL All-Star game in Jacksonville. They were also disappointed to find something else was not on board: the game ball and championship trophy. When the team was scurrying to leave the hotel in Fort Lauderdale, no one remembered to pack the trophy. The Jets had to send an assistant trainer back to retrieve it, and it arrived later in the afternoon, on a commercial flight.

Lindsay told Ewbank that as soon as he could get the team together, they would be honored with a ceremony at City Hall. Lindsay was asked about Namath, and said, smiling, "I'm for him." How about running against Namath for re-election? "I don't want to run against anyone right now," he said. There were chants of, "We want a parade for our boys!" The previous Friday, New York had held a ticker-tape parade for the Apollo 8 astronauts, but parades for sporting heroes were rare at the time—in the long history of ticker-tape parades in New York, which dated to the turn of the century, only 14 had been given for sports figures, and five of those had been for Olympic athletes. Four had been given for baseball teams (the Giants in 1954, the Yankees after championships in 1961 and '62, and the Mets at their birth in 1962), but none had been given for football, even the Giants. That wouldn't change for the Jets.

It was 8 a.m. on January 22 when, outside City Hall, a crowd began to gather—about 90 percent (by one estimate) truant teenagers, and most of them female. By noon, the crowd would grow to about 6,000, when the door of City Hall opened and Lindsay came out, striding through a cordon of police to a podium looking out at City Hall Park. He was met with, one reporter wrote, "solid booing, as though the Mayor was a Baltimore Colt." Just behind Lindsay, Joe Namath, in a gray plaid double-breasted suit, with broadsword tie and silver-buckled shoes, stepped forth and the booing was replaced by high-pitched cheers. The mayor addressed the crowd, lauding, "our conquering team." A chant of "Namath for mayor!" went up, and Lindsay was drowned out. Namath stood up, as if to hush the hyperventilating young ladies, and allow Lindsay to finish the official proclamation. Lindsay presented the Jets with cufflinks and tie clasps engraved with the city seal, and the team presented Lindsay with a LeRoy Neiman painting of Namath in action. Addressing the crowd, Namath said, "We're the new faces for the new generation."

We. Namath said. *Me and you. The rest of these stuffed shirts don't get us.* It was not long ago, fewer than four years, in fact, that Lindsay drew eager crowds like this (if slightly less hormonal), when his 100-plus storefront volunteer offices were packed with boys who had barely known a whisker and "Lindsay Girls" too young to vote. Those kids weren't Lindsay's anymore. Maybe what had happened to Fun City over the last four years had soured them on civic duty. Maybe they'd learned the hard lessons that a politician who promises to fix everything, can't. Maybe they looked at John Lindsay and saw the guy who couldn't prevent a school strike and ruined their entire year and so they booed him. Maybe they just liked Joe Willie's unapologetic self-centeredness. They belonged to Namath now. Lindsay was the stuffed shirt.

After City Hall plaza, Namath headed up to Mamma Leone's restaurant on 48th Street, where he was to receive a new sports car from *Sport* magazine for being named the game's MVP. Of course, the bulk of his adoring female fans knew that, and by the time Namath arrived at the restaurant in a city limousine, there was already another crowd gathered outside, trying to press through the police to get at Namath, jumping on the hood of the car just to have a look inside, holding out all manner of objects for him to autograph. "It was like a combined appearance by Frank Sinatra, the Beatles and Tiny Tim," reporter Joseph Durso wrote. Inside, Namath was supposed to hold a press conference but, heck, he'd been giving speeches all through lunchtime. Now it was afternoon, and Leone's had what Namath wanted to see most: a bar. The elation of the Super Bowl victory combined with the excruciating pain that the 1968 season had left in its trail—both knees hurting, a wrist injury in the Super Bowl itself, the concussion and broken finger courtesy of the Raiders, a jammed thumb—had Namath doing a good deal of self-medicating with Johnnie Walker Red. "I'm drinking a lot lately," he told Breslin, who asked whether he drinks all the time. "I might as well," Namath said. "I get the name for it whether I do it or not." With apologies to the press, Namath wound up at the Leone's bar, holding "impromptu interviews" with his adoring fans while "aggressive sports writers found themselves being elbowed out of earshot by the fair sex." Al Silverman, the editor of *Sport* and toastmaster for the event, said, "This is the largest crowd, from in town and out of town, we have ever had for the award luncheon. Maybe it is because Namath is the first back to be honored since Paul Hornung." Silverman smiled knowingly. Hornung, a Packers star, cultivated a winking, behind-the-scenes playboy image that Namath had brought to the fore. "I notice there are more women here than there ever has been. Even more than there were for Hornung."

For Lindsay, Namath's high coincided with his own low, such that all the expression of emotion the locals could muster for their Mayor was a guttural booing. All that had gone wrong in late 1968 was compounded in January by a devastating scandal uncovered by a *New York Times* investigation, which found stunning corruption, graft, and plain incompetence in Lindsay's Human Resources Administration anti-poverty agency, including three employees accused of embezzling millions of dollars into a Swiss bank account, a group of four men from Durham, North Carolina, who had managed to skim $1.75 million by programming a computer to print fake checks and a bizarre attempt "to steal $52,000 in HRA funds by the purchase of a Los Angeles house with a check made out to an apparently fictitious man who 'identified' himself by writing a false license plate number and the unlisted phone number of a movie star on the back of an HRA check."

Entering 1969, after he returned from his much-criticized vacation in the Bahamas, Lindsay had taken so many political bullets that those around him were certain he would not be running against Namath or anyone for the office of mayor in the fall, but would finish his term, settle in with a corporation or as a university president, and eventually re-enter politics seeking a spot in the Senate or the governor's office. But there was a problem with that approach, too. If Lindsay left city politics, especially with his popularity at an all-time low, he would give the appearance of abandoning New York, and would lose the base of city voters he would need to have a chance of winning any statewide office. Not long after he had supposedly made a decision not to run, Lindsay was reconsidering.

It was at the height of that reconsideration that disaster struck again. On the morning of Sunday, February 9, readers of the *Daily News* would have gotten their morning papers and, checking the weather report, found that "RAIN, WINDY AND COLD" was the forecast. But any reader could look out his window and see that forecast was way off. It had begun to snow at a little before 2 a.m., and by 5 a.m., the National Weather Bureau had changed course and called for a heavy snow watch. By 2 p.m., there were seven inches of snow, falling at the rate of an inch per hour. By the end of the night, there were fifteen inches of snow, with wind gusts topping 30 mph, pushing mounds twice as high in places. Caught unaware, the city was paralyzed. Snow crews did not get onto the streets until 9 a.m., which left the plowing well behind a normal schedule and made it impossible to clear highways. At Kennedy Airport, which closed at noon and recorded twenty inches of snow, there were 6,000 travelers stranded, and as food and drink quickly ran short at the airport, supplies were later airlifted in by helicopter. The Long Island Railroad was shut down. The westbound side of the Lincoln Tunnel shut down, which backed up bus service out of the city. There were about 1,000 cars stranded on the Tappan Zee Bridge, and officials had to send buses to evacuate the cars and carry people to Tarrytown, where they took shelter at fire stations and a church. Tragically, three people were found dead in a car at JFK, suffering carbon monoxide poisoning while trying to leave a parking garage, and forty-two deaths were attributed to the storm. Half of those deaths were in Queens.

While Lindsay could not be held accountable for the initial snow dump, he would face blame for what proved to be a very slow clearing of streets in the outer boroughs. Two days after the storm, many streets in Staten Island, Bronx and, especially, Queens were still unplowed, and Lindsay was being excoriated by Democrats for his failure to act faster. Francis Smith claimed that Lindsay had been slow to get sanitation men (who were responsible for snow removal) on the job on because he did not want to pay them Sunday double-time. He called Lindsay, "short-sighted, penny-wise and pound-foolish." Lindsay scoffed at the accusation, chalking it up to election-year grandstanding. But when Lindsay went to Queens, where sentiment toward him was frigid with snow or without, to survey the area on foot, he found a deep well of resentment for him, crystallized visually in the unpassable streets and audibly in the jeers he received. Later, Lindsay would recall that walk: "The reception I got was virtually unanimous," he said. "There were a number of suggestions about what I might do with myself, and there was a good deal of fascinating speculation about my ancestry." One woman shouted, "You should be ashamed of yourself. It's disgusting." Another onlooker yelled, "Go back to Gracie Mansion and enjoy it while you can, because you'll soon be out." At another point, Lindsay approached an elderly woman to talk, and she shrieked, "Get away, you bum!" Speaking to a crowd at a Lincoln Day dinner at the Hotel St. George in Brooklyn, Lindsay tried to lighten the mood by telling the crowd that Attorney General Louis Lefkowitz suggested he run for re-election. *Boooo!* "Louis, I'll be around till hell freezes over," Lindsay said, pausing for comedic effect, "and it did."

The snow cleanup, especially in Queens, remained slow, so that even on Wednesday, the third day after the snow, the borough was unpassable. It would be nine days before the city as a whole came out of a state of emergency. The Lindsay administration kept making appeals to New Yorkers, pointing to past reports that showed after a similar storm in 1961, Robert Wagner took just about the same amount of time clearing out the snow. But that was eight years ago, and that wasn't Lindsay. He was coming closer to a final decision on whether to seek reelection, and his experience taking verbal abuse made clear what he had already known: If he ran, it would be these people screaming at him who would oppose him most, and in order to have a chance at winning a second term, he would have to change the minds of some portion of them. Middle-class Queens folks. Angry white people.

. . . .

Mets manager Gil Hodges was supposed to meet with members of the media on February 10 in New York, but like the rest of the city, those plans changed because of the snow. For Hodges, it was just as well. If he had met with the writers covering the club, he would want to field questions about the players and the team's prospects. The writers, though, would only want to talk about something he'd rather avoid. The previous September, when the Mets were in Atlanta with five games left to play, Hodges began to feel sharp pains in his chest. It had been building for a few days, but it was in the second inning of a game that it became unbearable. He went back into the clubhouse with the team trainer to lie down. The Mets had been reasonably successful in his first season, breaking the club record for wins with 73 and boosting attendance. But the pressure of managing in his hometown, of maintaining his poise while trying to guide a group of young players stuck in a losing mind-set, was too much. "He had those pains for several days," one of his coaches said, "but he wouldn't admit it. He was smoking like crazy. Two, three packs a day. He was keeping it all inside." It was a heart attack. In the weeks, then months, that followed, speculation about Hodges's future as the Mets manager swirled. But he vowed to return, to get more exercise and cut out the cigarettes. "I'll be going along as if nothing ever happened," he said. "I feel fine."

At training camp in St. Petersburg, Florida, Hodges had a favorite trick for inducing the kind of discipline among his players that had been missing with the Mets before he was hired. Hodges himself was not much of a night owl—he was certainly no Casey Stengel—but he would, every so often, stay up late and stake out the team hotel to keep an eye on the comings and goings of his players, making note of curfews missed. One morning in spring, Hodges gathered his team together and announced that he knew curfew had been broken by four players, and rather than calling out their names, he expected each to pay a $50 fine privately, and he'd consider the matter closed. Hours later, bench coach Joe Pignatano whispered to him, "Hey, Gilly, you're going good. You've got nine checks already." On the field, Hodges had cause for optimism. The pitching staff, headed by Tom Seaver and lefty Jerry Koosman, would be the strength of the team, but the outfield of Ron Swoboda, Cleon Jones, and Tommie Agee (who had struggled through a miserable 1968, but still had the faith of Hodges) had the potential to produce runs, and the infield had some of the best gloves in the league. Backup outfielder Art Shamsky got a good sense of just how things had changed with the Mets after he suffered a back injury that kept him out of spring training. Once he was healthy, Hodges called him into his office. General manager Johnny Murphy was there, too. They wanted Shamsky to go to the Mets' Class AAA affiliate, Tidewater, to get some game action since he had played so little in the spring. He needed a spring training. *Spring training? To play for the Mets?* "I don't need spring training to play on this team," Shamsky said. He regretted it immediately. Hodges and Murphy just stared grimly. Shamsky, chastened, played eleven games for Tidewater.

Before the season opened, Hodges was asked to make a guess as to his team's win total. He thought 85 was a reasonable number, a 12-game improvement over the previous season. But he also knew that, in 1968, the Mets had gone 26–37 in one-run games, the kinds of games that came down to experience, avoiding mental errors, having just a bit more depth in pitching than the other guys. And luck. The Mets, he figured, were due for some luck. "If you win half of those," Hodges said, "you are a contending ball club." The gambling elements in Las Vegas were not so sure. The Mets were listed at 100-to-1 shots to win a championship. There was confidence in the clubhouse, though. Pitcher Al Jackson announced, "This year, we start out at No. 1, and we stay there." Agee considered that and said, "Hey wouldn't that be something if we won it all? That would shake them up." Cleon Jones, nodding, said, "Shake us up, too."

....

Two hundred miles to the southeast, at Yankees training camp, thirty-seven-year-old Mickey Mantle was ready to concede his turf to Joe Namath. Six weeks earlier, Namath had borrowed his locker, and by the time he left it, Namath had taken Mantle's status as leading scamp among New York sporting heroes. The two were friends, sharing a history of knee problems, an affinity for liquor, and their own ill-conceived fast-food restaurants (Broadway Joe's hamburgers on one side and Mickey Mantle's Country Cookin' on the other) that would hit the rocks disastrously within a year. In mid-February, they'd been partners in a celebrity golf tournament in California. But when Mantle settled in for Yankees spring training, he just didn't feel up to it anymore. He had hobbled through 144 games the previous season, hitting .237, bad enough to knock his career average from .302 to .298. If he were to come back, it would be to raise his average back up over .300, but he knew, everyone knew, another year would only send his average further downward. He called a press conference on March 1 and said, simply, "I'm not going to play any more baseball."

Mantle was the last of the Establishment Yankees. Elston Howard retired after performing backup duty in Boston the previous year. Roger Maris had hit a measly five home runs in St. Louis in 1968, and he quit, too. Whitey Ford had retired during the 1967 season. In the *Sporting News*, Jim Ogle wrote that Mantle "also pulled down the curtain in what has to be the most exciting, glamorous and legendary era ever enjoyed by an athletic team. . . . Now, with Mantle following Babe Ruth, Lou Gehrig and Joe DiMaggio into history, the Yankees are bereft of a superstar for the first time in almost half a century. With

Mickey gone, the New Yorkers become a nameless, faceless array moving into a new era without a leader and without glamour."

The Yankees were not a good team after 1964. But they had Mantle, at least. Now, there was a gaping hole to be filled on New York's baseball scene.

CHAPTER 18

Eating Crow

EVEN AS THE SNOWSTORM EMERGENCY lingered into mid-February, and the good people of Queens continued to curse his handsome face, Lindsay was measuring his strategy for reelection. His wife, Mary, was strongly against his running again, having been with Lindsay in Flatbush, when he had taken the worst verbal abuse of his first term and had to escape an angry mob with help of police. She didn't want her husband subjected to that kind of torment. Still, Lindsay had ordered polls taken in all five boroughs, broken down by ethnicity, to get a sense of where he stood. The numbers were not good. Collectively, his approval rating was in the twenties. The coalition of Jewish and minority votes he had built in the 1965 election had eroded, largely because whites in the city felt he had been too attentive to blacks. After the teacher strikes, the Jewish vote seemed a lost cause. But, while speculation about his future abounded, Lindsay reached out to Richard Aurelio, a brilliant political strategist who had been the chief of staff for Senator Jacob Javits. Aurelio had decided he'd had enough of Washington DC after Javits won reelection in 1968, and decided to go back to New York to, "make some money," he explained, "to give my family a better life." He went to work for Edward Gottlieb and Associates, a public relations firm, when Lindsay got in touch with him and asked if he would review the polls.

The number that stood out, the one that had discouraged Lindsay from running: 74 percent. That was his disapproval rating.

But to Aurelio, it was not so hopeless. Things had gone badly for Lindsay on school decentralization, but it was a liberal concept that most New Yorkers would support if the emotion of the Ocean Hill-Brownsville situation were removed. While there were those who would always resent him for spending so much time in minority communities, there were also those who would eventually realize that those communities had been neglected so long, they required extra attention from government. Lindsay's execution had been inept at times, but his ideas were in line with a majority of the city. "So I told him he should run," Aurelio said. "I told him that his policy priorities, were, essentially, the right ones. Liberalism was in jeopardy, and he was a strong and effective voice for it. He couldn't abandon these important issues."

Lindsay considered Aurelio's analysis for a moment and responded, "Well, if you feel so strongly, how about managing my campaign?"

Though rumors of Lindsay's impending entry into the fight for reelection popped up as early as mid-February, he would officially announce a full month later. In the meantime, he let the rest of the field make their introductions. On February 18, squat, feisty city comptroller Mario Procaccino, recognizable from his well-pomaded black hair and distinctive pencil mustache that ranked somewhere between David Niven and the Great Gildersleeve, announced his candidacy for the Democratic nomination. Lindsay had been working with Procaccino for the last three years and called him, "a good friend," but the newly minted candidate declared, "The citizens of our city have had more than enough of Fun City," and made clear that he would hit the Mayor on the issue of crime. Procaccino had a conservative, pro-police bent and was one of the few prominent politicians opposed to the addition of civilians to the police review board in 1966. Those credentials would appeal to a wide swath of voters. But Procaccino also had a habit of allowing himself to be easily (and almost comically) overcome with emotion, and during his first round of television interviews after announcing his candidacy, he wept, inexplicably.

Lindsay was given a surprise, too, when conservative state Sen. John Marchi of Staten Island announced a week after Procaccino that he, too, would enter the race, challenging Lindsay in a primary. This was odd. Few had actually heard of Marchi, and he had little chance of winning a citywide election. But he could win a primary. The problem was that Republicans in New York City just didn't have primaries for mayoral races. If there was a good enough candidate willing to take on a machine-backed Democrat in what was almost always a hopeless fight for mayor, the party would not want that candidate squandering resources on a primary battle. There had not been a Republican mayoral primary since 1941. Sticking with this line, President Nixon and Rockefeller placed calls, trying to talk Marchi out of running and leaving the path clear for Lindsay, who was the only hope of the Republicans holding on to City Hall. Marchi would not be moved. This forced Lindsay's campaign, for the first time, to really consider what made a New York City Republican, that rare and largely unstudied species, with only 628,000 registered voters. It was reported that the Jewish and minority vote made up only 12 percent of the New York City GOP, which meant, as one Lindsay aide said, "The only thing we're sure of, is that the average Republican enrollee is not a typical Lindsay supporter."

A crowd developed on the Democratic side, with liberal state Rep. James Scheuer, City Councilman Robert Low, Bronx Borough President Herman Badillo, state Rep. John Murphy and former Patrolman's Benevolent Association official Norman Frank (who termed Lindsay, "The most popular mayor in the world—outside of New York") joining the field by early March. They could smell blood in the water. The numbers any challenger could present to the voters were stark and easy to grasp. Under Lindsay, the crime rate had gone up 50 percent. Taxes went up, making New Yorkers the most-taxed citizens per capita in the country. Welfare replaced education as the city's top expense, reaching $1.5 billion, or 23 percent of the budget. Rents had skyrocketed. Six major municipal unions (police, fire, teachers, sanitation men, welfare, and transit workers) had either called strikes or initiated work slowdowns during Lindsay's three years in office. "The last six months of 1968," Lindsay later wrote, "had been the worst of my public life." That did not bode well for 1969. Yet, on March 18, Lindsay finally announced that he would seek reelection, both in a Republican primary and on the Liberal Party line, which gave him a fallback position should Marchi win the June 17 primary. Lindsay set off that afternoon, in one of the few nods he would make to the 1965 campaign, on a walking tour, eventually taking him to Brooklyn. In a reminder that, while everyone else might still be tired, Lindsay was not so fresh anymore, he was told that two women saw him pass and one said to the other: "He's sure aged a lot in four years!" Lindsay laughed.

A little more than three weeks after Lindsay made his candidacy official, the Democratic side would add one more major challenger: former Mayor Robert Wagner, who had been serving as ambassador to Spain. He was a surprise entry, but with Lindsay in trouble, Wagner saw a chance to reclaim his own legacy, which had been skewered by Lindsay four years earlier. Wagner seemed to be visualizing the naïve, untested 1965 version of Lindsay when he said, in announcing his candidacy, "I do not pretend or believe that I am so uniquely equipped that I can, through the exercise of my own powers, solve all the problems of New York City. I think it would be a foolish or an inexperienced man who would say that." Wagner was no fool, and he was not inexperienced. He also created a ripple of anxiety among the Lindsay people that he would pull away Liberal Party support and leave Lindsay, should he lose the Republican primary, without a home on the ballot. (The Liberals stuck with Lindsay as their candidate, however.) Author Norman Mailer, chilled at the prospect of a Wagner redux in City Hall, said, "Wagner represents mediocrity, dull greed, emptiness of vision, and an inability to confront any issue which is not situated under the table." So Mailer, with columnist Jimmy Breslin as his running mate, figured he'd add another layer of kook to an already uniquely bizarre primary season, entering the Democratic Party race with a platform seeking to designate New York City as the 51st State, and a simple slogan: "No More Bullshit."

In the run-up to the primary, Wagner appeared formidable. Though he did not have the support of blacks and other minorities that Lindsay could boast, Wagner did have strong liberal credentials, a base of left-over Democratic support and the backing of the city unions. Ironically, those unions actually got more favorable deals under Lindsay than they had under Wagner, but because the perception of Lindsay as an effete intellectual who thought he could talk over the heads of union members, and because Wagner had back-slapping friendships with union bosses, the rank-and-file would undoubtedly be behind Wagner. When voters finally went to the polls in June, there were some surprises in the results. Lindsay lost the Republican primary to Marchi, as expected, but the margin was only about 6,000 votes, 113,000 to 107,000. This was good news for Lindsay, an indication that there were still a sizable number of Liberal Republican votes to be had in the general election. The big shock came on the Democratic side, where a moderate-to-liberal coalition of voters could have easily brought down Procaccino, who finished with just 32.8 percent. But the field was just too deep. Procaccino had 255,000 votes, a large portion of them coming from blue-collar Italians who never had much use for Lindsay to begin with. Wagner had 224,000, and though he had not carried any boroughs, he polled steadily between 23–33 percent in all five. Herman Badillo, at 217,000 votes, had done better than expected, pulling in a large portion of the minority vote, winning Manhattan and nearly upsetting Procaccino in the Bronx. (This was especially impressive given the fact that Badillo had been accused of being in the race only to split the liberal vote with Wagner; if that was the case, he split it more completely than anyone could have imagined.) Mailer had garnered 41,000 votes, and Scheuer had 39,000—small totals, but if those two had dropped out, their liberal voting blocs could have swung either Badillo or Wagner past Procaccino.

For Lindsay, Procaccino's 32.8 percent of the Democratic vote mattered little. What mattered was that he had *not* gotten the other 67.2 percent—all those votes had gone to the four other mostly liberal candidates. The voters who cast those ballots might have had issues with Lindsay on a personal level during the past three years, but they probably lined up with Lindsay on policy. Lindsay had even pulled a near-split with Marchi. The voters of New York might not be ready to throw their enthusiasm behind Lindsay, but they didn't seem thrilled with the other options, and would have to take another look at Lindsay before casting a November ballot. In defeat, a deflated Wagner summed up the rest of the campaign and the diminished choices the race left for voters. Asked if he would support Procaccino, Wagner said, "That would be very doubtful." How about Lindsay? "God forbid," he said. That left only one other choice. "Maybe Marchi," Wagner said, "might be worse."

....

There were no indications, when the 1969 season opened for the Mets, that anything special was afoot. April 8 marked the eighth Opening Day in franchise history, and their record in the seven previous openers—they'd lost all seven—didn't inspire confidence. It looked as though the National League schedule-makers were trying to will the Mets into breaking that streak with the arrival at Shea Stadium of the Montreal Expos, themselves an expansion team playing their first-ever game. The Mets would have their strong, young ace, Tom Seaver, on the mound, facing Mudcat Grant, a twenty-one-game winner four years earlier who had become a journeyman reliever in his thirties, having made just four starting appearances the previous season. It felt, at least, like a day on which anything could happen, a bright, 66-degree day, with a crowd of 44,541 on hand, including Bob Wagner and Jets coach Weeb Ewbank, "the flush of Jet victory still on his ruddy cheeks." But two errors and a walk by Seaver set up two runs for the Expos in what was an all-too-familiar first inning for the Mets, and when Seaver was replaced after five innings, having given up four runs, the Met bullpen blew open and allowed seven more, too much for a valiant comeback to overcome. Game 1 went in the books as an 11–10 defeat, and after the game, Seaver said, "My God, wasn't that ridiculous?" Things would stay ridiculous for the first ten games.

The Mets bounced back to beat the Expos in their next two, but lost six of seven to fall to just 3–7.

One of the leading causes for that struggle was leadoff hitter and centerfielder Tommie Agee, and for Gil Hodges and the Mets, this was the kind of issue that could sink the rest of the year. The Mets had traded for Agee from the White Sox before the 1968 season, just two years removed from a season in which he hit 22 home runs and drove in 86 RBI, winning Rookie of the Year and earning an All-Star spot. But he had a tumultuous relationship with hard-driving White Sox manager Eddie Stanky, who was paranoid that Agee was spending too much time enjoying Chicago's social scene and not focusing on base-ball. Agee was in a bar called Flukie's on the South Side of Chicago in the summer of 1967, as he told it, when a detective slipped into a seat at his table. "The guy pulled a badge and told me I'd better not hit the ground in Chicago because he'd been watching where I went and what I did, even to my apartment. I guess the White Sox thought I was having an excess of night life." Agee was sufficiently spooked. He went into a terrible slump in the second half of the 1967 season with the White Sox (he hit .218 after the All-Star break) and when he was traded to the Mets, he was so eager to redeem himself that he heaped pressure on every at-bat. Agee again struggled, batting .217 in 1968. He was short with teammates and hard on himself. "I was depressed," Agee said. "A lot of times, I didn't want to go to the park." When he started 1969 with a .190 average in April, Hodges put Agee on the bench in an effort to get him to clear his head. "We've got to do something," Hodges said, resigned. As good as the Mets' pitching was, they were light on run-producing hitters, and Hodges needed Agee to return to his Rookie of the Year form if the Mets were going to make real progress in 1969. A break was called for.

Hodges looked wise when Agee was put back into the lineup in early May, and started swinging the bat easily. He went on a ten-game hitting streak that saw him post a .385 average with four home runs and 11 RBI, a stretch that ran to May 21. The Mets won that day, 5–0 behind a complete-game shutout from Seaver in Atlanta, moving their record to 18–18, the latest they'd been at .500 in any season in franchise history. After the game, New York reporters, who'd witnessed so much clownish baseball from the Mets in eight seasons, came barging through the clubhouse door, expecting an exuberant scene. But the young Mets were not impressed. Maury Allen of the *New York Post* got to Seaver first and asked, "Isn't it great to be at .500?" Great? Maybe for those who had been around in 1962, who knew what it was to lose 120 games. But this edition of Mets expected more from themselves. "No," Seaver told Allen. "It doesn't have any significance for me. I can't appreciate it. I'm looking beyond .500. Why don't you and Al Jackson and Ed Kranepool go celebrate?" Allen, perhaps sensing that his celebratory column had lost some steam, told Seaver, "You'd better appreciate it while you're there." But the Mets were resilient. On May 28, light-hitting shortstop Bud Harrelson, who would miss three weeks of the summer serving in the National Guard, knocked a game-winning single in the eleventh inning of a game that had seen Jerry Koosman throw ten shutout innings against the Padres. That game would spark an eleven-game winning streak. In the midst of that streak, the Mets' charter flight from San Diego to San Francisco was delayed by hours, and the plane was stuck in a holding pattern once it reached the Bay Area. Such a delay would normally engender big-league grousing from travel-weary ballplayers, but this was not a normal situation. The Mets were winning, and would be 29–23 after the final game of the streak. "Everybody's feeling too good to be irritated at anything," pitcher Jim McAndrew said.

Back home in New York, though, the Mets had been knocked out of the headlines on the sports pages. Even after most of the Jets had settled back to the normalcy of their offseasons, Joe Namath had kept pressing right on with his post–Super Bowl party. Namath was arrested in Miami in April on a series of traffic charges, including drunken driving, charges that were later dropped. Shortly thereafter, Namath made an appearance at his East Side bar/restaurant, Bachelors III, to pick up the Hickok professional athlete of the year award, where he claimed that if NFL teams like Atlanta, New Orleans, and the Giants were in the AFL, "they'd get killed." He also reported that his luxury apartment had been burglarized, and the $5,000 fur coat he'd worn for the cameras in the previous training camp—the coat that made furs for men a national fashion trend—was stolen. Namath wasn't too put out. "I don't think I'll bother getting another one," he said. "I never wore that one."

It was his appearance at Bachelors III on June 6, though, that drew global headlines and drowned out the enthusiasm around the Mets. In a teary press conference, Namath explained that NFL commissioner Pete Rozelle was forcing Namath to sell the bar, because of reports from the police and FBI that it had become a haven for gamblers and underworld figures. Namath was defiant. He didn't know any underworld types, and, he figured, if everyone who gambled in New York City were prohibited from entering bars and restaurants, there would be a lot of empty bars and restaurants. Still, Rozelle told him he would be suspended in two days if he didn't get rid of the place, reminding him that his contract contained a clause that stated he could not, "associate with notorious persons." Namath would have to sell. "I don't want to do it," he said. "I don't have any choice. The last thing I want to do is quit. But it's a matter of principle. I'm quitting."

. . . .

As the June primary approached, the Lindsay campaign had been planning for Bob Wagner as the Democratic nominee. That would have been a difficult prospect because, no matter how bad things had been getting under Wagner, they'd gotten worse since, and there would be pre-Lindsay nostalgia for the days when the mayor didn't walk around in Harlem or East New York and didn't appear on the cover of *Newsweek*, but did keep the trains running and the garbage collected. Democrats, though, had given them Procaccino. The name itself was a blessing—as a fellow Italian, Procaccino would be hurt by Marchi's presence on the ballot. It helped, too, that both Procaccino and Marchi were running on a message of law-and-order, and it was unclear how that would play in New York. Proccacino described to campaign audiences what he'd do if he caught a burglar in his home: "I wouldn't run for the handbook," he said. "I wouldn't call my lawyer; I'd just blow his brains out." Procaccino also declared that, "It's safer to be in Vietnam than it is to be in New York at 3 o'clock in the morning."

To Lindsay, and to many New Yorkers, the emphasis on order had the ring of heavy-handed over-policing. When confronted with questions about whether his policies would turn New York into a police state, Procaccino got angry. "I'm for security in our streets and safety in our homes, but that doesn't mean a Fascist state and you know it," he said. "The question in this town, as far as Mario Procaccino is concerned, is whether you are a good guy or a bad guy." Nationally, a campaign built on the theme of law-and-order seemed to be resonating. In Los Angeles, embattled Mayor Sam Yorty, whose politics had tacked sharply to the right, had won a primary over black candidate Tom Bradley by scaring voters with a campaign that dubiously linked Bradley with black radicals and Communists. There had been a similar result in a primary in Boston in 1967 (moderate Mayor Kevin White eventually prevailed), and again in 1969 in Minneapolis, where a police detective with virtually no political backing was elected on his law-and-order stand. Quoting what he called, "some Northern writer," segregationist former Alabama Governor George Wallace said of the trend, "what we're hearing now is, 'Wallaceism with a Yankee accent.' That's pretty good, I think."

Procaccino found himself wrapped in that same Wallaceist, "white backlash" cloak, a polite way of labeling him a racist. He fought that perception, sometimes in regrettable language. "If you think my record is that of a bigot," Procaccino said, "you're out of your mind—your cotton-picking mind." On June 22, five days after the primary, Lindsay appeared on *Meet the Press*. Host Gabe Pressman reminded Lindsay that he had chalked up his primary loss to "backlash, fear and the worst instinct of man" and asked him if those were all code words for racism. Lindsay deflected, carefully declining to name either Marchi or Procaccino, while still assailing the statements and ads that had been attributed to them. "The people who voted against me are not racists," Lindsay said. "People who voted against me by and large have a genuine concern, and they're worried about violence and they're worried—they do have fears. That has to be recognized and understood. One has to speak to those fears and answer their problems and discuss it. The way to do it is not simply to, for candidates and others, is not to appeal to those fears. And a good deal of that happened, of appealing to those fears. By constantly saying you're afraid and no one dares go out at night, and slogans of that kind, you do appeal to fears."

Poking at the nature of the campaigns of Procaccino and Marchi was an advantage for Lindsay, but did not address the mayor's biggest problem, which was summed up by Marchi: "A lot of people in New York would vote for the Boston Strangler if he were running against Lindsay." The toughest opponent for Lindsay was not so much Proccacino and Marchi, it was his own record. The way to change that, Lindsay's advisors felt, was television, and most remarkable aspect of Lindsay's 1969 campaign was his TV ads. He had to appeal to those alienated whites, and particularly Jews, who were inclined to support him, but felt betrayed by the shortcomings he'd shown in his first term. He would do that by making frequent campaign visits to the places where he'd lost the most support (Brooklyn and Queens) and letting the residents there vent and boo him. Once the emotion was out of the way, the thinking went, a rational conversation about priorities and policies could follow. And he would back up those conversations with the messages he was delivering in a wave television and radio spots. It was very targeted—this would not be anything like 1965, would not be flesh-pressing and Robert Price's 117 storefront volunteer headquarters.

This time, Lindsay didn't need to introduce himself, he needed to explain himself. Of the approximately $3 million he would spend in that campaign, about $2 million went to media and at least $500,000 to television. "We did not want to go anywhere John was going to get cheered," Aurelio said. "We wanted to go to the places where people were angry, in Queens and Brooklyn and the Bronx. The ads we did, we wanted to show that Lindsay understood that anger and was going to do something about it." The ads were well ahead of their time. Some of them appeared to be apology videos, though Lindsay never actually said he was specifically sorry for anything. But he would have to look into the camera directly and admit mistakes. He was not sure that was wise. Nothing like it had ever been done before in a political campaign. "He had to be talked into it," Aurelio said. "He didn't want to do it. He didn't like the idea of going in front of millions of New Yorkers and eating crow."

There were twelve ads in all. One played up Lindsay's role in fighting sulfur dioxide in the city, which had dropped 50 percent. Another championed his effort to add a fourth platoon of cops from 6 p.m. to 2 a.m., the most active times for crime. There were ads celebrating the city's battle against drug addiction, the success in scaling back rent profiteering, adding a commuter tax, and even an ad about the US involvement in Vietnam. Old Brooklyn Dodgers broadcaster Red Barber (who later joined the Yankees and was fired when he discussed their embarrassingly sparse crowd on the air in 1966) pitched in to go on camera walking in Brooklyn, lamenting the treasures the borough had lost, including the *Brooklyn Eagle* and Ebbets Field ("It's apartment houses now," Barber said). But he hailed Lindsay for fighting to get the Brooklyn Navy Yard back under city control. One controversial ad opened with jaunty music and road-trip video, suggesting every voter make a trip at least once before Election Day, "just across the river . . . *to Newark!*" The desolate scenes of Newark are accompanied by harsh, blaring horns and the kind of nerve-crawling music that could be expected in an Alfred Hitchcock film at the moment the long-dead corpse is revealed. The video shows plowed-over wreckage, broken windows, a burned-out building and the decapitated head of a child's doll, capped by the message, "If you want to see what's happened in New York since Mayor Lindsay took over, you have to see what hasn't happened." Newark's mayor termed it "unconscionable."

The most powerful of the ads, though, begins with a shot of Lindsay, up close, sitting on the porch of Gracie Mansion, his collar open. This would be his almost-apology. His first line: "I guessed wrong on the weather before the city's biggest snowfall last winter, and that was a mistake. But I put 6,000 more cops on the streets, and that was no mistake."

After a pause, he continued, his cadence increasing, "The school strike went on too long, and we all made some mistakes. But I brought 225,000 new jobs to this town and that was no mistake. And I've fought for three years to put a fourth police platoon on the streets, and that was no mistake. And I reduced the deadliest gas in the air by 50 percent, and I forced the landlords to roll back unfair rents. And we did not have a Detroit, a Watts, or a Newark in this city. And those were no mistakes."

Another pause. And then: "The things that go wrong are what make this the second-toughest job in America. But the things that go right are what make me want it."

CHAPTER 19

"A year ago I would have felt it was pretty hopeless"

Tommie Agee was sitting in front of his locker at Shea Stadium on July 7, flipping through his mail. The Mets had wrapped up June with a 19–9 record for the month, only their third winning month, out of forty-four, in franchise history—the last one had been the previous June, when they pulled together in the wake of Robert F. Kennedy's assassination. The Mets had just finished an eight-game road trip on which they won six games, their record stood at 45–34 and, yes, they were looking beyond .500. In St. Louis, the two-time defending pennant-winning Cardinals were 40–44 and struggling under the weight of expectations and bloated salaries. In Pittsburgh, the Pirates faded after a fast start. The Phillies had started the year with four straight losses, endured a nine-game losing streak in June and just didn't have the pitching to keep pace. The expansion Expos probably hit their peak with their Opening Day win over the Mets. At the top of the National League East sat the Cubs, 53–31, 5½ games ahead of the Mets. But Chicago would start a three-game series at Shea Stadium the next day, and Mets annals would theretofore record it as the first important series the team would play. The Mets had already acquired a distaste for the Cubs, whose manager, Leo Durocher, had needled their ineptitude in the past, whose pitchers were brash about throwing inside and whose star slugger, Ron Santo, would leap and click his heels at every Cub win, which the Mets considered bush league. "I want to beat them so badly," Agee said, "I don't know how to express it."

If there were doubts that the Mets might be on to something magical in 1969, the first game of the series might have removed them. Jerry Koosman, still working through a difficult shoulder injury and entering the game with just a 5–5 record, faced star Cubs pitcher Fergie Jenkins. Koosman still did not have his best stuff, but he was able to strand five baserunners in the first two innings, keeping step with Jenkins as the game went to the sixth, with the Mets holding a 1-0 lead on an Ed Kranepool homerun. But Koosman allowed runs in three straight innings, putting the Mets behind, 3–1 heading into the bottom of the ninth. "A year ago," Koosman said, "I would have felt it was pretty hopeless." Not this year, however. Ken Boswell doubled, followed by another double from Donn Clendenon—a power hitter acquired in June in a trade with Montreal— and a double from Cleon Jones, tying the score, 3–3.

With two outs and runners at second and third, Kranepool came to the plate. Kranepool's history with the Mets faithful was a checkered one. He had been a standout athlete at James Monroe High School in the Bronx, and signed with the Mets, who were desperate to cultivate a homegrown star, for a whopping $80,000 bonus, making his debut in a Mets uniform (he was a late-game fill-in for then-first baseman Gil Hodges) at the Polo Grounds in 1962 at age seventeen. But Kranepool had never developed into the slugger the Mets had foreseen, and he didn't develop into much of a batting-average hitter, either, a particular problem because he played first base, typically the defensive home for one of a team's best two or three hitters. Worse, Kranepool had an offseason job in a brokerage house, and was one of only two licensed brokers in baseball. (Pitcher and future Senator Jim Bunning was the other.) Fans resented him because he'd made a small fortune in the stock market and, according to one beat writer, "played like a man with money in the bank." But on this day, Kranepool was all Met. He took a curveball from Jenkins and lined it into centerfield, scoring Jones and giving the Mets an improbable win.

Where the Kranepool win against the Cubs might have taken some blind luck and divine intervention—this was the year in which Sandy Koufax asked Tom Seaver if God was a Met, prompting Seaver's famed reply, "No, but He's got an apartment in New York"—the second game was matter of sheer talent. Seaver would take the mound, carrying a 13–3 record and an ERA of 2.62, obviously on his way to the best year of his young career, and one of the best pitching seasons of 1969. Seaver himself had been a gift to the Mets, landing with the team after baseball Commissioner Bill Eckert determined that the Braves, who had drafted Seaver in 1966, had signed him after Seaver's season at the University of Southern California had begun that year, which was illegal under league rules. Seaver was placed into a special pool for teams willing to match the Braves' contract—$51,500—and, in the end only three (the Mets, Phillies and Indians) agreed to bid. Seaver was surprised anyone was making bids. He had been undersize until he got to college, and, he confessed, "I frankly thought I was too small. I had decided to become a dentist." But the three names were placed into a hat, and it was the Mets' scrap of paper that was chosen, forever altering history, in baseball and perhaps beyond.

On July 9, in front of 59,083 fans, Seaver put forth one of the greatest pitching performances Shea Stadium will ever see. He had all of his pitches—his rising fastball, his sinking fastball, his curveballs, his slider—working, and it was evident from the first batter, the Cubs' Don Kessinger, who struck out. Seaver then struck out seven of the first ten batters he faced and, from the Mets dugout, the idea that something special was happening set in. He closed the sixth inning by striking out pitcher Ted Abernathy looking, and Seaver had not only not allowed a hit, he had not allowed a baserunner. In the seventh, it was fly ball, fly ball, groundout, and still no runners. In the eighth, with the noise of the Shea Stadium crowd rising steadily like a tide, Seaver set down the heart of the Cubs' order, getting a fly ball from Ron Santo before striking out Ernie Banks and Al Spangler. When Seaver went to bat in the bottom of the inning, the ovation was so overwhelming, he could not even enter the batter's box until the frenzy quieted to a roar. Alas, in the ninth inning, facing redheaded rookie Jim Qualls, Seaver fired a sinker on his second pitch. It failed to sink, and Qualls, whose career would end with just 31 major-league hits, lined a single. Seaver would record the final two outs, and the Mets won, 4–0. Still Seaver admitted, "I felt empty, shocked, numbed. . . . I was too old to cry."

It was hard to be too disappointed in the wake of Seaver's near-miss perfect game. The Mets' win was their seventh straight and brought them within 3½ games of the division lead, and though they would lose the third game of the series, even in a loss there was something to be gained. After seeing the Mets play two of the season's best games to open the series, Cubs manager Leo Durocher watched the New-Yorkers commit a key error in a five-run fifth inning that paved the way to a 6–2 Chicago win. "Those," Durocher observed, "were the real Mets." That didn't sit well with the real Mets at all, and four days later, they were in Chicago, again facing the Cubs for a three-game series, and again taking two out of three games. This time, with the Mets gaining on his team, Durocher was snappish. Did the Mets' four wins in six games convince him that New York was a contender? "I don't dismiss anybody," Durocher said. Then Durocher played the part of questioner, asking reporters, who was in first place? When the answer came back, "Cubs," he harrumphed, "That's all." After Chicago, the Mets had one more series to contend with—four games in Montreal—before the All-Star break. They'd split their first two games with the Expos, but on the second day, there would be some good news out of New York: Joe Namath had come to his senses, would sell his share of Bachelors III and report to Jets training camp. The final day of the trip came on July 20, 1969, and history would record that the Mets split a double-header at Jarry Park. It would not show, though, that the Mets' charter plane had an issue with its oil system and that the team would have wait until another plane arrived. Of course, that plane was coming from Detroit, leaving the Mets no choice but to hunker down and have dinner in front of a grainy television.

History would, however, record what the Mets were watching: Apollo 11 had landed, and Neil Armstrong was taking one small step on the surface of the moon.

....

In a July article for *New York* magazine, Jimmy Breslin wrote a story under the memorable headline, "Is Lindsay Too Tall to Be Mayor?" It was a flighty concept at first pass, but put into the metaphorical sense, it was the very problem that Lindsay's campaign people had been worrying over since he'd decided to go for reelection five months earlier. Historically, New York's mayors had been men of average, or even short, stature. Breslin listed them: Jimmy Walker (5–8); William O'Brien (5–8½); Joseph V. McKee (5–9½); Fiorello LaGuardia (an announced 5–5 but actually closer to 5–2); Bill O'Dwyer (an actual 5–9, but given a little vanity and a great gift of language, an official 5–10); Vincent Impellitteri (5–8¾); Robert Wagner (5–8¼). Lindsay was 6–4, which meant he cut a dashing figure nationally, but bore no resemblance to the typical New Yorker. Voters wanted that in 1965, wanted someone tall and elegant and blue-eyed, able to rescue their city from the grim sameness of Bob Wagner and all their undersize mayors, someone who talked about fixing all of New York's problems, all at once.

When, three years later, nothing was fixed and things had actually gotten worse—there was more crime, more filth, more welfare—most New Yorkers did not want the White Knight anymore. "John Lindsay was a striking, handsome, cool, towering figure as he walked the streets of Harlem and was acclaimed across the country as future Presidential material," Breslin wrote. "But now, take Lindsay off the front pages of the *Washington Post* or *Los Angeles Times* or *Chicago Sun-Times* and put him on the Grand Concourse in the Bronx. Put him there with the schools closed and the garbage not picked up and the robberies and assaults way up. Put him there in a crowd of stumpy, bulging, balding Bronxites. Do this, and you do not have a towering figure anymore. You have a bony Protestant from Yale and Wall Street whose height makes him a conspicuous target for the stumpy little people who yell up at him, 'Lindsay, make the robbers go away or you go away!' . . . Suddenly it is not good to be so tall and handsome. 'Send Lindsay to a dance,' the cabdrivers yell."

Procaccino, though, was 5–4, lumpily built, stumbled over his words with regularity and frequently would have to pat dry his sweaty brow. Assailing Lindsay's Ivy League background and his Manhattanite concern for the poorer classes with whom he'd never really had to live or work or go to school, Procaccino coined the phrase "limousine Liberal." He resonated naturally with New Yorkers, and after the primaries, he had a sizable lead in the polls. He appeared, in caricature, on the cover of *Time* magazine, holding a city flag high in the middle of a downtrodden and anguished New York, in the style of Delacroix's French allegorical portrait, *Liberty Leading the People*. The story's headline was, "The Revolt of the Average Man," and Procaccino proudly reveled in his own averageness. "I'm not one of the select few," he said. "I am not one of the Beautiful People." Lindsay acknowledged that he had not given enough attention to the white middle class in New York, and Procaccino was drawing those voters. When he would make campaign appearances, speakers from trucks would ring out the message, "Mario, son of a shoemaker! He came up the hard way, just like you and me!" At a Lindsay gala, comedian Woody Allen mocked Procaccino, "in his undershirt, drinking beer and watching Lawrence Welk on television." Procaccino welcomed such ridicule.

For much of the summer, Procaccino's approach worked. His campaign aides mostly kept him on a controlled schedule, trying to keep him from saying too much—their feeling was that if they could keep Procaccino from flubbing in public, they'd clean up the anti-Lindsay vote and win. Late in the summer, Liberal Democrats who were inclined to abandon Procaccino and back Lindsay instead deferred, fearing that a Procaccino win would bring reprisals. "Some liberal Democrats," the *New York Times* stated in early September, "believe they can avoid endorsing any candidate for Mayor or can appear to be on both sides." That put Lindsay in a tough position. The Procaccino campaign did not want to debate Lindsay on television, for fear that their striking physical differences and Lindsay's self-assured speech would inspire more confidence in Lindsay. And Lindsay and his staff were under strict orders not to make any personal attacks on Procaccino. "He was too much an easy target for that," Aurelio said. "If you went after him, you would look like a bully and he would look more sympathetic. He had been comptroller, Lindsay had worked with him. We knew he would say some things eventually. The best strategy was to just wait and let him damage himself."

That damage started to come as Election Day drew near. According to political columnists Rowland Evans and Robert Novak, Procaccino had, "simply by staying unveiled . . . gained through the summer to increase his lead." But when Harlem Democratic leader J. Raymond Jones called Procaccino a "bigot" and a "coward" for his appeals to racist sentiment, and labeled his campaign "anti-black," Procaccino began to go on the offensive, saying, "These vicious insults cannot go unanswered." Procaccino's aides advised him to ignore Jones's attack, but Procaccino was, again, reduced to excess of emotion. "When he heard of it," Novak and Evans reported, "Procaccino dissolved into tears among campaign aides." Rather than keep a stiff upper lip, Procaccino reverted to some eighteenth century need to defend his honor. "He told friends," Novak and Evans went on, "he could not bear for his family to carry with them the shame of alleged cowardice." Procaccino called a press conference and lashed back, lumping Lindsay with Jones and demanding that Lindsay, under threat of a full investigation, show proof of racism on his staff. So it went for Procaccino, who had more and more trouble staying out of his own way and exposing his knack for painfully mangled flourishes. He said of City Council President Francis X. Smith, his running mate, "He grows on you, like a cancer." Most famously, Procaccino was addressing a group of minorities in Harlem when he declared to them, "My heart is as black as yours!"

Procaccino also made little attempt to court the liberal Democrats who were on the fence about his campaign. If he could have gotten, for example, Robert Wagner, to back him, he would have given his candidacy the kind of gravity it was lacking. Wagner did meet with Procaccino, but was concerned about what sort of policies he would bring to City Hall, and asked Procaccino for a "white paper" that broke down his positions. According to one observer, Procaccino told Wagner, "Why don't you cut the shit? You're the number one Democrat in this town and I expect your support." By the beginning of October, Procaccino's campaign was wavering, and a Quayle poll showed that Lindsay was slightly ahead, 35 percent to 33 percent, with Marchi at 12 percent. More and more prominent Democrats lined up behind Lindsay. Even some of the labor unions that had been so opposed to Lindsay over the past three years—John DeLury's sanitationmen, the Social Agency employees, the transit workers, the longshoremen—now threw their support behind the mayor. One Democrat who switched allegiance to Lindsay, Elinor Guggenheimer, had angrily quit the City Planning Commission just ten months earlier, said, "My criticism related to his inexperience. I think he's grown, he has matured in human understanding."

But Lindsay's team did not put too much trust in the Quayle poll—the Lindsay campaign had developed its own, very sophisticated polling, and even as Lindsay gained momentum, there were two outstanding trouble spots. One was the possibility that Marchi supporters, once it became clear that their man could not win, would jump to Procaccino, whose outlook was far more closely aligned with their own than Lindsay. That was, "the great, great danger," one Lindsay strategist said. The other was the undecided vote, which the Quayle poll put at 20 percent. Lindsay's polling further showed that undecideds were likely to be Jewish, a bloc Lindsay had spent most of the year courting, but still with only limited success.

He would get a tremendous boost with that bloc, though, at the end of September, when Israeli Prime Minister Golda Meir visited New York for three days to attend the United Nations General Assembly. Sensing an opportunity, the mayor arranged for a lavish black-tie dinner celebrating Meir, and rather than putting it in Manhattan, took the symbolic step of having it in a parking lot at the Brooklyn Art Museum, an outreach to the powerful rabbis in Brooklyn and Queens. The Department of Public Events spent $42,000, half its 1969 budget, on Meir's visit alone. The dinner took place on the Jewish holiday of Succoth, and a massive sukkah (a structure of branches and leaves hung with fruit; Orthodox Jews are required to take meals in the sukkah on the holiday) was erected. Lindsay was accused of playing politics with the guest list, which topped 1,200. "Of course there were politics," Aurelio said. "But that was only natural. We wanted to invite all of the major rabbis and Jewish figures in the city. It was only natural that they were political." When comedian and pianist Victor Borge stood up to perform during the dinner, he said, "Mrs. Meir and Mr. Mayor, you both have something in common. You're both running for election, and you're both dependent on the Jewish vote. Particularly you, Mr. Mayor."

Lindsay and Aurelio met with Meir before the dinner, and Lindsay made a passionate appeal to her about the upcoming mayoral election, and the importance it would have in keeping the Jewish community open to their tradition of helping their fellow man. They'd hoped that perhaps Meir would say something kind about Lindsay when she made her remarks later. At the dinner, Lindsay addressed Meir and said, "If you stand with the right of a small nation to live in peace with her neighbors, you stand with Israel. And Madam Prime Minister, all of the cheers, all of the tributes, all of us who have welcomed you and toasted you have only one real message—Madam Prime Minister, we stand with Israel." Throughout the evening, Meir was warm toward Lindsay. When meeting those gathered for the dinner, she continually referred to Lindsay as, "my good friend John." In making her speech, she said she wished, "I had Mayor Lindsay's eloquence to tell what is in my heart tonight." Lindsay and Aurelio were delighted and surprised. "We were just hoping she would mention his name," Aurelio said. "What she did instead, she practically endorsed him."

Having made progress on the Jewish vote, there was one more thing for the Lindsay campaign to address. Lindsay was still too tall. He did not cut the figure of a regular New Yorker. But there, he would get lucky. The Mets—the *New York Mets*, of all teams—were in a pennant race. And John Lindsay, whose sporting interests ranged from such regular-guy pursuits as tennis and yachting, was about to become the city's No. 1 Mets backer.

. . . .

On August 13, now returned from their moonwalk, the trio of astronauts who had manned the Apollo 11 voyage to the moon were given a ticker-tape parade in New York City. As they rolled up Broadway in a convertible, waving to their eager supporters on the street, Col. Michael Collins noticed the many signs the locals had made to welcome them. One stood out as his favorite, he said. It read: "We love the Mets. We love you more. Sorry, Mets."

Sorry Mets indeed. On the same day in Houston, the Astros completed a three-game sweep of the Mets, knocking out rookie pitcher Gary Gentry after just one inning of an 8–2 loss. That moved the Mets 9½ games behind the Cubs, and even put them into third place behind the Cardinals. The joy of the Mets' June and July performance was sapped, and it seemed that 1969 would go down as a good year for the Mets, one in which they made progress but ultimately fizzled. But when the Mets returned home to Shea Stadium after the Houston disaster, they immediately regained their rhythm. Tom Seaver got their ensuing homestand off to a good start with a 2–0 win over the Padres, and the shoulder trouble that he'd been dealing with after his near-perfect game was muffled under painkillers. He would, in his final eleven starts, go 10–0 with a 1.34 ERA. Jerry Koosman, too, had his shoulder troubles subside, and after he allowed seven runs to start the Astros series, he went 8–1 in his next ten starts with an ERA of 2.15. Gentry, hailed as a future Seaver by Gil Hodges, looked like it in September, when he went 4–1 in seven starts, with an ERA of 2.19.

The Mets won nine of ten games on their August homestand, and began to take notice of some strange events unfolding in Chicago. At the end of July, Cubs manager Leo Durchoer had begged out of two games because of a stomach ailment. But it was later discovered that Durocher had actually been at a summer camp in Eagle River, Wisconsin, visiting the stepson of his new wife. For Durocher—the irascible manager who once quipped, "Nice guys finish last"—the incident was a very public embarrassment, and he felt added pressure to push his team to a pennant. The Chicago media didn't help. In the *Sun-Times* columnist Jack Griffin pleaded for wins, writing, "Husbands and wives who have kept batting averages together all summer will go back to screaming at each other if the Cubs fall. . . . Sportswriters will shoot their typewriters. Televisions will be smashed all over Chicago. Millions will flee the city and hide in the mountains from the shame of it." The Cubs didn't heed the call, though. The pressure was cracking them. They entered September 4 1/2 games up on the Mets, with a critical two-game series at Shea Stadium looming. But before the Cubs arrived in New York, they were swept by the Pirates, and limped in ahead by only 2 1/2 games.

By now, Lindsay had put his stamp of approval on the Mets, hoping he would get a reciprocal political benefit. In September, political columnist James Reston wrote, "New York City is a jungle of human conflicts these days—over commerce, education, transportation, pollution, the churches, the races and everything else—but the Mets are now in the race for the National Baseball League pennant and they are almost the only unifying force in the Big City." Reston was right about that. But he also wrote, "Mayor Lindsay, running for re-election, is a minor character in this larger sports spectacular of New York. He has no forum like Shea Stadium." Reston was wrong there. Already, Lindsay had begun to identify his longshot, underdog campaign with that of the Mets. When *Time* magazine ran a story on the Mets' fight into the pennant chase, there was Lindsay, commenting, "No one likes to lose—I can tell you something about that. Of course we want them to keep on winning. That kind of spirit is catching. It makes everything seem possible."

The possible became the actual, starting when the Mets took the field against the Cubs on a drizzly, cold September 8 night at Shea Stadium. Durocher, described by one writer as "a firm believer in the efficacy of the skullbuster or knockdown ball," started the bottom of the first by having his pitcher, Bill Hands, throw inside at Tommie Agee's head. Agee hit the dirt, and tension between the Mets and Cubs dugouts built. Then Hands did it a second time. When Koosman, known for his hard fastball, took the mound to start the second inning, he did not hesitate. His first pitch zipped inside at Ron Santo and plunked him in the arm. He, too, hit the dirt, and Koosman had done his job—the Mets would not be pushed around. When Agee batted again in the third inning, with Bud Harrelson on first base, he drove a home run over the 396-foot sign in left-center field to put the Mets up, and then scored the game-winning run in the sixth inning when he streaked home ahead of a throw from Cubs right fielder Jim Hickman, diving in safe despite the protests of Durocher and catcher Randy Hundley. Koosman struck out thirteen on the night, and in the second game of the series, Seaver dominated, picking up his twenty-first win with a complete-game, 7–1 victory. That moved the Mets within a half-game of the Cubs, which took an already rattled Cubs team and pushed it into a meltdown.

Chicago went to Philadelphia after the two losses to the Mets, and pitcher Ken Holtzman, still upset about Koosman hitting Santo, popped off to reporters, saying, "They act like they can run the league. They think they can intimidate our guys. But they're not the only guys in the league who can throw hard at somebody." The problem for Holtzman was that he was the scheduled pitcher that night, and was busy thinking about the Mets. Unfocused, he went to the mound and walked six Phillies batters, yielding three runs in the loss. The Philadelphia fans, not usually known for good feeling toward their New York brethren, nevertheless began chanting, "Let's go, Mets! Let's go Mets!" during the game. That loss, coupled with the Mets' first win in their doubleheader sweep over the Expos, put the Mets, amazingly and improbably, into first place. The scoreboard at Shea Stadium read: LOOK WHO'S NO. 1 over the records of the Mets (83–57) and Cubs (84–58). Lindsay sent a telegram to Chicago Mayor Richard Daley (a South Sider and White Sox fan by birth), congratulating him on being the mayor of "The Second City."

The Mets kept winning, building a run of thirteen wins in fourteen games that stretched their lead over the Cubs to an insurmountable five games. On September 24, exactly one year after Gil Hodges suffered a heart attack, Gentry threw a complete-game shutout against the Cardinals, winning 6–0 and giving the Mets their 96th victory. It also clinched the Eastern Division title for the Mets, officially putting them in the playoffs and convincingly laying to rest eight years of laughable futility. At Shea Stadium, there was mayhem, with fans pouring onto the field, tearing at the turf, pulling up home plate and, relaxing with marijuana smoked in a pipe at the mound, what writer Larry Merchant called, "an urban Bethel." In the locker room, the sheer joy of the players' celebration stretched well into the night. "We drank most of the champagne, not like most of the celebrations where you spray it around the clubhouse," Ed Kranepool later told a television interviewer. "We were celebrating a victory." The following day at City Hall, Lindsay declared that the coming week would be designated "Mets Week" in New York, and recalled that in July, he had been asked by a Chicago newspaper who would win the N.L. East. "I stated that the Mets would win on the last day of the season in Chicago," he said, "at about 4 o'clock in the afternoon, behind a no-hitter by Tom Seaver and a grand slam by Cleon Jones." He paused and said, "I sincerely regret having underestimated them by so much." Lindsay added that by winning, the Mets "gave me the biggest lift since the day I entered Congress." But the Mets were just getting started.

CHAPTER 20

The Saints of Lost Causes

AFTER THE METS CLINCHED THEIR spot in the playoffs and were wrapping up the season and preparing to face the Western Division champion Atlanta Braves, Jimmy Breslin wrote a column for *New York* magazine. Breslin had chronicled the first season in Mets history in his book, *Can't Anybody Here Play This Game?* telling of late nights with Casey Stengel and the foibles of Marv Throneberry. He looked at the Mets of 1969, and the Mets of 1962. Then he looked at the New York of 1969, tried to envision it with Mario Procaccino as mayor, and saw the New York of 1962: "It is clear that in the campaign of 1969, Mario Procaccino is Marvin Throneberry. We are in the era of Tom Seaver and pennants and new stadiums and great successes. The time of Marvelous Marvin Throneberry has passed. Look at the newspaper. Look at the sport pages. Do you see the name Throneberry in the Mets lineup? Of course not. How, then, you must ask, can the city of New York elect Mario Procaccino, the Marvelous Marvin Throneberry of the Democratic party, to any office in the year 1969?"

Breslin was seated alongside John Lindsay on October 6, for Game 3 against the Braves, in a box next to the Mets dugout with Arthur Goldberg, the former Supreme Court Justice and Secretary of Labor under President Kennedy, who would be another well-known

Democrat to endorse Lindsay the following week. Lindsay was not Marv Throneberry, but nor was he Babe Ruth. "He was not a baseball fan," Richard Aurelio said. "He didn't like team sports very much. But the Mets were a big thing. If you're in a tough campaign like that, and something happens like the Mets start winning, you have to make yourself part of it." As one reporter had it, Lindsay adopted the Mets but "started to go out to Shea Stadium with groans like, 'Christ do I have to go out to the ballpark again?'" The Met rooters, however, were still not entirely sold on the mayor—when he was introduced to the crowd, he was, one report stated, "booed louder and longer than the Braves." Robert Wagner, a baseball fan who helped get Shea Stadium constructed after the departure of the Giants and Dodgers (for which he bore some everlasting guilt), had learned a thing or two about protocol for politicians at ballgames. After Lindsay was booed, Wagner shook his head and said, "Don't get introduced at ballgames. The people are here to watch baseball and don't want politicians interrupting." Procaccino was at the game, too, but was not presenting himself as very mayoral. He stood up to speak with reporters and announced, "It's the year of the moon, the Mets and Mario!" When he was finished with the press, though, Procaccino couldn't find his seat. One fan shouted, "Hey Mario, how you gonna find your office if you can't find your seat?"

The Mets had won the first two games in Atlanta, outslugging the powerful Braves, 9–5 in the opener and 11–6 in Game 2. In Game 3, Gary Gentry allowed a two-run home run to Hank Aaron in the first, then gave up a single and a double in the third before Hodges yanked him from the game in favor of Nolan Ryan. The Mets, though, collected 14 hits and scored seven runs, and Ryan allowed just two more in the final seven innings to secure a 7–4 win, putting the Mets into the World Series. After the game, Lindsay and his aides went down to the Mets locker room. What happened next is the subject of different interpretations. Immediately after the game, backup outfielder Rod Gaspar said, "I saw [Lindsay] come over and went to shake hands. Then I said to Tom [Seaver], let's get him. I've always liked him, he seems like a good man, and it's just something we decided to do on the spur of the moment." Mets reporter George Vecsey remembered, "Two bright-eyed Californians, Seaver and Gaspar, doused the sculptured features of the Mayor, who smiled under the shower and looked for the television cameras." Columnist Robert Lipsyte was a little more direct in his cynicism, writing, "[Lindsay] would course into the locker room behind a flying wedge of aides, remote, stone-faced. When the television camera's red light glowed, he would snap on a smile and stride up to congratulate the game's hero. . . . He materialized on television as somehow having been involved in the pennant race. Manager Hodges reportedly refused to endorse Lindsay. But when pitcher Jerry Koosman poured champagne on the mayor's classic head during a stagey televised locker-room party, he was also bestowing what was construed by the fans as an endorsement from the whole team." Aurelio said the decision to drench the mayor was entirely the Mets' own. "It really was not something that was staged," he said. "The players did it on their own. We were very happy with the result, obviously, but we did not plan it that way."

No matter how earnest Lindsay was, or how many other players got involved, the result was a photo that ran all over the city, and in many parts of the country: John Lindsay, standing next to Gaspar as he empties a bottle of champagne on his head, while Jerry Grote stands behind the Mayor, swirling the foam into his hair. Later, Lindsay would joke, "One of my opponents charged me with using the Mets for political purposes. This is completely untrue. If you don't believe me, ask Deputy Mayor Hodges or Judge Seaver."

. . . .

After finishing the sweep of the Braves in the Championship Series, the Mets had four days off before they faced the American League champions, the Baltimore Orioles, in the World Series. The Orioles were a powerhouse, winners of 109 games, and were heavy favorites over the Mets (one estimate had them rated 8-to-5 to win). Manager Earl Weaver liked to play for the home-run ball, and the Orioles had the kind of lineup that could deliver. They'd hit 175 during the regular season, third-most in baseball, and well ahead of the Mets' paltry 109. They'd scored 779 runs, almost a full run per game better than the Mets, who scored 632. Burly Orioles first baseman Boog Powell hit 37 home runs and drove in 121 runs, and wound up second in the MVP balloting, but Baltimore also had sluggers Frank Robinson (32 homers), Brook Robinson (23) and Paul Blair (26). The Orioles had pitchers who could match the Mets' staff, too. Two lefties, Mike Cuellar and Dave McNally, topped the rotation and had each won 20-plus games. Jim Palmer, just twenty-three and having battled injuries for much of his young career, had come back from six weeks off with a back injury to finish the season strong, going 16–4, including a no-hitter win over Oakland in August. Collectively, the Orioles had an ERA of 2.83, slightly better than the Mets' 2.99 ERA.

But this was getting to be tiresome for Charm City. It had been only nine months earlier that Baltimore had sent its beloved Colts to Miami to quell a small uprising from an inferior American Football League bunch out of New York, and that matchup wound up with the Jets winning Super Bowl III. Two months after that, the best team in pro basketball, the 57-win Baltimore Bullets, faced the Knicks in the NBA playoffs, and were handed a humbling sweep. When Gaspar, in the dizzy, champagn-ey Mets' locker room at Shea Stadium, predicted that the Mets would win the World Series in a sweep, some of the Orioles caught wind of it, and after they swept their series against the Twins in the A.L. championship, Frank Robinson shouted, "Bring on Ron Gaspar!" When a teammate chimed into correct him— "Rod, stupid,"—Robinson shouted, "Bring on Rod Stupid!"

The Mets' run was getting tiresome for their Shea Stadium tenants, too. When the Jets signed to share their home field with the Mets in 1964, they were in a decidedly weak position—the AFL was still a joke, and even with Sonny Werblin taking over, there was little leverage for the football club vis-à-vis baseball. The purpose of getting Shea built had been to fill the void left by New York's defecting National League teams, and the Mets treated the stadium as though it was their birthright. As part of the Jets' sublease, they were forbidden to play any football games at Shea Stadium while there was even a possibility of the Mets needing the field. It wasn't just that the Mets would get priority over the Jets when their game days coincided, it was that the Jets would be barred from using the stadium at all while the Mets were in the postseason, even if the Mets were idle or on the road. The Mets' intransigence on that issue had been the only thing preventing the Giants vs. Jets preseason matchup that so many football fans wanted to see. Earlier, in August, the Jets and Giants finally gave up on the stubborn Mets and found a neutral site at which to play so that when, for the first time in history, the Jets and Giants took the field to face each other in a game, it was at the Yale Bowl in New Haven, Connecticut. The game still drew 70,784 fans, and more important, the last inkling of NFL dominance in New York (Giants fans were disregarding the Jets' Super Bowl win as a fluke) was erased with a Jets 37–14 blowout that featured Joe Namath completing 14 of his 16 passes. It was also Waterloo for Giants coach Allie Sherman. The chants of, "Good-bye, Al-lie!" had grown more virulent and oppressive among home fans, and when the team finished the preseason schedule without a win, Sherman was fired and replaced by his former player, Alex Webster.

· · · · · · · · · ·

John Lindsay sent the Mets off to Baltimore on October 10 from the Marine Air Terminal at LaGuardia Airport, allowing the team to skip out on the crowds they'd draw if they'd had to use the main terminal. There was a crowd of 200 to cheer them onto the plane in the late afternoon, and Lindsay took the occasion to read the "Ode to the New York Mets," penned for him by speechwriter Jeff Greenfield:

Oh the outlook isn't pretty for the Orioles today,
They may have won the pennant, but the Mets are on the way.
And when Gil Hodges' supermen get through with Baltimore,
They'll be champions of the world—they'll win it in four . . .
The experts say they cannot win, but they'll just eat their words,
When Jones and Koos and Agee pluck the feathers off those Birds.

When Gentry shuts out Robinson and Ryan does the same,
The world will know the Mets have come to dominate the game.
With Harrelson and Kranepool, with Gaspar and with Weis,
With Grote, Shamsky, Boswell—we've got the games on ice.
And when we've got a manager like Gilbert Raymond Hodges,
We've got a team that makes up for the Giants and the Dodgers.
So good luck down in Baltimore, New Yorkers place your bets,
We know we've got a winner—with our Amazin' New York Mets.

As noted literary critic Art Shamsky commented, "It wasn't the most beautiful poem, but the Mayor did have good intentions." Lindsay waved a pennant and pinned a "We're No. 1" button on his son, John Jr., while a Dixieland band played, "Take Me Out to the Ball Game," and sheepish policemen asked Mets players for autographs. One reporter wrote, "Fun City never seemed so together."

Lindsay flew to Baltimore on the morning of Game 1, and was greeted at Friendship Airport and taken to a pregame reception hosted by Baltimore Mayor Thomas D'Alessandro III (brother of former Speaker of the House Nancy Pelosi). He sat in a box at Memorial Stadium with team owner Joan Whitney Payson, whose brother, Jock Whitney and his former *Herald-Tribune* partner Walter Thayer were among Lindsay's financial backers in his race for re-election. President Richard Nixon was not able to show for Game 1, and in his place, Spiro Agnew, the man Lindsay had seconded for the role of vice president at the Republican convention just fourteen months earlier, was slated to throw out the first pitch. (Commissioner Bowie Kuhn ultimately filled in for Agnew.) That meant the second pitch was thrown by Cuban Orioles ace Mike Cuellar, matched up against Seaver. Cuellar started by getting two outs in the first inning before allowing a single, which he made up for by striking out Donn Clendenon. Cuellar was sharp all afternoon, and until the seventh inning, the Mets were able to move a runner past first base against him. But even then, a bases-loaded, one-out rally produced only one run, on a sacrifice fly by Al Weis.

Seaver, on the other hand, stepped in to face his first batter, Orioles leadoff man Don Buford. The scouting reports told Seaver to pitch inside to Buford, and he laid his second pitch on the inside corner. Buford caught hold of it, hitting what broadcaster Curt Gowdy at first casually called "a high drive," but one which kept carrying. Right fielder Ron Swoboda thought he had it lined up, but when he leapt, the ball dropped over the fence, "ticking" Swoboda's glove, he said afterward. It was a home run, and the Mets trailed, 1–0. Seaver couldn't believe it. He was unable to find a comfort zone in the game, and in the fourth inning, allowed a two-out, three-run rally that put the Mets further behind, and they went on to lose the opener, 4–1, wiping some of the spit-shine off the Miracle Mets. "We are here," Brooks Robinson said after Game 1, "to prove there is no Santa Claus."

Robinson, who had been flawless making tough plays at third base in the first game, would regret poking at the Mets' aura. In Game 2, he came up with a big hit in the seventh inning against Jerry Koosman, knocking in the only run that Koosman would allow all game, to make the score 1–1. It was also the only hit that Robinson would muster in 19 at-bats in the series, leaving him with a batting average of .053. In the ninth inning of Game 2, the Mets mystique reappeared when 160-pound second baseman Al Weis—thirty-one years old, a career .222 hitter, who'd collected just 23 RBI all season—slapped a single to left field with two out, scoring Ed Charles from third and giving the Mets a 2–1 lead. In the bottom of the ninth, Brooks Robinson was back at the plate, with two outs, two runners on base and the game on the line. He grounded out to third base. *Ho-ho-ho!*

When the series moved to Shea Stadium for the first time in Game 3, under the threat of rain, Gil Hodges announced that if there was a postponement, he would skip Gary Gentry in the rotation and go back to Seaver. But good fortune continued to smile upon the Mets, and the weather held. So did Gentry, but only with the help of centerfielder Tommie Agee. In the fourth inning, with two men on and two out, Agee heeded the Mets' scouting reports and was shaded toward right field with Elrod Hendricks at bat. When Hendricks hit a swirling fly ball to left-center, Agee had to come on in a dead sprint for about forty yards, reaching over his head to make the catch. In the seventh, after Gentry lost control and walked the bases loaded, forcing Hodges to bring in Nolan Ryan in relief, Paul Blair lined a pitch to right-center field, and again, Agee had to sprint and, with the wind knocking the ball down, make another diving catch. Agee had also led off the game with a home run, pushing the Mets to a 5–0 win. "Few, if any," wrote Lowell Reidenbaugh in the *Sporting News*, "could doubt that any other outfielder ever had enjoyed a comparable afternoon in World Series play."

....

The New York Knicks were in Cincinnati on October 15, 1969. It was Moratorium Day, billed by activists as a nationwide day of mourning for those casualties suffered during the Vietnam War. It was also to be a day of massive protests against the war. Forward Bill Bradley and his roommate Dave DeBusschere decided to give the demonstration a look, following thousands of mostly college-age kids to the fountain at Government Square. Bradley chatted with the students. DeBusschere relaxed and took in the speeches and folk songs. "I was surprised by how orderly the whole thing was," DeBusschere later wrote. "I imagine some of the kids were just looking for an excuse to get out of classes, but most of them seemed pretty serious." That night, the Knicks played the Royals in the second game of their season, facing a Cincinnati team built around all-time great Oscar Robertson and tough-minded big man Jerry Lucas. DeBusschere was assigned to guard Lucas, and had done well to limit him to 13 points. As the game wound down, Royals coach Bob Cousy inserted Tom Van Arsdale into the lineup, and Van Arsdale got into a minor shoving match with DeBusschere. As the pair ran back down the court, Cousy yelled to Van Arsdale, "Next time DeBusschere shoves you, take his head off." To which DeBusschere said, "Why don't *you* come out of retirement and try it?"

The Knicks beat the Royals that night, as they'd beaten Seattle the previous night. They won in Chicago, and won again at home against Los Angeles and Phoenix, running their record to 5–0. Before the season, the Knicks had been projected as a contender, again. This time, the projections looked right. A tight, 112–109 loss to San Francisco at Madison Square Garden stopped the Knicks' opening winning streak, but only made them determined to start a new streak. They did, beating Detroit by 24 points on October 24. And the Knicks would not lose another game for five weeks, a run of 18 straight games. Their seventeenth consecutive win tied the league record, and came in Atlanta. Before the game, Bill Bridges of the Hawks approached slick-tongued Knicks guard Dick Barnett and informed him, "You guys ain't gonna tie any record against us tonight." To which Barnett replied, "What's the matter? Ain't you guys gonna play?" Whatever it was that had gotten hold of the Jets down the stretch of the 1968 AFL season, and the Mets over the course of the 1969 baseball season, had taken hold with the Knicks, too. Not only did they set a new mark for consecutive wins, they were 23–1 to start the year, also an NBA record. "It's like the gods are with them," Van Arsdale said. "It's like a nightmare."

. . . .

In New York City, John Lindsay had seized upon Moratorium Day as a chance to draw a sharp distinction among the city's voters between himself and his rivals, Marchi and Procaccino. It wasn't strictly a political tool for Lindsay. He genuinely believed that the Vietnam War was wrong, had spoken out against it as far back as his days in Congress and had begun to tie the war to urban issues—the wasted finances that could be used at home, the unfair proportion of soldiers who were poor and black, the precedent set by the government's wanton use of violence—as far back as 1967. He would stake some political capital on his opposition to the war, knowing that the bulk of New Yorkers were opposed to it. Procaccino mostly dodged talking about the issue, saying it had no place in a mayoral campaign. Marchi agreed with Procaccino, but left no doubt where he stood on peaceniks and the protest movement: "It is a strike against America." Lindsay set himself up with a full schedule on Moratorium Day, starting at 7:45 with a church visit, to be followed by fourteen speaking engagements at the widespread rallies around

New York, and closing with a visit to the St. Alban's Naval Hospital in Queens. Not only was he leading the anti-war fight in the city, but he ordered all flags on municipal property to be flown at half-staff to honor the war dead. That, it would turn out, was a bad idea. Police and fire stations all over the city refused to lower the flags. At Shea Stadium, Lindsay's order created a quandary for new baseball Commissioner Bowie Kuhn. Because the park was city-owned, the flags should have been at half-staff. But the Mets had invited a group of more than 200 war-wounded soldiers to Game 4, and before the National Anthem could be sung, the soldiers gathered near the flagpole in centerfield, almost daring a would-be flag-lowerer to approach. "They would have had to fight us first," one soldier said. Kuhn consulted with the Mayor, and it was agreed that Kuhn would issue a statement saying he had decided to keep the flags at full mast to, "promote the greatest amount of respect and quiet in the stadium."

By taking an active part in the rallies, which drew about 125,000 protestors in New York and more than 2 million nationally, Lindsay was also running the risk that violence could break out. "If there had been trouble—broken windows, calling cops 'pigs,' anything like that—Lindsay would probably be through," *New York Times* political columnist Richard Reeves wrote. There was no trouble, as Lindsay made stops throughout the city, speaking at City Hall, at the Brooklyn Borough Hall, to 1,000 New York University students, to 5,000 Fordham students and to 10,000 Columbia students before joining the main feature of the day, a rally at Bryant Park with Sen. Jacob Javits, Sen. Charles Goodell and former presidential candidate, Sen. Gene McCarthy. Counter-protestors held up a sign at City Hall reading, "Moratorium Day is for Commies and Pigs," and the head of the firefighters union, denouncing Lindsay's flag order, said, "No one has the right to order us to participate in this voluntary day of national disgrace." But among activists, Lindsay was greeted with cheers of "We Want Lindsay!" At all of his stops, he countered the notion that protest was unpatriotic. "This form of dissent," he said at Washington Square Park, "is the highest form of patriotism. . . . Those that charge this is unpatriotic do not know the history of their own nation and they do not understand that our greatness comes from the right to speak out—and from the willingness to exercise that right."

. . . .

Tom Seaver reported to Shea Stadium for Game 4 on Moratorium Day at about ten in the morning. He went through his normal routine, changing, seeing the training staff, cup of coffee, bantering with teammates. When he was ready to get into his uniform, Seaver went to his locker and was handed an eight-page pamphlet by fellow pitcher Tug McGraw, who asked Seaver if he had seen it. He hadn't. "They're giving it out outside the park," McGraw told him. Four days earlier, Seaver was quoted in a three-paragraph item in the *New York Times*, hidden near the bottom of Page 4, between ads for Saks Fifth Avenue and Bergdorf Goodman. Seaver was quoted saying that, should New York top Baltimore in the World Series, he would take out an ad in the paper reading: "If the Mets can win the World Series, we can get out of Vietnam." Seaver went on to say, "I think it's perfectly ridiculous what we're doing about the Vietnam situation. It's absurd! When the series is over, I'm going to have a talk with Ted Kennedy, convey some of my ideas to him and then take an ad in the paper. I feel very strongly about it." As Seaver recalled it, that was not quite what he'd said. He had been contacted by the Moratorium Day committee, and agreed to sign an advertisement that was being discussed that would read, "If the Mets can win the pennant, we can get out of Vietnam." He would be willing to talk with Sen. Kennedy about the war, but just to ask questions, he said, not to give his opinions. Seaver had been a reservist with the Marines for a year starting in 1962, and came out of the experience ambivalent about war. He felt the US involvement in Vietnam was wrong, that it was damaging to the American image abroad. "I wasn't opposed to all wars," he later wrote. "I wasn't a confirmed pacifist. But I did feel that this particular war was wrong."

He was stunned, then, to look over the pamphlet McGraw handed him. There was a picture of Seaver on it—he had expressly told members of the Moratorium Day committee they could not use his photo—

and the title, "METS FANS FOR PEACE," alongside a copy of the article from the *Times*. On the back of the pamphlet, cartoon B-52s were dropping bombs on the Statue of Liberty. It turned out, the pamphlet was not actually produced by the Moratorium Day committee at all. It had been the work of the Chicago Conspiracy. The group, which included heavyweight radicals Abbie Hoffman, Bobby Seale, and Jerry Rubin, was on trial for inciting the violence and riots that took place during the 1968 Democratic Convention. The following day, they sent Seaver a telegram, reading, "Our trial now taking place in the center court of the Chicago Federal building has been termed the World Series of Injustice. In this series we, like you, are the underdog. So from us eight underdogs of the world struggling against oppression, we offer our support. Up against the center field wall, Baltimore! Power to the New York Mets!" Seaver was dumbfounded. "The people are being misled by that, and I resent it," Seaver said, "Whatever I want to say or do will come after the World Series is over. I'm a ballplayer, not a politician. I'm not in favor of those pamphlets and I feel that I've been used. I'm an American citizen and I have my feelings. They shouldn't be blown out of proportion."

The pamphlet had little effect on Seaver's Game 4 focus. He gave up baserunners in the first three innings, but was able to escape any damage and retired 16 of 17 batters he faced into the ninth inning. A Donn Clendenon home run had given the Mets a 1–0 lead, and Seaver needed only two outs to put the Mets on the brink of the World Series championship. Instead, he gave up back-to-back singles to Frank Robinson and Boog Powell before Brooks Robinson hit a hard, fast-dropping line drive to right field. Swoboda, stockily built and not known for his glovework, charged hard and made a tumbling, acrobatic catch, hopping to his feet and hurling the ball toward the plate. Frank Robinson scored on the sacrifice, but Swoboda's hustling play gave the Mets some added life in the tenth. After Jerry Grote doubled, Hodges sent in J.C. Martin as a pinch-hitter and Gaspar as a pinch-runner. Martin's bunt died beautifully, designed to move Grote into scoring position. But Martin snuck a little too far inside the baseline, and when catcher Elrod Hendricks fired a throw down the line, it hit Martin and caromed out toward second base, allowing Gaspar to come across with the winning run over cries from the Orioles that Martin was guilty of interference. Seaver had come out with a ten-inning complete game win, allowing six hits. He'd have to deal with the pamphlet mess—hippie-hating veteran writer Dick Young of the *New York Daily News* would give him an earful—but more important, he had made up for the way he pitched in Game 1. "When that run scored, I was a kid again," Seaver said, "and my entire life flashed before my eyes. Every young ballplayer dreams of playing in a World Series and I was playing ball when I was nine."

. . . .

The next day, October 16, it was over. Jerry Koosman got a fly ball from Davey Johnson and watched it nestle into the glove of Cleon Jones at 3:17 p.m. to clinch a Game 5 win, 5–3, and finish perhaps the most stunning run in the field of athletics since Pheidippides hustled to Athens. The World Series champion Mets were back in the dark comfort of their locker room where the champagne oozed and gurgled for the third time in twenty-two days. Swoboda—about whom Casey Stengel said, "The right-fielder frightens me all the time," which is just what you want from a New York Met—sat by his locker, having knocked in the run that cracked open a 3–3 tie in the eighth inning. "This season," Swoboda said, "has been one high after another. We've gone higher and higher until you can't go any higher."

Out on the field, the New Breed fans were again wreaking havoc, hurling smoke bombs and firecrackers, pulling up bases and ripping out chunks of Shea Stadium sod—6,500 square feet worth, reportedly—which they would keep to commemorate the victory until nature wilted and eroded them. Gil Hodges, heart patient one year earlier, was so gripped by emotion he could not speak, and two of his coaches had to help him to a side room until he could collect himself. Mrs. Joan Payson, the matriarch of the Mets, who had been told by Young seven years earlier to expect nothing, now could only seem to murmur, as if she feared some cruel joke had been played, "Oh my, oh my. Oh my."

The singer Pearl Bailey bellowed into the Mets locker room with her own piece of sod and announced that it was her corsage, and grabbed Hodges and planted kisses on both of his cheeks, telling him that while all the Mets were marvelous, "You are the one." John Lindsay found Rod Gaspar and reminded him, loudly, "You said you'd win it in four straight," and Gaspar replied, "I didn't say which four . . ."

On Rikers Island, forty inmates, given a reprieve from their payment of various debts to society, were allowed to watch Game 5. "Society's underdogs watching baseball's underdogs," one observer quipped. In the sixth inning, some suggested Cleon Jones (on base because of a controversial hit-by-pitch that struck his shoe, as black polish on the ball supposedly proved) steal second with Donn Clendenon at bat. Another said that, no, Clendenon is too good a hitter. Clendenon homered, scoring Jones, and the wise prisoner, a teenager doing five months for grand larceny, said, "See, I told you it doesn't pay to steal." By the time the game was over, the convicts cheered, "Gil Hodges for Warden!"

On Wall Street, there was, according to one description, a spontaneous "avalanche of ticker tape, computer print-outs, toilet paper, Dow Jones broad tape, and over-the-counter pink sheets . . . piled up ankle-deep on the curbs." Such were the masses in the Financial District that the police closed Broad Street to traffic, and the old-timers said they'd not seen the likes of this since Lindbergh came back from Paris in 1927. A bus driver on Madison Avenue surprised waiting passengers by swinging open the door and telling them, heck, they could ride for free. The chant went up: "Gil Hodges for Mayor!"

The *New York Times,* acknowledging the hardships that come with life in New York City, said in an editorial, "All these insufferable conditions were tolerated by the uncomplaining citizenry, waiting in a comatose state for something to happen. Out of the blue it did, at Shea Stadium . . . when the New York Mets proved that everybody loves a loser even when winning the World Series."

And Swoboda, at his locker, distilling the meaning of the Mets: "We," he said, "are the saints of lost causes."

CHAPTER 21

"It is best not to plan on promises and dreams"

It was late afternoon on October 20, and Red Holzman was not even sure what he was doing here, strolling the grounds of New York's mayoral residence, Gracie Mansion. In the morning, he had been out in Queens, at a community recreation center called Lost Battalion Hall, where the Knicks held practice because Madison Square Garden was occupied. The place was dilapidated, and inspired some player grousing. "I think it was lost a long time ago," Dave DeBusschere joked, "and I don't know how the Knicks ever found it." The gym had wooden backboards and the showers were typically short on hot water. Holzman had to apologize to his players about the condition of the place, and explain that the team was working on finding a place to practice in Manhattan on days when the Garden was not available. Now, though, the Knicks had taken a step up in class. Gracie Mansion sits high on the Upper East Side, between 88th Street and FDR Drive, with a rolling lawn and a view of the Triborough and Hell Gate bridges over the East River. Holzman and his wife, Selma, did not typically spend their late afternoons sharing *bon mots* at champagne receptions, but this was a party held to honor the World Series champion Mets, and, as Holzman saw it, "I guess we were window dressing." Not entirely. Lindsay did emerge from his dalliance with the Mets with some endorsements, including one from Ron Swoboda. Knicks center Willis Reed publicly backed Lindsay, too. DeBusschere, though, also in attendance as part of the Knicks contingent, wasn't thinking politics. He palled around with diminutive shortstop Al Weis and poet-infielder Ed Charles, and finally, met Mayor John Lindsay. "Mr. Mayor," DeBusschere said, "I hope you'll be having a party like this for the Knicks next May." Lindsay probably knew less about basketball than he did about baseball—he would later declare the week of November 3, "New York Knickerbockers Week," which would have been a very nice honor, except that the Knicks were on a nine-day road trip that week.

As October progressed, it looked more and more like Lindsay, no matter his basketball vocabulary, at least would be living at Gracie Mansion in 1970. Voters trickled away from Mario Procaccino, and seeking to alter the dynamics of the race, he finally consented to a televised debate. But aides who had warned him to stay away from a TV showdown were shown to be right when Procaccino, facing the elegant Lindsay and the erudite John Marchi, came off as harsh and temperamental, obscuring his points with excitability. On the same day he was celebrating the Mets, Lindsay received the endorsement of the *New York Post*, giving him an essential run of all media endorsements (the right-leaning *Daily News* gave its endorsement to Marchi). "What thoughtful citizens have steadily recognized," the *Post* said in its endorsement, "is that Lindsay's insistence on truly being 'Mayor of all the people' including many who have long felt isolated and alone—has been his most impressive achievement." On October 25, the *Daily News* released its well-respected straw poll showing Lindsay ahead with 47 percent of the vote, compared to Procaccino at 31 percent and 19 percent for Marchi. Lindsay's resurgence not only put him back into control of the mayoral race, it caught the imagination of the rest of the political world (in an off-year election, New York's mayoral decision was among the most high-profile contests for national political junkies to monitor) and got his career, now as an unaffiliated Liberal-Independent candidate, again pointed toward the national stage. California Governor Ronald Reagan said that the path was now clear for Lindsay to run for president in 1972—as a Democrat. Sen. Eugene McCarthy, Democratic candidate for the 1968 Presidential nomination, foresaw the rise of a third party, with Lindsay at the helm. Columnists Rowland Evans and Robert Novak claimed that national Democrats were already prepared to hand over the party reins to Lindsay, if he'd be willing to make the switch from his Republican roots: "They do realize they are in deep trouble with a vacuum of leadership since the decline of Sen. Edward M. Kennedy. That is why they are looking toward Lindsay."

All Lindsay had to do was win on Tuesday, November 4. In an attempt to cinch the mayoralty, he had one more television spot to release, in which he would remind voters, yet again, that he had entered the race as an underdog, just as the 100-to-1 Mets had started the 1969 season—though, Las Vegas had Lindsay's betting line set as a 9-to-5 longshot to open, much better odds than the Mets had gotten, and by Election Day, Vegas listed Lindsay as the 5-to-2 favorite. (Yes, you could go to Vegas and bet on the New York mayor's race.) In the ad, Lindsay was sitting in his darkened City Hall office, lit only by his desk lamp, his sleeves rolled up and tie loosened. He said to the camera, "For one afternoon this fall, a baseball team brought this town together like it's never been brought together before. At 3:17, on a cool afternoon, a bunch of kids, named Koosman and Agee and Weis, brought about the Impossible Dream. And all of the sudden, New Yorkers forgot about their differences, and it showed me how close this city really can be. Well, the fact of the matter is, the Bay Ridge homeowner, and the Forest Hills schoolteacher, and the jobless teenager in Bedford-Stuyvesant are *not* natural enemies. There are people trying to divide this city, and we can't let them do that. The man in this office, who occupies this chair, has to reach all of the people in this city and bring them together. And if anyone tries to tell you it can't be done, remember the Mets. If they can do it, we can do it."

And Lindsay did finally do it, winning a reelection bid that seemed so farfetched seven months earlier when the snow was falling, or a year earlier when the teachers were striking. The margin was closer than the polls had predicted, with Lindsay (41.8 percent) finishing just ahead of Procaccino (35 percent), while Marchi (23 percent) had a decent showing.

Lindsay had done it. He won. But he returned to the office chastened, with a much better understanding that running the city required that he put away the lofty rhetoric that marked the outset of his first term. In his second Inaugural Address, he sounded more like the kind of politician he would have assailed in his first Inaugural Address: "This is the last day of the decade," he told New York, "and we have, all of us, been through much hope and much sorrow. And if we have learned anything from these 10 turbulent, unsettling years, we have learned not to assume too much, because assumptions have a way of falling before the merciless assault of facts. So it is best not to plan on promises and dreams."

....

On Saturday, December 20, Joe Namath was sitting at his locker at Shea Stadium, dejected. He had just put forth what was, arguably, the worst performance of his career. The whipping winds of Flushing Bay got the better of him, and he completed only 14 of the 40 passes he attempted, throwing three interceptions and failing, when given a first-and-goal from the one-yard line on a pass interference call, to push the Jets across for a touchdown. The Jets, following up their Super Bowl triumph of the previous January with a 10–4 regular-season record in 1969, now saw their season end with a miserable 13–6 playoff loss to Kansas City. Outside the locker room, having realized the political benefit of attaching oneself to local sporting success, John Lindsay strode past locker-room attendants and gathered reporters and first found Weeb Ewbank. "Next time," he told the coach, who, shook his head and, said, "Makes it a long winter when you don't win." Lindsay moved along to Namath's locker, cut through the phalanx of writers, television foofs and radio men, and found Namath, sullenly packing together chunks of Skoal tobacco, tucking them into his lip and spitting into a paper cup. "Joe . . . Joe . . . Joe," the Mayor said, Namath hesitating to so much as look up. When he finally did, Lindsay said, "I know what it is to lose. Let me remind you there's a next time."

"Yeah, but next time is a long way off for us," Namath said. "We've got to live with this all year." When he had stopped shaking Lindsay's hand, Namath was still talking, and said, "I just could not throw the damn football with that wind, this is certainly the end, there is no tomorrow."

In retrospect, Namath was right. He was speaking about the 1969 season, but he might well have been speaking about himself, about Lindsay and about the New York they had both entered just four years earlier, a New York that was trying to hold its center. New York was a city in crisis when Lindsay took over, and when his second term got underway, it was still a city in crisis. But, at least, for a brief period, during Lindsay's summer of 1968 ascendancy, it looked like that crisis could be resolved, that Lindsay's urban vision could be actualized through the power of his rolled-up sleeves and smiling strolls through New York's worst slums. While Lindsay represented a Fun City built on open-mindedness, a zeal for civic responsibility and high ideals put into dynamic action, Namath was the pure *fun* of Fun City. Away from the cameras, he was coping with the personal torment of a career spent plying the corporal arts with a body built on mangled underpinnings. But in front of those cameras, he was tanning by the pool, and putting back tumblers of scotch before the ice had time to melt in Upper East Side hotspots, and growing sideburns, and exploding the myth of the virtuous American athlete, and preaching a doctrine of living and letting live. Lindsay was often accused by detractors of being more style than substance; Namath, on the other hand, proudly put style over substance. The two arrived on New York's stage together in 1965, when everyone went to Toots Shor's (except, mostly, blacks and women) and by 1970, found themselves in a city where it seemed everyone was going to the Electric Circus.

The 1970s would not be kind to either man. When Lindsay told Namath after the 1969 playoff loss to the Chiefs that there would be a "next time," he was wrong. Namath would play seven more seasons with the Jets, but he would miss a third of the Jets' games, and even when he was on the field, he'd never quite be the same. He'd already had three knee surgeries before winning Super Bowl III, but in the years that followed, he would suffer a season-ending broken wrist, another devastating knee injury that caused nerve damage, a shoulder separation, and a snapped hamstring that caused so much pain, his body went into shock. The Jets would not finish better than .500 in any of those seasons, and would never get back to the postseason. Namath would close out his career by playing four games with the Los Angeles Rams in 1977. He remained an in-demand pitchman, but would embark on a mostly fruitless acting career and see several of the business ventures he enthusiastically backed—Broadway Joe's, a chain of Bachelors III bars—fail. Lindsay, too, found himself out of his depth in the 1970s. The racial tensions that had been stirred during the school strikes flared up repeatedly, flight to the suburbs accelerated, the welfare tally skyrocketed, the liberal social projects Lindsay touted made little impact, municipal employee pay kept rising and New York spiraled into a fiscal crisis. Lindsay did, finally, attempt to pull himself onto the national stage in 1972, after he had fully converted to the Democratic Party, but it was too late. He was the wrong man in the wrong time. He ran for president in 1972, focusing on primaries in Florida and Wisconsin. But he was a dismal fourth in Florida (6.5 percent), finishing well behind the winner, George Wallace, and was just as bad in Wisconsin, where he polled sixth, with 6.7 percent of the vote.

Namath came to New York in the mid-1960s by way of a working-class town in western Pennsylvania and the Bear Bryant finishing school in Tuscaloosa, Alabama. Lindsay was from the Upper West Side, Yale, and the Silk Stocking District. Their backgrounds, styles and constituencies were different, but there was, in both Lindsay and Namath, an inherent faith in the better angels of man—the kind of faith that both men, and the nation in general, seemed to lose as the more cynical 1970s unfolded.

Jets coach Weeb Ewbank, instrumental in bringing Namath to New York, reflected on his star quarterback years later, during Ewbank's last season with the Jets. "Joe's always been for the underdog and maybe that's one of his troubles. A guy comes by and tells Joe he's from Beaver Falls and mentions one or two names, and Joe's liable to pay his expenses in New York for two or three weeks. And don't think these guys aren't ready to do that, either. They're always around. I don't know whether that's a fault or not. That and the hell of a lot of trouble it is getting him up in the morning are his two biggest faults, and I still don't know if the other one's a fault. I don't think any of us coming from the background he and I did—not poor, but a hell of a long ways from being rich—I don't think any of us getting out of college and then having a guy dangle $400,000 at you for 3 years ... Well, what would you do with it? I don't know, maybe we'd be worse."

Joseph Viteritti, chair of Hunter College's Urban Affairs and Planning Department, worked for Lindsay in his youth. He remembered the mayor's approach and motivation: "He did support the underdogs in society, and he wasn't doing it for political reasons. It was political suicide, really, if you look at it. He embraced a constituency that had no power, that wasn't voting—blacks who came to New York in those days had no habit of voting, because they came from the South and they were not allowed to vote. Puerto Ricans were not voting. I think he genuinely felt that, as a privileged person, he owed it to the poor to try to make their lives better. Some people would call it guilt, but that was not it. It was a feeling of responsibility you have as a privileged person to give back and to help those who are not as privileged as you are. That is what made him tick. I think he was surprised when he got into office and he found out that not everyone felt that way, he was maybe naïve that way. He made some drastic mistakes in the way he went about it. But I think he really felt that responsibility to help others. I don't think that was make-believe."

. . . .

John Lindsay made good on the arrangement he'd worked out with forward Dave DeBusschere, who had told him seven months earlier at the mayor's party for the Mets that the Knicks would be back, expecting their own party in May. Now it was noon on May 15, 1970, and the Knicks had just completed what would go down as one of the greatest years a city has ever had in sports, adding their own championship to the Jets' upset over the Colts and the Mets' run through the Braves and Orioles in baseball's playoffs. The headlines might have been bigger for the Super Bowl and World Series, but the rise of the Knicks was an enormous boon to the NBA—the Knicks attracted more than a million fans, at home and on the road, in each of the two seasons from 1968–1970, the first team to achieve that level of popularity in league history. They made Madison Square Garden a celebrity destination at a time when the American public was only mildly grasping onto basketball. The guileful Harlem Congressman Adam Clayton Powell adopted them as his own, calling himself the team's chaplain and arriving in the locker room on occasion, accompanied by the stench of his cigar. Actors like Dustin Hoffman, Robert Redford, and Elliott Gould adopted the club, too, regulars sitting courtside among the packed houses.

Though those Knicks had their 23–1 start, the 60 wins and the best record in the NBA by four games, they were not like the rest of the league, where the back-and-forth pace could be dizzying and the defense haphazard. The Knicks averaged 115 points, a mediocre ninth (of fourteen teams) offensively, but they won because they played an intense, full-throttle defensive system that suffocated ballhandlers and required a mix of repetition, ESP and trust in teammates. The Knicks, reluctantly at times, bought in, and limited opponents to 106 points per game, by far the lowest in the league. Team captain Willis Reed led the Knicks with 21.7 points per game, which did not crack the NBA's Top 10, but so varied were his contributions that he was named league MVP. He was symbolic of how the Knicks played, an utterly different style of basketball, one that required depth, balance and yeoman's work ahead of individual accomplishment. "The fans here used to come to the Garden to watch Wilt Chamberlain and Bill Russell do their stuff," Reed said. "Now they come to watch us."

It was Reed, of course, who provided the Knick climax, and who did so at the perfect, back-to-the-wall moment. But there was an eerie foreshadowing to the way it all went down. Back in December, a writer had visited the team for a magazine story, and pointed out to Red Holzman that injuries seemed to be going around the NBA, even among star players. "Let's just imagine," the writer said, "for the sake of starting something, that somebody important on the Knicks, say Willis Reed, gets sidelined by one of those injuries that seem to be crippling everybody else in the NBA."

"I'm not going to worry about Willis falling into a manhole until it happens," Holzman said. "Don't talk to me about things like that. Talk to me about disasters and I'll listen."

"What's a disaster?"

"A disaster," Holzman said, "is when you get home and you're out of scotch."

But disaster did strike at the Garden, which was not out of scotch. It struck Willis Reed. The Knicks had clawed their way past (who else?) the Baltimore Bullets and star guard Earl Monroe in a seven-game series in the first round of the 1970 Eastern Conference playoffs, withstood a 34-point-per-game onslaught from twenty-two-year-old native New Yorker Lew Alcindor (who would become Kareem Abdul-Jabbar the following year) to beat the Bucks in the East finals, and faced the Lakers for the championship. But it was then that 100 games' worth of strain on Reed, who, at 6-foot-9 was shorter than most centers and relied on his physicality and agility to guard them, caught up to him. And it caught up to him as he was dealing with the toughest assignment of his career: Chamberlain. Reed was dealing with injuries in both knees, and as he played through that pain, he put increased pressure on his thighs and hips. Reed was having success over the first four games, averaging 32 points while holding Chamberlain to just 19 points per game, but, finally, on May 4, during his fifth game going head-to-head with Chamberlain, Reed pulled the tensor muscle in his upper thigh, and the pain got so bad he could barely lift his leg. Without Reed in Game 5, the

Knicks, "gambled and got lucky," Holzman said, by running a series of undersize forwards at Chamberlain and forcing 19 turnovers, but Holzman reminded reporters, "On another night, playing that gambling defense, we might have been killed." They didn't have to wait long for that night. It came on May 6 in Los Angeles, where, without Reed, Chamberlain dominated, scoring 45 points with 27 rebounds, and leading the Lakers to a 135–113 win in Game 6.

On the day of the decisive Game 7, Reed was back in the Knicks' training room as a steady stream of teammates came to check on him. They only needed twenty minutes out of him, they said. Just twenty minutes of him standing between Chamberlain and the basket, and they'd gamble their way through the rest. He would play, he said. "I can make it up and down the floor," he told his teammates. "I just can't jump." That'd be good enough. Just twenty minutes of getting up and down the floor. While the Lakers and Knicks took the floor for warmups, Reed remained back in the locker room, taking a 200-milligram shot of carbocaine in his knee and cortisone in his thigh. Lakers guard Jerry West, thirty-one years old and openly frustrated with his inability to be part of a championship team to that point, thought perhaps he was about to have a change in fortunes. Looking ahead to Game 7, West had said, "One game, and a season depends on it. So much is tied up in the way you shoot and the way you defend. And then there's that key player—that one key man." There was no question who that key man was for the Knicks. "If Willis Reed isn't ready to play," West said, "well, I'd say the Knicks are in a bad way."

The fans at the Garden were not sure Reed would be ready to play. At 7:34 p.m., the Lakers were harmlessly shooting around on one end of the court, when they began to hear a roar on the other end, one that spread throughout the entire arena. Reed, in his bright white warmup suit, was taking the court. Each time he took a practice shot, the crowd roared again. Chamberlain, standing near DeBusschere, looked on. "How do you like that entrance?" DeBusschere asked.

"Not bad," Chamberlain responded.

"It's good for the crowd, anyway," DeBusschere said.

Chamberlain nodded, "Good for your team, too."

Indeed. Reed was not able to move well laterally, and jumping was out of the question, but that almost didn't matter. Just seeing him on the floor gave the Knicks a lift, and deflated the Lakers. "That was what I noticed," said Frazier, who would lead the team with 36 points. "Before the game started, you could look at the other guys and see it on their faces. They were just looking at Willis, and I thought, I think we might have them here." Reed scored the Knicks' first two baskets, and didn't score again on the night. He played the first twenty-one minutes, and despite his lack of mobility, despite the wearing off of the painkillers in his leg, he stood behind Chamberlain and gave him elbows to the lower back, took elbows to the sternum, and stumbled and pushed and prodded and made Chamberlain as uncomfortable as he could, not letting Chamberlain get close enough to the rim to execute his favored finger-roll shots. The rest of the Knicks fed off his example. New York was up, 69–42 at halftime, and the outcome was never in doubt. They played out the second half, a mere exhibition for the jubilant crowd. The Knicks were champions, for the first time in twenty-four years. One Los Angeles writer, whose team had just finished as the runner-up for the seventh time without a championship, admired, "The Knicks blend into a perfect team and it doesn't matter who is playing."

If Mayor Lindsay was a marginal baseball fan and an opportunistic Jets fan, he was completely out of touch when it came to the NBA and the Knicks. That much was clear when the Knicks and 100 or so dignitaries from sports, entertainment and politics gathered on the lawn of Gracie Mansion, with Reed limping the grounds in his suit, downing a hot dog, while the Smith Street Dixieland Jazz band played. Lindsay stepped to the microphone, placed in front of the shrub-lined steps leading to the estate's front door. He'd had some remarks prepared to congratulate the Knicks on their first title in twenty-four years, but he first wanted to, rather somberly, wish good luck to three players who would no longer be with the Knicks: John Warren, Don May and Bill Hosket. "Unfortunately," Lindsay said, "three members of the team have been drafted by Uncle Sam." The mayor had misunderstood, however. The players were not drafted to fight in Vietnam. They had been chosen in the NBA's expansion draft. Hosket and May would leave the Knicks to play for the Buffalo Braves, and Warren was going to the Cavaliers. "I was drafted by Uncle Cleveland," Warren said, "not Uncle Sam."

Holzman, maybe summing up Lindsay's political life in general, forgave the blunder, observing that, the mayor "was well-intentioned, anyway."

....

The Knicks were an apt symbol of success in pro sports, not just in their era, but in any era. While New York was hailed for its incredible teamwork and the mastery of Holzman in guiding his group, later that year, a book chronicling the season—*Miracle on 33rd Street*, by Phil Berger—showed a much different side of the Knicks, one in which the locker room was distinctly divided between black and white players and where Holzman's self-effacing public image dissolved into occasional bouts of bitterness and antagonism toward players. "The feeling here," sixth man Cazzie Russell told Berger, "is that other than basketball, I don't particularly care about you, and I think Red is probably the cause of some of it, because that's basically how he feels." Such tensions are natural on any professional sports team, but when revealed—when the curtain goes up on the locker room charade—we're reminded of the fallacy of sports parables, in which so many seek comfort. Indeed, the celebration of Namath's swinging lifestyle eventually gave way to his struggle with alcoholism, at first private, then very public. The Mets did return to the World Series in 1973 (they lost in seven games), but they were mostly an unspectacular, slightly above-average bunch in the wake of their 1969 miracle. It didn't take long for dissension to kick in with them. After the season, thirty-six-year-old beloved infielder Ed "The Glider" Charles, was ready to quit baseball, and was offered a job in the Mets promotions department, in part to help rectify the reality that the team's front office was lily-white. But Charles had a falling out with general manager Johnny Murphy over moving expenses, and the deal fell through. There was word, too, that when seven Mets signed up to go to Las Vegas for a stint on stage at Circus Maximus in a vaudeville-style act, several players were resentful that Tom Seaver had brought his wife. A decade after their World Series title, the Mets would plant a story with Dick Young of the *Daily News* about Nancy Seaver expressing jealousy over the contract Nolan Ryan (who had remained Seaver's friend even after he was traded to the Angels in 1971) had gotten from California. That precipitated a nasty Mets-Seaver breakup.

The success of pro sports teams can't necessarily resolve the issues of the athletes who make up those teams, and it certainly can't fix the morass of issues that typically beset the cities in which those players perform. Even as the Knicks were winning the NBA championship in 1970, New York was quelling the hard-hat riot, in which a group of construction workers chanting, "All the way, USA!" attacked student demonstrators protesting the killing of four students at Kent State by Ohio National Guardsmen. Shortly thereafter, New York convened the Knapp Commission, which would, over the span of two years, collect testimony and issue a report on the widespread corruption and abuse in the New York Police Department. The Jets, Mets, and Knicks didn't fix New York, but for a stretch, at least, their successes saved John Lindsay and the city from their own failures, and brought together a divided city in which residents seemed increasingly unable or unwilling to understand each other. They could understand Joe Namath, though, and the Mets, and Willis Reed. "When you live in fires and funerals and strikes and rats and crowds and people screaming in the night," Jimmy Breslin wrote in 1969, "sports is the only thing that makes any sense."

Source notes

Chapter 1

2 "Bear Bryant runs that department." From the *Miami Times*, January 1, 1965.

3 ". . . the Longhorn guard who stopped the plunge." *The Sporting News*, January 16, 1965.

3 ". . . spanked for something bad" *Los Angeles Times*, January 2, 1965.

3 "I sent in all the plays ..." *Miami Times*, January 2, 1965.

3 ". . . shoulda, shoulda, shoulda . . ." Namath describes the final sequence of the 1965 Orange Bowl on page 98, in the book *Namath*, co-authored by Namath and Shawn Coyne. (New York: Rugged Land Publishing, 2006.)

4 ". . . scribbled his name on the papers." Maury Allen, *Joe Namath's Sportin' Life*, pg. 63. (New York: Paperback Library, 1969.)

4 "I'm going after that Namath kid from Alabama." Paul Zimmerman, *The Last Season of Weeb Ewbank*, pg. 14. (New York: Farrar, Straus and Giroux, 1974.)

6 "At least I'm going to give it a try." *The Sporting News*, January 16, 1965.

6 "in living color." *The Sporting News*, December 19, 1964.

7 "I decided to go with the Bears." *Kansas City Star* June 19, 2008.

7   "It was just me and these two guys in my room, right?" Namath and Coyne, pg. 117.

8   "Yeah, boy wants a LIN-coln Con-ti-NEN-tal!" Namath has told the story of the Cardinals' reaction to his contract demands in several places, including in *Namath*, HBO Sports Documentary, 2012; and on page 117 of Namath and Coyne; also on page 202 in Joe Namath and Dick Schaap, *I Can't Wait Until Tomorrow . . . Cause I get Better-Looking Every Day*. (New York: Random House, 1969.)

8   "Namath was going to be a really good athlete." *Broadway Joe and his Super Jets,* by Larry Fox, pg. 110. (New York: Coward-McCann, 1969.)

8   . . . consider forgoing the NFL to do so. Fox, pg. 111–112.

9   ". . . leaves, flowers and colors." Namath and Coyne, pg. 122.

9   "I really did." Namath and Schaap, pg. 204.

10   ". . . as far as you can without breaking it." Namath and Schaap, pg. 204.

10   "We know he wants to play in New York." *New York Post*, December 31, 1964.

10   ". . . tax advice on his impending windfall." *Sporting News,* January 15, 1965.

10   ". . . the greatest pilot film in TV history." Fox, pg. 116.

11   ". . . a pro team right now." *Sports Illustrated*, January 11, 1965.

11   ". . . I'm not paying this guy enough.'" Hirsch's interview about Namath appeared more than two years after the Orange Bowl, in the *Chicago Tribune*, September 7, 1967.

11   . . . a hotel just a few doors down. *Miami Times* January 3, 1965.

11   ". . . demeanor and attitude of Joe DiMaggio." *New York Times*, January 10, 1965.

12   ". . . a hole in the sole of his right shoe." *Miami Times*, January 3,1965.

12   ". . . Namath who was driving the attention." *Los Angeles Times*, January 5, 1965.

13 "What else are you going to do?" Quotes and descriptions of Beaver Falls, Pennsylvania, from Boston Globe, January 4, 1965; January 10, 1965; and January 11, 1965.

13 ". . . permission to date my daughter." *Atlanta Journal*, January 23, 1965.

13 ". . . a moment I have dreaded." *New York Times*, January 23, 1965.

14 ". . . We got no respect from these people." Namath and Coyne, pg. 124.

14 "Sort of looks like Ernest Borgnine." *Sports Illustrated*'s Monday Morning Quarterback, July 20, 2013.

14 "The men's room." Dr. Nicholas' story appeared in the *Sun-Sentinel*, November 17, 1986.

14 ". . . the hell he was thinking, but he split." Namath and Coyne, 125.

14 ". . . ever be able to play." *New York Times*, June 17, 2006.

14 ". . . get yourself another quarterback." *Sun-Sentinel*, November 17, 1986.

15 ". . . he actually signed for." *New York Herald-Tribune*, January 23, 1965.

15 "I am going to make it." *Sport*, August 1965.

Chapter 2

16 ". . . allowed to proliferate for decades." *Time*, November 12, 1965.

18 ". . . the most influential Washington audiences." *Atlanta Constitution*, December 19, 1964.

19 ". . . I never saw a man talk himself off the Foreign Affairs Committee so fast in my life." *Time*, November 12, 1965.

19 ". . . a little too curt and abrasive." *New York Times*, May 23, 1965.

20 ". . . beaten, shamed or dying men." *New York*, May 27, 1968.

20 ". . . living in metropolitan areas." *New York Post*, October 23, 1964.

21 ". . . all the way to the White House." Oliver Pilat, *Lindsay's Campaign*, pg. 9. (Boston: Beacon Press, 1968.) Pilat offers several

details of the luncheon at which Lindsay's potential run for Mayor of New York was discussed.

21 ". . . a raison d'etre for me to run." Richard Kluger, *The Paper*, pg. 702. (New York: Knopf, 1986.)

22 ". . . tell Jock to shove it up his ass." Kluger, pg. 701.

23 "Gave me a sleepless night." Author interview of Richard Aurelio.

23 ". . . get from here to there." *New York Times*, March 7, 1965.

24 ". . . their sense of people-politics." *New York Post*, May 15, 1965.

24 "And he never let us forget it." Nat Hentoff, *A Political Life: The Education of John V. Lindsay*, pg. 51. (New York: Knopf, 1969.)

24 ". . . for merely being there." *New York Times*, February 12, 1965.

25 ". . . future depends on its success in the cities." *New York Times*, May 12, 1965.

25 ". . . a real chance to win." *New York Times*, May 13, 1965.

25 ". . . the spear carrier for the bad guys." *Atlanta Constitution*, May 18, 1965.

26 ". . . who was turning five." Details of Lindsay's decision to run for mayor found in *New York Times Magazine*, May 23, 1969.

26 ". . . Brooklyn Republican politicians filtered in." *Village Voice*, May 20, 1965.

26 ". . . you are a fuddy-duddy." *New York Post*, May 14, 1965.

27 ". . . everyone else is tired." *New York World-Telegram*, May 14, 1965.

Chapter 3

28 ". . . a good day Saturday so much." From Jimmy Breslin's column, printed in the *Boston Globe*, December 13, 1964.

29 "The hell with it." *New York Times*, December 13, 1964.

29 "Those were the cartoons." *New York Post*, December 14, 1964.

30 ". . . against my ex-teammates." *New York Times*, December 14, 1964.

31 ". . . what they came to see." *Time*, November 30, 1959.

31 "I'll never forget that trade." From article on www.Redskins.com, by Mike Richman, December 16, 2011.

32 "Thanks for taking care of my folks." Details of Werblin's pursuit of Snell vs. the Maras' pursuit of Snell found in Fox, pg. 102.

32 ". . . he turns his back on Werblin." *New York Times*, December 22, 1964.

33 ". . . nobody cared about the Establishment." Allen, *Sportin' Life*, pg. 67.

33 ". . . unto themselves in Major League baseball." *Chicago Daily News*, December 27, 1964.

34 "I'm just a little bit madder." *New York Times*, August 14, 1964.

36 ". . . state paper Izvestia wrote." Congressional quotes and Russian news story found in *Sporting News*, August 29, 1964.

36 ". . . nearly 400 times greater?" *Boston Globe*, August 16, 1964.

36 ". . . the standings of the teams." *New York Times*, August 16, 1964.

37 "Some of the guys resented him." *New York Post*, October 18, 1964.

39 ". . . game in a bank vault." Houk quotes from Sporting News, January 2, 1965.

39 ". . . the Yankees must reach?" *New York Times*, October 18, 1964.

Chapter 4

41 ". . . all over Tuscaloosa to prove it." *Atlanta Journal*, January 1, 1965.

41 "Here he is about to go in the hospital and he's having a ball." Allen, *Sportin' Life*, pg. 71.

41 ". . . patron saint of difficult tasks." *Sports Illustrated*'s Monday Morning Quarterback, July 20, 2013.

41 ". . . the original injury occurred in October." Namath's surgery details can be found in *Time* magazine, February 5, 1965.

42 ". . . play pro football for four years." *Sporting News* Conversation with Joe Namath, January 27, 2012.

42 ". . . tapping of Joe Namath's knee." *Sports Illustrated*, October 17, 1966.

42   "... to have had a knee operation." The letters come from both the *New York Times*, February 6, 1965 and Allen, pg. 73.

43   "I guess it wound up a little over the top." Namath's description of his arrival in New York City and his first and second apartments are found in the *Wall Street Journal*, January 31, 2013; Namath's *Playboy* interview, December 1969; and the *New York Times*, December 13, 1967.

44   "... we ask them how far crazy is and they don't know." *New York Post*, November 25, 1964.

44   "Larry Grantham worked in a bank." The offseason jobs worked by Jets veterans were noted in *Sports Illustrated*, October 17, 1966; and in Don Maynard and Matthew Shepatin, *You Can't Catch Sunshine*, pg. 151–152. (Chicago: Triumph Books, 2010.)

45   "... an economic accident of the time." Werblin and Grantham quotes from the *Boston Globe*, January 11, 1965; and *New York Times*, January 10, 1965.

45   "... getting it while the getting is good." *New York Times*, December 31, 1964.

45   "... gets only maybe $18,000." *New York Times*, January, 1965.

45   "... a great harm to sports." *Hartford Courant*, February 18, 1965.

45   "... not even me, my wife says." *Atlanta Constitution*, January 4, 1965.

46   "That is just about it." Fox, pg. 119–20.

46   "The Continentals didn't fool around." *New York Post*, July 23, 1966.

46   "there never will be any dissension." *New York Times*, May 4, 1965.

46   "At least he's left that big green car behind." Fox, pg. 121.

47   "There were some guys that were pissed-off to see him." Schmitt quoted from *Namath*, HBO Sports Documentary, 2012.

47   "Your money weighing you down?" Namath and Schaap, pg 160.

47   "It was a good gag." *Playboy* interview, December 1969.

48 ". . . fight whomever had a problem with him." Namath has given several accounts of this story. One was in *Namath*, HBO Sports Documentary, 2012. Also, see Fox, pg. 127–28.

48 "He can't miss." *New York Times*, July 16, 1965.

49 "Joe was being Joe." Maynard and Shepatin, pg.163–164.

50 ". . . long ago decided on Namath as the No. 1 quarterback." *New York Daily News*, August 15, 1965.

50 ". . . 42,710 the previous year." *New York Times*, September 12, 1965.

50 ". . . how's Sonny taking it?" *Hartford Courant*, September 21, 1965.

51 "Eventually, this will all pay dividends." *New York Times*, October 18, 1965.

51 ". . . a successful rookie quarterback." *New York Times*, November 25, 1965.

51 "Not as a $400,000 quarterback." *Sporting News* January 1, 1966.

Chapter 5

52 ". . . strip to the waist and get into a bathing suit." *New York Daily News*, December 21, 2000.

52 ". . . I'm on his wagon wherever the hell it's going." Pilat, pg. 168.

53 . . . whenever the situation even remotely called for it. Chris McNickle, *To Be Mayor of New York*, pg. 201. (New York: Columbia University Press, 1993.)

54 "Mollen had, 'miserably botched,' his job." *New York Times*, March 6, 1965.

54 "Now we are looking for the bad government people." Pilat, pg. 138.

54 ". . . he can be downright impudent." *New York World-Telegram*, August 26, 1965.

55 "Lindsay is not Nixon." Pilat, pg. 14.

55 ". . . army of 30,000 volunteers." Sources differ on just how many volunteers Lindsay had working for him. The estimate of 30,000 was from *Time* magazine, November 12, 1965.

55 ". . . scion of an aristocratic old New York family" *New York Times*, May 23, 1965.

56 "Will Mr. Lindsay lend himself to such purposes?" *New York Post*, May 17, 1965.

56 ". . . Lindsay was an ungrateful son of a bitch." Richard Norton Smith, *On His Own Terms: A Life of Nelson Rockefeller*, pg. 473. (New York: Random House, 2014.)

56 ". . . Democratic way to clean the streets." *New York Times*, May 27, 1965.

57 ". . . taking care of 10 million lunatics?" and, "I've never been so scared in my life." *New York Times*, May 29, 1965.

57 ". . . more glass-holding than drinking." Pilat, pg. 61.

57 "I'm going to help you." *New York Times*, June 8, 1965.

59 ". . . Lindsay rises from banality, only to arrive at fatuity." Buckley's raps at Lindsay, and his press conference, can be found in the *Herald-Tribune*'s *New York* magazine, January 2, 1966. Also see William F. Buckley, *The Unmaking of a Mayor*, pg. 110. (New York: Viking Press, 1966.)

60 "I'd give up Saturday nights to watch him." *Village Voice*, October 28, 1965.

61 "Vote for Lindsay for more crime in the streets." *New York Times*, July 4, 1965.

61 "We have to kill him." Pilat, pg. 107.

61 ". . . credible enough to warrant a police detail for Lindsay." Woody Klein, *Lindsay's Promise: The Dream that Failed*, pg. 13. (New York: Macmillan, 1970.)

61 ". . . most hostile he had encountered in nearly six months campaigning." *New York Times*, October 27, 1965.

63 ". . . a rump Republican party and the press and Barry Gray!" Pilat, pg. 243.

63 ". . . perplexed and harassed." *New York Post*, October 29, 1965.

63 ". . . I do think this is a radical right thing." Pilat, pg. 312.

64 "... personally distasteful to share a platform with you." Lindsay's exaggerated charges against Beame, and Beame's respons found in the *New York Times*, October 22, 1965.

64 "... repugnant to everything I have been taught this country stands for." Religious mudslinging among the candidates found in *New York Times*, and *New York Daily News*, October 22 and October 23, 1965.

65 "... machine power and control in New York City." Video of the 1969 mayoral debate can be found at http://crooksandliars.com/gordonskene/politics-past-1965-new-york-mayoral-de.

65 "... live with the possibility they put Mr. Lindsay in office." *New York Times Review of Books*, October 30, 1966.

66 "... starts out from a lonely base." *New York Times*, November 8, 1965.

Chapter 6

68 "Gentlemen, we've just been fucked." John Helyar, *The Lords of the Realm, The Real History of Baseball*, ch. 23. (New York: Ballantine, 1995.)

68 "I certainly was not disappointed." Jimmy Breslin, *Can't Anyone Here Play This Game?*, pg. 51. (New York: Viking, 1963.)

69 "... you ain't doing a thing for me!" *Sporting News*, February 20, 1965.

70 "... on any track, wet or dry." *New York Times*, October 19, 1960.

70 "They don't want the old way." *New York Times*, October 19, 1960.

70 "You don't see me crying, do you?" George Vecsey, *Joy in Mudville*, pg. 30. (New York: McCall Publishing Co., 1970.)

70 "... given their dynasty a firmer footing than it ever had." *New York Times*, October 19, 1960.

71 "You better write down that lineup so I'll remember." Sporting News, April 18, 1962.

71 "In Chicago." Maury Allen, *The Incredible Mets*, pg. 49. (New York: Paperback Library, 1969.)

72 "We don't fool around." Vecsey, pg. 45.

72 "Stengel just shrugged before the question was even posed." Robert Lipsyte, *SportsWorld: An American Dreamland,* pg. 30. (New York: Quadrangle/New York Times, 1975.)

72 "It's the greatest since Ruth." *Sporting News,* June 9, 1962.

73 ". . . if he criticizes anyone, criticizes himself as often as not." *Sporting News,* July 11, 1964.

74 "He'll understand the Depression when they teach it to him in school." Breslin, pg. 95.

74 ". . . he's liable to drop it." Allen, *Mets,* pg. 47.

75 ". . . the Mets will start a winning streak." *New York Times,* April 28, 1963.

76 "Baseball, around the Mets, is fun." *New York Times,* October 18, 1964.

76 "Lots of people my age are dead." *Sporting News,* July 11, 1964.

76 "I haven't been there in a while." *New York Post,* May 5, 1964.

77 "Nobody sees me fainting." *New York Post,* May 11, 1965.

77 . . . stumbled and broke his hip. Accounts of Stengel's day leading up to the broken hip found in *New York Times,* July 26, 1965 and *Sporting News,* September 7, 1965.

77 ". . . you oughtn't to manage." *New York Daily News,* August 7, 1965, and *New York Times,* August 31, 1965.

78 "It looked like Toledo." *New York Post,* May 3, 1965.

78 "They don't have it anymore. That's for certain." *New York Post,* May 12, 1965.

78 ". . . like putting Billy Graham in charge of the Hell's Angels." *New York Times,* March 16, 2013.

79 ". . . postgame harangue triggered more rumors." *Sporting News,* May 7, 1966.

79 "I've left you a tough job. Best, Ralph." *New York Times,* October 3, 1966.

Chapter 7

81 ". . . as big a challenge, as assistant secretary of state." *The New Republic,* July 16, 1966.

81   "I've lived in buildings all my life." Sam Roberts (ed.), *America's Mayor: John V. Lindsay and the Reinvention of New York*, pg. 24. (New York: Columbia Press, 2010.)

81   "I think I can use you." Klein, pg. 19.

82   $312 million deficit for the fiscal year that would stretch into 1966. Charles R. Morris, *The Cost of Good Intentions: New York City and the Liberal Experiment*, pg. 137. (New York: W.W. Norton, 1980.)

82   ". . . acting as a receiver in bankruptcy." *New York Times*, November 18, 1965.

84   "You fuckers can deal with Quill yourself." Vincent J. Cannato, *The Ungovernable City: John Lindsay and his Struggle to Save New York*, pg. 79. (New York: Basic Books, 2001)

84   ". . . a raving Anglophobe." *Time*, January, 14, 1966.

84   ". . . as a congressman and then as mayor." Hentoff, pg. 54.

85   "Mike Quill looked at Lindsay and he saw the Church of England." *New York Herald-Tribune*, January 2, 1966.

85   ". . . little fruitful negotiations under such circumstances." *New York Times*, November 24, 1965.

85   ". . . do anything else with it that is handy." *New York Times*, and *New York Daily News*, December 2, 1965.

86   "This is going to be a bitch." Klein, pg. 41.

87   "leading the rest of the union delegation with him." Quotes from Quill and details of the Mayor's meeting with the union on December 31 come from Klein, pg. 47–48, as well as Jimmy Breslin's story in the *Herald-Tribune*, January 2, 1966.

88   ". . . no matter how severe the threat." *New York Post*, January 2, 1966.

88   ". . . a gesture which proved that the fun city had a fun mayor." *Herald-Tribune*, January 7, 1966.

89   "He looks like you!" Accounts of Lindsay's anger with MacMahon and his call to his brother in Klein, pg. 71, and *New York Times*, January 11, 1966.

89   "They know!" Lindsay's rails against the "power brokers" found in *New York Times*, January 12, 1966, and *Time*, January 21, 1966.

90 ". . . grass roots movement to bring back Vincent Impellitteri." *New York Times*, January 13, 1966.

90 ... about a 70 percent increase from the previous contract. On February 9, 1968, more than two years after the settlement of the transit strike, the *New York Daily News* pointed to the settlement as opening the way to large pay demands from other unions.

90 ". . . has worn the 'record' label." *New York Daily News*, February 9, 1968.

91 "did everything he could to end the strike." *New York Times*, January 26, 1966.

92 "He's a real operator, isn't he?" Klein, pg. 75.

93 "They've just never gotten along with each other." *New York Times*, January 1, 1967.

93 "We were discussing architecture and got in an argument." Smith, pg. 501.

93 "He doesn't seem to know what he doesn't know." Hentoff, pg. 109.

94 ". . . style that marked most city parks." *New York Times Magazine*, July 10, 1966.

94 "I'm testing the water!" *New York Post*, July 13, 1966.

94 ". . . act of making these spaces of quiet itself promoted harmony." *New York Times*, December 12, 2009.

95 ". . . sex everywhere, pornography everywhere." *New York Daily News*, January 8, 1967.

95 ". . . showcase for the American people." *New York Daily News*, January 8, 1967.

95 ". . . it's not even bad burlesque." *New York Daily News*, January 14, 1967.

96 "Wouldn't you rather play Henry II?" *New York Times*, May 17, 1966.

96 ". . . purpose of New York and other American cities." Roberts, pg. 87.

Chapter 8

97 "Holy shit. Don't start that shit." Namath and Schaap, 168–69.

97 ". . . two indispensable people in the organization, Joe and Matt Snell." Zimmerman, pg. 64.

97 "We don't want any of that stuff here." Namath and Schaap, 168–69.

98 "Go find your own bar." Zimmerman, pg. 62.

98 ". . . the entire country couldn't handle it." Zimmerman, pg. 64.

98 "I'm hoping to change. I'm trying." Zimmerman, pg. 62.

99 "We have been friends for a long time." Allen, *Sportin' Life*, pg. 132.

99 ". . . which was shortened to just, 'Nigger.'" *Playboy*, December 1969.

99 "It's so absurd." *Jet*, September 17, 1964.

100 ". . . from the leaders on the team." Zimmerman, pg. 63. Zimmerman observed Namath's behavior crossing racial lines at Jets training camp.

101 "Weeb looked a little shook." Namath and Schaap 168.

101 ". . . uncomfortable moment for Werblin turned to laughter. *New York Daily News*, January 7, 1967.

101 "The Private World of the Negro Ballplayer." Boyle's article was published in *Sports Illustrated* on March 21, 1960.

102 "Obviously it's not that way at all." Jim Bouton, *Ball Four*, pg. 280. (New York: Dell Publishing, 1970.)

103 "I just won't step on the field." *New York Post*, October 24, 1964.

103 ". . . what went on in New Orleans was more than they could be expected to take." Foss quote is taken from the Pro Football Hall of Fame website, at: http://www.profootballhof.com/history/2010/2/18/players-boycott-afl-all-star-game/

103 "There'll be no niggers on this ballclub as long as I have anything to say about it." Hirshberg's assertion cited at: http://sabr.org/bioproj/person/dce16a07

104 ". . . you've got good, hardworking, white people here." Griffith's speech is recounted at: http://www.startribune.com/sports/blogs/257189521.html

104 "They would be offended to have to sit with niggers." Allen Barra, *Yogi Berra: Eternal Yankee*, pg 194. (New York: W.W. Norton, 2010.)

104 "You're colored, and they don't want that." *Reggie Jackson with Kevin Baker, Becoming Mr. October, pg.* 5–6 (New York: Doubleday, 2013.)

105 ". . . regard them as watermelon-eating idiots." *Sports Illustrated*, July 1, 1968.

105 ". . . positions such as linebacker, offensive guard and quarterback." Meggysey's book, *Out of their League*, was excerpted in *Look* on December 1, 1970.

105 "There had been prejudice." *Hartford Courant*, November 10, 1968.

105 "'player power' could do nothing but hurt us." *Sporting News*, June 10, 1967.

106 ". . . every kind of job there is in the front office." *Sporting News*, June 24, 1967.

107 "Bring on the Packers." *New York Times*, November 1, 1966.

107 ". . . nothing I enjoy better than to show up those who belittle me." Donaldson and Namath quotes from *Sporting News*, October 22, 1966.

107 "But blondes, they come first." *New York Post*, July 25, 1965.

108 ". . . scrutinizing his press minutely for a few hours every day." Mamie Van Doren with Art Aveilhe, *Playing the Field,* pg. 239. (Newport Beach, Calif.: Starlet Suave Books, 2013.)

108 ". . . the people who make life stimulating for a bachelor." *Sports Illustrated*, October 17, 1966.

108 "Joe, you're the most beautiful thing in the world!" *Saturday Evening Post,* December 3, 1966.

108 . . . Frank Sinatra and Dean Martin, told the venerable weekly. *Sporting News*, November 5, 1966.

109 ". . . once last year that I couldn't talk." *Saturday Evening Post,* December 3, 1966.

109 "I thought about staying down." Ibid.

109 "This isn't high school." Ibid.

109-110 "... younger writers, all liberals and black militants." Lipsyte, pg. 177.

110 "Now it was out in the open." Allen, *Sportin' Life*, pg. 94–95.

110 "I don't give a damn." *Saturday Evening Post*, December 3, 1966.

111 "... booed by my family every time I came home." *New York Daily News*, October 31, 1966.

111 "... breed of fans is go on tearing him apart." *New York Daily News*, November 1, 1966.

112 "... on a pedestal and let everybody chop him down." *New York Daily News*, November 1, 1966.

112 "... from the monastic life of the last 10 days." *New York Times*, January 5, 1967.

Chapter 9

114 But there was no formal punishment. The incident at Joe's Place incident is recalled in the *New York Times*, March 1 and 2, 1966.

115 "... there would be instant mutual acceptance." *New York Post*, November 8, 1964.

115 "The cop on the street took it all as a criticism of himself." Morris, pg. 92.

116 "... you immobilize the police force." Quotes from Farmer and Cassese taken from the *New York Times*, February 15 and 16, 1966; also February 21, 1966.

116 "... their gripes and their shouting." *New York Times*, May 9, 1966.

117 "It was a vulgar, obscene advertisement if I've ever seen one." T.J. English, *The Savage City: Race, Murder and a Generation on the Edge*, pg. 160. (New York: HarperCollins, 2011.)

117 "Nothing could have been more likely to alienate middle-class whites." *City Journal*, Winter 1993.

119 "... and reached 20 percent by 1968." Jerald E. Podair, *The Strike that Changed New York: Blacks, Whites and the Ocean Hill-Brownsville Crisis*, pg. 15. (New Haven, Conn.: Yale University Press, 2002.)

119 ". . . 85 percent of those were in New York." From the Center on Puerto Rican Studies at Hunter College: http://centropr.hunter. cuny.edu/education/puerto-rican-studies/story-us-puerto-ricans-part-four

120 ". . . a shocking jump of 264 percent." Crime statistics are from: http://www3.istat.it/istat/eventi/2003/perunasocieta/relazioni/ Langan_rel.pdf

120 "I wouldn't want one living next door." *Saturday Evening Post*, September 7, 1963.

121 "But I don't like myself for saying it." *New York Times*, September 21, 1964.

121 ". . . in the weeks and months that followed. Wallace transcript, *Eyes on Prize*, located at Washington University Digital Gateway texts: digital.wustl.edu/e/eii/eiiweb/wal5427.0729.168mikewal-lace.html.

122 ". . . the higher-ups in the Muslim movement." Quote was in Jimmy Breslin's story about Malcolm X's murder, *Boston Globe*, Febraury 22, 1965.

123 ". . . some have begun to describe him as a new Malcolm X." *New York Times*, August 5, 1966.

124 "Blood gonna flow, whitey." Black Power quotes from *New York Times*, July 29, 1966. *Time*, July 1, 1966; *New York Post*, July 5, 1966.

124 ". . . even more abandoned by Government than do Negroes." *New York Times*, August 16, 1966.

125 ". . . hottest summer city residents ever had to swelter through." *New York Times*, July 14, 1966.

125 ". . . lowest employment in the city." Barry Gottehrer, *The Mayor's Man*, pg. 12. (New York: Doubleday, 1975.)

126 . . . empty cans and torn clothing. *New York Post*, July 11, 1966.

126 "I'm going to get out of here." (Accounts of rising tensions in Brooklyn found in *New York Post*, July 21, 1966, *New York Times*, July 20, 1966.

127 "I still hate his guts, but he's sure got balls." Accounts of the skirmishes can be found in Gottehrer, pg. 14; and *New York Daily News*, July 23, 1966.

128 "I think we're going to have a riot."Gottehrer, pg. 15.

128 ". . . to have Dean given a proper burial.) Gottehrer, pg. 27.

128 ". . . heading into the weekend, the police stayed put." Reactions to Dean's shooting and police presence found in *New York Times*, July 23, 1966; *New York Daily News*, July 22, 1966; *New York Post*, July 23, 1966.

128 ". . . much more in the ghetto than will brute force." *New York Times*, July 23, 1966.

128 ". . . but they followed orders." Klein, pg. 208.

129 ". . . they are colored people." Gottehrer, pg. 27.

129 ". . . I never cursed anyone before." *New York Post* ,July 22, 1966.

129-130 ". . . afraid to walk out of the house." *New York Times*, August 19, 1966.

130 ". . . a vote against Stokely Carmichael." *Time*, November 18, 1966.

131 ". . . this being a Fun City?" *New York Daily News*, November 9, 1966.

Chapter 10

133 " . . . a nut, an illiterate for two years?" Accounts of Ali's reaction to his change in draft status found in *New York Times*, February 18, 1966; *Washington Post*, February 18, 1966.

133 ". . . punks who picket and demonstrate against the war." *Washington Post*, February 23, 1966.

134 ". . . you can call me by my slave name, Cassius. JIM." *Sporting News*, November 19, 1966.

135 "He's just an idiot." Accounts of the Ali-Terrell pre-fight scuffle found in *Time* January 6, 1967; *New York Times*, December 29, 1966; *Chicago Tribune*, December 29, 1966.

135 "I don't play with the religion or the name." Cosell's interview with Ali is viewable at: https://www.youtube.com/watch?v=HMiSX8M3U2s

135 ". . . the eye he broke the vein in was standing in one spot." *USA Today*, November 23, 2009.

135 ". . . vicious demonstration of savagery." *New York Daily News*, February 8, 1967.

135 ". . . Uncle Tom nigger." Details of Ali's verbal assault on Terrell found in *New York Daily News*, February 7, 1967.

135-136 ". . . more apparent becomes his retrogression as a man. It's a pity." *New York Times*, February 8, 1967.

136 ". . . making the ring into a speaking rostrum." *Time*, February 17, 1967.

136 ". . . get mad at him and build up this fight?" *New York Times*, March 22, 1967.

137 "You saw men become beasts." *New York Daily News*, August 6, 1965.

137 ". . . made him truly happy." *New York Times*, February 16, 1967.

138 ". . . is this the last time Ali is going to be out there?" Author interview with Dave Anderson.

138 "I've gone onto the front pages." Thomas Hauser, *Muhammad Ali: His Life and Times*, pg. 167. (New York: Simon & Schuster, 1992.)

138 "I would join." *New York Daily News*, March 23, 1967.

139 ". . . considerable emotional impact, particularly among the young." *New York Times*, April 30, 1967.

140 "I don't need more to enjoy myself." *Playboy*, December 1969.

140 "Too many pretty girls in this world." Namath and Coyne, pg. 159.

141 ". . . and he had a tear in the lateral meniscus." *Hartford Courant*, December 9, 1965.

142 ". . . caused by the war in Vietnam." *New York Times*, February 20, 1966.

142 ". . . thank God a whole lot for giving me a chance to play." *Sporting News*, January 27, 2012.

143 ". . . the dubious that this is a limited war with limited objectives." The Senate hearing with Gen. Taylor is described in-depth in the

Boston Globe, February 18, 1966; and *Washington Post*, February 18, 1966.

143 ". . . most important issue for the nation." Dr. George Gallup, *The Gallup Poll, Public Opinion 1935–1971, Vol. 3*, pg. 2,026. (New York: Random House, 1972.)

144 ". . . lined the sidewalk six deep at places." *New York Daily News*, October 17, 1965.

144 ". . . widespread frustration and anger toward the war." *New York Times*, July 26, 1966.

145 ". . . it would become known as, 'Beyond Vietnam.'" Background details on preparation for King's speech are available at Stanford University's King Institute, which can be accessed online at: http://mlk-kpp01.stanford.edu/

146 ". . . 'justice and equality.'" *Chicago Tribune*, April 6, 1967.

146 ". . . but to deeper confusion." *New York Times*, April 6, 1967.

146 "... explode in racial violence this summer." *New York Times*, April 17, 1967.

Chapter 11

147 ". . . protecting his men from doing any work." Morris, pg. 120.

148 ". . . let's get out there and clean up this city." Versions of this story appear in *New York Times*, December 5, 1966; *New York Times Magazine*, January 1, 1967.

149 ". . . the city was still filthy." Details of how filthy New York still was are in the *New York Times*, December 27, 1966.

149 ". . . audience was shuffling in impatience." *Harper's* magazine, August 1968.

150 "New York City Mayor John V. Lindsay." Gallup, pg. 2059.

150 "It may be beyond reach." *New York Times*, August 7, 1967.

150 ". . . part of the white backlash, too." Reports on the activity of right-wing militants found in *New York Daily News*, October 31, 1966; *New York Times*, November 1, 1966.

151 ". . . Fun Crimes, Fun Mayor." *New York Times*, June 18, 2009.

151 ". . . the race issue to agitate his constituents." *New York Times,* May 18, 1967.

152 "You ask it, I will do it." Phone call between John Lindsay and President Johnson, July 27, 1967. Recordings and Transcripts of Telephone Conversations, LBJ Presidential Library, Ref. # 12009.

154 ". . . Gen. William T. Sherman banging on its gates." *Sporting News,* September 16, 1967.

155 ". . . cordial terms with sportswriters." *New York Times,* November 10, 1967; also, events described in Allen *Sportin' Life,* pg. 112–113.

155 ". . . the DiMaggios, the Mantles and the Ruths." *New York Times,* August 6, 1967.

155 ". . . three more years and $105,000 to the ongoing $427,000 deal." Fox, pg. 159.

156 ". . . what we wanted to hear from him." Fox, pg. 158.

156 ". . . Boozer's knee the surgery of which he was proudest." Sun-Sentinel, November 17, 1986.

157 "NFL source said anonymously." *Sporting News,* November 4, 1967.

157 ". . . a hard steak, in the morning." *New York Times,* December 19, 1967; also, *America's Game: The Super Bowl Champs,* NFL Films documentary, 2007.

158 ". . . he had been out all night." *America's Game: The Super Bowl Champs,* NFL Films documentary, 2007.

158 "Sometimes he threw five interceptions." Mark Kriegel, *Namath: A Biography,* pg. 220–221. (New York: Penguin, 2004.)

159 ". . . Werblin stayed with Namath's father." *New York Daily News,* December 17, 1975.

159-160 ". . . come out of college since Oscar Robertson and Jerry West." *New York Post,* May 3, 1965.

160 "It's simpler that way." Red Holzman with Harvey Frommer, *Red on Red,* pg. 70. (New York: Bantam Books, 1987.)

160 "Wood's wood." *New York Post,* April 26, 1968.

161 "I won't be able to feed her." *New York Times,* November 15, 1998.

161 "I want to start school straight." Holzman and Frommer, pg. 60.

161 "... didn't have a whole lot of respect for him." Marino Amoruso, *Gil Hodges: The Quiet Man*, pg. 60. (Middlebury, VT: Paul S. Eriksson, 1991.)

162 "... condones this form of wife-stealing." *Washington Post*, October 11, 1967.

162 "... pants were pressed, clean shaven every day." Tom Clavin and Danny Peary, *Gil Hodges*, pg. 288. (New York: New American Library, 2012.)

162 "... we're going home." Clavin and Peary, pg. 304.

Chapter 12

163 "... the difference between day and night." *New York Times*, January 2, 1968.

164 "... needs of the cities as a matter of first priority." *New York Times*, January 1, 1968.

164 "... from China by way of Canada." *New York Daily News*, April 13, 1968.

165 "... American society as now constituted." Michael Lipsky and David Olson, "Riot Commission Politics," *Transaction*, July 1, 1969. (*Transaction* was a journal of the social sciences now published under the title *Society*.)

165 "... That's how segregated Milwaukee was." From Fred Harris interview with Bill Moyers: http://www.pbs.org/moyers/journal/03282008/transcript1.html

166 "... repudiating his own commission, one his opponent supported." Lindsey Lupo, *Flak-Catchers: One Hundred Years of Riot Commission Politics in America*, pg. 144–145. (Lanham, Md: Lexington Books, 2011.)

166 "... Lindsay had you down and had his foot on your neck." Roberts, pg. 56.

166 "... retaliation to unfriendly Lindsay statements." Lupo, pg. 144–145.

166 "... Johnson in a head-to-head matchup for the White House in 1968." *New York*, May 28, 1968.

167 ". . . leave no stone unturned." *Washington Post*, January 6, 1968.

167 ". . . "bungled," opportunities for peace. *New York Daily News*, February 19, 1968.

168 ". . . and has a claim to it." Author interview of Joseph Viteritti, whose book included reference to the claim of Kriegel and Goldmark to the line, prompting Rosenthal to confide that he, actually, came up with the finished product.

169 ". . . conducted away by policemen." *New York Times*, February 3, 1968.

170 ". . . you don't have credentials." *New York Daily News*, February 8, 1968.

170-171 ". . . eight million people can find within themselves." *Time* February 16, 1968; *New York Times*, February 9, 1968.

171 ". . . a five-alarm blaze, damaging four houses." Scene description from *New York Times*, February 5, 1968.

171 ". . . nothing but garbage and rats." From a newsreel about the garbage strike, at: https://www.youtube.com/user/historycomestolife

171 ". . . let me tell you mine." *New York Daily News*, February 5, 1968.

172 ". . . he has chosen not to do so." *New York Times*, February 11, 1968.

173 ". . . he would have sent in National Guard troops." Reactions to the Gov. Rockefeller settlement with the USA found in the *New York Times*, February 14, 1968; and *Time,* February 23, 1968.

173 ". . . oppose him to a man if he seeks reelection." *New York Daily News*, February 26, 1968.

173 ". . . grim struggle for control of the Republican Party." *New York Daily News*, February 17, 1968.

174 ". . . I am not going to budge." *New York Times*, February 14, 1968.

174 "14.3 million square feet in 1970." Robert Bennett, *Deconstructing Post-WWII New York City*, pg. 54. (New York: Routledge, 2003.)

174 ". . . all the commercial development in the U.S." Joseph Viteritti, ed. *Summer in the City: John Lindsay, New York and the American Dream*, pg. 166. (Baltimore: Johns Hopkins University Press, 2014.)

175 "In New York, it's become cancer." Time, November 1, 1968.

175 ". . . the towers, with an airplane poised to fly into them." New York Times, May 2, 1968.

175 ". . . listen to the PA announcer." New York Times, February 15, 1968.

175 "Does he supply periscopes?" New York Daily News, February 23, 1968.

176 ". . . damn right they do." New York Times, February 24, 1968.

176 ". . . either burned down or blown up.: New York Daily News, February 16, 1968.

176 ". . . the country the Negro loves doesn't back." Lipsyte, pg. 128.

176 ". . . screaming for murder in the February night." Ibid.

177 ". . . better position hockey." New York Times, February 19, 1968.

177 ". . . fighting with us." New York Times, April 2, 1968. (Chamberlain was traded from Philadelphia to the L.A. Lakers in the offseason, so the Knicks would not fight with him, at least not until the 1970 NBA Finals.)

177 ". . . before the movie came out." Sporting News, February 23, 1968.

Chapter 13

178 ". . . 39 percent in January." Washington Post, March 21, 1968.

179 ". . . tipping point of rioting and looting." New York, April 11, 1988.

180 ". . . happening in other cities to happen in our city." New York Daily News, December 24, 2000.

180 ". . . see him moving through the crowd that spilled on the streets." Gottehrer, pg. 210.

181 ". . . someone to take a shot at him." Gottehrer, pg. 211.

181 ". . . before the riot, not after the riot." Breslin, New York Post, April 8, 1968.

181 ". . . Get him out of here!" New York Post, April 5, 1968.

181 ". . . memorials convened at the United Nations." New York Post, April 5, 1968; New York Daily News, April 6, 1968.

182 "... shoot the next Martin Luther King?" Jimmy Breslin column, *New York Post*, April 8, 1968.

182 "There is no other place for you to be." Breslin, *New York Post*, April 8, 1968; Daley details from *Chicago Reader*, April 4, 2002.

183 "... arsonists to kill and looters to maim and detain." *Chicago Reader*, April 4, 2002.

184 "'Lindsay for President' office had opened in Duluth." *New York Times*, June 15, 1968.

184 "... people are now aroused about the urban problems." *New York*, May 27, 1968.

185 "... any landlord we have in the city." *New York Post*, April 26, 1968.

185 "... evicted more than 7,000 Harlem residents from those properties." Jerry Avorn, *Up Against the Ivy Wall: A History of the Columbia Crisis*, pg. 13. (New York: Scribner, 1968.)

186 "... can really be a hippie." *New York Times*, December 6, 1964.

187 "... propaganda of a most vicious nature." *New York Times*, April 21, 1965.

187 "... they are inadequately informed about Vietnam." *New York Times*, April 28, 1965.

188 "... they're going to deal with the brothers on the street." *New York Post*, April 26, 1968.

188 "... we threw them out." *New York Times*, April 25, 1968.

188 "... university's good name intact." *New York Post*, April 26, 1968.

188 "... pity on this university." *New York Daily News*, April 25, 1968.

188 "... brutal bloody show of strength." *Columbia Daily Spectator*, April 30, 1968.

189 "... to justify violence in Vietnam." *New York Times*, May 5, 1968.

189 "... they're rejecting affluence." *Time*, April 28, 1967.

189 "At worst, it is no mind." Ibid.

189-190 "... instant gratification of needs." Details and a history of Dr. Spock's trial can be found: http://www.newenglandhistorical-society.com/trial-dr-benjamin-spock

190 "BEAUTIFY AMERICA, Get a haircut." *Los Angeles Times*, May 28, 1968.

190 "Get a haircut, you bum!" Schaap and Namath, pg. 106.

190 "Next month, Des Moines." *New York Times*, January 10, 1967.

190 ". . . a haircut using. 'cattle clippers.'" *Los Angeles Times*, May 31, 1967.

190 ". . . because his hair was too long." *Chicago Tribune*, February 7, 1968.

190-191 "We aren't anxious to see boys' hair becoming as long as girls." *Hartford Courant*, January 30, 1968.

191 ". . . drop in revenues the previous year." *Los Angeles Times*, April 14, 1968.

191 ". . . slap at the black athlete." *Hartford Courant*, January 9, 1969.

191 "We try to discourage it, but as subtly as possible." Ibid.

191 ". . . baseball player of all individuality." *Chicago Tribune*, November 8, 1968.

191 "That's ridiculous." *Hartford Courant*, November 26, 1968.

191 ". . . what the hell kind of history we've had." *Playboy*, December 1969.

192 "I'm just trying to be myself." Ibid.

192 ". . . anti-hero of the sports world." *New York Times*, December 26, 2003.

192 ". . . as symbols of a decade's decadence." Larry Merchant, . . . And Every Day You Take Another Bite, pg. 122–23. (Garden City, NY: Doubleday, 1971.)

192 ". . . like a yokel, or like guy who's in?" Hollywood Joe's warranted two feature stories, in *Time*, April 12, 1968; and in the *New York Daily News*, June 9, 1968.

Chapter 14

194 "I mean, that's a nice round number. Why not?" *New York Post*, April 10, 1968.

194 ". . . a lot of tickets with the interest." *New York Daily News*, May 22, 1968.

195 "... keep his name out of the papers." *New York Post*, June 18, 1968.

195 "He hated the idea he had partners." Milton Gross, *New York Post*, June 18, 1968.

195 "... decided they wanted to sell, too." *New York Daily News*, May 22, 1968.

196 "... running things by committee." *Sporting News*, June 8, 1968; *New York Times*, May 25, 1968.

196 "...undercut the authority of the coach." *New York Times*, May 24, 1968.

196 "...we can't do away with gals." *New York Times*, June 2, 1968.

196 "... if he thought it would help publicize his team." Fox, pg. 187.

197 "... Coach Ewbank has asked for." *Los Angeles Times*, September 15, 1968.

197 "But I can't change the way I am." Ibid.

198 "... can a thing like this happen in this country?" Quotes from Charles, Jones, Agee and Jackson from Dick Young's column, *New York Daily News*, April 7, 1968.

198 "... trying to kill each other off." *New York Post*, June 5, 1968.

198 "... really become this horrible?" *New York Post*, June 6, 1968.

198 "Who's next, John John?" *New York Daily News*, June 8, 1968.

199 "World War III if he attacked." World War III quotes from *New York Post*, May 11, 1967; *New York Times*, February 28, 1968.

199 "... panic buttons in the office phones of every U.S. Senator." *New York Daily News*, May 21, 1968.

199 "What kind of people are we?" *New York Post*, June 5, 1968.

200 "... deposited in the grave before yelling, 'Play ball!'" *New York Daily News*, June 9, 1968.

200 "This goes deeper than politics." Details and quotes from the Mets-Giants squabble taken from *New York Post*, June 5, 1968; *New York Post*, June 10, 1968; *Sporting News*, June 22, 1968.

201 "... they just can't be this stupid." *New York Post*, June 10, 1968.

201 "... I felt I would be hypocritical." *Sporting News*, June 22, 1968.

201 "Baseball's conscience apparently lies in its cash register." *New York Post*, June 10, 1968.

202 ". . . a spoiled brat on our hands, if we don't already." *New York Daily News*, February 22, 1968.

202 ". . . the decompression, back in a legislative job." *New York*, May 27, 1968.

203 ". . . he wants me in the city to cool it for him." Hentoff, pg. 211.

203 ". . . I intend to fulfill that contract." *New York Times*, June 11, 1968.

203 "That's the end of the conversation on this subject." Hentoff, pg. 210.

203 ". . . not be the one doing the asking, 'now or ever.'" *New York Times*, July 1, 1968.

204 ". . . why take on the third?" *New York*, May 27, 1968.

204 "He bridges the generational gap." *Washington Post*, August 1, 1968.

205 "Lindsay-for-Something headquarters." *New York Times*, August 4, 1968.

205 ". . . thereby keep me off the ticket." Hentoff, pg. 217.

205 ". . . Thurmond, took care of Percy and Lindsay." Reactions of Southern Republicans to liberal Vice Presidential candidates taken from the *Washington Post*, August 12, 1968.

205 ". . . wolf in sheep's clothing." *Time*, September 20, 1968.

206 ". . . the white knight of industrial-state Republicans." *Washington Post*, August 12, 1968.

206 "It is doubtful if Lindsay will ever have a better chance nationally . . ." Hentoff, pg. 219.

206 "... glorify the Spiro Agnews of the country." *New York*, July 28, 1969.

Chapter 15

208 "I'm just as ashamed of it as you are." Maynard from, *America's Game: The Super Bowl Champs*, NFL Films documentary, 2007.

209 ". . . throwing a football around once they got there." *New York Times*, July 21, 1968.

209 ". . . need two or three extra straws." Ibid.

209 "Everything else is incidental." Fox, pg. 189.

210 ". . . morale problem is obvious." *Look,* September 3, 1968.

210 ". . . team thinks of Broadway Joe." *Los Angeles Times,* September 15, 1968.

210 ". . . and I wasn't happy." Ewbank-Namath squabble details in Fox, pg. 195; Namath and Coyne, pg. 175; Namath and Schaap, pg. 187.

211 "That was one of the times I really hated Weeb." Namath and Schaap, pg. 187.

211 ". . . paved their way to popularity." *Atlanta Journal,* October 27, 1968.

211 ". . . Namath and Ewbank out of harmony." *New York Times,* August 15, 1968.

211 "This is the greatest honor of my life." *Los Angeles Times,* September 15, 1968.

212 ". . . he could easily win re-election as Mayor." *New York Times,* August 13, 1968.

212 ". . . futility which has usually beset American radicalism." *New York Times Magazine,* October 20, 1968.

213 ". . . confrontation with a sick society." *New York Times Magazine,* February 2, 1969.

214 ". . . white system that was failing to educate them." Ibid.

215 ". . . predicted there would be 300–400 teacher strikes nationally." Teacher pay and strike numbers taken from study in *Look,* September 3, 1968.

215 ". . . guard those teachers in our neighborhood from now on." *New York Times,* September 28, 1967.

216 ". . . person I have seen in my time in the city of New York." *New York Post,* October 30, 1968.

216 "You pale-faced Jew boy—I wish you were dead." Morris, pg. 218.

217 ". . . crowd surged forth." *New York Times,* October 16, 1968.

217 ". . . whether we can continue to survive as a city." *Time,* November 1, 1968.

218 ". . . heat coming from that chair." Namath on Michaels, from *America's Game: The Super Bowl Champs*, NFL Films documentary, 2007.

218 ". . . he thinks he can complete anything." *New York Times*, October 17, 1968.

218 "I fucking stink." Fox, pg. 205.

218 ". . . if Joe Namath fell off a bar stool and hurt his knee." *Sporting News*, August 31, 1968.

219 ". . . give them a shot to win some games for us?" Namath and Coyne, pg. 178.

219 . . . no-razor-till-title commitment. Details on the no-shaving group found in Fox, pg. 207.

219 "We were gonna get through this together." Namath and Coyne, pg. 177.

219 "WE SAVED SECOND PLACE FOR YOU." Fox, pg. 214.

220 ". . . entertainment value of your product." *Sporting News*, November 23, 1968.

220 "Man, let's talk about winning." *Hartford Courant*, November 12, 1968.

220 ". . . that a quarterback shouldn't say." *New York Times*, January 3, 1971.

221 ". . . the kind of stuff you pull in high school." Fox, pg. 216.

221 ". . . between players and officials." *Sporting News*, December 7, 1968.

222 "Don't be, we lost." Namath and Coyne, pg. 178.

Chapter 16

223 ". . . in favor of the plan, 'in principle.'" *New York Times*, October 24, 1965.

224 ". . . New York, not the Bahamas." *New York Times*, December 27, 1968.

224 ". . . hard as concrete in others." Maynard and Shepatin, pg. 227.

224 ". . . I just didn't like it." *Washington Post*, December 29, 1968.

225 ". . . the worst in the league." *Hartford Courant,* December 26, 1968.

225 "It was bent three ways." *New York Post,* December 30, 1968.

225 "Hey, Joe, you broke your finger!" Namath and Coyne, pg. 184.

225 ". . . put him in a fog for 30 minutes." *Boston Globe,* December 30, 1968.

226 ". . . willing me back out there." Namath's excursion into the trainer's room described in Namath and Coyne, pg. 184; and Fox, pg. 229.

226 "'60 G'—that is, a deep bomb to the goal line." Maynard and Shepatin, pg. 235.

227 ". . . defined that Jets team, that Jets era." Author interview with Dave Anderson.

227 "We're going to beat those guys, huh?" *Washington Post,* December 30, 1968.

227 "That should be enough." *New York Times,* December 30, 1968.

227 ". . . get the hell out of here!" *Baltimore Sun,* December 30, 1968.

228 ". . . there is little hope for progress." *New York Times,* November 16, 1968.

229 ". . . the opponent was Walt Bellamy of the Knicks." Red Holzman and Leonard Lewin, *My Unforgettable Season,* pg. 75. (New York: Tom Doherty Associates, 1993.)

230 ". . . coming back to your old home town." *New York Times,* January 12, 1969.

230 ". . . got stony silence." *New York Times,* December 21, 1968.

230 ". . . we really came together and took off from there." Author interview of Walt Frazier.

231 ". . . he might be the only athlete who never lied to me." Anderson interview.

231 ". . . bullshit papers print about you." *Playboy,* December 1969.

231–232 ". . . willing to pay $135,000 per minute." *New York Times,* February 9, 1969.

232 "Who cares if they didn't like me?" Marty Ralbovsky, *Super Bowl: Of Men, Myths and Moments,* pg. 3. (New York: Hawthorn Books, 1971.)

232 "... us on the same field as the Green Bay Packers." *New York Times*, January 2, 1968.

232-233 "... as the presidential candidate." *Washington Post*, December 31, 1968.

233 "I might sound like I am boasting and bragging, and I am." *New York Times*, January 3, 1969.

233 "... knock him out of the football game." *New York Times*, January 5, 1968.

233 "... sleep in the morning, that's the thing to do." *Washington Post*, January 7, 1969.

233 "... kick the shit out of our team." *Hartford Courant*, January 8, 1969.

233 "... defused by fellow Colts and Jets at the bar." *New York Times*, January 8, 1983.

233 "... bought the drinks for Michaels' table." *Hartford Courant*, January 12, 1969.

234 "... better quarterback than Morrall." *New York Times*, January 5, 1969.

234 "... real good doesn't have to talk." Smith and Ray quotes from Namath and Schaap 59–60; *New York Times*, January 10, 1969.

234 "I don't see any reason why we shouldn't be." Allen, *Sportin' Life*, pg. 157.

235 "I'll guarantee you." Details from the famed Namath "guarantee" from Dave Anderson, *Countdown to Super Bowl*, pg. 163. (New York: Random House, 1969.)

Chapter 17

236 "Well, he's said it to me a lot of times." Zimmerman, pg. 149.

237 "... in and around New York." Details of media picks from Allen, *Sportin' Life*, pg. 156.

237 ... more conservative, picking Baltimore, 38–0. *Atlanta Constitution*, January 12, 1969.

238 "If they did, I figured, they were dead." Namath and Schaap, pg. 55.

238 ". . . loosens you up good for the game." *New York*, April 7, 1969.

238 ". . . but my stomach wasn't." Allen, *Sportin' Life*, pg. 160,

239 ". . . cursing themselves in their huddle." Anderson, pg. 222.

241 ". . . eat their pencils and pads." *Sporting News*, January 25, 1969.

241 ". . . Colts 11- or 12-point favorites." *Washington Post*, January 15, 1969.

241 ". . . Colts into doubting they could win." *New York Times*, January 14, 1969.

241 "What a blow to clean living." *Washington Post*, January 13, 1969.

241 Ewbank just looked, saying nothing. Zimmerman, pg. 149; and Anderson, pg. 244.

241 ". . . lovely few days we had all but forgotten." *New York*, April 7, 1969.

242 . . . later in the afternoon, on a commercial flight. *Washington Post*, January 14, 1969.

242 "I don't want to run against anyone right now." *Los Angeles Times*, January 14, 1969.

243 ". . . as though the Mayor was a Baltimore Colt." *New York Times*, January 23, 1969.

243 "We're the new faces for the new generation." *Washington Post*, January 23, 1969.

244 "I get the name for it whether I do it or not." *New York*, April 7, 1969.

244 "Even more than there were for Hornung." Description of Namath's *Sport* awards ceremony from *New York Times* and *Washington Post*, January 23, 1969.

244-245 ". . . the back of an HRA check." *Chicago Tribune*, January 19, 1969.

246 Half of those deaths were in Queens. Snow and travel details found in *New York Daily News*, *New York Post* and *New York Times*, February 10–12, 1969.

246 ". . . penny-wise and pound-foolish." *New York Post* February 11, 1969.

246 ". . . speculation about my ancestry." Lindsay obituary, *New York Times*, December 21, 2000.

246 "Get away, you bum!" *New York Daily News*, February 13, 1969.

246 ". . . till hell freezes over . . . and it did." *New York Post,* February 13, 1969.

247 "He was keeping it all inside." *Sporting News,* October 12, 1968.

247 "I feel fine." *New York Post* April 11, 1969.

248 "You've got nine checks already." Vecsey, pg. 171.

248 ". . . played eleven games for Tidewater." Art Shamsky with Barry Zeman, *The Magnificent Seasons,* pg. 108. (New York: Thomas Dunne Books, 2004.)

248 ". . . you are a contending ball club." Clavin and Peary, pg. 320.

249 "Shake us up, too." *New York Post,* February 26, 1969.

250 ". . . a leader and without glamour." *Sporting News,* March 15, 1969.

Chapter 18

251 . . . her husband subjected to that kind of torment. Aurelio interview.

252 . . . 74 percent. That was his disapproval rating. Aurelio interview; and *Life,* November 14, 1969.

252 "He couldn't abandon these important issues." Aurelio interview.

252 ". . . he wept, inexplicably." Procaccino press conference details from *New York Post,* February 19, 1969.

253 ". . . not a typical Lindsay supporter." Jewish and minority portion of GOP vote, *New York Post,* February 28, 1969. Quote from *New York Times,* March 2, 1969.

253 ". . . outside of New York." *Time,* March 28, 1969.

253 "Rents had skyrocketed." *Time,* March 28, 1969; and *Time,* 10–3, 1969.

253 ". . . the worst of my public life." John Lindsay, *The City,* pg. 22. (New York: W.W. Norton, 1970.)

254 "He's sure aged a lot in four years!" *New York Times,* March 19, 1969.

254 " . . . issue which is not situated under the table." *New York Times,* April 17, 1969.

256 "Maybe Marchi might be worse." Wagner's thoughts on mayoral prospects from the *New York Times*, June 18, 1969.

256 ". . . the flush of Jet victory still on his ruddy cheeks." *New York Times*, April 9, 1969.

256 "My God, wasn't that ridiculous?" Tom Seaver and Dick Schaap, *The Perfect Game: Tom Seaver and the Mets*, pg. 61. (New York: E.P. Dutton and Co., 1970.)

257 ". . . the White Sox thought I was having an excess of night life." *New York Post*, October 15, 1969.

257 "A lot of times, I didn't want to go to the park." Vecsey, pg. 191.

257 "We've got to do something." *New York Times*, April 19, 1969.

258 ". . . appreciate it while you're there." Seaver and Schaap, pg. 62.

258 ". . . too good to be irritated at anything." *New York Times*, June 10, 1969.

259 ". . . I never wore that one." *New York Times*, April 30, 1969.

259 "But it's a matter of principle. I'm quitting." Allen, *Sportin' Life*, pg. 12.

260 ". . . Vietnam than it is New York at 3 o'clock in the morning." *New York Times*, August 10, 1969.

260 ". . . whether you are a good guy or a bad guy." *New York Post*, February 18, 1969.

260 "'Wallaceism with a Yankee accent.'" *Time*, June 27, 1969.

260 ". . . you're out of your mind—your cotton-picking mind." *New York Times*, June 19, 1969.

261 ". . . Boston Strangler if he were running against Lindsay." *New York Times Magazine*, November 2, 1969.

262 ". . . He didn't like the idea of going in front of millions of New Yorkers and eating crow." Aurelio interview.

Chapter 19

265 ". . . I don't know how to express it." Allen, *Mets*, pg. 119.

265 ". . . I would have felt it was pretty hopeless." Vecsey, pg. 187.

265 ". . . played like a man with money in the bank." Ibid.

266 "I had decided to become a dentist." *Time*, September 5, 1969.

267 "I was too old to cry." Seaver and Schaap, pg. 136–37.

267 "That's all." Durocher's terse press conference found in *Chicago Tribune*, July 17, 1969.

267 ". . . in front of a grainy television." Vecsey, pg. 198.

269 "Send Lindsay to a dance." *New York,* July 28, 1969.

269 ". . . one of the Beautiful People." *Time*, October 3, 1969.

269 ". . . drinking beer and Lawrence Welk on television." *New York Times, Magazine*, November 2, 1969.

269 ". . . can appear to be on both sides." *New York Times,* September 8, 1969.

270 ". . . just wait and let him damage himself." Aurelio interview.

270 ". . . gained through the summer to increase his lead." *New York Post,* October 1, 1969.

270 ". . . insults cannot go unanswered." *New York Times,* September 11, 1969.

270 ". . . shame of alleged cowardice." Ibid.

270 ". . . proof of racism on his staff." *New York Post,* October 1, 1969.

270 "He grows on you, like a cancer." *New York Times,* August 10, 1969.

271 ". . . the number one Democrat in this town and I expect your support." McNickle, pg. 230.

271 " . . . he has matured in human understanding." *New York Times,* October 23, 1969.

271 ". . . the great, great danger." *Wall Street Journal*, October 14, 1969.

271 ". . . $42,000, half its 1969 budget." *New York Times,* December 31, 1969.

272 "It was only natural that they were political." Aurelio interview.

272 "Particularly you, Mr. Mayor." *New York Post,* October 1, 1969.

272 ". . . Madam Prime Minister, we stand with Israel." Ibid.

272 ". . . Mayor Lindsay's eloquence to tell what is in my heart tonight." *Time*, October 10, 1969.

272 "What she did instead, she practically endorsed him." Aurelio interview.

273 "We love you more. Sorry, Mets." *New York Times*, August 14, 1969.

274 " . . . hide in the mountains from the shame of it." Glenn Stout and Richard Johnson, *The Cubs*, pg. 279. (Boston: Houghton Mifflin, 2007.)

274 "He has no forum like Shea Stadium." *New York Times*, September 12, 1969.

274 "It makes everything seem possible." *Time*, September 5, 1969.

274 " . . . believer in the efficacy of the skullbuster or knockdown ball." *Life*, September 26, 1969.

275 " . . . not the only guys in the league who can throw hard at somebody." *New York Times*, September 12, 1969.

275 " . . . the Mayor of, 'The Second City.'" Allen, *Mets*, pg. 127.

276 " . . . an urban Bethel." Vecsey, pg. 215.

276 " . . . underestimated them by so much." *New York Times*, September 26, 1969.

276 " . . . since the day I entered Congress." *Sporting News*, October 11, 1969.

Chapter 20

277 " . . . to any office in the year 1969?" *New York*, October 6, 1969.

278 " . . . you have to make yourself part of it." Aurelio interview.

278 " . . . Christ, do I have to go out to the ballpark again?'" *New York Times Magazine*, November 2, 1969.

278 " . . . if you can't find your seat?" Wagner and Procaccino quotes found in the *New York Times*, October 7, 1969.

278-279 " . . . we decided to do on the spur of the moment." *New York Times*, October 7, 1969.

279 " . . . looked for the television cameras." Vecsey, pg. 227.

279 " . . . by the fans as an endorsement from the whole team." Lipsyte, pg. 46.

279 " . . . but we did not plan it that way." Aurelio interview.

279 " . . . Deputy Mayor Hodges or Judge Seaver." *New York Times*, October 26, 1969.

280 "Bring on Rod Stupid!" Vecsey, pg. 230.

282 ". . . the Mayor did have good intentions." Shamsky and Zeman, pg. 148.

282 ". . . Fun City never seemed so together." Vecsey, pg. 235.

284 ". . . a comparable afternoon in World Series play." *Sporting News,* November 1, 1969.

284 "Why don't you come out of retirement and try it?" DeBusschere, pg. 53–54.

285 "Ain't you guys gonna play?" Holzman and Frommer, pg. 91.

285 "It's like a nightmare." Holzman and Frommer, pg. 92.

285 "It is a strike against America." *New York Post*, October 15, 1969.

286 "They would have had to fight us first." *New York Times,* October 16, 1969.

286-287 ". . . the willingness to exercise that right." Lindsay Moratorium Day details come from the *New York Post*, October 15, 1969; and *Washington Post*, October 16, 1969.

287 "I feel very strongly about it." *New York Times,* October 11, 1969.

287 "But I did feel this particular war was wrong." Seaver and Schaap, pg. 55.

288 "Power to the New York Mets!" *New York Times,* October 17, 1969.

288 "They shouldn't be blown out of proportion." Vecsey, pg. 241; and *Associated Press*, October 16, 1969.

289 "I was playing ball when I was nine." *New York Post*, October 16, 1969.

289 "The right-fielder frightens me all the time." *New York Times,* October 21, 1969.

289 "We've gone higher and higher until you can't go any higher." *New York Post,* October 17, 1969.

289 ". . . to a side room until he could collect himself." Clavin and Peary, pg. 346.

289 "Oh my." *New York Times,* October 17, 1969.

290 "You are the one." *Washington Post*, October 17, 1969.

290 "Gil Hodges for Warden!" *New York Post*, October 17, 1969.

290 "Gil Hodges for Mayor!" *New York Times,* October 17, 1969.

290 "... everybody loves a loser even when winning the World Series." *New York Times,* October 19, 1969.

290 "... saints of lost causes." *New York Post,* October 17, 1969.

Chapter 21

291 "I guess we were window dressing." Holzman and Lewin, pg. 106.

292 "... I hope you'll be having a party like this for the Knicks next May." Dave DeBussschere, *The Open Man,* pg. 59. (New York: Random House, 1970.) Details of the Knicks' makeshift Queens practice facility also from DeBusschere.

292 "... his most impressive achievement."*New York Post,* October 20, 1969.

293 "That is why they are looking toward Lindsay." *Washington Post,* November 7, 1969.

293 "... bet on the New York Mayor's race." *Washington Post,* November 3, 1969.

295 "... this is certainly the end, there is no tomorrow." Jets postgame locker room scene in *Sporting News,* January 3, 1970; and *New York Times,* December 21, 1969.

297 "I don't know, maybe we'd be worse." Weeb Ewbank on Namath from Zimmerman, pg. 36.

297 "I don't think that was make-believe." Author interview of Joseph Viteritti.

298 "Now they come to watch us." *Time,* December 5, 1969.

299 "A disaster is when you get home and you're out of Scotch." *Sports Illustrated,* December 8, 1969.

300 "... playing that gambling defense, we might have been killed." *New York Times,* May 5, 1970.

300 "... carbocaine in his knee and cortisone in his thigh." Reed quotes and details from *New York,* April 19, 1993; and the *Los Angeles Times,* May 9, 1970.

300 "... the Knicks are in a bad way." *Los Angeles Times,* May 7, 1970.

301 "Good for your team, too." DeBussschere, pg. 259–60.

301 "I think we might have them here." Frazier interview.

301 "... a perfect team and it doesn't matter who is playing." *Los Angeles Times*, May 9, 1970.

302 "... Uncle Cleveland, not Uncle Sam." *New York Times*, May 17, 1970.

302 "... was well-intentioned anyway." Holzman and Lewin, pg. 294.

303 "... the only thing that makes any sense." *New York*, April 7, 1969.

Index

A

Abruzzese, Ray, 44, 154
AFC East championship, 112
AFL. *See* American Football League
Agee, Tommy, 197
Agnew, Spiro, 232, 241
Alabama games, ix, 1–4, 8, 10–13, 49, 238
Alford, Lynwood, 98
Ali, Muhammad, 132–134, 136
Allen, Dick, 98, 99
Allen, Maury, 32, 76, 110, 258
Allen, Mel, 38
Allyn, Arthur, 34
American Football Conference, 106
American Football League (AFL), 4, 6, 7, 9,
    10, 32, 51, 106, 193, 195, 209, 224, 226, 228,
    233–235, 280
American League, 33, 37, 67, 101, 162
Anderson, Craig, 125
Anderson, Dave, 138, 227
Anderson, David, 188
Angell, Roger, 35
Anti-semitism, 216
Antwine, Houston, 157
Apple, R.W., 23
Arizona Republic, 104
Armstrong, Henry, 136
Atkinson, Al, 208, 226
Atlanta Braves, 35, 103, 106, 266, 277, 278,
    279, 298
Atlanta Constitution, 237
Atlanta Journal, 41, 211
Auburn, 1, 153
Aurelio, Richard, 22–23, 251

B

Baby and Child Care (Spock), 189
Bailey, Pearl, 290
Balboa Stadium, 9
Baltimore Colts, 241, 243, 280
Baltimore Sun, 227
Barber, Red, 79, 262

Barnett, Dick, 177, 285
Beame, Abe, 53
Belafonte, Harry, 146
Bell, Daniel, 189
Berger, Phil, 302
Berkeley Free Speech movement 1964, 186
Berra, Yogi, 36, 67, 76
Beverly, Randy, 208
Biggs, Verlon, 219
Bisher, Furman, 42
Black athletes, 102, 104, 105, 176, 191, 212
Black, Joe, 106
Black Muslims, 121, 122, 126,
    132–135
Black Panther party, 150
Blanchard, Johnny, 77
Blanda, George, 226
Bliss, Ray, 55
Blocker, Charles, 198
Boozer, Emerson, 208
Boston Globe, 12, 225
Bouton, Jim, 78, 102
Bowman, Steve, 2
Boyle, Robert, 101–102
Bradley, Tom, 260
Breslin, Jimmy, 206, 216, 241, 268, 277
Briscoe, Marlin, 105
Broderick, Vincent, 115
Brownell, Herbert, 81, 118, 206
Browns, 28, 30, 34, 227
Bruno, Larry, 13
Bryant, Bear, 2, 3, 7, 99
Buckley, Charles, 62, 64, 65
Buckley, William F., 59–61
Buffalo, 32, 110, 111, 112, 156, 217, 218, 219,
    220, 224
Busch, Gussie, 37
Butkus, Dick, 45

C

CALCAV. *See* Clergy and Laymen Concerned
    About Vietnam

Cannon, Jimmy, 109–111, 134
Cardinals, 7–10, 14, 37, 105, 161, 201, 264, 273, 276
Carlos, John, 212
Carlsmith, Merrill, 125
Carmichael, John, 33
Carmichael, Stokely, 123
Cassese, John, 116
Charles, Ed, 197, 201, 283, 292
Charlotte Observer, 153
Charlotte Sportsman's Club, 153
Chicago White Sox, 34
Christian Science Monitor, 168
"City in Crisis" theme, 21, 80
Civil War, 182
Clendenon, Donn, 290
Clergy and Laymen Concerned About Vietnam (CALCAV), 145
Cleveland, 28, 29, 45, 106, 125, 128, 144, 165, 302
Clinton, DeWitt, 20
Coil, Ed, 229
Colts, 227, 233, 234, 236, 237–241
Columbia Broadcasting System (CBS), 34–36, 64, 67
Committee for a Reasonable World Trade Center, 175
Condon-Wadlin Act, 83, 170
Congress of Racial Equality (CORE), 114, 187, 188
CORE. *See* Congress of Racial Equality
Costello, Timothy, 58, 64
Costello, Vince, 28, 29
Craig, Roger, 68
Cronin, Joe, 33
Cronkite, Walter, 169
Crow, Jim, 117
Cubs, 68, 199, 200, 264, 265, 266, 267, 273–275

D

Daily News, 68, 139, 150, 169, 173, 193, 210, 245, 292, 303
Daley, Arthur, 36, 70, 135, 196
Daley, Richard, 182–183
Dame, Notre, 44
Davidoff, Sid, 81
Davidson, Ben, 220, 225
Davis, Al, 225
Davis, Alvin, 24
Davis, Sammy, Jr., 24, 52
Dean, Eric, 127
DeBusschere, Dave, 284, 291, 292, 297
Decentralization process, 214
DeChamps, Leonard, 181

DeLuca, Sam, 98, 155, 156
DeLury, John, 147, 169, 170, 173
Democratic Convention, 212, 288
Dempsey, Jack, 11
Derrick, Mel, 153
Devaney, Bob, 191
Diller, Phyllis, 52
DiMaggio, Joe, 11, 12, 14, 16, 136
Dodgers, 34, 67, 68, 69, 73, 96, 101, 161, 278
Donaldson, Jack, 107
Donovan, Ed, 229
Dreyfuss Corporation, 148
Durocher, Leo, 267, 273
Durso, Joseph, 244

E

Eckert, Bill, 266
Eckert, William, 197, 199
Edwards, Harry, 176
Eisenhower, Dwight D., 56
Ellis, Jimmy, 137
Evans, Rowland, 205, 270, 293
Ewbank, Weeb, 4, 44, 49, 50, 98, 101, 109–111, 153, 155, 196, 207, 208, 211, 220, 221, 224–226, 236–238, 242, 256, 294, 297

F

Farmer, James, 116
Felt, Irving, 175, 228
Finley, Charles O., 34
Finney, Ben, 223
Fino, Paul, 151
Fitzgerald, Scott, 16
Folley, Zora, 136
Fonda, Henry, 52
Foss, Joe, 103
Frazier, Joe, 138
Frazier, Walt, 177

G

Galamison, Milton, 114
Garagiola, Joe, 67
Gaspar, Rod, 278
Gibson, Bob, 37
Gilbert, Rod, 177
Gleason, Jackie, 1, 14
Golden Gloves, 132, 137
Goldwater, Barry, 18, 55
Goldwyn, Samuel, 141
Goodman, Roy, 52
Goostree, Jim, 2
GOP Convention, 184, 203
Gordon, Cornell, 156
Gotbaum, Victor, 170
Gottehrer, Barry, 21, 81, 179

Gottlieb, Edward, 251
Graham, Billy, 1, 95
Graham, Otto, 211
Grange, Red, 12
Grantham, Larry, 44, 45, 98
Grant, M. Donald, 223
"Great Society" program, 119, 130
Grier, Rosey, 198
Griffin, Jack, 274
Griffith, Calvin, 78, 103–104
Gross, Milton, 201
Grote, Jerry, 161

H
Haley, Alex, 123
Hamill, Pete, 124
Hands, Bill, 274
Harlem Globetrotters, 103
Harvard Law, 81
The Hate that Hate Produced, 121
Hawley, William, 113
Heidi game, 224, 226
Heisman Trophy, 44
Hendricks, Elrod, 288
Hentoff, Nat, 93
Herald-Tribune, 16–18, 21, 22, 125
Herman, Dave, 32
Hickman, Jim, 275
Hill, Winston, 97, 100
Hirsch, Joe, 43
Hirshberg, Al, 103
Hodges, Gil, 289
Hoffman, Abbie, 288
Hoffman, John T., 20
Hofheinz, Roy, 36
Holtzman, Ken, 275
Holzman, Red, 159–161, 291, 299, 300, 302
Hood, James, 99
Hosket, Bill, 301
Houk, Ralph, 36–39, 78–79
Houston Chronicle, 154
Houston Colt .45s, 35, 36, 67
Hoving, Thomas, 81, 94
Howard, Elston, 77
Howell, Jim Lee, 30
Huarte, John, 44
Hudock, Mike, 47
Hudson, Jim, 208, 238
Huff, Sam, 30–31
Hughes, Richard J., 151
Humphrey, Hubert H., 217
Hunt, Lamar, 6

I
Interstate Highway System, 119

Irish Civil War, 82
Irish Republican Army, 82
Iselin, Phil, 194, 207

J
Jackson, Al, 76, 197
Jackson, Reggie, 104
Jacobs, Paul, 189
Jacoby, Tamar, 117
Javits, Jacob, 19, 22, 92, 179, 251, 286
Jenkins, Fergie, 265
Johnson, Davey, 289
Johnson, Lyndon, 91, 178
John, V., 32
Jones, Cleon, 197, 290
Jones, J. Raymond, 270
Jurgensen, Sonny, 45

K
Kaese, Harold, 36
Keane, Johnny, 67, 78–79
Kempton, Murray, 26, 27, 53, 54
Kennedy, Bobby, 92, 198
Kennedy, Jack, 24
Kennedy, John F., 18, 19, 55, 178, 190
Kennedy, Robert F., 22, 150, 178, 264
Kennedy, Ted, 241
Kerner Commission, 164–168, 183
Kerner, Otto, 152
Kheel, Theodore, 163
King Football, 33
Kinney, Charles, 164
Kirk, Grayson, 184
Klein, Woody, 61, 81, 85, 86, 89
Knicks, 159–161, 228–230, 284–285, 291–292, 298–303
Knox, Chuck, 8
Koman, Bill, 105
Koosman, Jerry, 258, 279, 289, 293
Koppett, Leonard, 39, 76
Kraft, Joseph, 63, 204
Kramer, Jerry, 241
Kranepool, Ed, 200
Kriegel, Jay, 81, 115
Kriegel, Mark, 158
Kubek, Tony, 78
Kuhn, Bowie, 286

L
Ladd, Ernie, 109
LaMotta, Jake, 136
Landry, Tom, 30
Lardner, John, 70
Lassiter, Ike, 220, 225
Latino communities, 115

Lefkowitz, Louis, 246
Lillis, Donald, 5
Lincoln, Abraham, 55
Lindsay, George, 23–26

Lindsay, John V.
  administration, 81, 214, 244, 246–247
  campaign, 52–57, 62
  inauguration, 87
  mayoralty, 17–27, 80–96
  Monterey Club, 57
  Special Theater District, 95
  Transit Authority, 83, 85, 86
  urban racial issues, 131
Lipsyte, Robert, 79, 176, 279
Little City Halls series, 80
Lomax, Louis, 121
Lombardi, Vince, 30, 107
Louis, Joe, 136
Lowery, Robert, 81
Lucas, Jerry, 284
Luther King, Martin, 121, 123, 144, 163, 182
Lynch, Lincoln, 128

M
MacMahon, Douglas, 89
Mahoney, George P., 205
Mailer, Norman, 53, 60, 254
Malcom X, 121–123
Malone, Vivian, 99
Mantle, Mickey, 69, 77
Mara, Tim, 32
Mara, Wellington, 32
Marcus, James L., 95
Maris, Roger, 77, 249
Marshall, Al, 56
Marshall, George, 103
Martin, J.C., 288
Martin, Townsend, 5, 194
Maynard, Don, 44, 48–50, 112, 208, 226, 301
Mayoral race 1965, 52
McAndrew, Jim, 258
McCarthy, Eugene, 178, 198, 293
McDonough, Will, 13, 225
McGraw, John, 69
McGraw, Tug, 287
McGrory, Mary, 143
McKissick, Floyd, 144
Meggyesy, Dave, 105
Meir, Golda, 271
Merman, Ethel, 53
Metophiles, 75, 202
Michaels, Walt, 218
Mike, Bite, 4
Miller, Marvin, 201

Modell, Art, 45
Modzelewski, Dick, 28
Moerdler, Charles, 148
Mollen, Milton, 54
Monterey Club, 57
Moratorium Day, 285, 287–288
Moses, Robert, 94
Muhammad, Elijah, 121, 122
Muhammad, Herbert, 138
Murphy, Johnny, 248
Murray, Jim, 134
Murtaugh, Danny, 104
MVP, 3, 210, 224, 240, 243, 280

N
Namath, Joe
  and Ali, 139–140
  Bachelors III, 258, 259, 267, 296
  Cardinals' approach, 7, 8
  deal with Jets, 10–12
  early life, 12–13
  knee injury, 2–4, 15, 41, 46, 49, 141, 156, 157, 296
  knee surgery, 14, 42, 112, 193
  and Jet's racial divide, 99–106
  Los Angeles Rams, 296
  salary, 11–12
  Super Bowl, 232, 233, 238, 241, 244, 296
  in training camp, 48, 97
National Baseball League, 71, 274
National Football Conference, 106
National Football League (NFL), 4–7, 10, 28–31, 45, 103, 105, 106, 209, 227, 258, 280
National Guard, 165, 172, 216, 258
National League, 67, 71, 76, 101, 193, 256, 264
National Rifle Association, 198
NBA, 175, 177, 229, 298, 299, 301, 303
NBC, 5, 6, 221, 222
NCAA, 191
Neal, Charlie, 68
Negri, Gloria, 12
Negroes, 97, 99, 101, 102, 103, 105, 114, 117, 120, 121, 123, 124, 138, 139, 167, 176
Newsweek, 124, 190, 259
New York Athletic Club, 176, 212
New York City Landmarks Preservation Commission, 174
New York Daily News, 168, 289
New York Giants, 5, 10, 13, 29–34, 67–69, 72–76, 79, 96, 107, 200, 201
New York Jets
  Buffalo rivalry, 32, 110–112, 156, 217–219
  Patriots rivalry, 47, 157, 217
  racial divide, 97, 106–107
  under Werblin ownership, 4–5, 8–13, 32,

43–50, 97, 101
New York Herald-Tribune, 16
New York Mets, 67–79, 104, 106, 161–162,
  197, 199–202, 247–248, 256–259, 264–268,
  272–293, 302, 303
New York Post, 124, 258, 292
New York's State Psychological Association,
  189
New York Times, 5, 70, 135, 138, 139, 155, 186
New York World-Telegram, 26
NFL. *See* National Football League
NHL, 106, 175, 177, 228
Nicholas, Jim, 14, 41, 42, 156
Nigro, Ken, 227
Niven, David, 252
Nixon, Richard, 1, 55, 166, 202–203, 217, 232,
  282
Novak, Robert, 205, 270
NYAC, 176, 212
NYPD, 115, 152, 182, 183

O

Ocean Hill board, 213
O'Connor, Frank, 91, 116, 131, 202
O'Donnell, Harry, 93, 148
Ogle, Jim, 249
Olsen, Jack, 104, 105
O'Neill, Edward, 90, 131, 173
Orange Bowl, 1–4, 8, 10, 11, 238
Orioles, 34, 36, 37, 78, 279, 280, 281, 282, 283,
  289, 298
O'Rourke, Edward, 172

P

Parilli, Babe, 218, 226, 234
Parmiter, Charles, 154
Patrolmen's Benevolent Association (PBA),
  116, 117
Patterson, Floyd, 135
Paulson, Dainard, 47
Payson, Joan, 68, 70, 282, 289
PBA. *See* Patrolmen's Benevolent Association
  (PBA)
Peekskill Military Academy, 46
Philbin, Gerry, 208
Phillies, 37, 68, 76, 98, 197, 264, 275
Piersall, Jimmy, 72
Plunkett, Sherman, 47, 101, 207, 225
Polo Grounds, 5, 32, 71, 75, 265
Porter, Cole, 16
Powell, Adam Clayton, Jr., 62
Powell, James, 114
The Power of Positive Thinking (Peale), 189
Probus Management, 208
Procaccino, Mario, 91

Q

Qualls, Jim, 267
Quill, Mike, 82–91, 163

R

Racism, 65, 99–102, 106, 115, 117, 118, 120,
  125, 126, 130, 131, 144, 150, 182, 213, 296
Rangers, 175, 177, 228
Reagan, Ronald, 149, 173, 186, 204, 293
Reed, Wills, 298–300
Reeves, Richard, 286
Republican National Committee, 55
Reston, James, 18, 187, 274
Reuss, Henry S., 35
Revolutionary Action Movement, 150
Rican, Puerto, 119, 126, 128, 179, 297
Richardson, Willie, 239
Richards, Paul, 68
Rifkin, Hyman, 211
Robbins, I.D., 54
Robinson, Frank, 288
Robinson, Jackie, 101
Robinson, Wilbert, 69
Rockefeller, David, 175
Rockefeller, John D., 145, 148
Rockefeller, Nelson, 19, 22, 23, 92, 93, 116,
  166, 179, 202
Rohan, Jack, 188
Rome Olympics 1960, 137
Romney, George, 166
Roosevelt, Teddy, 55
Rose, Alex, 58
Rosenbloom, Carroll, 236, 237
Rosenthal, A.M., 90
Rote, Kyle, 240
Rozelle, Pete, 32, 241, 259
Rubin, Jerry, 288
Rush, Clive, 31
Russell, Bill, 106
Russell, Cazzie, 159
Ruth, Babe, 11
Ryan, Frank, 45

S

Sanders, James, 96
Santo, Ron, 265
Sauer, George, 208, 240
Sayers, Gale, 6–7
Schaap, Dick, 88, 97
Schmeling, Max, 134
Schmitt, John, 47, 239
Seale, Bobby, 288
Seaver, Tom, 287
Senate Foreign Relations Committee, 142

Shanker, Albert, 215, 216
Shea Stadium, 5, 43, 50, 71, 77, 106, 110, 218, 223, 224, 264, 274, 276, 278, 281, 283, 286, 287, 289
Shepherd, Jean, 186
Sherman, Allie, 29–31, 38
Shula, Don, 236
Sinatra, Frank, 243
Smith, Clarence, 180
Smith, Francis X., 242, 246, 247, 270
Smith, Tommie, 212
SNCC, 123, 150, 187, 188
Snedeker, Jeff, 225
Snell, Matt, 31, 32, 44, 101, 195, 207, 208, 240
Snider, Duke, 72
Society for the Prevention of Niggers Getting Everything (SPONGE), 127–128
Spock, Benjamin, 189, 190
SPONGE. See Society for the Prevention of Niggers Getting Everything
Sports Illustrated, 42, 47, 101, 104, 108, 237
Stanky, Eddie, 257
Stengel, Casey, 68–73, 76, 77, 104, 223, 248, 277, 289
Stinchfield, Frank E., 141
Student Afro-American Society, 188
Student Non-violent Coordinating Committee, 123
Students for a Democratic Society (SDS), 185, 186
Super Bowl, 106, 208, 227, 230, 232, 233, 238, 239, 244, 294, 298
Swoboda, Ron, 75, 283

T
Taliaferro, Mike, 32, 156
Terrell, Ali, 134, 135
Thayer, Walter, 17
Thimmesch, Nick, 20, 202, 204
Titans, 5, 48, 194
Torres, Jose, 52
Transit Authority, 83, 85, 86, 163
Transport Workers Union, 83, 163
Truman, Harry, 141
Twombly, Wells, 154

U
UATF, 180
UFT, 215 216
Uniformed Sanitationmen's Association (USA), 169
Urban Action Task Force, 179
Urban Design Group, 95
Urban League, 150

V
Van Doren, Mamie, 107, 108
Vietnam War, 132, 168, 178, 187, 190, 284, 285
Viteritti, Joseph, 297

W
Wagner, Bob, 52, 54, 57, 58, 62, 77, 84, 87, 89, 129, 259
Wagner, Robert, 17, 21, 22, 80–82, 179, 247, 254, 270, 278
Wallace, George, 2, 99, 260
Wallace, Mike, 121
Wallace, William, 211
Warren, John, 301
Washington Post, 152, 167, 204
Washington Redskins, 31, 103
Washington Star, 143
WCBS, 65
Weaver, Earl, 279
Weiss, George, 70, 71, 74, 76, 104
Werblin, Sonny, 4–6, 8–12, 16, 31, 32, 40, 42, 43, 45, 46, 50, 97, 101, 111, 140, 141, 155, 159, 194–196, 210, 223, 235, 238
White, Bill, 105
White, Lee, 208
White, William S., 25
White Sox, 34, 37, 79, 191, 198, 257
Whitney, Jock, 17, 21–22, 282
Williams, Gertrude, 113
Wilson, Ralph, 32
Wirtz, Willard, 91
Wismer, Harry, 5
Wood, Dick, 45
Wood, Gary, 29
World Boxing Association, 132
World-Telegram Sun, 81
World Trade Center, 175

Y
Yankees, 14, 33, 35, 38–39, 67–79, 104, 117, 242, 249, 250
Yankees-Columbia Broadcasting System (CBS), 34–36
Yankee Stadium, 28, 31, 38, 39, 69, 79
Yawkey, Tom, 103
Young, Dick, 68, 194, 289

Z
Ziff, Sid, 12
Zimmerman, Paul, 100, 194